William G. Beale

Opinions of the Corporation Counsel and Assistants

From January, 1872, to March, 1897

William G. Beale

Opinions of the Corporation Counsel and Assistants
From January, 1872, to March, 1897

ISBN/EAN: 9783742837318

Manufactured in Europe, USA, Canada, Australia, Japa

Cover: Foto ©Suzi / pixelio.de

Manufactured and distributed by brebook publishing software
(www.brebook.com)

William G. Beale

Opinions of the Corporation Counsel and Assistants

OPINIONS

OF THE

CORPORATION COUNSEL AND

ASSISTANTS

FROM

January, 1872, to March, 1897.

Published by direction of the City Council under the supervision of
the Corporation Counsel.

WILLIAM G. BEALE,

Corporation Counsel.

Compiled and Edited by
EDWARD S. DAY,
Assistant Corporation Counsel.

Press of W. B. CONKEY COMPANY.

In compiling this book reference has been made to all the records of opinions now preserved in the office of the Corporation Counsel. These records date back to the time of the Chicago fire, all earlier records having been destroyed. It has been the purpose to include only opinions having some general or permanent interest for the City Council and the executive officers of the corporation.

OPINIONS

OF THE

CORPORATION COUNSEL AND ASSISTANTS

FROM

JANUARY, 1872, TO MARCH, 1897.

October 31, 1874.

Hon. S. S. Hayes, City Comptroller.

Sir—

The following communication, from you to the corporation counsel, has been turned over to me, with instructions to prepare an opinion as requested.

"Hon. T. Lyle Dickey, Corporation Counsel.

"Dear Sir—

"I desire to call your attention to an ordinance passed by the common council of June 22, 1874 (page 259 C. P.), amending the ordinance concerning billiard tables, ball alleys and shooting galleries. Also to an ordinance concerning same passed June 29, 1874 (page 281 C. P.), and request your opinion as to my duty in regard to these rebates.

"1st. Am I to pay the money to such parties as have taken out licenses since April 1, 1874, and prior to the passage of this ordinance June 22, 1874?

"2nd. If so, to what fund shall same be charged?"

"Respectfully,

"S. S. HAYES, Comptroller.

"By J. A. FARWELL, Chief Clerk."

The powers of the common council in relation to the subject matter, and specified in the city charter, are as follows:

"To license, regulate and suppress billiard tables."

"To authorize the mayor, or other proper officer of the city, to grant and issue licenses, and direct the manner of issuing and registering thereof, and the fees to be paid therefor. Laws and Ord. Chapt. VIII, Sec. 10, paragraph 8-13."

In the exercise of this power the following provision, contained in the revised ordinances of 1873, was passed.

"The mayor of said city is hereby authorized to issue a license to any person or persons desiring to keep and use a billiard table or

3

tables, alley or alleys, gallery or galleries mentioned in section 9, upon such person or persons paying to the city collector the sum of $25 for each table, alley or gallery aforesaid, which license shall expire on the first day of July of each year; and all such licenses shall be issued in the manner and be in accordance with the conditions, provisions and restrictions named and provided in Chapter XXVI of these Revised Ordinances, entitled "Licenses," so far as the conditions, provisions and restrictions of said chapter may be applicable thereto (and not in conflict with the provisions hereof); and all licenses granted under the provisions of this section may be revoked at any time by the mayor, for any cause which he may deem good and sufficient."

Section 9 of the same chapter imposes a penalty of $5 for each and every month that any person shall keep for gain a billiard table, except as provided in Section 10, quoted *supra*.

March 24, 1873, an ordinance was passed by the common council which provides as follows:

Section 1. That all licenses issued by the authority of the city of Chicago, after the passage of this ordinance, shall be issued for a term which will expire on the last day of March next subsequent to the issue thereof.

Sec. 2. When any license is issued after the first day of April in any year, the same shall be issued upon the person applying therefor paying for the same the number of twelfth parts of the same, or price fixed by any ordinance for a yearly license as will equal the number of months which will elapse between the date of the application for license and the first day of April next thereafter, provided, however, that in determining the price to be paid, the month in which the application is made shall be counted and included in the number of months to elapse.

June 29, 1874, an order was passed by the common council as follows:

Ordered, that the city comptroller be, and he is hereby directed to grant rebates on all licenses issued to persons to have and to keep for gain, any billiard table, pin alley or shooting gallery, and which said licenses expire on the 31st day of March, A. D., 1875, such rebates to be made in such sum or sums as shall fix the fee charged for all such licenses, at the sum fixed in the ordinance entitled "An ordinance amending Section 10 of Chapter XXVIII of the Revised Ordinances, entitled misdemeanors," and passed June 22, 1874.

October 19, 1874, the following resolution was passed by the council: "Whereas, no rebates have been made to those parties up to the present time; therefore, be it

"Resolved, that the comptroller be and he is hereby ordered to pay the sum of $15 to all the proprietors of billiard tables in this city who paid the amount of $25 for billiard licenses for the year A. D. 1874."

The following is all the legislation upon the subject, necessary to be considered in the present inquiry.

The first and most important consideration is, as to the power of the common council in the premises. The power granted by the charter is to regulate, license and suppress and prohibit, and to authorize the mayor or other proper officer to license. Under this grant of power the common council had, beyond question, the power to pass the ordinances of January 20, 1873, providing for licenses for the keeping of billiard tables, for gain, and prohibiting the keeping of such tables, for gain, without license. After the ordinance went into effect then, the keeping of a billiard table, for gain, without a license, was an unlawful act, and subjected the keeper of such table to a penalty of $5.00 per month, or $60 per annum.

By the ordinance passed March 24, 1873, still in force, a license issued after the first day of April in any year expires on the last day of March on the succeeding year, in other words the license when issued is a license to keep a billiard table, or billiard tables, as the case may be, until the first of April next ensuing the date of the license. Such license for such time is the consideration for which the person licensed pays his money. The consideration passes the very instant the license is delivered.

The fee for a license for each billiard table from April 1, 1874, to April 1, 1875, was $25.00 by the ordinance of January, 1873, and by that ordinance licenses expired on July 1st in each year, and no matter how long after July 1st a license was applied for, there was no rebate, the full fee for license, $25.00, was required to be paid. But by the act of March 24, 1873, it was provided, that licenses should expire on the last day of March, next succeeding their dates, and if issued after April 1st, the fee was fixed at such proportion of $25.00, as the unexpired time bore to a year. Such was the fee paid by persons receiving a license, after April 1, 1874, and before June 22, 1874, when the ordinance was passed reducing the license fee to $10.00.

The latter ordinance is prospective in its operation, and, indeed, in its terms. In Section 1 the following language is used: "The intent and meaning of this section, being that billiard tables * * * shall be charged a license of $10.00 each per annum."

Again, Sec. 2: "This ordinance shall be in force and take effect from and after its passage."

Suppose that the ordinance of June 22, 1874, instead of reducing the license fee to $10.00, had increased it to $50.00, would the city have a claim upon the persons licensed after April 1, 1874, and before June 22, 1874, for the difference? Clearly not. In such case persons licensed would rightfully say, I have paid a full consideration for my license, as fixed by the city ordinances, and nothing more can be demanded of me. So, also in the case of the city. It has given full consideration for the fee-paid, and nothing more can be demanded.

The fee, having been paid into the city treasury in accordance with law, becomes and remains the money of the city. To pay it back would be simply a donation, and I know of no authority in the common council to make a donation from the city treasury for any purpose. My opinion is, that the order of June 29, 1874, and the resolution of October 19, 1874, are ultra vires and void, and that the duty of the comptroller is to refuse to pay any rebates on billiard table licenses. Respectfully,
FRANCIS ADAMS

March 1, 1875.

To the Honorable H. D. Colvin, Mayor.
Dear Sir—
You ask "is it lawful to draw money from the sewerage fund to pay for the filling of a street for the protection of a sewer * * * when there is not sufficient depth of earth on the street for the protection of the sewer?" I think it is. The placing of earth over a sewer is as essentially a part of the work of constructing the sewer as is the digging the ditch. The fact that a sewer is in or under a street does not affect the question. Respectfully,
T. LYLE DICKEY,
Counsel to the Corporation.

December 16, 1875.

Hon. S. S. Hayes, City Comptroller, etc.
Sir—
The following communication from you to the counsel to the corporation, of date December 6, 1875, has been by him referred to me for an opinion:
I desire your opinion in writing upon the following points:
First. Is the real estate belonging to the "University of Chicago" exempt from special assessments for any and all purposes, as well as general taxation by virtue of Section 10, of "An Act incorporating the University of Chicago," approved January 30, 1857?
Second. Is the property of the Woman's Home exempt from taxation and special assessments, either or both, by virtue of "An Act to amend an act entitled an act to authorize the incorporation of Unitary Houses," approved February 25, 1867, and for the benefit of the Woman's house, approved April 16, 1869? Respectfully,
S. S. HAYES, Comptroller.

The section of the charter of the University of Chicago, which, it is claimed, exempts the university from special assessments, is as follows:
"The tract of land, not to exceed one hundred and sixty acres on which the university is erected, belonging to the said university, is

hereby declared exempt from taxation or assessment, for any and all purposes whatever."

The act was approved January 30, 1857. This section cannot operate and exempt the property of the university from special assessment unless the word "assessment," in the section, is construed to mean special assessment.

The rule of construction in cases of this class is very clearly and forcibly enunciated by the supreme court of the United States in the case of the Ohio Life Insurance Assessment Company vs. G. H. Howard, p. 435, in the following language:

"The rule of construction in cases of this kind has been well settled by the court, the grant of privileges and exemptions to a corporation are strictly construed against the corporation and in favor of the public. Nothing passes but what is granted in clear and explicit terms. And neither the right of taxation nor any other power of sovereignty which the community have an interest in preserving, will be held by the court to be surrendered, unless the intention to surrender is manifested by words too plain to be mistaken. This is the rule laid down in the case of Billings vs. The Providence Bank, and affirmed in the case of Charles River Bridge Company.

Nor does the rule rest merely on the authority of adjudged cases. It is founded in principles of justice, and necessary for the safety and well-being of every state in the Union. For it is a matter of public history, which this court cannot refuse to notice, that almost every bill for the incorporation of banking companies, insurance and trust companies, railroad companies, or other corporations, is drawn originally by the parties who are personally interested in obtaining the charter; and that they are often passed by the legislature, when, from the nature of our political institutions, the business is unavoidably transacted in a hurried manner, and it is impossible that every member can deliberately examine every provision in every bill upon which he is called upon to act.

On the other hand, those who accept the charter have abundant time to examine and consider its provisions, before they invest their money, and if they mean to claim under it any peculiar privileges, or any exemption from the burden of taxation, it is their duty to see that the right or exemption they intend to claim is granted in clear and unambiguous language. The authority which this court is bound under the constitution of the United States to exercise, in cases of this kind, is one of its most delicate and important duties. And if individuals choose to accept a charter in which the words used are susceptible of different meanings—or might have been considered by the representatives of the state as words of legislation only, and subject to future revision and repeal, and not as words of contract—the parties who accept it have no just right to call upon this court to exercise its high power over a state upon doubtful or ambiguous words, nor upon any supposed equitable construction or inferences made from other provisions in the act of incorporation. If there are equitable considerations in their favor, the application should be made to the state and not to this court. If they come here to claim an exemption from their equal share of the public burdens, or any peculiar exemption or privilege, they must show their title to it—and that title must be shown by plain and unequivocal language."

The rule here laid down, and which has been announced in other decisions by the same tribunal is substantially, that if from the language used in the act, the exemption is doubtful; then there is no exemption.

The decisions of the supreme court of the United States in this class of cases are of the highest authority, involving as they do the construction of the provision in the federal constitution that no state shall pass any law impairing the obligation of contracts. Exemption from special assessments is clearly not granted by the university charter in plain and unequivocal language, it is not granted in express words, nor can it in my judgment, be reasonably implied from the words used.

It is a fundamental rule of construction that words must be taken in their ordinary signification. The word assessment in its ordinary sense means an appraisement or valuation of property. The word is not used in Article IX of the constitution of 1848, which relates to revenue, but the word "assess" is used in Section 5 of the article, and, as used, refers solely to taxation, which word does not, as our supreme court has frequently decided, include special assessments.

The word assessment as used in revenue acts passed while the constitution of 1848 was in force uniformly relates solely to taxation, and in acts passed under the same constitution conferring power upon the corporate authorities of cities, etc., to levy special assessments, the words "special assessments" have been uniformly used. Thus the word assessment whether taken in its ordinary sense, or as it is used in the constitution of 1848, or in acts of the legislature passed while that constitution was in force, does not mean or include in its meaning special assessments made to defray the costs of local improvements.

Our supreme court, speaking of public grants to private persons, say: Where there is a doubt the construction is made most favorably for the sovereign. Again, public grants should not be extended by implication in favor of the grantee, beyond the natural and obvious meaning of the words employed, even if by such construction the object of the grant is entirely defeated.

Hills, et al., vs. The County of St. Clair, 2 Gilen. 227-228:

I am, for the reason stated, of opinion that real property of the university of Chicago is not by virtue of Section 10 of the act of incorporation, cited supra. exempt from special assessments.

WOMAN'S HOME.

The Woman's Home was organized under a general law for the incorporation of "Unitarian homes," approved February 25, 1867. This act did not purport to exempt from taxation or special assessment the property of any corporation which might organize under it, but Section 1 of an act approved April 16, 1869, to annul the act approved February 25, 1867; and for the benefit of the Woman's Home, provides that all the property, real and personal, of the Woman's Home, a corporation located in Chicago, and organized for benevolent purposes, under the general act aforesaid, together with all the stock of said corporation, is and shall forever remain exempt from taxation for state, county, town and municipal purposes, so long as said corporation shall in good faith, continue to carry out the purposes of its organization and shall not declare "or pay any dividend on its stock, etc." Public laws 1869, 409. The act does not purport to exempt the property of the Woman's Home from special assessment, but only from taxation, which word, as I have already stated, does not, as construed by our supreme court, include special assessments.

The general assembly had power, under the constitution of 1848, to exempt from taxation such property, as it might deem necessary, from school, religious and charitable purposes. Con. 1848, Art. IX, Sec. 3.

This necessarily left to the legislature the power of determining within reasonable limits, what was a religious or charitable purpose. In the case of the Woman's Home, the general assembly evidently decided that the corporation was established for a charitable purpose, and I have no doubt that it was in the power of the general assembly to grant the exemption.

If this exemption had been granted in the law of incorporation of the Woman's Home, then the question might arise, whether the privilege of exemption from taxation was not a contract between the corporation and the state, binding upon the state so long as the corporation should "in good faith continue to carry on the purposes of its organization." In such case the purpose of the organization might be held a sufficient consideration for the grant of exemption.

But at the time of passage and approval of the act of 1869 the Woman's Home, as appears from Section 1, of the last act was a corporation, incorporated under the general law of 1867. There was, therefore, no consideration for the privilege of exemption conferred by the act of 1869, and, consequently, no contract between the state and the corporation that such exemption should continue. It was in the language of the law a privilege *bene placitum*, and the law granting it was subject to repeal at any time.

Rector of Christ Church, etc., vs. County of Pennsylvania, 24, How, 300.

Ohio Life & Trust Co. vs. Debolt 16, Ib. 416.

The constitution of 1870, Art. IX, Sec. 3, provides that such property as may be used exclusively for charitable purposes may be exempted from taxation, *but such exemption shall be only by general law.*

Section 1 of the schedule to the constitution continues in force laws not inconsistent with the constitution. By necessary implication laws inconsistent with the constitution were repealed by its adoption. The act of 1869 exempting from taxation the property of the Woman's Home relates solely to the Woman's Home. It is not in any sense a general law, and so inconsistent with Section 3, Article IX, of the constitution and in my judgment was repealed by the adoption of the constitution.

If, therefore, the property of the corporation is exempt from taxation, such exemption must exist by virtue of some law passed since the adoption of the present constitution.

The only provision for the exemption from taxation of the property of charitable institutions of which I have any knowledge, which has been enacted since the adoption of the constitution is contained in the general revenue law in force July, 1872, and is as follows:

"All property described in this section to the extent herein limited, shall be exempt from taxation—that is to say, all property of institutions of purely public charity when actually and exclusively used for such charitable purposes, not leased, or otherwise used with a view to profit."

Whether the property of the Woman's Home is exempt from taxation under this provision, depends upon whether it is an institution "of purely public charity."

I understand that board and lodging are furnished by the corporation to women, at comparatively low rates, and that this is the chief, if not only ground, upon which it can claim to be a charitable institution.

If this be true, I am of the opinion, that it is not an institution of purely public charity, within the meaning of the law, and that its property is not exempt from taxation.

Respectfully,

FRANCIS ADAMS, Attorney for the City.

FINANCE COMMITTEE OF COMMON COUNCIL.

January 4, 1876.

Gentlemen—

The following communication from your committee has been received:

"The Law Department is requested to inform the committee whether the council has the power to remit city taxes to individuals who have been assessed for an amount greater than the value of their property."

II

The question is a general one and before answering it I think it best to state the sense in which I understand it, in order that there may be no misapprehension in regard to my opinion. I understand the question to relate to the taxes of 1875, the warrants for the collection of which are now in the hands of the town collector, and I understand the word "remit" to be used in the sense of absolving or discharging parties from liability to pay to the collectors such part of the taxes levied against them, as may have been extended on an overvaluation or assessment of their property.

I am of the opinion that the council has not the power specified in the question of your committee and will state briefly some of my reasons for this opinion.

The tax in question was levied under Section 111 of the present charter, and the general revenue law of the state. Section 111 provides as follows:

"The City Council or Board of Trustees, as the case may be, shall on or before the second Tuesday in September (August) in each year ascertain the total amount of appropriations for all corporate purposes, legally made, and to be collected from the tax levy of that fiscal year, and by ordinance levy and assess such amount, so ascertained, upon the real and personal property within the city or village subject to taxation, as the same is assessed for state and county purposes for the current year. A certified copy of such ordinance shall be filed with the county clerk of the proper county, whose duty it shall be to ascertain the rate per cent. which upon the total valuation of all property subject to taxation within the city or village, as the same is assessed and equalized for state and county purposes, will produce a net amount not less than the amount so directed to be levied and assessed; and it shall be the duty of the county clerk to extend such tax, in a separate column, upon the book or books of the collector or collectors of the state and county taxes within such city or village."

There has been no appropriation of money to be used in remitting taxes, or in refunding taxes, if already paid.

By Section 112 of the charter the taxes are to be collected and enforced in the same manner, and by the same officers as state and county taxes, etc.; that is by the town collectors while the warrants remain in their hands, and by the county collectors after the warrants are returned to them.

The duties of these officers, the town collectors and the county collectors, are prescribed by statute. They look to the warrants for their authority, and the manner in which the warrants shall be executed is specifically and expressly prescribed by law. When the warrants are issued, the collectors are bound to execute them in the manner prescribed by law; the city council has no right to change them; and no action of the council subsequent to the receipt of the warrant by the collectors is binding on collectors.

To remit the tax would be in effect to change the warrant. Suppose that a town collector after the city council should remit a tax set down in his books, were to execute the warrant by distress and sale of goods and chattels of the person taxed, as prescribed by law, would an action of trespass lie against the collector? Clearly not. His warrant and the law would furnish a complete vindication and the action of the city council in opposition to these would be held a nullity.

But there is another consideration, which, in my judgment, is conclusive of the question.

The power to remit "to individuals who have been assessed for an amount greater than the value of their property" necessarily includes the power to determine the value of the property before the council could intelligently exercise the power to remit, it would be necessary for the council to sit as a board of revision of an assessment made by officers designated by law for that purpose. This the city council has no power to do. In the language of the supreme court in the case of Spencer vs. The People, etc., Legal News, page 215, "To do so would seem to be to abrogate the power of ascertaining the value of property for taxation, which ascertainment of value the constitution declares shall be by some person or persons designated by the General Assembly and not otherwise."

The city council has not been designated by the general assembly as a body to determine the value of property, for the purpose of taxation. For the council to do so, therefore, would be in violation of the constitution.

Whether there is any remedy in cases of excessive assessments, and, if so, what such remedy is, are questions which I shall not discuss in this opinion, but that the city council has *not* the power to remedy the wrong by remitting taxes for which warrants have been issued, I have no doubt.   Respectfully,

FRANCIS ADAMS.

November 15, 1876.

J. A. Farwell, Esq., City Comptroller.

Dear Sir—

In your communication of November 11, 1876, you ask for a written opinion upon the following question: In reference to the manner in which payments should be made of the compensation or damages, awarded in cases of condemnation of land for streets:

1. "When only a portion of the assessment has been collected can the Comptroller pay damages for property taken, pro rata?"

I understand this to mean that when the money collected is insufficient to pay the total amount of damages awarded, whether the comptroller should make a payment on each piece of land condemned in the proportion which the total amount collected bears to the total amount of damages awarded. My answer is no; and for this reason: The city cannot, under the law, take possession of any piece of property condemned until the whole amount of the compensation awarded in respect to it has been paid, so that *pro rata* payments on all the pieces condemned should be made as indicated in your questions, and no more should be collected. The city would never acquire the right to take possession of a single piece of the land condemned and the money would have been expended fruitlessly.

2. "Is he (the Comptroller) required to pay any party in full when he has sufficient funds to the credit of the assessment, but not a sufficient amount to pay the entire amount due every person when property has been condemned?"

3. "If he is required or even authorized, under the law, to pay any person before the entire amount is collected, when should he commence paying? i. e., has he the discretion to pay at random according as he chooses?"

Ans. There is no provision of law requiring payment of the compensation for one of the number of pieces of land condemned for a street, before the sum total of compensation for all the pieces condemned have been collected, neither is there any law prohibiting such payment. The law is silent on the subject; it remains, therefore, a matter of expediency, and of discretion on the part of the city, and in my opinion, each case should be determined by itself, and no arbitrary or invariable rule should be adopted and applied to all cases indiscriminately.

The comptroller should not pay "at random." For instance when a street is ordered to be extended between certain *termini* the payments should be so made that each piece paid for and taken possession of by the city would be a continuation of the street in the direction proposed, in other words, the pieces next to the *terminus* of the street ordered to be extended should first be paid for.

By making payments in this way the city will have a *quid pro quo* in the money expended, even though sufficient to pay for all the pieces condemned should never be collected.

4. "Is the city under the law, the custodian of the funds, or should all collections be paid into court?"

Ans. Under the law the city may either pay the money into court or pay to the person entitled to receive it.

If there is any doubt about the person entitled to receive it, it should be paid into court, where parties having conflicting or adverse claims, may have this claim passed on by the court.

5. "If the city makes its payment can it require parties to furnish a deed, and is not the better course to take a deed?"

Ans. Under the law the city cannot insist on a deed, but it is the better course to request and take deeds.

Respectfully yours,
ELLIOTT ANTHONY, Corporation Counsel.

January 5, 1877.

John A. Farwell, Esq., City Comptroller.

Dear Sir—

In reply to yours of the 4th instant, in which you call my attention to an item in the appropriation ordinance of March 22, 1876, as follows: For rents of armories for the use of the police force and for the first and second regiments of Illinois State Guards, as part of said police force, and then ask me:

1st. Whether the first and second regiments of the Illinois State Guards are a part of the police force of the city.

2d. If they are not, had the city council a right to make an appropriation for their benefit, and

3d. Whether the city is liable to said regiments for the amount of appropriation for armories whether said armories have been used by the city or not.

I answer:

1st. That these military companies designated as the First and Second Regiments of the Illinois State Guard are not a part of the police force of the city at all—are not under the control of the city—and have no connection whatever with the police force—but are state organizations, and are a body of men who have associated themselves together for military purposes solely.

2d. By Article V, Section 42, of the city charter, the powers of the city council are defined, and by the second clause of that section the council have the power to appropriate money for corporate purposes *only*, and provide for payment of debts and expenses of the corporation.

3d. To appropriate money to defray the expenses of military companies which may be organized in our city under the state laws would not be an appropriation for corporate purposes, and I am, therefore, of the opinion, that the city could not be liable to these regiments for the expenses of providing them an armory.

4th. I do not think that the fact that some of the police had drilled in these armories, or one of them, can make the city liable, as I do not understand from your communication that these armories have ever been rented by the city at all, but have been as I understand rented by these regiments, and on their responsibility.

It may be that they relied upon the appropriation which you specify, and I do not say but what the city may, for drilling its police force, rent a building or buildings for that purpose, but it is well settled that the powers of a municipal corporation are limited by its charter and the city council can exercise only such powers as are expressly given it or are fairly implied in or incident to the powers so expressly granted, and every person or body of men in dealing with the municipal corporation is bound to take notice of the powers which it possesses. Yours respectfully,

ELLIOTT ANTHONY, Corporation Counsel.

John A. Farwell, Esq., City Comptroller.

Dear Sir—

My opinion is asked—

1st. As to whether any portion of the amount appropriated last year by the city council, by the general appropriation ordinance for the fiscal year from January 1, 1876, to December 31, 1876, under the head of "Indebtedness Fund," can be used for any purpose or indebtedness incurred prior to the year 1876, and if so, whether any portion can be used for any indebtedness incurred subsequent to the year 1876."

2d. Whether there is any authority for the mayor and comptroller or the treasurer to pay any salaries for the year 1877 or on account thereof, before the passage of the annual appropriation bill, and before the salaries are fixed

3d. If the authority does not exist, can the city council legally authorize the proper officers to make any advances whatever to any officer or employe of the city, before the salaries are fixed in the annual appropriation bill, and if this can be done, whether any of "Indebtedness Fund" can be used for this purpose?

In answer to these inquiries, I would say—

1st. That the "Indebtedness Fund," is, if I am correctly informed, a fund provided to pay any general indebtedness of the city not otherwise specifically provided for, and should strictly be applied to any general indebtedness existing at the time of the appropriation ordinance. If this fund is a general contingent fund then it can be used to pay any of the existing debts of the city which the city may order paid, but I take it that what was intended by particularly specifying this fund was to pay such indebtedness as was not otherwise particularly enumerated, and provided for and could be applied to pay such indebtedness as existed in 1876.

2d. As to the second question I answer, I think there is a doubt whether you have the right to make advances on account of salaries before the same are fixed, and that it would be the most judicious under any circumstances to have an order passed authorizing the same.

3d. That the city council has the right to authorize advances to be made to city officers on account of salary when there is enough money belonging to the city in the treasury, I have no doubt. The council by so doing do not fix salaries, and that even they can do by the act of 1873, found in the pamphlet edition of the city charter, page 74, *before* the passage of the general appropriation bill. The only legal objection which can be brought against it is that it would prevent any other appropriation being made for that purpose, and that all appropriations of every sort, character and kind must be made by one ordinance and at one time, and that during the first quarter of the fiscal year. But what I am contemplating is that there are some funds somewhere belonging to the city, which can be taken for the time being and applied for the purpose of paying on account of salaries until the appropriation is made; and as you particularly mention the indebtedness fund, I assume that fund has not been used for the purpose for which it was originally appropriated, and some portion of it is still on hand; if there is not, then why specify that fund any more than any other fund which may have been appropriated and exhausted? If that fund and all other funds provided by last year's appropriation bill have been exhausted and used up, then the city has not got a cent, and the only thing it can next do is to borrow in some manner enough money to pay on account of salaries until the appropriation bill can be passed; and then there is no question but what the city would have the right to borrow on account of the appropriation, or against it.

4th. Our charter has established, what our Supreme Court calls in the case of the Trustees of Lockport vs. Gaylord, 61 Ill., page 276, "the pay as you go policy," but it has coupled with it the impossibility of ever getting the money to carry it out until one year after the same goes into effect, and the only way that cities can conform strictly to it, will be to suspend their function for a year, and wait until all the taxes have been collected which are to provide for appropriations and paid into the treasury. There are several provisions in the old city charter which authorized the common council both to borrow money and also to transfer, with the consent of those immediately in charge of the same, any funds except the indebtedness fund, the school tax fund, and such assessments, etc., see particularly Section 48-49, page 426 of Revised Ordinances, to any other account to be replaced within three months, etc., but it is very doubtful whether this provision and several others with which you are perfectly familiar, found on pages 425 and 426 of the Revised Ordinances, have not been repealed by the adoption of the new charter, which has provided a complete financial system for the city.

Of course if there are unexpended balances in the city treasury left over at any time by reason of reduction of expenses in any of the departments, or by reason of reduction in salaries, then these balances would become a portion of all the public funds of the city, and by the provisions of Article V of the city charter, subject to the control of the city council, and could be applied to defray any legitimate expenses of the city government.

I have consulted with M. F. Tuley, Esq., late corporation counsel, in regard to the powers which the city possesses to pay salaries and defray the expenses of the city government during the interval which elapses from the expiration of the fiscal year to the time when the new appropriation bill should be passed; and he is of the opinion that there is an implied power on the part of the city to borrow money to bridge over the interval, and that the general assembly contemplated such emergency, and that there is no other way to do it except to borrow money or to let the city government remain in a state of suspended animation until funds are provided by the city and collection of the taxes, or to wait until the appropriation bill is passed, and then borrow on the strength of the same.

His opinion is expressed in the following terms:

"In view of the fact that the city charter contemplates that there must be an interval of time between the end of the fiscal year for which appropriations have been made, and the passage of the new appropriation bill, during which interval the city government must be run, I am of the opinion that there is an implied power to borrow money to meet indispensable and necessary expenditures during that interval of time, such moneys to be paid out of the appropriation when made and collected. This, of course, does not refer to public improvements, or other expenditures, which can be deferred until the appropriation bill is passed."

Payments to officers and employes may be made on account, until appropriation is made, which when made will govern as to entire fiscal year. If this practice should, however, be attempted it would prevent the same questions, that were so elaborately discussed last year in regard to borrowing money by issuing city certificates, and I therefore think that under all the circumstances, by far the best course to pursue will be to pass the appropriation bill as soon as possible and then borrow against that.

Yours truly,

ELLIOTT ANTHONY, Corporation Counsel.

City Law Department, Chicago, Feb. 2, 1877.

June 22, 1877

John A. Farwell, Esq., Comptroller.

Dear Sir—

I am informed that the county treasurer has declined to pay over to the city, until satisfactorily indemnified against loss, its proportion of taxes collected from parties who have paid their taxes to him *under protest* and with notice that they would litigate his right to the taxes so paid. I am requested to give you my opinion as to the right of the treasurer to hold moneys thus received in his possession, until indemnified to his satisfaction against any contingent liability.

I cannot imagine what right the treasurer has to hold money, paid under protest, any more than funds received without such notice. It is well known that written notice protesting against the validity and justice of the tax collected are frequently served upon the town and other collectors, but it has never been seriously urged as an excuse to retain tax funds in their hands. Last year, owing to the general dissatisfaction with the assessment on personal property, the town collectors had hundreds of such protests and notices, but their lawyers, without exception, advised them that they had no right to hold the funds so collected, or to demand any protection other than that given them by law.

2

I presume, however, the cases to which Mr. Huck refers are those where bills have been filed against him and the town collector to void or rebate the tax, and praying for an injunction. In all these cases that have been tried, the injunctions have been denied and in some cases the parties have prayed appeals. It is not necessary for me to give an opinion as to the merits of these cases. In fact, I have not examined the bills, as none of them has been tried since my appointment as counsel to the corporation; but this is immaterial.

Mr. Huck has received this money as collector; he is not legally restrained by injunction or other process from paying it over. In accepting the office he accepted its risks as well as its profits. The law prescribes how he shall pay it over and at what time; he has no discretion but to obey the law.

The collector's warrant protects him to the same extent as an execution does the sheriff, and even admitting that any of the pending suits should be successfully pressed, the city or county, as the case may be, would be liable to refund the money so paid. I think Mr. Huck, if his attention is particularly called to this matter, will not persist in his refusal.　　Respectfully,

JOSEPH F. BONFIELD, Corporation Counsel.

July 12, 1877.

Hon. John L. Thompson, Chairman Com. on Judiciary, City Council.

Dear Sir—

I am requested by you to give an opinion to the Committee on Judiciary—"Does the power to appoint the standing committees of the Council reside by law in the Mayor or in the Council?"

The mayor of the city as such has no power or authority to interfere with the deliberations of the city council, or to appoint its committees, except under express authority of law, the powers and duties of the mayor and council being naturally distinct, as the executive and legislative branches of the government.

The doubt, if any existing, as to the power of the mayor to appoint the standing committees arises (no doubt) from the fact that the mayor is by the charter made the presiding officer of the city council.

The section is as follows: "The Mayor shall preside at all meetings of the Council, but shall not vote except in a case of a tie, when he shall give the casting vote."

The powers of the presiding officer of any deliberative body when appointed by the body itself, can be in the nature of the case only such as are conferred upon him by the body of which he is a member, and the appointment of the standing committees is not a right by virtue of his office, but by virtue of the rule of the body, or a custom acquiesced in by the members as a usage, but which may at any time be revoked.

The matter of appointing standing committees by supreme legislative bodies being entirely in the control of the body differs widely. In this country it is the almost invariable practice to confer upon the presiding officer the appointment of all committees.

Cushing says: "Of all the infinite variety of methods which may be adopted and practiced in the appointment of committees, two only need be mentioned particularly as peculiar to the legislative assemblies of this country. The first of these which prevails very extensively with us and is in more frequent use than any other method, is the appointment of committees both permanent and occasional by the speaker. * * *

"The only other method which is occasionally practiced with us, is that of the *viva voce*, or a suffrage."

It may be asked, does the fact that the mayor is made presiding officer of the council by law and given a vote in case of a tie, confer upon him any rights not incident to the office of a presiding officer appointed by the body itself? It cannot be so construed, and while it is evident the legislature intended to clothe the mayor with all the power incident to the office of presiding officer in any legislative body, in the absence of express authority to appoint the standing committees, the power to make the appointment resides in the city council. I am, therefore, of the opinion, that the power to appoint the standing committees of the council, in the absence of any rule of that body conferring the right upon its presiding officer, resides in the council. Very respectfully,
JOSEPH F. BONFIELD, Corporation Counsel.

July 30, 1877.
Math. Benner, Esq., Fire Marshal.
Dear Sir—
In response to your communication as to the liability of the city for damages from sparks from fire engines, I would advise that payment be refused in all such cases. The matter has never been decided, though I believe the corporation not liable.
Yours truly,
JOSEPH F. BONFIELD, Corporation Counsel.

December 1, 1877.
D. S. Mead, Esq.,
Secretary Department of Public Works.
Sir—
The following communication from you of date November 20th has been received:
"Will you please furnish this department with your opinion as to the legal rights of the owners of dock property to permit vessel owners to lay at such dock in such manner as to obstruct navigation and what authority, if any, has the city to cause the removal of such vessels and keeping the river channel clear for the free passage of the same."

Chapter XV of the Revised Ordinances gives to the harbor master ample power to prevent the mooring or anchoring of any vessel, craft or float at any slip or dock so as to prevent the passage of any other vessel, craft or float or to order and if necessary cause the removal or change of location of any vessel, craft or float.

This ordinance was passed under and by virtue of the act of February 13, 1863, which conferred ample power to pass ordinances. Laws & Ord. 407.

Laws and ordinances in force at the time of the adoption by the city of the general law for the incorporation of cities and villages were, by the latter act, continued in force after such adoption until repealed or amended.

The ordinance in question has not been repealed or amended in respect to this subject matter under consideration.

The powers conferred upon the council in respect to the river and harbor by the general incorporation law are as large and comprehensive as the powers conferred by the special charter. Rev. Stat. 220, Sec. 62, paragraphs 33, 34, 38 and 39.

The ordinance then is valid and in full force and effect if the legislature could constitutionally confer the power in the exercise of which it was passed.

Without citing authority on the point, it is sufficient to say that I have examined the question, and have no doubt of the constitutionality of the provisions of the charters on the subject.

Chapter XV. therefore, of the Revised Ordinances, p. 41, is in full force, and the powers therein conferred upon the harbor master may be legally exercised.

Respectfully,

FRANCIS ADAMS, Assistant Corporation Counsel.

December 3, 1877.

John A. Farwell, Esq., City Comptroller.

Dear Sir—

I am requested to give you my opinion upon the power of the comptroller to invest the moneys of the sinking funds of the city.

The charter provision establishing a *sinking fund* for the payment of *school bonds*, is found on page 472, Tuley's Laws & Ordinances, Section 5. It is provided that "An annual tax of not exceeding one-fourth of a mill on the dollar on the assessed rate of all taxable real and personal estate in said city, shall be levied and collected as a sinking fund to pay said funds at their maturity and for the payment of such bonds as may have been previously issued for schools or school purposes. Such sinking fund when collected shall be invested first in school bonds and if they cannot be obtained then in city bonds."

The provisions for the *general sinking fund* are as follows: The common council shall also annually levy and collect a tax of one mill on the dollar on all real and personal estate in said city made taxable

---

by the laws of this state, to provide a sinking fund for the liquidation of the general bonded debt of the city, which amount shall be invested in the purchase of the bonds of said city, if they can be purchased upon satisfactory terms. All city bonds so purchased shall be immediately retired and canceled.

Tuley's Laws & Ord., p. 473, Sec. 2.

The provision for a *sewerage sinking fund* is as follows: "It shall be the duty of the said board to direct the comptroller of said city to invest the amount heretofore raised, or hereafter to be raised, to provide a sinking fund for the liquidation of said bonds, or other bonds of the city of Chicago; and in like manner to invest the interest received on such last mentioned bonds and to invest and reinvest said sinking fund, and all proceeds thereof in such manner as to make the same available for the liquidation of the said bonds."

Tuley's Laws & Ord., p. 567.

The provision for the *River Improvement Sinking Fund* is the same as the *Sewerage Sinking Fund*.

Laws & Ord., p. 540.

The fifth clause of Section 1 of the revenue act of 1873, known as "Bill 300," practically repeals the above charter provisions relating to sinking funds and is as follows: "Fifth: To provide for a sinking fund or funds for the payment of the general or special indebtedness of the city, and no city shall hereafter contract any debt without at the same time providing for the annual levy and collection of a direct tax sufficient to pay the interest and the principal when it falls due. All money raised for any sinking fund shall be invested in the purchase of bonds of said city—such purchases to be made from time to time and directed by the mayor, and all bonds so purchased shall be immediately retired and canceled."

This act is declared by the Supreme Court to be unconstitutional (8 Legal News, p. 330), and I am, therefore, of the opinion you have the power to invest the sinking fund as originally provided, and as set forth in the charter provisions above cited.

Respectfully,

JOSEPH F. BONFIELD, Corporation Counsel.

February 6, 1878.

Hon. Monroe Heath, Mayor.

Dear Sir—

I am requested to give you an opinion as to the power of the mayor to suspend fines for violations of city ordinances, and if he has not such power to state where it lies.

The old city charter provides as follows: "Neither the mayor nor common council shall remit any fine or penalty imposed upon any person for the violations of the laws or ordinances of said city, unless two-thirds of all the aldermen authorized to be elected should vote for such release or remission, but the mayor shall be authorized in his discretion to release from imprisonment any person committed to the bridewell or house of correction or county jail for violation of the ordinances of said city, by virtue of the judgment of said police court.

Laws & Ord. 1873, Sec. 8, p. 513.

The only provisions in the present city charter touching on the power of the mayor in such cases is as follows: "He (the mayor) may release any person imprisoned for violations of any city ordinance and shall report such release with the cause thereof to the council at its first session thereafter." Art. XI, Sec. 9.

Under Section 6, Article I, of our charter, all laws or parts of laws not inconsistent with the provisions of the act shall continue in force and be applicable to any city the same as if such change of organization had not taken place.

The clause above referred to of the old charter empowering the city council by a two-thirds vote to remit any fine or penalty imposed upon any person for a violation of the laws and ordinances of a city, must be considered as yet in force.

I am, therefore, of the opinion, that the power to remit fines for violation of city ordinances reposes solely in the city council, and that it requires a two-thirds vote of that body to legally cause such remission. Respectfully,

JOSEPH F. BONFIELD, Corporation Counsel.

July 26, 1879.

T. T. Gurney, Esq., City Comptroller.

Sir—

In answer to the annexed communication from you I would say that in cases where land has been condemned for a street or alley under existing laws, the city has no legal right to demand a deed of the condemned premises, sufficient title for the contemplated public use being acquired by means of the proceedings to condemn and payment in accordance with them.

In cases of streets the city has usually procured deeds, when the owners were willing to execute them, but in cases of condemnation for alleys, I think it unnecessary to be at the trouble of having deeds executed, and as I have already stated, the city has no right to insist on conveyances in any condemnation case.

Respectfully,

FRANCIS ADAMS, Corporation Counsel.

October, 1879.

Hon. Carter H. Harrison, Mayor, etc.

Dear Sir—

In answer to your question whether the city has the power to retire city bonds when due, by the reissue of other bonds for a like amount, and at the same or a lower rate of interest, I will say that there is no doubt as to the power.

Tuley's Laws and Ord., p. 424, Sec. 43.
City and Village Incorporation Law, Art. V, Sec. 6, paragraph 6,
The substitution of new bonds for old ones is not increasing indebtedness.
City of Galena vs. Corwith, 48 Ill., 423. The same rule applies to bonds not yet matured, but, as city bonds are at a premium, it must be evident that they cannot be retired prior to maturity.
Respectfully,
FRANCIS ADAMS, Corporation Counsel.

November 20, 1879.
T. T. Gurney, Esq., City Comptroller.
Dear Sir—
You have requested my opinion on the following questions, viz.: Whether the limitation or taxation of two per cent. on the valuation of the preceding year, contained in Sec. 1, Art. VIII of the City and Village Incorporation Act, as amended, applies to taxes for school purposes, or whether it applies only to taxes levied for municipal purposes exclusive of school purposes, so that taxes may be levied for corporate purposes other than school purposes, to the extent of the limitation expressed in the section, and for school purposes in excess of such limitation. Section 1 of Article VIII of the general law for the incorporation of cities and villages, as amended by act approved May 28, 1879, and in force July 1, 1879, after authorizing a levy each year, of the total amount of appropriation for all corporate purposes, legally made, contained the following proviso: "Provided, the aggregate amount of taxes levied for any one year exclusive of the amount levied for the payment of bonded indebtedness, or the interest thereon, shall not exceed the rate of two per centum upon the aggregate valuation of all property within such city or village, subject to taxation therein, as the same would equalize for state and county taxes of the preceding year." Bradwell's Laws, 1879, p. 623, Sec. 43 of the School Laws, as amended by act approved June 3, 1879, in force July 1, 1879, Ib., page 216, provides: "Section 43. For the purpose of establishing and supporting free schools for not less than five nor more than nine months in each year and defraying all expenses of the same of every description; for the purposes of repairing and improving schoolhouses, of procuring furniture, fuel, library and apparatus, and for all other necessary incidental expenses in each district, village or city, anything in any special charter to the contrary notwithstanding, the directors of such district and the authorities of such village or city, shall be authorized to levy a tax, annually, upon all taxable property of the district, village or city not to exceed two per cent. educational and three per cent. for building purposes, to be ascertained by the last assessment for state and county taxes."
The statute containing the two per cent. limitation was approved

May 28, 1879, and that amendatory of the school law, June 3, 1879, so that if there be any irreconcilable repugnancy, the latter act must prevail, being the last expression of the legislature on the subject.

But if there is no irreconcilable inconsistency, then they must be so construed that both shall have effect.

Section 1 of Article VIII, as amended, applies solely to the levy of taxes for corporate or municipal purposes.

In the case of Spright vs. The People, ex. rel., etc., 87 Ill., page 595, the court say: "The constitution, Art. VIII, Sec. 1, directs that the general assembly shall provide a thorough and .efficient system of free schools, whereby all children in this state may receive a good ·common school education. There is no limitation in that or any other article as to the agencies the state shall adopt in providing this system."

The court then, after expressing the opinion that the legislature may designate such persons for the levying of school taxes, as may be conducive to the public interest, say: "All laws, whether in city charters or elsewhere, designed to affect free schools,. may be regarded simply as school laws, as a part of the law intended to carry out the mandate of Art. VIII, Sec. 1 of the constitution, and although they may require the boundary lines of cities to be adopted as lines for the formation of school districts, and that city officers shall perform the duties of school officers, yet this is for convenience only, and the districts thus to be formed, and the officers thus required to perform duties, are to .be regarded simply as agencies selected by the state to provide a system of free schools. Although the limits and officers of the two corporations (that for strictly city purposes and that for the purpose of providing free schools) are the same, their purpose and objects are different, and they are, in fact, *separate and distinct corporations.* The one has its existence and is limited in the powers it may exercise *by its charter proper;* the other *by the school law.*"

Here the court clearly distinguishes school purposes from the corporate purposes of cities.

In the case of Fuller vs. Heath, et. al., the court, commenting on the provisions of the special charter of the city of Chicago, in force prior to the adoption of the present constitution, say: "The law on this subject in force at that time, whether embodied in form in the charter of the city, or in amendments to the charter, or in laws not purporting in form to be a part of its charter, must be regarded as a part of the school laws, *not as strictly a part of its charter for strictly city purposes.*"

These cases decide, *first,* that the city, in levying taxes for school purposes, acts merely as the agent of the state to carry into effect the provisions of Art. VIII, Sec. 1, of the constitution; and *secondly,* that in levying such taxes it does not act in its character as a municipal corporation levying taxes for its municipal or corporate purposes.

Both the opinions cited were published prior to the passage of the statutes in question, and must, therefore, be presumed to have been within the knowledge of the legislature, at the time the statutes were passed.

There is another circumstance which evinces that it was not the intention of the legislature to include taxes for school purposes in the limitation prescribed by Sec. 1, Art. VIII of the charter.

Section 43 of the school law of 1872, only conferred the power of levying taxes for school purposes on school directors; no taxes could be levied under that law by boards of education, in cities having over one hundred thousand inhabitants, but in such cities taxes for school purposes were to be levied by the city council.

Rev. Stat. 1874, pp. 960, 978.

Section 43 of the school law as amended, not only confers the power to levy school taxes on *school directors*, but also confers the power on cities, and the limitation of taxation prescribed by the section is two per cent. for educational, and three per cent. for building purposes, thus clearly indicating, as I think, the intention of the general assembly that the limitation upon taxation in the general municipal incorporation law, for the corporate purposes of cities, should not include school taxes.

My opinion, therefore, is that taxes for school purposes are not included within the limitation prescribed by Section 1 of Article VIII of the charter as amended, and that the only limitation upon taxation for school purposes is that prescribed by Section 43 of the school law, as amended, and by Sec. 12, Art. IX of the constitution.

Respectfully,

FRANCIS ADAMS, Corporation Counsel.

LAW DEPARTMENT.

Chicago, Feb. 2, 1880.

To the City Council of the City of Chicago—

Your honorable body has referred to this department a petition requesting, "the use for ten years of one hundred feet front, by two hundred feet deep, on the lake front, for the purpose of building thereon an armory for the 2d regiment."

The opinion asked is "as to right of city to make lease of Lake Park, and if lease should be made, whether city's interest would be jeopardized."

In answering the questions propounded by your honorable body, it is unnecessary to inquire as to the title to the land east of Michigan avenue, as at present occupied, as whether the title is in the city or state does not affect the question. The premises referred to in the petition constitute either part of Lake Park, as heretofore established, o͙r part of Michigan avenue, as being an accretion to such avenue as established by the canal commissioners, by plat recorded July 20, 1836.

. Whether it be part of the street or part of the park, the authority of the city is the same. In neither case has the city the power to grant the permission requested. This is true upon all established principles, and without regard to special legislation on the subject. But legislation is not wanting. The general assembly, by act passed in 1861, amendatory of the city charter, provided, that neither the common council of the city of Chicago nor any other authority, should ever have the power to permit any encroachments on the land lying within four hundred feet east from the west line of Michigan avenue, without the assent of all persons owning lots or lands on said avenue.

This provision was re-enacted in 1863. Laws and Ordinances, 1873, p. 456, Secs. 57 and 58.

My answer to the questions propounded by the council are, therefore, as follows:

First. The city has no power to make a lease of any part of Lake Park.

Secondly. If the city were to make such lease it would not, in my opinion, jeopardize the city's interest in the Lake Park, for the reason that it would be *ultra vires* and void.

The question whether the council should do that which it has no legal power to do, and which, if done, would be in legal contemplation as if not done, I leave to your honorable body to determine.

FRANCIS ADAMS, Corporation Counsel.

June 1, 1880.

Mr. Harrison.

Dear Sir—

I stated to the committee that the council was the judge of the election and qualification of its members, and that its action in the matter is conclusive, but that a committee upon a mere reference to it of papers, as of the returns of an election and affidavits, as in the present case, without any instructions from the council, had not power to go into the whole matter, but that the committee's report should be based solely on the papers committed to them by the council. The council could, of course, give to the committee as ample power for the purpose of investigation as the council itself possesses, but this is not done by a mere reference of particular documents. In reference to your suggestion that the former council was a canvassing board, but that the present acts in the capacity of judging of the election and qualification of its own members, I would say, that in legal contemplation there is no former or later council, the council being a continuous body. It is made the duty of "the city council" to ascertain and canvass the returns and declare the result—charter, Section 57—and inasmuch as that has not been done in the case under consideration, it is the duty of the council to do it.

In conclusion I will say that the council has all the power in the premises which Congress has in like cases, and may, if it sees fit so to do, exercise its powers by committees.   Respectfully,

FRANCIS ADAMS, Corporation Counsel.

June 2, 1880.

Mr. E. P. Barrett, Chairman Committee on Elections.

Dear Sir—

I am informed that your committee to whom was referred the election returns from the 7th precinct of the 14th ward, are about to make a report, upon the hypothesis that my opinion as expressed at a meeting of the committee, is that under the order of reference the committee can only count the votes as they appear on the face of the returns.   If the committee think that such is my opinion, I must certainly have failed to make myself understood, as I entertain no such view.   I informed the committee that their report must be based on the matters referred to them, viz., the returns including the tally papers and the affidavits presented to the council, and that the committee might make such report as might seem to them just, after an examination of the matter.

It is evident that this would not limit the committee to acting in the capacity of mere tellers, so that they could only report the number of votes for each candidate, as such votes appear upon the face of the returns.   For instance, the committee might, upon an examination of the returns and the affidavits referred to them, report that it appeared to the committee from such examination that the returns had been altered, and that they should be rejected, or unless the apparent alterations were explained to the satisfaction of the council they should be rejected.   The only doubt which I had, when called before your committee, was whether your committee had power, under the order of reference, to examine witnesses in relation to the returns.   This is a question of parliamentary law, which I have not examined, and which had not been presented to me, prior to the time I was called before the committee, and my impression was that the committee had not the power, and I so stated.   Since then, however, I have examined the matters, and have come to the conclusion that my impression was erroneous.   What induced my mistake was that there was no formal order of reference to the committee made by the council, no instructions, and no express powers conferred.   In legislative bodies it is usual to make a formal order of reference including instructions to the committee.   In the present case, when the returns came before the council for examination and canvass, affidavits were presented to the council attacking the returns, and Alderman Throop moved that the returns and affidavits be referred to the committee on elections, and that no result be declared, which motion prevailed.   The object of the reference, although not expressed, clearly was, that the committee might examine and investigate in relation to the returns and the affidavits, and the subject matter thereof. In such case the rule is thus stated by Cushing: "When the object or one of the objects of a select committee is the investigation of facts, it may, without any express authority for that purpose, examine all witnesses that may appear, and all papers that may be brought before it, and all records to which it can obtain access in the prosecution of its inquiries."—Cushing's Manual, Sec. 1901.

The same rule, in my opinion, applies to a reference to a standing committee. I think such examination should be oral, and not by affidavits. The committee could not, of course, examine the ballots, such examination being beyond the power of the council.

Respectfully,
FRANCIS ADAMS, Corporation Counsel.

June 23d, 1880.
D. C. Shorey, Esq., Chairman of Judiciary Committee.
Dear Sir—

I have received from your committee a communication containing certain questions, which, with my answers thereto, are as follows:

First. Has the city council, under the charter, authority to prevent the emission of smoke from the smoke-stack of any steamboat, or locomotive, or from any chimney not connected with a private residence, within the city limits, as provided in the bill for an ordinance herewith submitted to you?

The charter confers upon the city council the following powers:

"To regulate the police of the city or village, and pass and enforce all necessary police ordinances."

Sec. 63, Sub-sec. 66th.

" To declare what shall be a nuisance, and to abate the same; and to impose fines upon parties who may create, continue, or suffer nuisances to exist."

Ib. Sec. 63, Sub-sec. 75th.

The first provision cited vests the council with police power within the jurisdiction of the municipality.

The police power is the most comprehensive power known to civil government. Mr. Justice Redfield says: "This police power of the state extends to the protection of the *lives, limbs, health, comfort* and *quiet* of all persons, and the protection of all property within the state. According to the maxim, *Sic utere tuo ut alienum non laedas*, which, being of universal application, it must, of course, be within the range of legislative action to define the mode and manner in which every one may use his own as not to injure others," etc. Shaw, C. J., says: "Every holder of property, however absolute his title, holds it under the implied liability that his use of it shall not be injurious to the *equal enjoyment* of others having an equal right to the enjoyment of their property."

Cooley on Cons. Limit, Sec. 572, 573 *et seq*.: also Northwestern Fertilizing Co. v. Village of Hyde Park, 70 Ill., p. 631.

The liquor traffic is within the police power. Schwuchow v. City of Chicago, 68 Ill., 444.

I have no doubt that if the emission of dense smoke, as described in the first section of the bill submitted to me, is detrimental to the health, comfort or ordinary enjoyment of the public, it can be prevented by the exercise of the police power.

NUISANCES.

The power to declare what shall be a nuisance and to abate the same, etc., is a valid power. Held, that in the exercise of such power a municipal corporation may declare the selling of intoxicating drinks a nuisance, and provide for its abatement. Goddard vs. Town of Jacksonville, 15 Ill., 588. President et al. vs. Holland et al., 19 Ib., 276. Block vs. Town of Jacksonville, 36 Ib., 301.

Held, also that the declaring the running at large of hogs, within the municipal limits, a nuisance, and imposing a penalty therefor, is a valid exercise of such power. Roberts v. Ogle, 30 Ill., 459.

The council, however, cannot, in the exercise of the power to declare what shall be a nuisance, arbitrarily declare that to be a nuisance, which cannot be such, in the nature of things. C. R. I. & P. R. R. v. City of Joliet, 79 Ill., 25.

The subject of the declaration must be something which may be a nuisance in *fact*. The question is whether dense smoke issuing from the smoke-stacks of steamboats and locomotives may be a nuisance.

The supreme court in this state, in Wahle v. Reinbach, 76 Ill. 322 quotes with approval the following language: "Any business, however lawful, which causes annoyance that materially interferes with the ordinary comfort, physically, of human existence, is a nuisance that should be restrained, and smoke, noise and bad odors, even when not injurious to health, may render a dwelling so uncomfortable as to drive from it any one not compelled by poverty to remain."

"Whatever is offensive, physically, to the senses, and by such offensiveness makes life uncomfortable, is a nuisance."

Smoke such as described is, as I think, clearly within this definition. Other authorities might be cited, but when I find the law unequivocally stated by our own supreme court, I deem it unnecessary to look farther. I am of the opinion that the city council has the power to declare the emission of smoke as described in the question a nuisance, and to prohibit it by ordinance.

Secondly: "If the city council has the power to prevent the emission of such smoke, is the said bill for an ordinance sufficient in form to effect that purpose?"

I think the ordinance obnoxious to criticism in the following particulars:

First: Section 1 of the proposed ordinance declares the emission of dense smoke from the smoke-stack of a steamboat or locomotive or from any chimney *not connected with a private residence* a nuisance.

By implication the emission of dense smoke from a chimney connected with a private residence is not to be regarded as a nuisance. This makes the question of nuisance or no nuisance depend, not upon the emission of dense smoke, but on the place whence it is emitted. I think the public would find it difficult to understand how dense smoke issuing from the chimney of a building where no one resides is a nuisance, while like smoke in like volume issuing from the chimney of a building occupied as a residence is not a nuisance. I think, also that the section savors too much of special legislation.

Section 2 limits the jurisdiction of the magistrate to cases in which complaint may be made by the commissioner or officers of the health department, thus putting it in the power of the commissioner to prevent prosecution by merely omitting to complain.

Another objection is, that the requiring the complaint to emanate from the health department is an implication, that the emission of dense smoke is not to be deemed a nuisance, unless detrimental to health, whereas it may be a nuisance by producing physical discomfort, although not injurious to health.

Section 3 is difficult to understand. It provides: "It it shall appear in evidence that some proper and efficient device or apparatus has been attached to the furnaces, then the above fine may be remitted." Device proper and efficient for what purpose? To prevent the emission of dense smoke? This can hardly be, because if such a device were used there would be no emission of dense smoke, and consequently no fine.

Then, no fine can be imposed until the evidence is all heard, so that after the imposition of the fine nothing can appear in evidence. If the intention is that, if it shall appear in evidence, that a proper and efficient device or apparatus to prevent the emission of dense smoke from the chimney, has been attached to the furnaces since the action was commenced, then the action shall be dismissed at the defendant's costs, it should be so expressed. Respectfully,

FRANCIS ADAMS, Corporation Counsel.

March —, 1881.

To the City Council of the City of Chicago—

Your honorable body Feb. 21, 1881, referred to me an ordinance in relation to the vaccination of children attending schools in the city, for an opinion as to the power of the council to enforce the same if passed. The substance of the ordinance is that children shall not be permitted to attend any school in the city, public or private, who have not been vaccinated within seven years last past. Sub-section 78th of , Section 63 of the general charter vests the city council with power "to do all acts and make all regulations which may be necessary or expedient for the promotion of the public health or the suppression of disease," and Sub-section 66 of the same section vests the council with power "to regulate the police of the city or village, and pass and enforce all necessary police ordinances."

The bill for the ordinance, if passed, will not only be a sanitary regulation but a police ordinance.

In other words, the ordinance may be passed under either the 66th or 78th clauses of Section 63, or under both. The power of the council under Sub-section 66 of Section 63 is discussed in my opinion to the council of date, June 23, 1880. Council Pro. 1880, p. 107, to which I respectfully refer your honorable body. The power conferred by Sub-section 78 of Section 63 in relation to the public health is couched in the most comprehensive terms. The court of appeals of the state of Maryland commenting on a provision substantially the same in the charter of the city of Baltimore says: "The transfer of this salutary and essential power is given in terms as explicit and comprehensive as could have been used for such a purpose. To accomplish, within the specified territorial limits, the objects enumerated, the corporate authorities were clothed with all the legislative powers which the general assembly could have exercised."

Of the degree of necessity for such municipal legislation the mayor and city council of Baltimore were the exclusive judges. Dillon on Mun. Corp., Sec. 95.

If the council has power to pass such an ordinance, it follows necessarily that it can be enforced, but this is not left to inference, as the charter expressly confers the power to "enforce all necessary police ordinances."

That vaccination is a material, if not a certain preventive of small pox is, as I am informed, the almost universal opinion of the medical profession, also, that vaccination in the majority of cases is necessary at least once in seven years until attainment of majority.

Upon consultation with the health commissioner and examination of the bill submitted to me, I have concluded that there are some defects in it, and have, therefore, drafted a new bill, which I enclose with this communication. Respectfully,

FRANCIS ADAMS, Corporation Counsel.

April 19, 1881.

To the City Council of the City of Chicago—

Your honorable body passed, March 2, 1881, the following order:

*   *   *   *   *   *   *

The charter of the city does not contemplate the maintenance of water works and furnishing of water to parties outside the city limits. This is manifest from the provisions of the charter in regard to the levying of taxes for water works, and water rates which can only be levied on property within the municipal limits. It is also manifest from other provisions of the charter. If, however, the water works of the city are of such capacity that water may be supplied to persons outside of the city limits without inconvenience to citizens of the city, I am of opinion that the city might safely contract for furnishing water outside of the city limits. In such case the contract price might be fixed by the council, at its discretion, and a bond might be taken to secure the payment of the amount agreed on, and also, the water meter might be placed inside the city limits, so that, in case of non-payment, the water could be promptly shut off. Respectfully,

FRANCIS ADAMS, Corporation Counsel.

June 16, 1881.

Mr. Frank A. Stauber, Chairman Committee on Schools.

Dear Sir—

Your Committee has referred to me a resolution referred to your committee by the city council, requesting my opinion on the following questions, viz.:

Whether the city council has any power to prescribe how books shall be purchased by the city of Chicago or board of education for the use of the public schools of the city?

Whether the city council can compel a purchase of all books to be used by the pupils in the public schools, the same to be owned by the city or board of education?

Whether the city council can compel the board of education to purchase all books and keep them for the use of pupils attending public schools?

My answer to each and all of these questions is, no.

Section 80 of the school law of 1877 prescribes the duties of the board of education. Among the prescribed duties are the following:

"To prescribe the books to be used and the studies in the different schools."

"To prescribe the method and course of discipline and instruction in the respective schools, and to see that they are maintained and pursued in the proper manner."

The board of education derives its power from the statute, and such powers as are not conferred by the statute it cannot exercise. The power to purchase books for the use of pupils is not conferred by the statute either on the board of education or the city council.

The city council has no power whatever in the matter under consideration.

The statute expressly provides: "Schools in such cities shall be governed as hereinafter stated, and no power given to the board shall be exercised by the city council." Revised Statutes, 1877, page 920.

Respectfully,

FRANCIS ADAMS, Corporation Counsel.

June 20, 1881.

To the City Council of the City of Chicago—

Your honorable body passed June 13th, 1881, a resolution requesting an opinion from me on the following question, viz.: "Whether the City Council possesses the authority to compel the gas companies of this city to lay down gas mains, where so ordered to do by the council?"

I am of opinion that the city council possesses no such power. The Chicago Gas Light & Coke Company was incorporated by act approved February 12, 1849, which was amended by act approved February 9, 1855, and the People's Gas Light & Coke Company was incorporated by act of February 12, 1855, amended by act of August 30, 1858, and February 2, 1865.

Laws & Ord. 1873, pp. 172-176.

The gas companies do not derive their right to lay gas mains and pipes in the public streets. That power is expressly conferred by the acts of the general assembly.

Laws & Ord. 1873, p. 172, Sec. 2; pp. 174-5, Secs. 2 and 5.

The extent of the power of the council is to establish proper regulations for the protection of the streets, and to prevent damages, etc.   Respectfully,

FRANCIS ADAMS, Corporation Counsel.

October, 1881.

Hon. Carter H. Harrison, Mayor.

Dear Sir—

I have received from you the following communication:

"I understand that the Staats Zeitung Company claim that they have a right to publish city matters under an old ordinance never repealed. Please examine and let me know; also as to whether we should put in German paper special assessment advertisements."

I have read the communication from the Staats Zeitung Company to the city council on the subject referred to.

The statement in that communication that the city council by the adoption of the report of a minority of a committee awarded "the contract for printing city claims to the Staats Zeitung" is correct. This was done April 4, 1879, Council Proceedings 1878-9, p. 555.

No contract in writing was made with the Staats Zeitung Company, but after the award of the council such matters as were desired to be printed in the German language were sent to the Staats Zeitung for publication, and were published in that paper, and the publications were paid for at the rate mentioned in the company's bid, viz: 24 cents per square inch. This has continued nearly to the present time.

No contract was made by the city with the Staats Zeitung Company or any other German paper for the publication of matters required to be published, for the fiscal year 1880 or 1881, nor has any

3

such contract been awarded to any German paper for either of those years.

The Staats Zeitung Company claims that the contract having been awarded to it for the year 1879, and not having been awarded to any other company or newspaper for the years 1880 and 1881, and it having published matter required to be published in the German language during the fiscal year 1881, and down to the present time, and having been paid therefor at the rate mentioned in its bid accepted by the city in 1879, there is an implied contract on the part of the city to continue to publish in the Staats Zeitung matters required by any law or ordinance to be published, until a contract shall be let after the second Monday of December, 1881, as prescribed by the revised ordinances. The question is whether this position is correct.

I think it unnecessary in considering this question to discuss section 1664, article 4, of the municipal code, because, as to that section, I concur in the view taken in the communication of the Staats Zeitung Company, viz.: that what is there prescribed to be done, is to be done in the month of December next succeeding the date when the ordinance took effect, which will be December, 1881.

The company bases its claim solely on the ordinance of August 31, 1876, as amended by the ordinance of January 20, 1879 (Council Proceedings 1876, p. 181; lb. 1878-9, p. 357), the action of the council awarding the contract in 1879, and the other circumstances above stated. The reasoning of the communication is, in my opinion, so far correct, that if the claim cannot be maintained on the basis above stated, it must fail.

Section 1 of the ordinance of August 31, 1876, provides that "the city printing and publication of those matters and things required by law or any city ordinance to be printed or published shall be done in the English and German languages."

Section 2, as amended by ordinance of January 20, 1879: "All publications in newspapers now, or which may hereafter be required to be done by any law or ordinance, or by direction of the City Council, or any officer of the city authorized to have such work done, shall be, under contract, let to the lowest bidder. Provided, however, that in determining who is the lowest bidder, the circulation of the bidder's newspaper within the limits of the City of Chicago, may be taken into consideration."

Section 3 relates to job printing.

Section 4: "The City Comptroller shall at once advertise and let such contracts for the unexpired portion of the present fiscal year, and annually thereafter he shall, at the beginning of the fiscal year, advertise and let such contracts for such fiscal year, and shall submit the bids received by him and his action thereon to the City Council for its approval."

The last section contemplates an annual advertisement and letting of the contracts for printing, and it shall be let only for the current fiscal year, and that it shall be subject to the approval of the council.

Thus by the very terms of the ordinance the contract could not be let for a longer period than the current fiscal year.

But such a contract could not be let for two or three years for another reason. Appropriations are made during the first quarter of the fiscal year, and for the fiscal year, and the charter expressly prohibits the making of any contract, or the incurring of any expense by the city, unless an appropriation shall have been previously made concerning such expense.

Mun. Code, p. 32, Sec. 91.

A contract might possibly be made involving large expense, and which from its nature could not be performed within a year, provided a previous appropriation were made for the necessary outlay for the current year, but a contract capable of completion within the current year, as for printing, cannot, in my opinion, be made to extend beyond the year.

This was the view taken by Judge Drummond in the case of Garrison v. The City of Chicago and the People's Gas Light and Coke Company, which involved the question of the validity of a contract between the city and the gas company to furnish the city with gas for two years.

Elliott Anthony, Esq., then corporation counsel, supported the proposition that such a contract was invalid, by a large mass of authorities.

It is clear that the ordinance of 1876 intends a contract in writing, and it is, to say the least, an exceedingly loose manner of transacting public business to let such matters rest in merely verbal or implied contracts. But waiving the fact that there was no contract in writing, and admitting that there was a sufficient contract between the city and the Staats Zeitung Company, it was only a contract for the then fiscal year, viz.: the year 1879, and under the charter and the ordinance of 1879 could not have been for a longer period. The contract with the Staats Zeitung Company expired with the fiscal year 1879. The city comptroller advertised for bids for the city printing early in January, 1880, as provided by the ordinance of January 12, 1880. He reported the bids received by him to the city council, naming the Arbeiter Zeitung as the lowest bidder. This report was referred to the committee on printing.

Council proceedings, 1879-80, p. 358.

The Staats Zeitung Company was one of the bidders, thus inferentially admitting that its contract with the city had expired.

A majority of the committee on printing reported in favor of awarding the contract to the Volksfreund, but the report was not concurred in, and the matter was deferred from time to time, and no final action was ever taken in the matter by the council.

C. P., 1879-80, pp. 407, 433, 441, 455, 464.

There has been no advertisement for bids for the year 1881, as provided by the ordinance of 1876, but the printing has, as before stated, been done by the Staats Zeitung Company.

Under the facts, as stated, there is not, in my opinion, any implied contract on the part of the city to continue to cause publications to be made in the Staats Zeitung until December, 1881, or for any time whatever.

But this question is presented by, the facts, viz.: There having been no contract made with the German newspaper for the year 1881, is there any authority to make publication of city matters in any German newspaper?

There are certain things required to be published by the statute (or charter), as, for instance, imposing any fine, penalty, imprisonment or forfeiture,' or making any appropriation, and special assessment notices. Mun. Code, pp. 26 and 45, Secs. 65 and 142.

There may be other matters required to be published by the statute, but these are sufficient to illustrate the argument.

Now matters required to be published must be published in the English language, whether there has been any contract for their publication in accordance with the ordinance of 1876 or not.

The statute is imperative in this regard.

The publications required by the statute are English publications only, because if a statute provides for a publication, being silent as to the language in which it shall be made, it is the same as if it prescribed an English publication in express words. The statute also provides that publications shall be made "in a newspaper published in the city or village."

Mun. Code, p. 26, Sec. 65; p. 34, Sec. 98; p. 45, Sec. 142.

The statute therefore means publication in one newspaper printed in the English language. This view is fortified by the fact that the general assembly by acts amendatory of the city charter, approved February 13, 1863, and March 9, 1867, respectively, provided for the publication in a German newspaper of ordinances and other proceedings and matters required to be published.

Laws and Ord., 1873, p. 398, Secs. 23 and 24.

This legislation would have been wholly unnecessary if the mere power to publish ordinances and other matters included the power to publish ordinances and other matters included the power to publish them in the German language without special and express authority so to do. But the provision of the amendatory acts of 1863 and 1867, as to publications in the German language, became inoperative upon the adoption by the city, in April, 1875, of the act of 1872, the present charter.

Mr. Grinnell, the present city attorney, expressed this opinion in an opinion to the city council dated February 16, 1880.

A statute authorizing publications in one newspaper, and in the English language only, is, in my opinion, clearly inconsistent with a statute authorizing publications in two newspapers, one English and the other German.

Richard S. Tuthill, Esq., who was city attorney in 1876, gave an opinion to the council dated July 15, 1876, that the provision in the former special charter referred to would become inoperative upon the exercise by the council of the power conferred by Sub-section 94 of Section 62, of the act of 1872, viz.:

"To provide by ordinance that all the paper, printing, stationery, blanks, fuel and all supplies needed for the use of the city shall be furnished by contract let to the lowest bidder."

The council in passing the ordinance of August 31, 1876, acted upon Mr. Tuthill's opinion, in establishing the corporation newspaper, which existed only by virtue of the section above cited in the charter of 1863.

The council ever since the passage of the ordinance of August 31, 1876, have, in omitting to designate a corporation newspaper, acted upon the hypothesis that the sections referred to in the former special charter are no longer in force.

It will be seen that I go further than Mr. Tuthill, in holding that the adoption of the act of 1872, *ipso facto*, and without any action on the part of the council, rendered inoperative the provisions in the acts of 1863 and 1867 above referred to. I am of opinion, therefore, that publications in the German and any other language than the English are unauthorized by the statute, and that it is not within the power of the city council to authorize such publications, at the expense of the city. It is a familiar rule that a municipal corporation can exercise only such powers as are granted in express words or by necessary implication.

As said by Mr. Justice Black of Pennsylvania, "A doubtful power does not exist, because whatever is doubtful is decisively certain against the corporation."

It may be asked where is this power to stop, if it is to be exercised at the discretion of the council? If the council can, without express authority so to do, cause publications to be made in German, why not in Dutch, French, Hebrew, Bohemian and Sanscrit? Why not in all languages? Respectfully,

FRANCIS ADAMS, Corporation Counsel.

October 12, 1881.

Wm. S. Young, Jr.,
    Chairman Judiciary Committee.
    Dear Sir—
    I am asked by your committee for an opinion on the question contained in the following resolution, viz:
    "Resolved, That the Judiciary Committee report to this Council if the Mayor can legally act as Commissioner of Public Works."
    I will assume that the question is asked with reference to the

present state of affairs, as otherwise it would be merely speculation. The council October 31, 1881, passed the following ordinance:

Be it ordained by the city council of the city of Chicago:

Section 1.   That all the powers and duties devolved by ordinance on the commissioner of the department of public works be and the same are hereby devolved upon the mayor of the city until a commissioner of the department of public works shall be appointed and qualified.

The council has, beyond question, the power to pass this ordinance.   The office of commissioner of public works is not a charter office, but one created by the council in pursuance of authority conferred by the charter, and which may be abolished by the council at any time, and its duty devolved upon any other city officer.

The charter in prescribing the duties of the mayor provides:

He shall perform all such duties as are, or may be prescribed by law, or *by the city ' ordinances.'"*

The office of commissioner of public works being temporarily vacant, the council has seen fit, by the ordinance above quoted, to impose upon the mayor the duties heretofore required to be exercised by the commissioner of public works by the ordinance creating the department of public works.

The mayor, in exercising such duties, is not, in contemplation of law, acting as commissioner of public works, but as mayor.

He is performing, as mayor, duties hitherto imposed upon the commissioner.   He is not, under the ordinance, commissioner of public works, *de jure* or *de facto*.   Respectfully,

FRANCIS ADAMS, Corporation Counsel.

October 17, 1881.

Hon. Carter H. Harrison.

Dear Sir—

In your communication of this date you inform me that suits have been brought against a number of livery stable keepers in violation of Art. XII of the revised ordinance, in relation to licenses, etc.; that the parties sued claim that the ordinance is invalid on the ground that it is unreasonable, and propose that a test case shall be made and a final decision obtained before the institution of further prosecutions, and you ask my opinion as to the validity of the ordinance, and whether the proposition of the livery men should be entertained.

Before answering these questions, I will briefly state the provisions of the ordinance in reference to the subject matter.

Section 1146 prohibits the keeping or using for hire, for the carrying or conveying of persons within the city of Chicago, any vehicle or carriage of any description whatever without a license.

Section 1147 authorizes the issuance of a license to any resident of the city over the age of twenty-one years, to keep and use for hire, for the conveyance of persons any vehicle or carriage, such as is mentioned in Section 1146, of which such person is the owner, upon executing a bond as prescribed by Section 1149, in the penal sum of five hundred ($500) dollars, and paying a license fee as prescribed by the ordinance.

This section would seem to require a bond for each vehicle, or carriage licensed.

By Section 1148 licenses may be transferred.

Section 1151 requires every person to have painted on each licensed vehicle or carriage his name and the number of his license.

Section 1152 requires that every vehicle or carriage for the conveyance of persons (except on the busses running on established lines) shall, when driven or used for hire, or standing in any public place, etc., in the night time, have lighted lamps with plain glass fronts, with the number of the license painted thereon, etc.

Section 1155 provides that no person, except a licensed owner, shall drive any vehicle for the conveyance of passengers for hire or reward without being licensed as a driver, nor shall a licensed driver drive any vehicle, except that for which he is licensed, nor shall any owner permit any licensed driver to drive any vehicle except the one for which he is licensed.

Section 1155 provides that no vehicle shall have more than one driver, who shall be licensed, etc.

By Sub-section 4, of Section 1160, livery stable keepers are required to pay, as a license fee, two and fifty one-hundreds ($2.50) dollars, for each vehicle kept by them for hire for the conveyance of passengers.

To recapitulate, the ordinance purports to impose on livery stable keepers the following duties:

1.   They must take out a license for each vehicle owned by them, and used for hire, for the conveyance of passengers.—Section 1146.

2.   They must pay a license fee of two and fifty one-hundredths ($2.50) dollars for each vehicle licensed, and give bond in the penalty of $500 for each vehicle licensed.—Sections 1149, 1160, Sub-section 4.

3.   The name of the owner and the number of the license must be plainly painted in a conspicuous place on the outside of each vehicle, and, in the night time, each vehicle must have conspicuous lamps, with the number of the license thereon.—Sections 1151 and 1152.

4.   Not only must each vehicle be licensed, but it must have a licensed driver, and no driver can drive any vehicle except that for which he is licensed, nor can there be more than one licensed driver for any vehicle.—Sections 1154 and 1155.

The ordinance seems to make no distinction between the keepers of hackney coaches and cabs which stand in public places and are used for the conveyance of passengers from place to place in the city (just as express wagons are used for the conveyance of merchandise, etc.) and vehicles kept by livery stable keepers in their business.

A buggy or a carriage kept by a livery-stable keeper, which never occupies a public stand, but is used solely for hire to persons applying at the stable, is placed by the ordinance on the same ground as a hackney coach or cab, which is as much a public conveyance as a street car.

If the keeper of a livery-stable uses a coach owned by him as a hackney coach, then he is *quoad hoc* a hackman, and the regulations as to hackmen apply.

But in respect to vehicles not used thus publicly, but strictly in the livery business, viz: for hire at his place of business, he is neither a hackman nor a cabman, and the ordinance in placing him, as to such vehicles, upon the same ground, and subjecting him to the same regulations as hackmen and cabmen, ignores a distinction which is recognized in the charter.

The charter confers upon the city council the following power:

"To license, tax and regulate hackmen, draymen, omnibus drivers, carters, cabmen, porters, expressmen, and all others pursuing like occupations, and to prescribe their compensation."

Mun. Code, p. 21.

"To tax, license and regulate auctioneers, distillers, brewers, lumberyards, livery-stables, public scales, money changers and brokers."

Mun. Code, p. 25.

The charter in these grants of power clearly distinguishes between livery-stables and hackmen and cabmen.

I suppose no one would contend that the council has power to prescribe the compensation to be paid to keepers of livery stables, for vehicles hired to private persons, and not used as hackney coaches or cabs.

Webster defines "livery-stable" as "a stable where horses are kept for hire and where stabling is provided."

In the present common acceptation of the word it means a stable where not only horses but vehicles are kept for hire. It is well known that by far the largest and most profitable part of the business of the keepers of livery stables is the hiring of buggies, and of carriages to persons who desire to use the vehicles as their own for the time being, as ostensibly private vehicles, and who prefer them to a public conveyance, such as a hackney coach or cab. The ordinance will, I think, materially and detrimentally affect this source of profit, by making these ostensibly private vehicles conspicuously public.

I am of opinion that the ordinance is unreasonable, in that it requires a livery-stable keeper to have one licensed driver for each vehicle owned by him, and also, in providing that no driver shall drive any vehicle except that for which he is licensed. The proper regulation of livery-stables certainly does not require such legislation, and in my judgment it is unreasonable and oppressive.

I think the power conferred by the charter to license livery-stables authorizes the council to require that the keepers of such stables shall pay a license, and that it is a proper exercise of the power to make the number of horses or vehicles kept a criterion of the amount to be paid, as by requiring a certain sum for each horse, or vehicle, but I do not think that the charter authorizes the application to keepers of livery-stables, in respect to vehicles not used as hackney coaches, or cabs, such regulations as may be necessary and proper in the case of hackmen and coachmen.

I am inclined to the opinion that what the city council actually intended was to place the keepers of livery-stables, in respect to vehicles used by them as hackney coaches and cabs, upon the same footing as hackmen and cabmen, but strictly speaking the intention must be ascertained from the language of the ordinance itself, and that places them upon the same footing as to all vehicles.

I think the ordinance should be amended so as to except vehicles kept by livery-stable keepers, other than those used by them as common hackney coaches or cabs, from the provisions applicable to hacks and cabs.

The police court attorney informs me that the pending suits are for violations of the ordinance, by carrying on business without a license. I have already said that the requiring a license to be taken is a legitimate and reasonable exercise of the power conferred on the council, by the charter, and I am unable to perceive how it can logically be urged in defense of these suits that other provisions of the ordinance not sought to be enforced by the suits are unreasonable, nor how many of the suits can be made a test as to whether provisions, the consideration of which is not involved in it, are reasonable. I therefore think that the proposal to make one of the pending suits a test case should be rejected. Respectfully,

FRANCIS ADAMS, Corporation Counsel.

October 18, 1881.

Mr. Patrick Sanders, Chairman, Committee on Gas Lights.

Dear Sir—

Your committee has referred to me a bill for "An ordinance concerning gas companies" for an opinion as to whether the bill if it becomes an ordinance, can be enforced.

The bill is in terms applicable to all persons, firms, and incorporated companies engaged in the manufacture of illuminating gas.

Section 1 requires an annual license to be taken out, and the payment into the city treasury of $50.00 for such license, under a penalty of not less than one hundred nor more than two hundred dollars.

Section 2 prescribes a standard for gas, viz.: "Gas which burning at the rate of five cubic feet per hour shall emit a light equal to that produced by eighteen standard sperm candles, each burning at the rate of one hundred and twenty grains per hour."

Section 3 makes it the duty of each person, firm, or corporation engaged in the manufacture of illuminating gas to publish every day in an evening city newspaper the illuminating quality, "by candle power of the gas manufactured that day."

Section 4 provides, substantially, that the charge for gas shall be in proportion to its illuminating power, etc.

Section 5 requires an affidavit to be filed with the city clerk by every manufacturer of illuminating gas, on the first Monday in October of every year, showing that the provisions of Section 4 have been complied with.

Section 6 imposes a penalty of not less than one hundred nor more than two hundred dollars for each violation of the ordinance.

It is well known that the "Chicago Gas Light & Coke Company" and "The People's Gas Light & Coke Company," which are incorporated companies, supply illuminating gas to the city, and that they are the only companies supplying such gas. This being true, the conclusion must be that the ordinance is intended to operate on these companies, as, otherwise, it would be without practical effect.

The power to pass the bill in question must be conferred by the charter of the city, or some statute, else it does not exist.

The gas companies cannot be regulated, or compelled to take out a license, unless the power to license, or regulate is expressly conferred. Such power is not conferred by the charter of the gas companies, the charter of the city, or any law of which I have any knowledge.

The only power of regulation conferred upon the city in the premises' is to regulate the openings in the streets, alleys, and public grounds, for the laying of gas mains and pipes, and erecting gas lights.

I am, therefore, of opinion that the council is powerless to pass the bill.

The council, however, in consenting by ordinance to the erection of gas factories, and the laying of pipes in the streets by new companies, has power to impose such regulations as it may see fit to impose.

Mun. Code, Art. V, Sec. 1, Sub-sec., 13.

Respectfully,
FRANCIS ADAMS, Corporation Counsel.

December 8, 1881.

Hon. Carter H. Harrison, Mayor, Etc.

Dear Sir—

You have asked of this department an opinion as to the power of persons owning improvements on property which abut on the streets of the city to build or extend the same over the lot line and in or upon the street and to maintain the same there when so built or extended, and the rights and powers of the city in the premises.

Under its charter the city is empowered to "prevent and remove encroachments or obstructions upon its streets."

By Section 1995 of the Municipal Code it is provided that "no person shall erect or place any building, in whole or in part, upon any street, alley, sidewalk * * * within this city, under a penalty of fifty dollars."

By Section 1996, Municipal Code, it is provided that the commissioner of public works shall notify in writing the owner of any building so obstructing such street to remove the same within the time fixed within said notice, which shall not be less than three nor more than thirty days, under penalty of not less than twenty-five dollars nor more than one hundred dollars, and a further penalty of ten dollars for every day the same shall so remain.

Whenever the owner after such notice shall refuse or neglect to remove such obstruction, or if the owner cannot be readily found for the purpose of such notice, it is provided in Section 1997, Municipal Code, that the commissioner of public works may have the same removed, and may recover the expenses thereof from the owner.

While these are excepted from the general rule that a street cannot be encroached upon by individuals owning property thereon, certain portions of buildings, such as porticos, bay windows to dwelling houses, cornices, steps, etc., it is clear that the extension of show windows in business buildings upon and over the streets or sidewalks of the city, beyond the lot line, is illegal.

It is further the opinion of this department that the city has ample power to abate such nuisances by virtue of the sections herein cited, and that no further ordinance on the subject is necessary.

Yours respectfully,

F. S. WINSTON, JR., Asst. Corporation Counsel.

January 22, 1882.

Mr. H. F. Sheridan, Chairman of the Committee on Railroads.

Dear Sir—

The petition of the Chicago, Cook County, Passenger Dummy Railroad company for an ordinance granting to the company the privilege to construct and operate an elevated railway on certain streets in the city, together with a draft for the ordinance asked for by them, has been referred to me by your committee, for an opinion as to whether the city council has power to pass such an ordinance except upon a petition of the owners of property fronting or abutting on the streets named in the proposed ordinance. It is not stated in the petition how the company became incorporated, but it is to be presumed that it became incorporated under the general laws of the state for the purpose of constructing, maintaining and operating elevated ways or conveyors.

Consideration of the question presented requires an examination of the history of legislation in this state, in regard to the construction and operation of railways in the streets.

The framers of the constitution were anxious to prevent injury to property holders by the construction and operation of railways in the

streets of cities and among other things, provided that no law should
be passed by the general assembly granting the right to construct and
operate a street railroad in any city, town or incorporated village, without requiring the consent of the local authorities, having the control of
the streets or highways proposed to be occupied by such street railroad.

    Constitution, Art. XI, Sec. 4.

The legislature of the state, acting in harmony with the spirit of
the constitutional provision referred to, by an "Act to provide for the
incorporation of cities and villages," approved April 10, 1872, which is
the present city charter, provided that the city council in cities should
have the power to permit, regulate or prohibit the locating, constructing or laying the tracks of any horse railroad in any street, alley or
public place, but such permission should not be for a longer time than
twenty years, and the act further provided, as a protection to the property owners, that the city council should have no power to grant the
use of or the right to lay down any railroad track in any street of the
city to any steam or horse railway company except upon a petition of
a majority of the owners of more than one-half the frontage of the
street.

    Mun. Code, Sec. 63, Sub-sec. 90.

At the same session of the legislature an act was passed entitled:
"An act concerning corporations," which, among other things, authorizes corporations to be organized for the purpose of operating horse
and dummy railroads, but it will be noticed by the 28th section of that
act that it is provided that nothing therein contained shall be construed
to allow the construction and operation of any street railroad in any
city, town, or incorporated village, without the consent of the local
authorities thereof. Afterwards an "Act in regard to horse and dummy
railroads," approved March 19, 1874, was passed, authorizing the incorporation of horse and dummy railroads, and it will be observed that
this act requires that the consent of the city shall be given before any
street can be occupied for any such purpose.

By "An act in regard to elevated ways and conveyors," approved
April 7, 1875, corporations are authorized to be organized under the
general incorporation law for the purpose of operating elevated ways
and conveyors, but the act carefully provides that streets are not to be
occupied for that purpose, except with the consent of the city council
of the city in which it is proposed to construct and operate such elevated ways and conveyors.

These provisions of the several acts of the legislature referred to
necessarily lead to inquiry relative to the conditions upon which the
city council is authorized to grant the consent required by the acts.

First: Are the provisions of the act to provide for the incorporation of cities and villages, approved April 10, 1872, which is the present city charter, applicable to the granting consent to the use of
streets for the construction and operation of railways operated by
other than horse and steam cars?

It does not appear from the petition or from the proposed ordinance by what power the company seeking the ordinance proposes to operate its railway, and I am not advised whether it is to be operated by electricity, compressed air, steam or other means. It is to be noticed that the company only proposes to operate its projected railroad by the use of electric motors, if practicable, and if not practicable, I suppose it intends to operate it by some other power. But conceding that the company does not intend to operate its proposed railway by either steam or horse power, the question is whether the provisions of the act mentioned are applicable to every street railroad by whatever power operated.

The provision of the city charter prohibiting the council from granting the right to lay down railroad tracks in the streets of the city, except upon a petition of the owners of property fronting on the streets or part of streets proposed to be used for railroad purposes, applies in terms only to steam and horse railroad companies, and it is, therefore, argued that the provision does not extend to, or include, railroad companies which may operate their roads by other than horse and steam power. I am constrained to say that I think this is a very superficial view of the matter. The evident intention of the provision was to prevent damage to the property abutting on the street, by the construction and operation of the railroads in the streets, by placing it in the power of the owners of more than one-half of the frontage to prevent such construction and operation by withholding their consent. It is not the power used which constitutes the damage, if any, but the railroad and the operation of the cars thereon, by whatever power operated.

If, for instance, the railroad on State street was an injury to the property abutting on the street when operated by horses attached to the cars, it is clearly no less an injury now that it is operated by an endless cable moved by steam power, the power being applied not on the street, but on the private grounds of the railroad company. When the city incorporation act of 1872 was passed there were no railroads in the state operated by any other than horse and steam power, and no railroad companies, except horse railroad and steam railroad companies, and elevated railways, or railways operated by other than steam or horse power, were little, if at all, known. Hence the general assembly included in the language of the prohibition all railroads then generally known. The general assembly, by the prohibition in question, assumed that, as a general rule, the construction and operation of a railroad in the streets of a city are an injury to the abutting property.

Dwarris, in his work on statutes, a standard work acknowledged to be the highest authority by all the courts of this country, as well as England, says: "A statute may be extended by construction to other cases within the same mischief and occasion of the act, though not expressly within the words." Numerous instances are given by the writer of the application of the rules. As for instance, a statute of Richard II., Chapter III, gives a writ of error in reversion to a tenant for life or by courtesy. It was held that, although the statute speaks only of reversions, remainders were also to be taken within the purview thereof.

Plowden says: "The best way by which we can form a judgment whether a case is within the statute is to suppose a law maker present, and you asked him the question, Did you intend to include this case? Then you must give yourself such answer as you suppose he, being an upright, reasonable man, would give, and if he did mean to embrace it, you. may safely hold the case to be within the statute." A further example is cited. A statute was passed relative in terms solely to the Bishop of Norwich, but it was held to extend to all other bishops. So a statute was passed relative to the warden of the Fleet, and was held to extend to all jailers. A statute was passed relative to executors, and it was held to extend to administrators.

The rule of the English court is well expressed in the case of the Dean of York vs. Middleburgh, 2 Younge & Jervis, 196, in which Baron Alexander says: "It is by no means unusual in construing a statute to extend the enacting words beyond their natural import and effect, in order to include cases within the same mischief, where the statute is remedial."

It is the mode of construction familiar to every legal person.

The rule is well expressed in the case of The People vs. The Utica Insurance Co., 14 Johnson, 380, in which the court say: "Such construction ought to be put upon a statute as may best answer the intention which the makers had in view, and this intention is sometimes to be collected from the cause of necessity of making the statute, and sometimes from other circumstances. And whenever such intention can be discovered, it ought to be followed with reason and discretion, although such construction seems to be contrary to the letter of the statute. And such construction ought to be put upon it as does not suffer it to be eluded."

In 36 N. Y. Reports, p. 46, a statute authorizing an assessment for the curbing and guttering, was held to embrace flagging, although flagging was not especially named in the act.

The rule mentioned is distinctly stated by the Supreme Court of this state in O. & M. Railroad Co. vs. Brubaker, 47 Ill., 462. The action in that case was against the railroad company for killing an ass, and the only question raised was whether that animal fell within the protection of the statute which requires railroad companies to erect and maintain fences sufficient to prevent cattle, horses, sheep and hogs from getting on the railroad. The court said: The statute was a remedial one, imposing a reasonable duty upon railroad companies and furnishing a remedy to parties injured, in case their duty was not performed. Its object was to protect domestic animals and there could be no doubt the legislature intended to protect mules and asses, although not mentioned in the act, as well as horned cattle, horses, sheep and hogs. In view of the well-settled rule, it seems to me that the city charter should be so construed as to require a petition of the property-owners in every case in which a railroad is proposed to be constructed or operated in the streets without regard to the mode of power proposed to be used. It has been suggested that the act of April 7, 1875, relative to elevated ways and conveyors, dispenses with the provisions of the city charter, so far as they require a petition of the property-owners. It seems to me, however, that all of the statutes relative to the use of streets being in pari materia, should be construed together.

The last act mentioned is not in any manner inconsistent with the charter of the city, and consequently does not repeal any part thereof. It is true that the act of 1875 requires the consent of the city, but when the inquiry is made upon what terms or conditions the city is authorized to consent, reference must necessarily be had to the city charter. Dwarris on Statutes, p. 235, says: "That a remedial statute shall be extended to later provisions made by subsequent statutes, and that a statute may extend to matters of subsequent creation." And Lord Coke said that an act made of late time shall be taken with the equity of an act made long before. Numerous instances are given in which a subsequent act has been held to be governed by the provisions of a previous one.

In my judgment, the legislature did not intend by the passage of the act of 1875 to dispense with the salutary provision of the city charter requiring a petition of the property-owners.

I am, therefore, clearly of the opinion that the city council has no power to pass such an ordinance as is petitioned for by the Cook County Passenger Dummy Railway Company, except upon a petition of the owners of the land representing more than one-half of the frontage of the streets sought to be used for railroad purposes.

Respectfully,

FRANCIS ADAMS, Corporation Counsel.

June 13, 1882.

Mr. M. Ryan, Chairman Committee on Wharves and Public Grounds.

Dear Sir—

Your committee has asked my opinion as to whether the city council can legally pass the following resolution:

"Resolved, That the Mayor and Comptroller be and they are hereby authorized to grant a temporary permit to the Baltimore and Ohio Railroad Company to occupy and use that space on the Lake Front north of the Exposition building and the north line of the Armory buildings, between the space between the railroad tracks and the Armory buildings, for temporary purposes only, upon such terms, payments and conditions as in the judgment of said Mayor and

Comptroller will be proper, conditioned, however, that said company so receiving such permit shall remove therefrom at any time upon order of the City Council or the Mayor."

The proposed resolution contemplates an agreement between the city and the railroad company, for occupancy by the latter of the premises described in the resolution, for a time and for the rent to be specified in the agreement, the agreement, however, to contain a provision that it may be terminated at any time, at the option of the city.

Such an agreement would be a lease, and the question is whether the city has such interest in the Lake Front that it can legally lease any part of it. There is no act of the legislature in force authorizing the sale or leasing by the city of any part of the Lake Front, nor is there any act in force defining the power of the city in the premises.

I have examined the question with a good deal of care and in all its aspects, not only since the resolution under consideration was referred to me by your committee, but formerly, and am unable to arrive at any other conclusion than that the city has not such interest in the property, or control over it, as that it can lease any part of it to any individual or corporation, to the exclusion of the public.

There are a number of questions involved in the determination of the main question asked by your committee, which I have not thought it necessary to discuss at length in this opinion. I will say, however, that considering all questions involved in the view most favorable for the exercise of the power, I am of the opinion that the city council cannot legally pass the proposed resolution.

Respectfully,

FRANCIS ADAMS, Corporation Counsel.

August, 3, 1882.

Alexander Kirkland, Esq., Superintendent of Buildings.

Dear Sir—

You have asked my opinion as to the construction of Section 999, Municipal Code, and more particularly with reference to whether a shed or privy may be attached to the main building on any given lot.

Upon mature deliveration, I am of opinion that no frame shed can be attached to such main building, and my reasons are as follows:

1. The language of the section is, "Such sheds and privies shall be separate buildings." I am aware of the strength of the argument that this means "separate from each other." But upon consideration this meaning would only apply to a case where there is no main building on the lot. For if there is a main building and to this the shed or privy may be attached, then while they may be separate from each other, they are not "separate structures;" because they are attached to and form a part of another structure, to-wit: the main building.

2. On the other hand, if we say the clause means the shed and privy are to be "separate from each other," what is to become of that portion of the section which authorizes the shed and privy being under the same roof? If such a construction be accepted, then the section is conflicting. And it should be so constructed, if possible, as to be harmonious.

3. If the shed be allowed to be joined to the main building and there be an opening from one to the other, then the shed becomes practically a part of the main building, and it would practically allow the extension of dwelling houses, for example, to an additional area of 256 feet; then under Section 1046 this addition might be raised to the height of the main building. This, it seems to me, is not contemplated in the ordinance.

4. If the shed be made thus a part of the main building, it would be difficult to prevent its being used as a part of "a dwelling" or for "business purposes," both of which are expressly forbidden.

5. The word "shed" is defined by Webster as a temporary structure "*an out building.*" This would seem of itself to exclude the idea of its being an addition to or a part of another building.

6. The ordinance relating to frame buildings is obviously for protection against fire. In construing the ordinance therefore, its object is to be borne in mind and that construction given which will more effectually accomplish that object. If these frame sheds are more apt to spread fire when joined to another building than when "separate structures," this fact may properly be taken into consideration in construing a doubtful point in the ordinance.

The corporation counsel agrees with me in the conclusion which I have reached on this point. Very respectfully,

F. S. WINSTON, JR., Assistant Corporation Counsel.

November 20, 1882.

To the City Council of the City of Chicago—

Your honorable body, November 13, 1882, referred to this department a resolution requesting an opinion as to whether "the keeping of large numbers of cattle in the stables and yards of the various distilleries within the city limits is a nuisance, within the meaning and intent of Section 1626 of the Municipal Code."

Section 1626 in terms declares to be a nuisance the keeping or using any yard, pen, place or premises within the city of Chicago "in or upon which more than three head of cattle or swine shall be confined or kept at any one time."

The keeping of cattle or swine in excess of three, in the stables or yards of distilleries within the city, is a nuisance within the meaning of the section. * * * Respectfully,

FRANCIS ADAMS, Corporation Counsel.

4

April 7, 1883.

De Witt C. Cregier, Esq., Commissioner of Public Works.

Dear Sir—

I have considered your communication of date April 5th inst., inquiring whether it is within the power of the commissioner of public works to define the districts within which street sprinkling is to be done, and to assign a district to one person and prohibit other persons from sprinkling in the district so assigned, etc.

I am of the opinion that this can be practically accomplished. The water and water works are under the charge of the commissioner of public works.

Mun. Code, Sec. 558.

All the hydrants constructed for the purpose of extinguishing fires are public hydrants, and no person can open any of the hydrants, or draw water from them, without special permission so to do from the commissioner of public works, except members of the fire department, for the purposes of that department. Ib., Sec. 2043. This being true, I am of opinion that it is within your power to define sprinkling districts, and to refuse to authorize more than one person or firm to draw water from the public hydrants within a district, for the purpose of street sprinkling, and I think that the rule that such authority shall be given to the person who shall first procure a majority of the frontage on the streets in the district would be a reasonable rule. The system indicated would practically exclude all others than the party authorized, to use the hydrants in a given district, from sprinkling in the district, because without the use of the hydrants the sprinkling, as I understand it, cannot be done.

It is true that the plan suggested would not prevent other persons from obtaining licenses under Mun. Code, Sec. 2040, but, unless they could also obtain from the commissioner authority to use the public hydrants, their business would be of no benefit to them.

Respectfully,

FRANCIS ADAMS, Corporation Counsel.

May 5, 1883.

To the City Council of the City of Chicago—

Your honorable body has referred to this department a petition from a committee of "The Brotherhood of Stationary Engineers, No. 1, of the City of Chicago," asking your honorable body "to pass an ordinance compelling all persons in charge of steam boilers in the City of Chicago to be examined by a competent board of examiners, and, if qualified, to be licensed as engineers."

The petition contains a draft of an ordinance, which is suggested as the one desired by the petitioners. Section 1 provides for the appointment of a board of competent and practical engineers, etc., whose duty it shall be to examine each, and if found qualified, deliver to him a certificate of qualification. Section 2 provides that if the

applicant be found incompetent or unfitted, etc., a certificate of qualification shall be denied.

Section 3 provides that no person shall use or manage in the city
any steam boiler subject to inspection by the city except an engineer
who shall have received a certificate, as aforesaid, nor shall any person employ any other person who is not an engineer, qualified, as
aforesaid, to manage or use any steam boiler in the city.

The sections above are printed, and accompanying them are, in
writing, what purport to be certain provisions as to the appointment
of the board, the grades of licenses, etc, which it is unnecessary to
notice in detail.

The order of reference directs this department to report an order
as requested by the petitioners.

The ordinance asked for is of so unusual a character that I have
deemed it my duty to examine whether the council has the power
to pass it. The council can exercise no power not granted in the
charter, either in express words, or by necessary implication. The
only powers granted by the charter in respect to steam boilers are to
prevent their dangerous construction and condition, to cause them to
be removed and placed in a safe condition, when dangerous, and to
provide for their inspection.

Mun. Code, p. 23, paragraphs 63 and 67.

This power the council has already exercised. Mun. code, p.
221-223.

There is no power granted by the charter to license engineers
nor to determine by ordinance the qualifications of persons who shall
have charge of steam boilers, nor to provide that they shall be
licensed engineers, nor to compel them to submit to an examination.
The law seems to have left the responsibility for any injury which
may result from the negligence or incapacity of persons in charge of
steam boilers to them and their employers.

I am, therefore, clearly of the opinion that your honorable body
has no power to pass any such ordinance as that requested by the
petitioners, and that to do so would only involve litigation and expense resulting in a judicial decision declaring the ordinance void.

Respectfully,

FRANCIS ADAMS, Corporation Counsel.

July 5, 1883.

Dr. Swayne Wickersham, Chairman of Finance Committee.

Dear Sir—

Your committee have referred to me the following resolution:

"Resolved, that the Law Department report to this council what
funds, if any, can be taken from the City Treasury, so that the same
may be applied toward the completion of the new city hall."

Section 3 of Article VII of the city charter, after limiting the annual corporate expenditures, contains the following provision: "Pro-

vided, however, that nothing herein contained shall prevent the City Council or board of trustees from ordering, by a two-thirds vote, any improvement, the necessity of which is caused by any casualty or acci-dent after such annual appropriation is made, etc." Then follows au-thority to borrow money for such purpose, which, of course, is un-necessary when there is unappropriated money in the treasury suffi-cient to meet the expenses of the proposed improvement. The com-pletion of the city hall is an improvement, and the city council is the judge as to whether the necessity for such completion has been caused by any casualty or accident, since the passage of the appro-priation bill for 1883, and the judgment of the council in that regard, expressed in proper form, will be, in my opinion, conclusive.

It has been decided that a declaration by the legislature, ex-pressed in a law, that an emergency exists requiring that the laws should take effect immediately, is conclusive, and that the courts cannot inquire as to whether the declared emergency did in fact exist.

Section 22 of Article IV of the constitution prohibits the passage of local or special laws in certain enumerated cases, and then pro-vides: "In all other cases where a general law can be made appli-cable, no special law shall be enacted."

This provision is contained in the constitution of the state of Indiana, and was from that constitution adopted into ours. The Supreme Court of Indiana, prior to the adoption of our constitu-tion, held that under the provision the general assembly is the judge as to whether a general law be made applicable in the particular case.—Gentile vs. The State, 26 Ind., 410-15.

The city council, then, if of the opinion that the casualty men-tioned has arisen as above stated, may, in my opinion, so declare, and order the completion of the city hall, and that the amount of money necessary to be expended for that purpose during the present fiscal year shall be paid out of any moneys in the city treasury not other-wise appropriated.

I enclose with this communication an ordinance, to be used in the event that your committee shall decide to recommend the com-pletion of the city hall.   Respectfully,

FRANCIS ADAMS, Corporation Counsel.

October 16, 1883.

DeWitt C. Cregier, Esq., Commissioner of Public Works.

Dear Sir—

I have just received from you a communication in which you ask the following questions:

"Can the damages which may be occasioned by the construction of a viaduct be legally ascertained in advance of its construction?" And, if so, "What is the proper mode of proceeding?"

This is not the first time that these questions have occurred to me.   The numerous suits which have been brought and the judgments which have been recovered against the city for damages alleged to have been occasioned to private property by viaducts, especially since the decision of the Supreme Court in the Rigney case, led me to consider the subject long since. In the report of the law department to the city council of date January 1st, 1883, pp. 4-5, you will find this language: "In view of the decision on the Rigney case, it is impossible to make even an approximate estimate of an appropriation for a viaduct, in advance of its construction, unless the damages be ascertained by some proceeding in court. We, therefore, advise that, hereafter, no viaduct shall be constructed by the city without first having an ascertainment, by proper proceedings in court, of the damages which will be occasioned by the construction."

My opinion is that damages which may be occasioned by the construction of the viaduct can be substantially ascertained in advance of its construction, by legal proceedings. My reason for using the word "substantially" will appear hereafter.

The mode of procedure is that prescribed by Article IX of the city charter in reference to local improvements, such as the opening of a street. The only differences which I can perceive between proceedings for the opening or extension of a street under Article IX and proceedings to ascertain damages which may be occasioned by the construction of a viaduct are as follows:

When a petition is filed for the opening of a street, in pursuance of an ordinance passed for that purpose, the private property necessary to be taken for the improvement has been ascertained and is described in the petition. It usually consists of parts of lots or pieces of larger tracts of land, and if the owner of the remainder of the lot or tract claims damages, he should be heard as to his claim. If any one claims damages to a lot or tract of land, none of which is proposed to be taken for the improvement, and which consequently is not described in the petition, he must file a cross-petition setting up his claim. In the case of a petition to ascertain damages which may be occasioned to private property by a proposed viaduct, no property is, in most instances, required to be taken for the improvement, and in describing the property in respect to which damages may be claimed, it is manifest that it could be described only with approximate accuracy. It would be impossible to anticipate all property in respect to which the owners might claim damages. All property abutting on the viaduct or its approaches, however, or in such a situation in reference to it that it might, by possibility, be injuriously affected, could be described on the petition, and this would attain substantially the object proposed.

The modus operandi would be as follows: The department of public works would prepare plans and specifications of the proposed viaduct, showing its dimensions, its approaches, longitudinal and lateral, their proposed elevations of grade, the material to be used and the mode of construction, and report to the city council an ordinance ordering the construction of the viaduct, and the ascertainment of the damages, by filing a petition, as in the case of street openings. The ordinance should describe the property in respect to which the damages are proposed to be ascertained, just as in cases of street openings, the ordinance describes the property proposed to be taken. If it is proposed that the cost of the viaduct shall be paid by special assessment, so far as property can be found benefited thereby, the ordinance should so provide, or if by general taxation only, the ordinance should so provide.

Upon the passage by the city council of the ordinance the subsequent proceedings would be substantially the same as in cases of street openings. There would, of course, be some differences in the details occasioned by the differences in the improvements, but these can be considered when the occasion arises. A viaduct being a local improvement, I have no doubt that the expense of it can be raised by special assessment, to the extent that property can be found specially benefited thereby. Respectfully,

FRANCIS ADAMS, Corporation Counsel.

October, 27, 1883.

Hon. Carter H. Harrison, Mayor.
Dear Sir—

You have referred the following resolution, passed by the council October 22, 1883, to this department.

* * * * * * *

In reply to your question whether the social clubs of this city can be successfully prosecuted for selling liquor without a license, we beg leave to report:

We assume the following state of facts to exist in the case of each of such clubs: That it is organized under Chapter XXXII of the revised statutes, as a corporation "not for pecuniary profit;" that its object is simply a social one; that it is supported by contributions of its members, and managed by a board of directors, employing a steward or other person, who is paid a salary by the club; that its liquors and other supplies are purchased by the club, as a collective body, and sold to the individual members, and to no one else; that the profit, if any, arising from such sales does not accrue to the steward, or other individual, making the sale, but belongs to the collective body, the club, and is shared in by each indivual member thereof, including the individual to whom such sale is made; that no sale whatever is made to any individual not a member of the club, and not entitled to share in its profits. This last hypothesis does not, however, exclude the case of a stranger partaking of the hospitality of the club at the expense of a member.

Assuming the above state of facts to exist in the case of each of said clubs, the question is whether, by selling liquor in the manner described, without a license, they are thereby "common nuisances," within the meaning of the dram shop act, or fall within the city ordinances.

It is to be remembered that the dram shop act and the ordinances in question are penal and must be strictly construed.

Fentz vs. Meadows, 72 Ill., 540.

People vs. Peacock, 98 Ill., 172.

A case similar to the one before us was decided by the Supreme Court of Massachusetts in Commonwealth vs. Smith, 102 Mass., 144, when the question was raised whether a social club was within the meaning of the statute against selling intoxicating liquors. The court held that it was not "if the liquors really belonged to the members of the club, and had been previously purchased by them, or on their account," and was sold only to them. That it made no difference "that the person who is to make the distribution delivers them in small quantities and keeps his account by means of tickets or checks."

The court there likened the case to one where a number of gentlemen club together and import a quantity of wine and afterwards distribute it among themselves. The same question arose, in the year 1881, in the case of Seim vs. State of Maryland, 55 Md., 556. The steward of the Concordia Club, Baltimore, was prosecuted for selling liquor to a club member, in violation of the liquor law, prohibiting the selling or giving away of liquor on Sunday. It was there held that the liquor laws "have never been construed as applicable to social clubs." Speaking of the Concordia Club, the court says:

"The society is not an ordinary corporation, but a voluntary association or club united for social purposes; each member must be elected, and each is joint owner of the property and assets, and entitled to the privileges of the society as long as he remains a member. Among these privileges is that of partaking of the provisions and refreshments provided for the use of the members. These are not sold to him by the corporation, but furnished to him by the steward, upon his paying into the common fund what is equivalent to the cost of the article furnished, and what is so paid is expended in keeping up the supply for the use of the members. Such a transaction is not a barter or sale in the way of trade, and therefore not within the purview or meaning of the act of 1866."

The precise question was raised also in England, in 1882, in the case of the Grosvenor Club, London. It was held by the court (Queen's Bench) that the club, in order to sell liquor by retail to its members, did not require a license under the English license laws.

Graff vs. Evans, 51, L. J. R., M. C., 25. The English license law is similar to our dram shop act.

There is, on the other hand, a decision by Judge Lowell (U. S. vs. Wittig, 2 Low. 466 to the effect that a club falls within the terms of the U. S. Revenue Act and must take out a United States revenue license. In his opinion, however, he points out the difference between a license required by a revenue act and that required by a penal statute. There is, of course, a marked distinction between a license imposed for revenue, and one imposed for regulation. The licenses required under our state law and city ordinances have been repeatedly held to be for the purpose of regulation, an exercise of the police power. Those imposed by act of congress are for revenue simply.

The weight of the authorities is clearly to the effect that no saloon license can be exacted of the social clubs of this city, selling liquor or other supplies to their members, in the manner assumed in this opinion. The fact that no license has, in the past, been required of them in this city, nor so far as I have been able to ascertain, in other localities, may fairly be considered as evidence that none were necessary. On the other hand, it is equally well settled that any attempt to evade the liquor laws by the subterfuge of clubs organized for that purpose, will not be tolerated by the law.

Commonwealth vs. Smith, *supra*.

Rickert vs. People, 79 Ill., 85.

Yours respectfully,

FREDERICK S. WINSTON, Jr., Asst. Corporation Counsel.

January 10, 1884.

T. T. Gurney, Esq., Comptroller.

Dear Sir—

In your communication under date of January 5, 1884, you state:

"I am instructed by the committee on printing and finance to request your written opinion as to whether those matters and things required by law or any ordinance of the city to be published in a newspaper must be published in the German as well as the English language, as required by Article 41 of the Municipal Code?"

"Also, are publications in the German, or any other language than the English language authorized by the statute, and if so, has the city council the power to authorize such publications at the expense of the city?"

1. By an amendment of the old city charter passed March 9, 1867, the legislature required the city to publish "in the newspaper printed in the German language having the largest daily circulation, the proceedings, notices and ordinances of said city, and the departments thereof."

By the act of March 10, 1869, the council was required to "designate the German newspaper for the publication of the official proceedings, etc."

The above are the only enactments of the legislature requiring the city to publish in a German as well as an English newspaper, the matters and things required by statute to be published, and such publication, under the former charter of the city was undoubtedly *essential*. The question arose, however, in 1876, whether this obligation existed since the organization by the city under the general incorporation act of 1872. In an opinion, given July 15, 1876, Mr. Richard S. Tuthill, at that time city attorney, held, substantially, that these provisions ceased to be binding upon the city upon its organization in 1875, under the charter of 1872. An opinion to the same effect was given to the council by the present city attorney, Mr. Grinnell, in 1880. To the same effect was the opinion given by Mr. Adams, then corporation counsel, in November, 1881.

I fully agree with the conclusions reached by these gentlemen and without again setting out the reasons therefor will simply state, that there is now no statutory requirement compelling the city to publish in a German, as well as an English, newspaper, the matters and things required to be published.

2. It being clear that there is no statutory *obligation* upon the city to make such publication, your remaining question is, whether the city council has the *power* to authorize them. I am of the opinion that it has. For example, the city has the undoubted power to advertise in the papers for bids upon contracts. This is done under Section 50 of Article IX, of the charter, which gives the city the power to prescribe, by ordinance, the manner of letting contracts. Under this, the council may provide for advertising in any or all of the newspapers. The city, in this regard, possesses the power in common with all other corporations, to pursue the businesslike method of advertising for bids when contracts are to be let.

If in the judgment of the council, a class of contractors or bidders, not to be reached through an English newspaper, can be notified by means of a German paper, the city has clearly the right to advertise in such German paper.

As to the other matters and things required by law to be published, the case seems to me equally plain. Take, for example, the publication of ordinances imposing a fine, penalty, imprisonment or forfeiture, required by Section 3 of Article V of the charter. The object of this requirement is obviously to give notice to the public of the passage of an ordinance, imposing a fine or imprisonment, before undertaking to punish offenders for its violation. So far as this notice is made obligatory by the charter, it is confined to publication in an English newspaper. But it cannot be seriously doubted that the council has the power, in its discretion, to provide for giving such notice also to that large class of citizens who rely upon papers published in the German language for information and news.

Upon this point I entirely concur in the opinion given to the city council by City Attorney Grinnell, February 16, 1880, to the effect that the council has full power under Clause 94, Article V, of the charter, to provide for all printing and publishing which, in its discretion, is required. This clause gives the council the right "to provide by ordinance, that all the paper, printing, stationery, blanks, fuel and all the supplies needed for the use of the city, shall be furnished by contract, let to the lowest bidder."

I agree with the city attorney in the opinion that the term "printing," as here used, includes "publishing" and that the council has full power over the subject.

In short, I am of the opinion that there is no statute now in force which makes it obligatory upon the city to make publications in a German newspaper, but that the city council has the power to provide for such publication if, in its judgment, the interests of the city and the public require that such publication should be made.

Publication in a newspaper printed in the English language is compulsory and is the publication required by statute. Whether any publication should be made in a German newspaper, and if so, to what extent; whether all or any of the advertising done by the city, shall be in the German, as well as in the English language; whether all or any of the city ordinances, or the formal notices of assessments and like matters shall thus be published—these are matters which are in the discretion of the city council. Yours respectfully,

F. S. WINSTON, Jr., Acting Corporation Counsel.

February 7, 1884.

Mr. P. Sanders Chairman Committee on Streets and Alleys, S. D.
Dear Sir—

Your committee has referred to this department a petition and ordinance in relation to ceding Michigan avenue from Thirty-fifth street to Thirty-ninth street to the South Park commissioners for a boulevard.

You inquire as to the validity of the statute of April 9, 1879, enabling park commissioners to take city streets, with the consent of the city, and the property owners, for drives to public parks, and also as to your committee's "rights in the matter."

The validity of the statute referred to was involved in the case of *The People ex rel.* vs. *John R. Walsh*, 96 Ill., 232, and the act was there sustained."

The statute being a valid one, the question remains whether it authorizes the passage and acceptance by the board of the ordinance before your committee. Prior to the taking effect of the act of 1879, the city had no power to divest itself of its control over any other streets, nor had the park commissioners the right to accept such a grant. This was held in the case of Kreigh vs. City of Chicago, 86 Ill., 407, where there was raised the question as to the validity of the ordinance of June 1, 1874, surrendering certain streets of the city to the West Chicago Park Commissioners. The court there, speaking through Chief Justice Scholfield, used the following language: "The authority to establish and open streets, and improve and keep them in repair, as the public necessities require, is vital to the well being of municipal corporations; and it is never to be presumed that the legislature, having invested them with this power, has, at the same time, authorized them to surrender it to others over whose acts they can exercise no control. *It devolves on those who assert the existence of such an extraordinary authority to prove it by the clear letter of the law."*

Subsequently to this decision, the passage of the act of 1879 was procured. In accordance with that act, the council passed the ordinance of June 23, 1879, ceding to the South Park commissioners that part of Michigan avenue, extending from the south line of Jackson street to the south line of Thirty-fifth Street and that part of Thirty-fifth Street extending from the east line of Michigan Avenue to the east line of Grand Boulevard. On July 15, 1879, the park commissioners passed a resolution, taking such parts of said streets, "being parts of connecting streets leading to and connecting with the South Park" for the purpose mentioned in the act, that is, for a public boulevard or driveway connecting the park with the city. The city having ceded and the commissioners having taken this one continuous route, the question is, whether the city may grant, and the park take, another route, at the same time retaining the one now in use. There is not, as we understand it, any proposal to return to the city that part of Thirty-fifth street which connects Michigan Boulevard with Grand Boulevard. Were the act of 1879 silent on the point, it might, perhaps, be assumed that the city, having granted such portion of Thirty-fifth Street as a connecting link between Michigan Avenue and the park would have the right to grant another route from that point to the South Park. But the statute contains an express limitation upon the subject (Section 1): " *And, provided further,* that such connection or improvement shall embrace only such street or streets as are necessary to form *one continuous improvement."* It being remembered that the power in question is an "extraordinary" one and must be shown by "the clear letter of the law," it seems obvious that the city has no further right to grant, nor the park to accept, another portion of the city's streets for the purpose of forming another connection between the city and park. There is already "one continuous improvement," by way of Thirty-fifth Street; it is difficult to perceive the meaning of the proviso just quoted, if it is not a limitation upon the power of the city and park to grant and accept a second and difficult route.

Under any other interpretation of the statute, the city might grant and the park receive any number of the city's streets leading toward the park or connecting with Michigan Avenue, and the city be thus divested of its streets, and the same be converted into so many pleasure drives or boulevards. The proviso referred to is apparently designed to guard against such a result, and would seem to prohibit the further surrender of the city's streets. .Respectfully yours,

F. S. WINSTON, Jr., Acting Corporation Counsel.

Feb. 1894.

M. Ryan, Esq., Chairman Committee on Fire and Water.
Dear Sir—
Your committee has referred to this department, for information as to its legality, the matter of exemption of certain institutions from

water taxes. The rebate or exemption is made under an ordinance passed by the council July 30, 1883, which is as follows:

It has been urged that this ordinance is void because in violation of Section 3 of Article VIII of the constitution, as follows:

"Neither the general assembly nor any county, city, town, township, school district or other public corporation, shall ever make any appropriation or pay from any public fund whatever, anything in aid of any church or sectarian purpose, or to help support or sustain any school, academy, seminary, college, university or other library or scientific institution, controlled by any church or sectarian denomination whatever, nor shall any grant or donation of land, money or other personal property ever be made by the state or any such public corporation, to any church or for any sectarian purpose."

The power of the council in regard to water taxes is found in Article X of the charter. Section 3 of that article provides:

"The City Council or Board of Trustees shall have power to secure all needful rules and regulations concerning the use of water supplied by the water works of said city or government, and to do all acts and make such rules and regulations for the construction, completion, management or control of the water works, *and for the levying and collecting of any water taxes*, rates or assessments, as the said city council or board of trustees may deem necessary and expedient," etc.

It will be seen that the legislature has given to the council plenary control over the subject of water taxes and it would seem to possess ample power to make the exemption called for by the ordinance unless prohibited by the clause of the constitution above quoted.

From a careful examination of the authorities the conclusion has been reached that the ordinance in question is not obnoxious to this provision of the constitution.

It will be observed that the provision referred to is as binding upon the legislature as upon the city. "Neither the general assembly nor any county, city, town, township, school district, or other public corporation," etc., is the language of the section. Yet the legislature has passed laws exempting from taxation charitable institutions, churches and institutions of learning and their validity has never been questioned.

Rev. Statutes, Chap. CXX, Sec. 2.

The laws, it is true, are authorized by another clause of the constitution (Art. IX, Sec. 3.), but if the clause in question were to be construed so as to forbid the exemption of property belonging to such institutions from taxation by the state then the taxation would be inconsistent. For it would authorize in one section what it forbids in another. Section 3 of Article VIII cannot, then, be fairly construed as forbidding the general assembly or any public corporation from exempting from taxation the charitable or religious institutions of the state.

The exemption in the ordinance is an exemption from a tax or an assessment, as much so as is the exemption from a school tax, a city, county, town or state tax, provided for by the statutes of the state. This tax may be levied upon improved real estate, even when no water is used. Art. X. Sec. 3 of charter. The tax when collected goes to maintain and improve the system of water works, just as the school tax is used for school purposes or the city tax to meet the expenses of the municipality.

In exempting institutions of charity and learning from the water tax the city followed the example of the state which exempts the same from all other taxes. The state goes further and exempts all church property used for public worship.

The case of Nichols vs. School Directors, 93 Ill., 61, was a bill for injunction by a tax payer against the directors of the school district, to restrain them from granting to certain religious sects the use of the public school house. It was claimed that the statute authorizing such action, by the school directors, conflicted with Article VIII, Section 3 of the constitution, being the one here under consideration, and also with certain other similar provisions of the constitution. But the Supreme Court denied the claim. The opinion adds:

"Religion and religious worship are not so placed under the ban of the constitution that they may not be allowed to become the recipient of any incidental benefit whatsoever from the public bodies or authorities of the state. That instrument itself contains a provision authorizing the legislature to exempt property used for religious purposes from taxation; and thereby, the same as is complained of here, there might be indirectly imposed upon the taxpayer the burden of increased taxation, and in that manner the indirect supporting of places of worship."

In that case the directors of the public school house granted the use of the same to a religious sect; gave to a particular church the use of public property for a purely sectarian purpose. It is a much stronger case than the one under consideration. Here, the exemption from the water tax is not made for any religious or sectarian institution, *as such;* or *because* such institution is a religious or sectarian one. The exemption is for any and all charitable and educational institutions not conducted for private gain or profit. It is true, all or nearly all of these institutions are under the control of religious sects, but if such would be for charity or learning and be not conducted for private gain, it makes no difference what may be its creed or sect; whether Presbyterian, Catholic, Hebrew or Baptist. So far as this exemption from taxation is concerned the essential is that it be conducted for charity and not for private gain, the creed or want of creed is an incidental matter which in no way affects the exemption.

In considering the effect of the clause of the constitution here in question upon the act providing for the industrial school for girls in the case of County of McLean vs. Humphreys, 104, Ill., 378, the Supreme Court uses the following language:

"It is the unquestioned right and imperative duty of every enlightened government, in its character of *parens patriæ*, to protect and provide for the comfort and wellbeing of such of its citizens as, by reason of infancy, defective understanding or other misfortune or infirmity, are unable to take care of themselves. The performance of this duty is justly regarded as one of the most important of governmental functions, *and all constitutional limitations must be so understood and construed as not to interfere with its proper and legitimate exercise.*"

In that case, it was argued that the act was in violation of the constitution because it required that suitable provision should be made for the religious instruction of the inmates, avoiding, as far as practicable, sectarianism. But the court did not sustain the argument, holding *inter alia.*

"In the present case there is no pretense for the claim that the institution to which the subject of the controversy was committed was, or is, organized or conducted in the interest of any *particular* church or religious organization."

So with this ordinance; it makes no distinction in favor of any particular sect or religious organization. The very definition of the word "sectarian," "peculiar to a sect, bigotedly attached to the trusts and interests of a denomination" (Webster), of itself demonstrates that an ordinance applicable to no one sect or organization cannot be called "sectarian.",

In the case of Cook County vs. City of Chicago, 103 Ill., 646, the Supreme Court has before it the ordinance of September 22, 1879, respecting water taxes, as follows:

"That the Commissioner of Public Works be and he is hereby authorized and empowered to remit and rebate the water tax or rates assessed against property used and occupied fully for charitable and educational purposes.'

The ordinance was vigorously assailed in that case as illegal and void, but the court, while it did not directly pass on the question, impliedly upheld it, in saying that the county did not come within its provisions.

There is yet another consideration in regard to this clause of the constitution. It is not seriously contended that the exemption from the water tax is an "appropriation or pay from any public fund," within the meaning of the first part of the section. This is evident from the fact that the ordinance contains an express proviso to the effect that no tax which has been once collected shall be paid back to any such institution. The claim seems rather to be that the ordinance falls within the inhibition of the latter part of the section that no "grant or donation of land, money or other personal property shall be made to any church for any sectarian purpose."

Assuming this exemption to be a grant of personal property, it is not made to a church nor is it made for any sectarian purpose.

The gift of free water to the Protestant Orphan Asylum, St. Luke's Hospital, or Mercy Hospital, or to the Lutheran Free School or the Brothers' Industrial School, is not a grant to aid the respective sects which happen to control these institutions, in any sectarian purpose. It is granted to them because they are charitable or educational, and are not carried on for private gain. It is difficult to understand upon what basis this ordinance can be considered "sectarian." It gives the same privileges to all institutions of charity and learning without regard to sect, and is entirely in harmony with the laws and policy of the state.

It may be added, in conclusion, that the power to exempt persons or institutions from the payment of this tax should be strictly guarded, and never exercised save on the best of grounds. An ordinance granting such exemption must be a general one, applicable alike to all of a class, and no discretion should be left to an executive officer to exempt or not as he pleases. Yours respectfully,

F. S. WINSTON, Jr., Acting Corporation Counsel.

I approve of and agree with the foregoing opinion.

JULIUS S. GRINNELL, City Attorney.

February 16, 1884.

W. J. Onahan, Esq., City Collector.

Dear Sir—

In reply to your favor of the 12th inst., requesting an opinion as to your power and duty in regard to the collection of water taxes, and whether the same are a lien upon the land and buildings against which they are assessed, I beg to reply:

By Section 3 of Article X of the present city charter, the council is given the power to "make all needful rules and regulations concerning the use of water * * * and for the levying and collecting of any water taxes, rates or assessments, as the said City Council may deem necessary and expedient."

It is further provided that the water taxes may be assessed upon any lot, having a building thereon, which abuts upon a street in which a water pipe is laid, and that the same when so levied "shall become a continuing lien," thereon, which may be "collected or enforced in such manner as the City Council may by ordinance prescribe."

Under this power the council has provided two methods of collecting the tax: First, by shutting off the water in case of nonpayment, and second, by a warrant against the parties liable. The first means of enforcement is in the hands of the commissioner of public works. Mun. Code, Art. LXV.

To collect the delinquent taxes by warrant, the following method has been adopted: The council each year passes an ordinance levying or assessing the tax for that year, as established by ordinance upon all lots, having a building thereon, which abut upon streets having a water pipe. Such ordinance provides that a warrant shall issue to the city collector, commanding him to collect the water taxes unpaid on April 30th of that year, out of the personal property of the owner either of such lot or of the building on the same.

Under such warrant, it becomes your duty to give six days' notice by publication in a newspaper of the receipt of the warrant and requesting immediate payment, and that after the expiration of twenty days you will levy on the goods of those who fail to pay. In case of failure to pay, the warrant commands you to levy and sell the personal property of the persons liable for delinquent tax.

The parties against whom your warrants run are the owners of the land or of the buildings, or either of them.

You have nothing to do with tenants; the remedy on your warrant is against the landlords.

The remedy against the tenants of property—the actual consumers of water—is in the hands of the water department, by shutting off the water. It may be said in passing that, inasmuch as the great majority of the leases provide that tenants shall pay the water tax, it is made the duty of such department to enforce the shut-off ordinances in case of delinquency and not allow the matter to run along until there shall have been a change of tenancy.

But when the matter reaches your hands you have to deal only with the owners of the property.

As to your query whether the tax is a lien upon the land and buildings against which it is assessed, it may be answered that the charter expressly so provides. But the council has adopted only one method of enforcing this lien, viz.: by the issue of a warrant against the personal property of the owner of such land or buildings.

There is no method now prescribed by ordinance for selling the real estate in case of delinquency.

Prior to the adoption of the present charter, there was a method provided for the sale of the real estate, as in cases of special assessment where the tax could not be collected out of personal property.

Laws & Ord., 1873, p. 526, et. seq.

This provision was contained in the old city charter, but no similar provision has been adopted by the council under the powers granted by the general incorporation act.

You ask as to your power to collect the delinquent tax which accrued for the year 1876-7.

The council passed an ordinance January 29, 1877, levying the water tax for the year from April 30, 1876, to May 1, 1877, upon the lots and buildings against which it was assessed.

Council Pro., 1876, p. 327.

Under the ordinance of April 7, 1879, as amended by ordinance of October 27, 1879, a warrant was issued to you to collect the taxes for the year 1878-9, and also the "water rents or assessments remaining unpaid for any previous year or years."

The warrant provides that you shall "make the total amounts set opposite the said several lots, or parcels of land, out of the goods and chattels of the respective owners of said lots or parcels of land, etc."

This authorized you to collect of the owners of said lots or buildings the water tax of 1876-7.

In cases where the property was sold by those who owned it at the time of the assessment, the warrant does not authorize you to proceed against the personal effects of the purchaser. The lien is against the property and might perhaps, if proper ordinances were passed, be enforced against the property. But it does not become a personal liability upon one who purchases the property subject to such lien. As no method has been adopted for enforcing the debt against the land or buildings, you can proceed only against the personal property of those who own such land or buildings at the time of the assessment. Where property is owned to-day by those who held the same at the time this lien accrued, you should notify them of your warrant and your duties under it and insist upon immediate payment.

You should proceed in like manner against those who owned the property at such time and have since alienated. If such tax cannot be collected from those who actually consumed the water or from those who owned the premises against which the tax was assessed, at the time of such assessment, it may be that an ordinance could be so framed as to enforce the remedy against the land and buildings by sale as in cases of special assessment.

Before such an ordinance be passed, it might well be considered whether it is good policy that purchasers of property against which these liens have been allowed to accumulate in years prior to their purchase, should be compelled to pay for water not used by them or their tenants, and of the assessment for which they were no doubt ignorant at the time of their purchase.

The present remedies would seem to be ample if the usual warrants issued each year were duly pressed as in cases of warrants for the collection of personal property taxes. Respectfully yours,

F. S. WINSTON, Jr., Acting Corporation Counsel.

April 3, 1884.

T. T. Gurney, Esq., Comptroller.

Dear Sir—

In answer to your question as to the remedy in case of the neglect or refusal of a town collector to pay over to the city its taxes at or before the time of making his final settlement, I beg to reply.

Section 167 of the revenue act provides the town collector shall make a final settlement of city taxes, "at or before the time fixed in this act for paying over and making final settlement for state and county taxes collected by them."

Section 169 of the same act requires a return of the tax books and a final settlement on or before March 10th, with a proviso that the

5

county collector may notify the town collectors upon what day, within twenty days after March 10th, they shall appear at his office and make the settlement.

By Section 174 of the act it is made the duty of the county collector, in case the town collector does not comply with these requirements, to *forthwith* institute suit on the bond of the latter, and in such suit not only the taxes not turned over may be recovered, but 25 per cent. upon the same may be recovered as damages.

By Section 262 of the same act, the city itself is empowered to institute suit upon the bond of any collector in case of his failure to turn over the taxes received for the use of the city.

Yours respectfully,

F. S. WINSTON, Jr., Corporation Counsel.

April 14, 1884.

J. H. Hildreth, Esq., Chairman, Streets & Alleys, W. D.

Dear Sir—

In answer to your questions as to the charter provision requiring, "A petition of the owners of the land representing more than one-half of the frontage of the street, or so much thereof as is sought to be used," before an ordinance can be granted to a horse-railway company to lay its tracks in such street, I beg to reply.

1. As the provision is for the evident purpose of protecting the property owner there is no objection to his signing a petition for two or more companies. If any number of the companies obtain the consent of a majority of the owners, it makes no difference that the same parties sign all petitions. The section of the charter is a limitation upon the power of the council. Were it not for this provision, the council would have the power to grant such a right of way without any petition. A majority of the property owners uniting in a petition, the limitation is removed, and the council has the power, when two or more companies have the consent of the same property owners, to grant the right of way to either or both.

2. A property owner who signs such a petition has, in my judgment, the right to withdraw the consent thereto at any time before the passage and acceptance of the ordinance. Such withdrawal need not necessarily be in the formal shape of a written withdrawal, but may be evidenced in other ways, for example, by signing a remonstrance against the passage of the ordinance after affixing his name to the petition. The consent, by petition, of the property owners is a condition precedent to the action of the council and if, before the council acts, there is not the consent of the owners of more than one-half the frontage on the street, the ordinance cannot legally be passed.

Respectfully yours,

F. S. WINSTON, Jr., Corporation Counsel.

June 2, 1884.

To the Honorable the City Council of the City of Chicago.

Gentlemen—

In response to the resolution passed by you May 28, 1884, asking for information as to your power to prohibit the posting of obscene pictures, etc., I beg to reply:

By the 17th and 18th clauses of Article V. of the charter, you have the right to control the posting of advertisements in the public streets. By the 45th clause of the same article, you have the power "to prohibit the * * * exhibition of obscene or immoral publications, prints, pictures or illustrations." There can be no question as to your power in the premises.

By an ordinance passed March 5, 1883, you prohibited any one from engaging in the business of bill posting without obtaining a license. As no one can lawfully post any bills or advertisements in the city, save the licensed bill posters, the simplest way of remedying the evil complained of, seems to be to reach the bill posters. I accordingly submit, at the request of the alderman who introduced the resolution, an ordinance to that end.   Respectfully submitted,

F. S. WINSTON, Jr., Corporation Counsel

September, 1884.

To the Honorable the City Council of the City of Chicago.

Gentlemen—

There were passed by the city council on October 17, 1884, the following orders:

1. "There being a doubt in the minds of some property owners as to the power of the city council to assess property to rebuild sidewalks,

Therefore, be it ordered, that the Law Department is hereby requested to communicate to this council the law on the subject, also the bearing of the recent decision of the Supreme Court on this subject."

2. "Ordered, that the corporation counsel be requested to inform the council whether any method can be adopted by the city for the building and repairing of sidewalks, which shall be less expensive and more expeditious than proceeding in the courts by special assessment."

In response to the first request, it may be briefly and emphatically stated that there can be no doubt in the mind of any one, who knows the law, as to the power of the city to assess property for the building of sidewalks. The power is ample, complete, and beyond dispute or denial. The decision of the Supreme Court referred to in your order in no way militates against the authority given by the constitution and the statutes to assess property for the construction of sidewalks and other public improvements. The case in question, *City of Chicago vs. Crosby*, decides only that a city cannot compel property owners to build sidewalks by the process of penal ordinances; that the fee of the streets being in the city, it is for the city to build the sidewalks. This has always been the law in this state, and it was only upon a suggestion from the citizen's association that a test case was carried to the Supreme Court by the prosecuting attorney and the attorney of the association, in the hope of obtaining a decision different from those previously given by the Supreme Court. The court, however, adhered to this law as previously understood. But while this is the law, it is not at all inconsistent with the equally well settled principle that the city, while it is obliged to build sidewalks and keep the same in repair, can do so at the expense of the property owner by assessing his real estate for the cost of such improvement. In other words, the decision concerns only the *method* by which the property owner may be made to pay the cost of such improvement—that he cannot be compelled to construct a sidewalk by fining him if he does not do so; but that his property may be made to bear the cost of the improvement by the proceeds of assessment.

In reply to your second query, whether a better method cannot be adopted by the city for the building and repair of sidewalks, I beg to suggest a complete and radical change in the whole system of sidewalk building and repair. The matter has received my close and careful consideration, and I make this recommendation in the belief that, if properly managed, it would be of the greatest advantage to the city, the property owners and the taxpayers.

The chief objections to the present system of special assessment proceedings are the delay and expense they necessarily entail. They have often been a matter of complaint from the citizens and in your honorable body. You are obliged to have an estimate made of the cost of the improvement, including the cost of making the assessment. You must give the property owner fifteen days in which to build. A petition must be filed in court, and upon this the court appoints three commissioners to make the assessment roll. This roll must be made and filed in court ten days before the term at which there is to be a final hearing upon the matter. Notice of the proceedings must be given, not only by mail, but also by posting notices and by advertising. Affidavits and certificates must be filed of such notice, and if notice is not given in time, the matter is continued for a term of court. If any one objects to the assessment, the case must be set for trial and a hearing had before a jury. After their verdict there may be a new trial granted by the court, or the matter may be tied up for several months by an appeal. Without going further into the details of special assessment proceedings, it is evident from practical experience that they cause, in many cases, very great delay—notwithstanding the conceded efficiency and excellency of our special assessment department.

The change which I would suggest is that, instead of proceeding by the clumsy and expensive method of special assessment, you should build and repair sidewalks, hereafter, by the method of special taxation of abutting property.

This is authorized by an act of the legislature in force July 1, 1875, which will be found on pages 113 to 116 of the Municipal Code. The *modus operandi* under this act is briefly as follows: An ordinance is passed providing for the sidewalk desired and the property owners are given thirty days in which to construct it in accordance with the ordinance. At the end of thirty days the city may at once construct the sidewalk, and the cost of the same is taxed against the lots by the city clerk. This official thereupon issues a warrant to the city collector, who proceeds and collects the tax.

The advantage of this method appears to be saving of time and expense by the avoidance of all court proceedings. By either method the property owner is compelled to bear, not only the entire expense of constructing the sidewalk, but also all of the expenses of collecting such cost; any saving in the process of making such collection is a saving to the property owner. A diminution in the time in which a sidewalk is allowed to remain out of repair is a benefit not alone to the public using the streets, but must be a positive saving to the city of a portion of the money required to meet claims for the damages growing out of defective sidewalks.

It seems clear to me, upon theory, that the new method should be less expensive and more expeditious than the old. Not content with a theoretical view of the matter, I have written to ascertain how the new system is found to work in practice. I enclose herewith a letter received from the City Attorney of Bloomington, where the plan of special taxation has been in vogue for some time. You will observe that he finds the method to be "simpler, more expeditious and far better in every respect than the special assessment plan."

If such should prove to be the experience here, it would be a great step toward the betterment of our highways. As the change suggested is a radical one, I would advise that the matter receive full discussion and consideration at your hands before any action is taken thereon. Any further information desired upon the subject by the counsel or committee will be furnished by this department. I have the honor to be,   Respectfully yours,
                    F. S. WINSTON, JR., Corporation Counsel.

September, 1884.
Theodore T. Gurney, Esq., Comptroller.
    Dear Sir—
    You state that the West Town collector refuses to collect the city taxes for 1883 without compensation from the city for such services, and ask whether you have any authority to allow such compensation without action by the council on the subject.
    The decision of the Supreme Court to which you refer in your communication, *Ryan*, vs. *The People, ex rel.*, was an action on behalf

of the town of West Chicago to recover from the town collector the two (2) per cent. of the city taxes which have been retained by him and which, it was claimed, should have been turned into the town treasury.

The clause of the statute in question was as follows: "Each town or district collector shall be allowed a commission of two per cent. on all moneys collected by him, to be paid out of the respective funds collected; *provided,* that all excess of commissions and fees over fifteen hundred dollars shall be paid into the town or district treasury."

The Supreme Court held that the legislature had not the power to require, and did not in fact intend to require, that any portion of the city taxes should be paid into the town treasury. The words "district treasury" in the statute mentioned, they held to mean city treasury; and all taxes over and above the $1500.00 should be turned over respectively to the town and city treasury, etc. A rehearing, however, has been granted in the case, and it is impossible to say to what extent, if any, this opinion may be modified or changed. Assuming it to be the law, then all that a town collector can legally demand in return for his services and the large responsibility assumed by him and his bondsmen, is the sum of $1500.00.

Inadequate as this may appear, I by no means understand that he is at liberty, having accepted his office and taken the oath, to refuse to perform his duty or any part of his duty. I take it, there would be a liability against him and his bondsmen for any gross neglect of duty, whereby the city failed to receive its taxes. There are, however, as you suggest, certain practical aspects of the matter to be regarded. If a town collector is to receive only $1500.00, he will collect enough to pay him this amount as commission and is apt to be somewhat dilatory and easy going with the balance. As I understand the record, largely over ninety per cent. of the collections of personal property taxes have in the past been made by town collectors; that it is rare that the county collector has been able to collect any large amount of personal property taxes, which have been returned to him as delinquent by the town collectors; that taxes paid to the town collectors are received by the city in December, January and February, and those paid to the county collector not until after the tenth of March; that any delay in collecting may result in the loss of the tax from failures and other causes. The town collectors, receiving their books by December 10, are obliged to turn them over to the county collector by March 10, with a list of those from whom they have been unable to collect. The latter official is allowed by law one (1) per cent. upon all taxes collected by him, including those upon real estate, which are a mere matter of sale of delinquent property.

Other things being equal, the city could well afford to pay the town collectors what it is obliged to pay to the county collector if the former fail to fully execute their warrants. For the former collect where promptness and efficiency are vital, and the city receives from them its taxes several months earlier. It is to be remembered that if the city does not pay the town collector and he fails to collect, the city is then bound to pay the county collector for such collections.

As a legal proposition, I cannot advise that any official should be paid more than he is allowed by the letter of the law. As a business question, looking at the matter from the standpoint of the city's financial interest, there is much that might be said.

In the past, there has always, I understand, been retained from the city two (2) per cent. of its taxes. In some cases this has been kept by the town collector; in others, it has been paid into the town treasury; in no case has the city received it. As the Supreme Court is at present advised, this should be paid neither to the town collector nor to the town, but belongs to the city.

There is, of course, nothing to prevent the city from voluntarily paying this, or a part of it, toward the collection of its taxes, and the council, last spring, appropriated $65,000.00 for the collection of city taxes. A portion of this will have to be used in paying the county collector his one per cent. upon taxes returned as delinquent by the town collectors and subsequently collected by him. The balance is at your disposal, as the financial officer of the city, to use for the collection of the revenue of the city as may seem to you most advisable.

Should you and the mayor conclude that the city's interests demand that an inducement be offered the town collectors to insure the prompt collection of the city taxes, I would venture to offer a few suggestions.

The amount to be paid should not exceed one per cent., which is what the city must pay if the taxes are collected by the county collector. The amount should be in lieu of the two (2) per cent. claimed both by the town collectors and the town treasurers, so that if the Supreme Court should hereafter decide that the two per cent. belongs to the town, the city would be liable only for the difference; and if the court should say that it belongs to the collector, then the city is so much ahead. If, however, the city shall once get this two per cent., less the amount paid the collector, I have little fear but what it will be able to hold it.

Any allowance made the collectors should be further conditioned upon the prompt turning over of the money as fast as collected, so that the yearly dunning of town collectors may be dispensed with. Whatever arrangement you may decide to make should be uniform with all three collectors of the respective towns, so that there may be a clear understanding that no two per. cent. is to be hereafter retained from the city treasury, neither by the town nor by the town collector.

This communication has been longer than intended, but the question is somewhat involved and its practical importance to the

city demands a careful consideration of the subject.   I have the
honor to be,   Your obedient servant,

F. S. WINSTON, JR., Corporation Counsel.

September 19, 1884.

John Riordan, Esq., Chairman Committee on Police.

Dear Sir—

Your committee has referred to me for an opinion an order
appropriating one hundred thousand ($100,000.00) dollars from
the saloon license fund for the purpose of increasing the police force
of the city.

The necessity of an increase in the number of police seems to
be conceded by all.   It has been repeatedly claimed in the reports
of the department, and seems never to have been so keenly felt as at
present, when the demands upon the force from fairs, shows, exhibitions and the numerous political gatherings are so great that they
can, with the unmost difficulty, be met.   The approach, too, of cold
weather, with its usual concomitant of tramps flocking to the city, and
of vast numbers of men thrown out of employment, calls for an increase of police to properly protect the property, persons and lives of
our citizens.   That the city has in the past been able to do as well as
it has, with the limited force at its disposal, is a matter of much
gratification and is doubtless due to efficient management and the
use of the patrol system.

The demand for an increase was acknowledged and partly met
by the council appropriating last spring $75,000.00 for one hundred
and fifty additional patrolmen.   The mayor was compelled, against
his wishes, to veto the item, in order to bring the appropriation
within the limit fixed by law.   The amount of money to be derived from saloon licenses was at that time an unknown quantity, and
upon it no definite calculation could be based.   It has since become
evident that the sum to be received by the city from this source will
far exceed the estimates of the finance department and of the city
council.   From this fund it is now sought, by the order before me,
to appropriate $100,000.00 for the purpose mentioned.

While I concur in the general sentiment that the appropriation
desired is greatly needed, I am of the opinion that it cannot, under the
law, be made at this time.

By Section 2, Article VII, of the city charter, the council is required, prior to April 1st, to pass the annual appropriation bill, in
which must be included the amounts "necessary to defray all necessary
expenses and liabilities of such corporation."   The legislature has
further provided that, "no further appropriations shall be made at any
other time within such fiscal year, unless the proposition to make each
appropriation has been first sanctioned by a majority of the legal
voters of such city or village, either by a petition signed by them, or at
a general or special election duly called therefor."

This language is clear and unmistakable. Before the additional appropriation can be made it must be sanctioned by the voters of the municipality. The only exception, provided by the charter, to this rule is contained in Section 3 of the same article, as follows: "Nothing herein contained shall prevent the city council or board of trustees from ordering, by a two-thirds vote, any improvement, the necessity of which is caused by any casualty or accident happening after such annual appropriation is made."

This has been construed to cover appropriations in case of an epidemic of small-pox or an expected visit of cholera and even to the case of appropriations for the new city hall or to bridges, necessitated by accidents happening after the passage of the annual bill. But it cannot be extended any further. It will not cover an appropriation for additional police, the necessity for which was foreseen when the annual ordinance was passed. Such an appropriation is not called for by "any casualty or accident happening after such annual appropriation is made." It is, therefore, not within the law.

A misapprehension seems to exist with some who suppose that the additional appropriation may be made upon an "emergency," and that the council is the judge of what is an emergency. But there is no such term used in the charter. There must be "a casualty" or "accident," happening after the passage of the annual bill and I, by no means, understand that the council has the discretionary power to say that a casualty or accident has occurred when, in fact, there has been none.

I therefore recommend that the order be placed on file, as unauthorized by the city charter. As the matter is deemed of considerable importance, I will go further and, at the request of the police department, indicate a method by which the appropriation, if desired and needed, may lawfully be made. It is, in brief, that the consent of the people shall first be obtained. As pointed out by the section of the charter quoted from above, an appropriation may be made, after the first quarter of the municipal year, if sanctioned by a majority of the legal voters of the city. Three methods are pointed out by which this consent may be had. The method of obtaining a petition of a majority of the voters of this metropolis is open to objections; as the vast labor required, the uncertainty as to the genuineness of the signatures and a number of different legal questions. A special election might be called, but this would be a matter of great expense, and there could hardly be obtained, in this mode, a full and fair expression of the will of the people. There is approaching, however, an election, which will call out the full vote of the city. The election to be held in November is a general one and the vote to be then cast will be presumed to be the expression of all the legal voters of the city.

The People vs. Garner, 47 Ill., 246.
Melvin vs. Lisenby, 72 Ill., 64.

At this time there may be submitted to the people the question whether the council may appropriate a part of the funds derived from saloon licenses towards the increase of the police force. At that period of the year the necessity for an increase will be best appreciated.

Should the people sanction the appropriation, the council is then authorized to appropriate the amount voted for that purpose. It is to be noted that the council must first pass a proper order fixing the amount of the appropriation to be submitted for approval at the polls, the county clerk must give due notice and all the other requirements of the statutes must be observed. I am not aware that such a question has ever been submitted to the voters of the city, although similar appropriations for state purposes have been voted upon, and great care must be exercised in fully complying with the law. If the council should see fit to pursue this method and will designate the amount to be voted upon, the proper papers can be drawn by this department.

I have the honor to be, yours respectfully,

F. S. WINSTON, JR., Corporation Counsel.

October 11, 1884.

W. J. Onahan, City Collector.

Dear Sir—

You ask for an opinion as to the legal distinction between commission merchants and brokers so that you may know from whom you should require license fees and from whom not.

In the case of Braun vs. City of Chicago, the Supreme Court, in upholding the validity of the license fee required of merchandise brokers, defines a broker as one "who is engaged for others in negotiating contracts relative to property with the custody of which he has no concern." A factor is likewise described as one "who sells property of others when he has its possession." The city has the power, under the charter, to require a license of brokers, but has no power to exact such license from those who are exclusively factors. The above definitions must, therefore, be your guide upon this question.

An individual engaged in selling the goods of others for brokerage or commission must take out a license, provided he has not the custody of the property; otherwise, if the goods are in his custody, he is not obliged to take out a broker's license. There will doubtless arise cases where a person is engaged principally in the business of selling goods on commission and having the same in his possession, but who also sells goods, on commission, of which he has not the custody. From these a license fee must be demanded. This was expressly held in the case referred to above. Braun was a commission merchant and held the custody of the property; but it turned out that he was also engaged in selling, on commission, property of which he did not have possession. The court held that he must take out a license in that he was, not only a factor, but also a broker. Because, therefore, a man calls himself a commission merchant, it does not follow that he is exempt from the payment of the license fee. The question is, in each case whether the individual is a broker within the legal meaning of that term as above defined. If he does any business as a merchandise broker he must take out a broker's license, notwithstanding the principal part of his business is the selling of goods consigned to him and in his possession. Respectfully yours,

F. S. WINSTON, JR., Corporation Counsel.

December 5, 1884.

Elmer A. Sperry, S. S. Badger and Geo. L. Crossman, Committee.

Gentlemen—

Your committee, representing a number of electric lighting companies in the city, has formally requested my opinion whether electric lights may lawfully be allowed outside of buildings and overhanging the city streets. You state that the city electrician has refused to permit the hanging of these electric lights outside of any building and extending beyond the building line, acting under Section 2022 of the code, which prohibits the putting up or construction of any electric conductor in the streets or alleys of the city. Sections 1957 and 1958 of the code, to which you refer, permit, by implication, the suspending of signs and lanterns over the sidewalks of the city under certain restrictions. It is unnecessary to decide whether this is broad enough to allow the suspension of electric lights in a similar manner; for it is clear that electric conductors come within the express prohibition of Section 2022 of the code. Any privilege which might be claimed under Sections 1957 and 1958 would, therefore, be negatived by Section 2022. The council, moreover, has recently passed certain orders aimed against the erection of these electric lights, and has required the superintendent of city telegraphs to prevent both their construction and maintenance. It is to be remembered that the streets of the city extend from building line to building line, above and below ground, and that the control of the city's streets is exclusively vested by law in the city council. Its orders in regard to their use cannot lawfully be disobeyed by any city official.

I am somewhat reluctantly forced to the conclusion that the city ordinances do not allow the privileges asked for, as I thoroughly appreciate what you say in regard to the public interest in having the streets lighted by private enterprise as well as by the usual gas lamps. There should be, however, certain regulations in regard to the subject to insure the safety of life and property and the entire matter must necessarily be regulated by the city council.

Should the companies which you represent see fit to ask for the passage of a proper ordinance upon the subject, you can count upon my indorsement and aid, and I am assured by the superintendent of city telegraphs that he will also approve of any proper measure which shall allow the use of electric lights on the exterior of business blocks within the city. I have the honor to be,

Very respectfully yours,

F. S. WINSTON, JR., Corporation Counsel.

January 2, 1885.

John Gaynor, Esq., Chairman Committee on Railroads.

Dear Sir—

Your committee has referred to me, "for a proper ordinance," certain petitions relative to heating street cars.

Being informed that street cars were heated, in winter, in certain cities, I telegraphed, upon the receipt of your communication, to the law departments of the following cities: Minneapolis, Dubuque, Brookyln and Indianapolis, to ascertain the character of legislation upon this subject in force at those places.

From each of them I received replies to the effect that there was no ordinance or city regulation requiring the heating of street cars, and that, where heated, the same was done voluntarily by the companies.

So far as I have been able to ascertain, there is no municipal legislation upon the subject; at least, in those cities to which my attention has been called as having heated street cars.

The proposed legislation being somewhat unique in its character and the terms of your reference, calling simply for a "proper ordinance," being rather vague in its specifications, it has been a matter of some difficulty to draft an ordinance which shall meet with the approval of your committee and of the council.

The ordinance herewith submitted, in its first section, makes it the duty of all persons and corporations to provide for their cars, other than open or grip cars, a suitable heating apparatus.

By Section 2, this apparatus must be provided for the cars during the months of November, December, January, February and March in each year. You can add to, or deduct from, the number of these months as you may deem advisable. The kind of apparatus is left to the choice of the companies, so long as the same is reasonably effective in heating the car. It would not do for the city to undertake to prescribe the use of any particular patent or monopoly.

As it would be unreasonable for the city to require that the apparatus should be operated at all times during the months aforesaid, the period of operation is fixed in the ordinance by standard thermometers. You may require that a difference shall be made when the weather is dry and clear or wet and stormy, and the height of the thermometer is left blank for you to fill in. Section 2 also contains a proviso allowing a reasonable time for putting the apparatus in operation when there is a sudden change in the weather.

By Section 3 it is made the duty of the corporations, now operating street cars in the city, to begin forthwith to apply such an apparatus to their cars. They are to be allowed a reasonable time, to be fixed by your committee by filling out the blank, in which to begin their operation.

Changes or modifications of this ordinance may suggest themselves to your committee and can be incorporated in the draft submitted.

The question of the power of the council to pass such an ordinance has not been directly submitted to me and I have not, therefore, given it an extended examination. I understand that the companies in question deny that the power exists, but my own impression is that a reasonable ordinance upon the subject would be upheld by the courts. There can be no doubt of the right of the legislature to control and regulate the subject and I believe that sufficient power has been delegated to the municipal authority, under certain sections of the city charter, to sustain any ordinance of this character. But this will be a question for the courts.

I have the honor to be, very respectfully yours,

F. S. WINSTON, Jr., Corporation Counsel.

January 19, 1885.

John F. Dalton, Esq., Chairman Committee on Judiciary.

Dear Sir—

In response to the request of your committee as to the city's power to compel parties using water meters to pay the cost of keeping the same in repair, I beg to reply:

The city council is given, by Section 3, of Article X, of the charter the power:

"To make all needful rules and regulations concerning the use of water supplied by the water works of said city or village, and to do all acts and make such rules and regulations for the construction, completion, management or control of the water works, and for the levying and collecting of any water taxes, rates or assessments, as the said city council or board of trustees may deem necessary or expedient."

This, as you will perceive, is very broad language and would seem to give the council discretionary control of the subject.

Under this power, the council has required certain kinds of establishments to use water meters.

Mun. Code., Sec. 2041.

These meters, formerly furnished by the city, are now paid for by the party using the same. If the city may compel the property owner to purchase a water meter, it would certainly seem as though it could compel him to keep the same in repair. Your committee will, of course, recognize the fact that the city, in furnishing water to the people, stands about on the same footing as a merchant selling goods to his customers. It may charge practically what it pleases for the water and may impose all sorts of conditions upon those using the same. If it charge for the purchase of meters it would seem to necessarily follow that it may charge for keeping the same in repair.

As regards Section 3, I am not so clear. It relates to back charges, where the department has made the repairs and has not collected the cost of the same. Where the department of public works has voluntarily repaired water meters it is not altogether clear that an ordinance can subsequently be passed compelling such payment. But the section was inserted so as to draw no distinction between repairs made in the past and those to be made in the future and also to enable the department to collect outstanding bills. You will notice that this section applies only to cases where the party now using the meter is the same who was using it when the repairs were made.

In conclusion, I may state that I am of the opinion that the council has the power to require property owners to pay for keeping water meters in repair, but express no opinion as to the policy of such a regulation, that being a matter for your committee and the council to determine.

I have the honor to be, very respectfully yours,

F. S. WINSTON, Jr., Corporation Counsel.

March 16, 1885.

Mr. W. J. Onahan, City Collector.

Dear Sir—

In regard to your inquiry concerning the liability of one firm of Nichols & Co., of New York, under the wholesale malt liquor dealers' ordinance, to pay a license of $500.00 a year to the city, I am of the opinion that the license should be required of them for the following reasons:

They claim exemption upon the ground that the constitution of the United States prohibits any imposts or duties being levied by a state upon imports and that they deal exclusively in imported Bass ale in the original packages. The reply to this petition is that the license required by the city, under the authority of the state, is not a tax nor an impost; it is simply a license fee required of all who pursue a certain occupation, namely, that of wholesale malt liquor dealers. It has been repeatedly held by our Supreme Court that such license fees are not taxes and not, therefore, subject to the constitutional provisions regarding taxation. The charter power under which the city requires of wholesale malt liquor dealers $500.00 license merely authorizes the council to license, regulate and prohibit the dealing in liquor and not to tax such occupation. While, of course, these licenses bring a revenue to the city, yet they are sustained by the courts not under the taxing power, but under the police power of the state and city. Wiggins Ferry Co. vs. E. St. Louis, 107 U. S. 365. Hence, it follows that the city, in requiring a license fee of those engaged in selling malt liquors wholesale, does not, in a legal sense, impose a tax or an impost or duty upon the liquors themselves. The fee is required of a certain occupation and is not imposed upon the goods themselves. All of our wholesale malt liquor dealers are required to pay this license, and I am aware of no reason why dealers in foreign ales should be exempt. The decision referred to by Nichols & Co. has been modified by more recent decisions of the United States Supreme Court, and

I consider the law as settled that a license fee may be demanded of those who sell malt liquor, although in the original packages.

Respectfully yours,

F. S. WINSTON, Jr., Corporation Counsel.

April 8, 1885.

Alderman Sanders, Chairman Committee on Public Buildings.

Dear Sir—

In reply to the request of your committee for an opinion as to the power of the council in the matter of a proposed ordinance for regulating the location of livery stables I beg to reply:

The council under the charter has the undoubted power to regulate the location of livery stables, blacksmith shops and foundries, but an ordinance passed under that power has to conform to certain principles which govern all municipal legislation. The ordinance submitted to me would, I fear, not be sustained by the courts.

In the case of Tugman vs. City of Chicago, 78 Ills., 405, the Supreme Court considered the validity of an ordinance which prohibited the erection or operation of distilleries, slaughter houses, soap factories, "in any building not now used for such purposes." The Supreme Court held that the ordinance was invalid because it did not apply to distilleries, etc., already in existence. The court held that the ordinance was void because it drew the distinction between establishments already in operation and new establishments that might be put up. And the court says that the ordinance tended to create a monopoly. You will notice that the case is almost precisely similar to the ordinance which you have submitted to me. The same doctrine is held in the case of City of Chicago vs. Rumpff, 45 Ills., 90; in Mayor vs. Thorne; 7 Paige, 261; in Dillon on Mun. Corps., Section 256; in Cooley's Constitutional Limitations, 200. Upon the same ground the Appellate Court declared invalid Section 1258 of the code prohibiting the storage of lumber within the city except upon the border of navigable water.

In conclusion I may say that there appears to be great need of some such ordinance as that submitted to me and I am inclined to think that one could be drafted to cover the subject. If, therefore, your petitioners will call upon me I may be able to assist them in framing an ordinance which will be legal. Yours truly,

F. S. WINSTON, Jr., Corporation Counsel.

May 5, 1885.

W. J. Onahan, Esq., City Collector.

Dear Sir—

You ask me who are compelled to pay a license fee as keepers of restaurants under the law.

The city charter authorizes the imposition of license fees upon what are called "keepers of ordinaries" and the word "restaurant" is nowhere mentioned. An ordinary is defined to be a dining room or an eating house where a fixed price is charged for meals, in contradistinction to one where each dish is charged separately. The council, of course, had no power to require licenses of those who do not fall within the meaning of the word "ordinary" and the fact that it undertook, in the ordinance, to so define the word as to include restaurants, conducted upon what is known as the European plan, is necessarily without effect, as beyond the power conferred by the charter.

Although the ordinance is illegal in so far as it applies to restaurants conducted as above mentioned, it is valid as to ordinaries.

There has been no decision of any court of record upon this ordinance, but Justice Kersten, as I am informed, very properly adopted this construction in a case brought before him some time since. You will require licenses then, of all who keep ordinaries as above defined, and whose gross daily receipts average at least fifteen dollars, the minimum figure specified by the ordinance.   Respectfully yours,

F. S. WINSTON, Jr., Corporation Counsel.

July 9, 1885.

E. F. Cullerton, Esq., Chairman, Finance Committee.

Dear sir—

Your committee ask my opinion as to the liability of the city in cases where taxes have been erroneously collected, on account of the property being exempt or the taxes twice paid.

Section 268 of the Revenue Law provides, as follows: "If any real property shall be twice assessed for the same year, or assessed before it becomes taxable, and the taxes so erroneously assessed shall have been paid, either at sale or otherwise, or have been twice paid by different claimants, the county board, on application of the person paying the same, or his agent, and being satisfied of the facts in the case, shall cause the State and County taxes to be refunded pro rata by the State and County; and the city and incorporated town or village taxes and special assessments, by the city or incorporated town, village or other proper authorities or persons."

Under this, I am informed that the custom, in many counties of the state, is for the county collector to retain money in his hands belonging to the city or town and refund the same to the claimant upon order of the county board.

At any rate, it has been repeatedly decided that the city must refund taxes which have been wrongfully collected as specified in Section 268. In a recent case before Judge Shepard the city was ordered to refund to a tax buyer the proportionate amount of the taxes levied upon St. Luke's hospital, which is exempt as to property worth less than $50,000.00. In a case before Judge Gary the city was compelled to refund to a tax buyer the proportionate amount paid by him where the taxes had been paid by the owner before the sale.

This being the general principle, I would advise that each case be investigated by the comptroller to ascertain the facts and that too much reliance be not placed upon the certificate from the county board or county clerk. Then, let the amount required to meet such claims be included in the appropriation bill for the ensuing year.

Yours very respectfully,

F. S. WINSTON, Corporation Counsel.

September 2, 1885.

To the Honorable The City Council of the City of Chicago.

Gentlemen—

Your honorable body has referred to me the papers in the contested election case of Monear v. Doerner, as alderman from the sixth ward, with the following request for an opinion:

"As to the right of the City Council to compel the attendance of witnesses in the matter of taking depositions."

The question is a somewhat novel one in this state and my answer must be based mainly upon the consideration of analogous principles. By Section 6, Article LII, of the charter, it is provided, "the city council shall be judge of the election and qualification of its own members."

In the case of Linear vs. Rittenhouse, 94 Ill., 208, the Supreme Court uphold this grant of power and declare that this cause leaves no jurisdiction in the county court over the contest of seats in the city council. The court there say of certain sections of the election laws:

"These sections point out the mode, and we can see no great inconvenience by a few slight changes, in rendering it entirely practicable for the city council to try such a contest. The petition can be filed with the city clerk, the notice can be given to appear before the city council, and depositions taken and returned to the council under these sections, and a trial had by that body."

The city council having, therefore, exclusive jurisdiction over the contest of election of one of its own members, it seems to me that the power in question necessarily implies the power to compel the attendance of witnesses upon the question. For if the council cannot compel the giving of evidence by witnesses, their power of making a judicial inquiry in the matter would be a barren one. Hence, I conclude that a power is vested in the council to compel the attendance of witnesses in such cases as a necessary corollary to the conceded power to hear and determine as a quasi judicial tribunal, the contest of election of its members.

But there is no legislation and no method adopted by the council to compel the attendance of witnesses before the officer who takes the depositions. Section 1241 of the code provides that the testimony shall be taken "in the manner and as provided for taking depositions in cases in chancery." But the statute which provides for the attachment of witnesses for refusing to attend and testify in other cases is not broad enough to cover contests pending before a city council. Hence, I therefore conclude that legislation on the part of the city

6

council is necessary before there can be any compulsory attendance of witnesses in the case of a contest of election. Such legislation should be general in its character and provide for all such emergencies. If it is the desire of the council, I will endeavor to frame an ordinance which shall cover the subject.   Respectfully submitted,

F. S. WINSTON, Corporation Counsel.

October 7, 1885.
OSCAR C. De WOLF, Esq., Commissioner of Health.
Dear Sir—

Your letter of September 2, 1895, concerning your power to have discontinued the business of manufacturing tobacco in a tenement house where the same is detrimental to the residents of such tenements, has been mislaid and my attention just called to the matter.

In my opinion you have the power under Sections 1491 and 1492 to put an end to such a nuisance if, as a matter of fact, the same is detrimental to the health of the people in the building. If such be the state of facts, you may prosecute under the code or compel the parties to so conduct the business that they will not injure their neighbors.

Respectfully, submitted,

F. S. WINSTON, Corporation Counsel.

December 22, 1885.
To the Chairman and Members of the Committee on Streets and Alleys, S. D.
Gentlemen—

You desire my opinion whether Shields avenue, between Thirty-first and Thirty-third streets, is a public street of the city and whether the fences erected across the same by the base-ball club may be torn down as an obstruction to the street.

The department of public works requests me in answering these questions to embody in my answer a statement of the general principles of law applicable to such matters for publication in the council proceedings as a guide to the department in similar cases. The question is constantly asked of this department by property owners and city officers as to what constitutes a public street or alley of the city, so as to authorize the removal of obstructions therefrom and the usual exercises of the jurisdiction of the city over the same. I, therefore, take this occasion to explain the rules which govern such cases.

The case of streets which have become such by twenty years of travel or by proper condemnation proceedings requires no explanation. Aside from these, to constitute a public street, alley or highway, two things as requisite: (1) A dedication, or donation, by the owner of the land and (2) an acceptance, or taking, by the municipal authorities. The dedication may be one of two kinds; a statutory dedication or a common law dedication. In the former, the property owner makes and acknowledges a plat in conformity with the statute and places the same on record and the certificate attached to the plat will generally show whether or not the same conforms to the statute. A common law dedication is where the platting is defective or where the owner by some affirmative act, shows an intention to dedicate. For example, where he sells lots abutting on the street shown by an unrecorded plat or where he builds sidewalks or erects fences on the line of the street.

When a street or alley has been dedicated by the owner, it is further necessary that it shall be accepted by the city authorities in order to constitute a public street or alley of the city.

Marcy v. Taylor, 19 Ill., 634.

Rees v. Chicago, 38 Ill., 322.

Trustees v. Walsh, 57 Ill., 370.

The reason for this rule of law is obvious. The city is responsible for its streets and is bound to keep them in good condition. If the mere dedication were sufficient to constitute a public street a burden and responsibility would be thrown upon the city which it might not care to assume and ought not to assume. As was well said by the eminent jurist, Judge McAllister, speaking for the Appellate Court:

"The municipal authorities would at once be subject to the duty of exercising reasonable care and diligence to keep the same in a safe and suitable condition for travel and all the ordinary uses of public streets. It would hardly be tolerated that every enterprising speculator who happened to own, or control outside real estate, could thus impose such a burden upon the municipality."

Your own experience will tell you how extensive are the duties and responsibilities of the municipality with respect to its streets and the sense of the rule which gives the city the option of refusing to assume these burdens as to any given street or until the street may be needed by the public, is apparent.

Until the street has been accepted by the city, the owner may at any time, so far as the municipality is concerned, withdraw his dedication and vacate the street.

Littler v. City of Lincoln, 106 Ill., 353.

Village of Winnetka v. Prouty, 107 Ill., 218.

A lot owner, however, who has bought with reference to the proposed street, may prevent the vacation or the withdrawal of the dedication. But it must be a lot owner whose access to his property is cut off by the vacation of the street.

Chicago v. Union Bldg. Assn., 102 Ill., 379.

Littler v. City of Lincoln, 106 Ill., 353.

Even where a street has been both dedicated and accepted, it may be abandoned by the public and the municipality so as to preclude its further use as a street.

Peoria v. Johnston, 56 Ill., 51.

Winnetka v. Prouty, 107 Ill., 218.

The acceptance of a dedication may be shown in a great variety of ways. The more usual are ditching, grading, repairing, curbing, paving, laying sidewalks, sewers, drains or water pipes, or the erection of lamp posts or the exercise of like jurisdiction through order of the city council or by municipal officers duly authorized for that purpose. There is practically no limit to the evidence which will prove an acceptance by the city, but the highest evidence is, of course, exercise of the charter power over city streets through an order of the city council.

In this connection, I have been asked by the commissioner of public works whether the approval of a plat by a city officer is an acceptance by the city of the streets and alleys shown thereon.

Under the act of 1863, all plats before being recorded were required to be approved by the board of public works, where streets or alleys were dedicated. The object of this requirement is stated in the act to be, "in order to secure a uniform plan in the laying out of such streets and alleys."

By Section 5, Article X, of the present city charter, the council is authorized to provide that all proposed sub-divisions shall, before being recorded, be submitted to some officer of the city for approval. Under this power, the superintendent of assessments has been made ex-officio examiner of subdivisions and is required to certify his approval of plats.

Municipal Code, Sec. 608.

The object of these enactments is obviously to secure uniformity of street lines in all subdivisions and I do not understand that the mere approval of a plat by a city official at once imposes upon the municipality the duty and responsibility of the charter and improving all streets and alleys in such subdivision. If the city were sued for damages arising from the defective condition of an alleged street, where the same had been platted and the plat approved, but the city had in fact never undertaken to excercise any jurisdiction over such platted street, this latter fact would certainly be set up as a defense to the action, and, in my judgment the defense would be sustained. If the city is not bound to keep an alleged street in a reasonably good condition, it is because such platted street has not become a public street of the city.

The view that the mere approval of the plat is not of itself an acceptance of the streets shown thereon is borne out by the fact that the city comptroller is specified in the code as the officer who shall, upon a certificate from the council to the corporation, accept streets and alleys ceded to the city.

Municipal Code, Section 526.

In my judgment, the proper construction of the requirement that plats shall be approved, is in order that all new subdivisions shall be laid out with regard to the adjacent property, to the end that the municipality, when it gets ready to accept and improve the new streets, may find them uniform in line and width with the old streets of the city, but that the approval of the plat does not, instantly, throw the burden upon the city of caring for the streets and alleys contained in the subdivision.

Applying the above rules to the case in question, we have the following: The property was originally owned by the Canal Trustees, who did not plat this street, but sold the property in blocks bounded by other highways. The platting of Shields avenue, between Thirty-first and Thirty-third streets, appears from the records to have been made in 1872 by order of the Circuit Court in a certain suit then pending. The dedication, therefore, may fairly be assumed to have been made in conformity with the statute and to constitute a statutory dedication. The plat was also approved by the board of public works under the act of 1863, referred to above.

The facts as to acceptance by the city are reported to me as follows: Shields avenue, between the points in question, has until within a short time been a part of a cabbage garden. It is several feet below grade and the city has never made improvements of any kind upon the same. It has, in a measure, been recognized by turning the curb on Thirty-first street and building a cross walk on Thirty-third street, where Shields avenue is shown on the plats. But the locus in quo has never been in the practical possession of the city and the municipality has not yet manifested its intention of placing the street, south of Thirty-first, in the catalogue of public highways upon which is expended the public money. It would, therefore, be improper, under the decision of the Appellate Court, in a similar case, to proceed by force to remove the fences until the dedication has clearly been accepted by the legislative branch of the municipal government.

City of Chicago vs. Gosselin, 4 Bradw., 570.

But the dedication is still open to acceptance and if the council desires to take Shields avenue, between the streets mentioned, it may now accept the street and order it thrown open to the public.

I enclose herewith the draft of an order which may be passed if the council, in its discretion, desires to open the street to public travel. The passage of the order, it must be remembered, makes this a public street and the city liable for a failure to place and keep it in a reasonably good condition. Respectfully submitted,

F. S. WINSTON, Corporation Counsel.

December 26, 1885.

To the Honorable, the City Council of the City of Chicago.

Gentlemen—

At your last regular meeting you requested my opinion whether a valid ordinance could be passed requiring property owners and tenants to keep the sidewalks in front of their property clear of snow and ice and to report back such an ordinance, if I considered the same within the power of the council to enact.

You are doubtless aware that our Supreme Court has twice decided that the city cannot, under its mere police power, require abutting property owners to keep the sidewalks free from snow and ice.

Gridley v. City of Bloomington, 88 Ill., 557.

City of Chicago v. O'Brien, 111, Ill., 532.

The court holds that the sidewalks are as much the property of the city as the roadway; that the duty devolves upon the city to clean the sidewalks; and that the municipality cannot, under the general "police power," require the property owners to perform this work. These decisions are not in line with those of other states and it is generally held that such an ordinance is legal and binding.

Mayor v. Maberry, 6 Humph. 368; Washington v. Nashville, 1 Swan, 177; White v. Nashville, 2 Swan, 364; Bonsall v. Mayor, 19 Ohio, 418; Paxon v. Sweet, 13 N. J., 196; Woodbridge v. Detroit, 8 Mich., 274; Boston v. Shaw, 1 Metc., 107; Lowell v. Hadley, 8 Metc., 180; Goddard's case 16 Pick., 504.

The Supreme Court of this state, in its latest decision upon the question, stands four to three against the validity of section 1955 of the code, which requires all property owners to clean their sidewalks, and we can but submit to that ruling until such time as the court may conclude, if ever, to adopt the rule in force in other states.

The inconvenience caused by the Illinois decisions is obvious. It is impracticable for the city to clear its eight hundred and nine miles of sidewalk after every snow storm. The cost of such work would be appalling and no large city ever undertakes so great a responsibility. Moreover, it is cheaper and better for the property owners to themselves keep their sidewalks clear rather than to be taxed for that purpose. It may fairly be assumed that the great majority of the people would gladly comply with a requirement that their sidewalks should be kept passable if they know that their recalcitrant neighbors would be forced to do likewise.

As the law now stands you are unable to pass an ordinance which shall reach all property owners alike, but you may, in my judgment, enact a law which will be effective in the great majority of cases. This is not to be done as an exercise of the "police power," but as a requirement of a consideration from those citizens who receive certain privileges from the public, represented by the municipal government. You are aware that the owners and occupants of most houses and buildings in this city occupy a portion of the sidewalk space. The sidewalk area is used for coal or other storage purposes, space is taken for steps or entrances to basements and for other purposes. But the street is the property of the city, from building line to building line, and the city may altogether refuse the use of any part of the same for these purposes or may accompany the grant of such privileges with any reasonable condition. It strikes me as only fair and right that those who receive from the public the privilege of using any part of the city's property should, in return, be required to keep the sidewalks in good condition for use by the public.

Under the existing ordinances it is unlawful for any property own-er to use the area beneath the sidewalk without a permit from the de-partment of public works. These permits may be conditioned upon this provision and such provision may, by order of the council, be attached to any outstanding permits. As a matter of fact, few property cwners have as yet taken out these permits and they now occupy the sidewalk space without authority of law.

Upon the above theory I have drawn the ordinance submitted herewith, which explains itself. It does not, it is true, reach sidewalks in front of vacant lots or in front of houses which are set back from the street, where the sidewalk area is not used for coal vaults or other purposes. But I predict that it will be found effective, if properly en-forced, to meet nearly all cases of improved property and will certainly cover the business streets.

The condition of our sidewalks in winter is not creditable to a metropolitan city and I hope the proposed legislation will, to a great extent, at least, remedy the evil.

Equally important with an ordinance on this subject is a provis-ion for its strict enforcement and I submit an order directing the police department, in detail, how to enforce the legislation contemplated.

Respectfully submitted,

F. S. WINSTON, Corporation Counsel.

December 31, 1885.

Hon. Carter H. Harrison, Mayor.

Dear Sir—

In response to your question whether you have the power to ex-amine and pass upon charges against officers of the city, I beg to re-ply:

The power to remove officers of corporations, municipal and other, for reasonable or just cause, has been considered settled ever since the judgment of Lord Mansfield in the leading case of the King v. Richardson, 1 Bur. 517. The doctrine has been accepted in this state in the cases of the People v. Chicago Board of Trade, 15 Ill., 112 and Sturgan v. Board of Trade, 96 Ill., 441. The power exists even where it is not expressly conferred, but the city of Chicago has, also, to meet provisions upon the subject.

By Section 7, of Article III, of the city charter the mayor is given the power to remove any officer appointed by him, on any formal charge, whenever he shall be of the opinion that the interests of the city demand such removal, but such removal may be disapproved of by the city council by a two-thirds vote. This obviously presumes an examination by the mayor of the charges preferred. Again, by Section 500 of the Municipal Code, the council has provided that "The Mayor shall supervise the conduct of all the officers of the city; *examine the grounds of all reasonable complaints made against any of them*, and cause all their violations of duty and other neglects to be promptly punished or reported to the proper tribunal for correction.

The law thus devolves upon you the duty of hearing and examining charges against city officers. You are made the tribunal to pass upon these questions and as no method of procedure is pointed out by the law, "the substantial principles of the common law as to proceedings affecting private rights must be observed."

People v. Bearfield, 36 Barb., 254.

Murdock v. Academy, 12 Pick., 244.

Dillon on Mun. Corps., Sec. 253.

Your actions in the premises are judicial in their nature.

People v. Cooper, 57 How. Pr., 395.

In the performance of this duty the law requires that the accused shall be given personal notice of the charge; that the charges against him shall be specifically stated; that he shall have a reasonable time to answer the charges and to produce his testimony and that the evidence on both sides shall be heard.

Dillon on Mun. Corps., Secs. 254, 255 and notes.

Upon such a hearing the oath may be administered to witnesses by any officer authorized to administer oaths. This includes yourself, as you are empowered by Section 16, Article VI, of the city charter, to administer oaths upon all lawful occasions. The hearing of charges against a city officer, which is required by the courts to be conducted according to the "substantial principles of the common law as to proceedings affecting private rights," is plainly a lawful occasion for the administration of oaths; indeed, the taking of evidence, which is to deprive any officer of his reputation, his office and his means of livelihood, without the sanction of an oath, would hardly be tolerated. It is a mistaken idea to suppose that testimony is given under oath only in court proceedings; for example, notice the cases of testimony in an aldermanic contest, taken before a notary public, and of charges against a patrolman investigated by the superintendent of police.

It is my opinion, therefore, that you not only have the power, but it is made your duty by statute and ordinance, to hear and examine charges against city officers other than those elected by the people, and that the testimony at such a hearing may and should be under oath. Respectfully submitted,

F. S. WINSTON, Corporation Counsel.

April 12, 1886.

To the City Council of Chicago.

Gentlemen—

By an order passed last Thursday, you called for my opinion upon a series of questions regarding the effect of the city election law upon the provisions of the city charter. It is impossible for me to do full justice to the subject in the limited time allowed and as the questions have not yet been decided by the courts of this state, this opinion is but my personal judgment in the matter, based upon what I know to have been the intention of the framers of the new law and upon the application of general principles to the particular points involved.

Taking up your questions seriatim, I answer, as a matter of law, your first query in the negative. The city election law does not undertake to make any change in the term of office of aldermen or any other officers. Practically, however, it may operate in seating the aldermen-elect earlier than would have been the case if the law were not enforced. Members of the council are elected and qualified. After a city election held under the city charter, the returns were required to be made to the city clerk within two days; it "thereupon" became the duty of the council to canvass and declare the result. The performance of this duty being at times delayed, it resulted in the aldermen-elect being sometimes deprived of their seats for an unreasonable length of time. Under the city election law, the canvass of the votes is directed to be made within seven days after the close of the election. In other words, the new law makes an immediate declaration of the result of the election imperative and hence shortens the term of those aldermen who were not promptly seated after the city elections of 1884 and 1885. But for this the sitting aldermen have no redress if their term be shortened, as their failure to serve for two full years is owing to the neglect of the council to promptly perform its duty in declaring the result of the elections in 1884 and 1885.

You next inquire, "when can the aldermen elect take their seats?" When the board of canvassers finishes its canvass and the result is declared and entered of record in the county court, and a certified copy of such record filed with the county clerk, it becomes the duty of that officer to issue, upon application, the certificate of election to those who have been declared elected aldermen. Having received their certificates of election, it becomes the duty of the aldermen-elect to take the oath of office prescribed by Section 4, Article VI, of the city charter, and they are entitled, thereupon, to take their seats as members of the city council.

Your third question is whether the new law repeals the power of the council to judge of the qualifications of its own members. To the question as asked, I answer that the power of the council to judge of the "qualifications" of its members is not repealed by the new law. By Section 6 of Article III, of the city charter, the council is made the "judge of the election and qualifications of its own members" and there is no provision in the new law which provides for any new or different tribunal to pass upon the qualifications of aldermen to serve as such. You do not ask me as to the effect of the new law upon the power of the council to judge of the "election" of its members and I, therefore, refrain from the discussion of the interesting question as to whether there may now be an aldermanic contest of election before the city council.

The council being still the judge of the qualifications of its members, you ask whether this power may be exercised after the alderman-elect has received his certificate and taken the oath of office. The answer to this question must plainly be in the affirmative.

Your last query embraces the effect of the new law upon the various provisions of the charter and as to the extent of such effect. The question has a very wide scope and I cannot pretend to give a complete answer within the limited time allowed me. Speaking in broad terms, the new law divests the council of its power of providing for city elections and ascertaining and declaring the result of the same and places that power in the hands of officers of the county court. It further undertakes to prescribe such rules and regulations in regard to the ballot, to ensure a fair and honest expression of the will of the electors, as have not heretofore been in force through the general election law of the state.

Coming down to details I believe I can best demonstrate how the new law has affected the charter provisions by contrasting the methods under the latter with those now in force.

Under the charter, it was the duty of the council to locate the polling places, and select judges of election. This duty now devolves upon the county court and its officers. The manner of conducting and voting at the election was formerly the same, substantially, as in the case of the election of county officers under the general election law of the state. It is now regulated in detail by the city election law.

The ballots were counted and the returns were made out, and, with the ballots, were returned to the city clerk. The ballots are now destroyed and the returns are made to the election commissioners, the county clerk and the city comptroller. Formerly, it was the duty of the council to act as a canvassing board and to declare the result of the election. This duty now devolves upon a special board of canvassers, consisting of the county judge, the city attorney and the election commissioners. In case of a tie, the result is to be determined now by lot before the board of canvassers instead of before the council, as formerly. It is made the duty of the city clerk to notify aldermen of their election. This he formerly did, acting as the clerk of the body which declared the result of the election. It is rather a curious question whether this duty still devolves upon that officer, now that the result is declared by another tribunal and the certificates of election are issued by the county clerk. Certainly, it would seem a matter of supererogation for him to notify those who have applied for and obtained from the county clerk their certificates of election. But if it is sought to declare the office vacant, for a failure to qualify under Article IV of this charter, I am inclined to think it would still be necessary to show that the officer-elect had received notice of his election from the city clerk. The requirement that the council shall. cause notice of elections to be given remains unrepealed.

To sum up, the power of the council over what may be called

the preliminaries of an aldermanic election, except the giving of notice for the same, is now vested in other hands. After such election, the council formerly had the power to pass upon the same, first, as a canvassing board and second, in its judicial capacity. This distinction I pointed out at length to you in my opinion last spring concerning the returns from the third precinct of the third ward. The first of these powers is taken away by the new law; how far the second is divested, if at all, I do not now feel called upon to explain at length, in the absence of a specific request upon that point. The effect of the city election law upon your political powers may be fairly illustrated by saying that it has practically placed your body in the position, upon this subject, of the house of representatives or state senate at Springfield. An alderman, like a state senator, now receives from the proper official a certificate of election which is prima facie evidence of his election. The qualifications of each may then be inquired into by the body of which he is a part but each is entitled to act until ousted by the legislative body after due inquiry and investigation.

Respectfully submitted,

F. S. WINSTON, Corporation Counsel.

May 26, 1886.

Hon. T. T. Gurney, Comptroller.

Dear Sir—

In your communication, dated May 25, you request my opinion in writing as to the power of the council to allow rebates upon saloon licenses, to apply upon future licenses; also, how far the comptroller is liable for respecting the order of the council in the premises.

I was at first inclined to doubt both the legality and propriety of allowing rebates to be applied upon future licenses. If this ordinance had not received the sanction of all subsequent councils, thus indicating their unqualified approval, and if this system of rebate had not proved both equitable and fairly satisfactory during the twenty odd years that it has been in operation in this city, I might still question the propriety, if not the legality, of the ordinance in question.

After the taking effect of the Harper high license law, which prohibits cities from issuing saloon licenses at less than "at a rate of $500 per annum," the question was raised whether licenses might be issued for periods of less than a year at proportionate rates.

This question was answered in the affirmative by the then corporation counsel in an opinion published in the council proceedings of February 25, 1884. Thereupon the council proceeded to divide the license year 1884-5 into three periods, for the purpose of saloon licenses, and have followed the custom ever since.

By these ordinances it is made the duty of the city collector to exact from every applicant payment for the entire period, without regard to the time when he commences business. Thus, a man who applied on April 1, 1886, for a saloon license was obliged to pay a license running from December 1, 1885, to April 30, 1886. It is understood that this method was adopted to insure payment in full from those saloon-keepers who are dilatory in taking out their licenses. About the same time as the passage of the ordinances dividing the license year into periods, the council adopted the corresponding policy of allowing to those who commenced business after the beginning of one of these licensed periods and paid for the whole period a proportionate rebate, whereby the surplus or over-payment which is made is allowed to be applied in part payment for a succeeding period.

The first order after the Harper law went into force was passed July 28, 1884, by a vote of ayes twenty-nine, noes one; the next by a unanimous vote and all since by a like unanimous vote. Prior to the passage of the Harper law a similar practice was in vogue ever since 1862.

The legislation in this city, by the council, upon this subject of saloon licenses for nearly a quarter of a century, demonstrates that it is, and has been, the policy of the law-making power to require of saloon-keepers that they pay for licenses at the rate of $500 per annum and no more.

As a matter of financial policy, the council has deemed it advisable to require of every applicant for a license payment in full for the period without regard to the time in such period when he begins business. The over-payment, or surplus, is allowed to be credited to him upon a subsequent license, in case he is granted one, and upon his convincing the authorities that he is clearly entitled to such rebate.

There are some objectionable features to the policy hereinabove delineated. It is easy enough to find fault with this license system. It is quite another thing to substitute an improvement. No other method has suggested itself to me, nor has any been offered for my consideration that is not equally objectionable, if not more so, from the legal aspect of the case, than the one that has received the assent of all administrations and councils since its first introduction. The legal objections to this system apply with equal force to all others that have been so far submitted. As a mere matter of law, or legal abstraction, a proposition may not be tenable, yet when applied to a particular situation of affairs and taken in connection with the surrounding circumstances its adoption may be necessitated by the exigencies of the case, and, therefore, justified, viewed from the highest legal standpoint.

This license system simply amounts to a case of over-payments, placed to their credit to be used only in certain way, i. e. upon a new license. It is not properly the case of money appropriated for, or paid out to the licensees.

It is to be objected that the Harper law requires an advance payment at the rate of $500.00 per annum and that a party, who takes out a license for the highest period from May 1 to August 1, 1886, and pays for the same in part by a rebate from the third period of the preceding year, 1885, does not comply with that law. The answer readily suggests itself as follows:

The amount of money he is allowed as rebate is a surplus payment upon the license of such third period of 1885 and may be fairly considered in law, as an advance payment to that extent upon the license for such first period of 1886. I think that the courts will sustain this view of the case.

If the rebate system is illegal the question can easily be tested by an action against one of the licensees, and until the courts decide that the rebates cannot lawfully be allowed, I shall uphold the legality of the various ordinances now in force.

Your second query, properly the most important to you personally, as to your liability in case the ordinance should be declared illegal by the courts, I answer somewhat at length, as the advice contained herein is applicable to many other cases in your department.

The enforcement of the ordinances, that is the will of the city as expressed in its ordinances, is placed in the hands of certain officials whose duties are well defined. Having accepted a public office the incumbent is bound to properly discharge the duties imposed upon him by law. This involves no great danger, no insufferable hardships. If the officer has acted in good faith in the exercise of his official functions he will ordinarily be protected, even though he exceeds his authority. On the other hand, if an official refuse to perform his duty, the municipality has thereafter no power to indemnify him, even when desirous of so doing. So long as you obey the law, as expressed in and by the ordinances passed by the council, you will be protected.

The courts so hold to guard the best interests of the municipality. The wisdom of distinguishing between an erroneous but bona fide act and an absolute refusal to act is too obvious to need further elucidation. There are exceptions to this general rule of protection of officers in the discharge of their duties, but it must be a very clear case of *illegality*, that would justify your non-compliance as a public officer with the mandates of the council, especially where it has, as in this instance, sanctioned the ordinance by its repeated approval.

Respectfully yours,

FRANCIS A. HOFFMAN, Jr., Corporation Counsel.

June 7, 1886.

Honorable Carter H. Harrison, Acting Commissioner of Public Works.

Dear Sir—

At your request I have examined the question whether the commissioner of public works can issue a permit, for the construction of a tunnel under the bed of the river at Taylor street in this city, to the gas companies (several of which have applied for permits) and herewith respectfully submit the following opinion.

Article V of the act of the legislature of this state, under which the City of Chicago is incorporated, enumerates the powers of the city council. The following paragraphs (quoted verbatim) of Section 1, of said Article V, bear directly upon the question submitted to me for decision:

"Thirteenth—To regulate the openings therein for the laying of gas or water mains and pipes, and the building and repairing of sewers, tunnels and drains, and erecting gas lights; provided, however, that any company heretofore organized under the general laws of this state, or any association of persons organized, or which may be hereafter organized for the purpose of manufacturing illuminating gas to supply cities or villages, or the inhabitants thereof, with the same, shall have the right, by consent of 'the Common Council (subject to existing rights), to erect gas factories, and lay down pipes in the streets or alleys of any city or village in this state, subject to such regulations as any such city or village may by ordinance impose.

"Twenty-eighth—To construct and keep in repair bridges, viaducts and tunnels, and to regulate the use thereof.

"Seventh—To lay out, to establish, open, alter, widen, extend, grade, pave or otherwise improve streets, alleys, avenues, sidewalks, wharves, parks and public grounds, and vacate the same.

"Ninth—To regulate the use of the same.

"Tenth—To prevent and remove encroachments or obstructions upon the same.

"Eleventh—To provide for the lighting of the same."

It seems to me that there can be no question as to the power of the city council in the premises. From a careful examination of the statutes and decisions of the courts I am of opinion that permission to construct the tunnels in question must be obtained from the city council, and that you have no authority to act in the premises, in the manner requested by said companies. Application must be made to the council not to you. The city council alone has power to permit the construction of said tunnels.

This city exists now by virtue of the general act passed in 1872. It can exercise all the powers therein granted by express words or fair implication. Among the powers delegated to this city under said act are those hereinbefore stated. (Vide Art. V. Sec. 1, of said act).

They refer to the authority of the council over tunnels and streets. It is true, that this power, like all other municipal powers, is derivative, depending solely for its existence and exercise upon legislative enactment; nevertheless the right to regulate the use of streets and the construction of tunnels is practically unlimited. In these respects the council is virtually endowed with sovereign power, confined, of course, to the trusts for which these extraordinary powers were conferred.

By the above general act the legislature gave the control and supervision of the streets and tunnels of this city to the council and has also designated the manner in which such control shall be exercised.

Paragraph 96, Section 1, Article V, of said act, authorizes the council to "pass ordinances, rules and make all regulations proper or necessary to carry into effect the powers granted therein."

Some of the gas companies, notably the Chicago Gas, Light & Coke Company, contend, that because they receive their charter direct from the legislature they are not required to go to the council for permission to build said tunnel. The Chicago Gas, Light & Coke Company for instance claims that the following provisions of its charter confer upon said company the right to construct the tunnel in question, "to lay pipes for the purpose of conducting gas in any of the streets or avenues of this city."

If there were a bridge at Taylor street this company might lay gas pipes under said bridge, beneath the bed of the river: Bridges are considered in law, parts of streets and treated the same as streets. Bridges are highways over water; the fee of such portions of the Chicago river, as are crossed by bridges, is in the city of Chicago. The city may devote the river, the soil covered by it and its banks for the entire width of the street to any use which in the judgment of its authorities shall be most promotive of the public interests, subject only to the easement for navigation.

Let us even assume for argument sake, that the existence of a bridge over the river is not a pre-requisite to constitute Taylor street a thoroughfare across said river. A rather violent assumption by the way. Can it be seriously contended that this company has a right, under its charter, to construct a tunnel at that point? If there, why not at any and all other points on Taylor street, and every other street in the city? If by the term to "lay pipes" in the streets is included the power to construct tunnels, then clearly the right is given to build tunnels the whole length and breadth of every street in Chicago.

Nor can the phrase in the charter of said company "to erect all necessary works and apparatus" be twisted into a meaning conferring, any such right as claimed by the company.

"Courts adopt a strict rather than liberal construction of powers. It is a well settled rule of construction of grants by the legislature to corporations, whether public or private, that only such powers and rights can be exercised under them as are clearly comprehended within the words of the act, or derived therefrom by necessary implication, regard being had to the object of the grant. Any ambiguity or doubt arising out of the terms used by the legislature must be resolved in favor of the public."

But it may be said, that although the charter of this company does not grant the power to build tunnels in *express words*, yet that power is *essential* to the declared objects and purposes of the company; that the building of the tunnel under the river is essential in order to convey the illuminating gas to other divisions of the city separated by the river from their gas works; therefore authorized under their charter. It undoubtedly would be *convenient* for the companies to tunnel the river in order to run gas mains to some other division of the city, but it must be more than convenient, the tunnel must be *indispensable*, in order to warrant such a construction of grant. There is no *such necessity*. The company is not restricted by its charter in the number of gas works; it may have as many as it pleases, one or more in each division of the city; hence can supply gas to all inhabitants of this city without crossing the river with its pipes at any point whatsoever.

The claims of the gas companies are wholly unfounded and pretentious; they vanish when properly investigated; they have no legal existence. The whole subject matter must be regulated by ordinance. The council is the only properly constituted authority in the premises. No tunnels under the river at Taylor street, or at any other street in the city, can be built without its sanction.

Respectfully submitted,

FRANCIS A. HOFFMAN, Jr., Corporation Counsel.

July 2, 1886.

To the Chairman and Members of the Committee on Railroads.

Gentlemen—

If I understand the question of your chairman correctly, I was asked to state under what circumstances the council is authorized to repeal an ordinance.

For general purposes of legislation the city council has full power to repeal an ordinance. The power to make includes the power to repeal. The council may in all cases rescind and annul an ordinance so long as the same has not been accepted and acted upon. The repeal of an ordinance is valid when specifically authorized by the granting ordinance itself. The ordinance may also be annulled when the beneficiary has violated the provisions of such ordinance. If the grant in the ordinance is not a franchise, but a mere license, the ordinance may be lawfully repealed.

It is hardly necessary to give additional instances to illustrate the above proposition. Whenever the passage of an ordinance is obtained by fraud in which the party benefited participated, such ordinance may be annulled by repeal, as it is a thoroughly well settled principle of law that fraud vitiates everything tainted with it.

There is, however, a limitation to the general rule that an ordinance may be repealed, which is of the greatest importance to bear in mind, viz: an ordinance granting rights and privileges which the council has a right to grant, cannot ordinarily be annulled after acceptance, whenever the granting ordinance in effect amounts to a contract. Whether an ordinance can be entirely retracted by repeal thereof depends upon the fact whether or not the particular ordinance constitutes a contract. If the grant have the elements of a contract it cannot be annulled by repeal. The city cannot repudiate a fair contract which has been made and which it was authorized to make. The city is bound the same as an individual by the grant and contract it has made.

There is no power to repeal such an ordinance, and the repealing ordinance would be void and of no effect.

I deem it superfluous to cite decisions upon the foregoing propositions of law. Their application depends upon the facts in each case.

Whether a given ordinance can be annulled by repeal cannot be definitely known until the court of last resort has passed upon the question.   Respectfully submitted,

FRANCIS A. HOFFMAN, Jr., Corporation Counsel.

October 23, 1886.

W. J. Onahan, Esq., City Collector.

Dear Sir—

The pressure of other business has prevented an earlier answer to your inquiry of October 2, concerning "Bucket Shops." You ask my opinion whether they should be licensed as brokers and be required to pay a license fee of $25.00 per annum.

The case is a delicate one to decide as it would seem on its face, that they should either be compelled to take out licenses as brokers, if enengaged in a legitimate broker's business, or suppressed, if engaged in an illegal occupation.

My understanding of the nature of these concerns is, that they are places where persons are engaged in betting on the rise and fall in the prices of grain, pork or stocks; where the proprietor charges a commission on the alleged sale and purchase, but where, in fact, nothing is sold or bought. These transactions are undoubtedly against both the policy and the letter of the law.

Whether the proprietors of such places can be punished under the criminal code, I do not undertake to decide, but the city ordinances on the subject of gambling are not, in my judgment, sufficiently broad to cover the offense. I am informed that an effort has been made more than once to amend the criminal code of this state to more explicitly cover cases of this kind.

Whether the proprietors of the "bucket shops" are or are not amenable to the criminal law of this state, it is certain that their occupation is one which ought not to be allowed to continue.

There is no form of gambling so demoralizing to the community. The pretense of an analogy between their transactions and the legitimate buying and selling of the board of trade only adds to the seductiveness of this method of gambling. It must lead many to gamble who would hesitate before risking their money on the turn of a card.

In view, therefore, of the character of this business, what is your duty as city collector as to issuing to these people city licenses to do business as "brokers." Clearly you should decline to throw around them the protection afforded by a license from the city. If the city has the power to issue licenses to them and does so, these

7

licenses would protect them against prosecution under the state law.
Gardner v. People, 20 Ill., 430.
Berry v. People, 36 Ill., 423.
Moreover, I doubt whether they can be called "brokers." To
constitute a broker one must be engaged in the negotiation of the
purchase or sale, upon a commission of some articles or things. As
I understand it, these people make but a pretense of selling or buying
the article or thing in question. Neither they nor their principals have
anything to sell and the "trades" are closed out on the difference in
price and the objects of purchase never change hands. Undoubtedly
the keeper of the so-called "bucket shops" would very willingly
waive this defense and pay the small license fee for the responsibility
and protection a license from the city would give.

But my advice to you is to decline to issue licenses to them and
to leave them amenable to whatever action may be taken under the
criminal law of the state either as it now reads or as it may be
amended by the legislature. Respectfully yours,
FRANCIS A. HOFFMAN, Jr., Corporation Counsel.

October 28, 1886.
To the Chairman and Members of the Committee on Bridewell.
Gentlemen—
You have referred to me a communication from the inspector of
the house of correction to the city council as to the employment of
prisoners in the bridewell, and ask the following question:

What control, if any, the city council has over the affairs of the
bridewell, and whether the board of inspectors of the bridewell can be
controlled in the management of the affairs of said institution by any
ordinance, order or resolution that may be passed by said city council.

The Board of Inspectors of the House of Correction was created
by an act of the legislature, approved April 25, 1871. By that act
it is provided that they shall be appointed by the mayor, that officer
being ex-officio a member of the board, by and with the consent of the
legislative authority of the city. The act in question defines the
powers and duties of these inspectors but does not undertake to vest
in them the jurisdiction and control over the House of Correction, exclusive of the commands of the city council.

On the contrary the act makes them practically city officers.
Their appointment must be confirmed by the council; their appropriations of money must be sanctioned by that body; their books and
records are open to the inspection by a committee of the council; to
that body they must also make their reports; their expenses are to
be paid by appropriations made by the legislative body and the act
contemplated throughout that the House of Correction is to be managed by the Board of Inspectors and the Superintendent, but subject
always to the direction and supervision of the legislative body of the
city.

Moreover the act provides, "all provisions of law and ordinances authorizing the commitment and confinement of persons in jail, bridewells and other city prisons, are hereby made applicable to all persons who may or shall be under the provisions of this act, sentenced to such House of Correction."

Obviously this means that the council may pass ordinances concerning the employment of prisoners in the House of Correction.

If there were any question of the power of the council under this act the question would be settled by another consideration. This act just referred to was approved April 10, 1872, and adopted by the city of Chicago April 23, 1872. By this statute, being the city charter, the council is given the following power:

To establish and erect calabooses, bridewells, houses of correction and work houses, for the reformation and confinement of vagrants, idle and disorderly persons, and persons convicted of violating any city or village ordinance, and make *rules* and *regulations* for the *gov erment of the same*, and appoint necessary keepers and assistants."

If the council have not the right to make rules and regulations concerning the House of Correction, by virtue of the act of 1871, they seem clearly to possess that right under the subsequent act of 1872.

Again, by an act of the legislature, approved and in force April 12, 1879, the city council was given express power to provide that prisoners committed to the house of correction, for violation of city ordinances, shall be required to work not exceeding ten hours a day.

The city council has, in fact, exercised these powers and the ordinances will be found collected under Article XXX of the Municipal Code. Among these ordinances will be found one requiring the superintendent of the House of Correction "to put the prisoners to the work which they are respectively best able to do, not to exceed ten hours for each working day."

The communication from the inspectors of the House of Correction is entirely in order and it is the duty of the council, having sufficient power in the premises, to say how the prisoners of the Bridewell shall be employed.   Yours respectfully,
        FRANCIS A. HOFFMAN, Jr., Corporation Counsel.

                                                January 14, 1887.
W. Guthrie, Esq, Inspector of Steam Boilers.
        Your inquiry of 13th inst. at hand. It is your duty under the ordinance to inspect all boilers "used for the generation of steam power or for heating or steaming purposes." I do not understand that it makes any difference as to your duty that a boiler is in a private residence.   Yours, etc.,
        O. H. HORTON, Corporation Counsel.

March 14th, 1887.

Hon. Charles H. Schwab, Comptroller.

Dear Sir—

I am in receipt of your letter of March 10th, 1887, which reads as follows:

Geo. M. Haynes, Esq., Corporation Counsel.

Dear Sir—

I desire your written opinion as to whether I can legally pay city employes whose salaries are fixed by the city council, extra compensation for services rendered after office hours. If not, would any action of the finance committee favoring its payment legalize it.

Yours truly,

CHARLES H. SCHWAB, Comptroller.

In reply will say that it is well settled that no person can receive compensation twice for the same labor performed. The statute is very plain upon this question. Hence I am clearly of the opinion that for work done as extra work *within* the regular working hours no extra compensation can be allowed. Work done and performed after the expiration of the regular working hours does not come within the rule and this should be paid for, whether performed by a regular employee of the city or not.

It has been the custom for years to close the offices of the various departments of the city at 4 p. m. This is or was originally intended as a regulation as to the time in which the public might have access, but it has grown into a practice and custom so strong that without any affirmative order of the heads of departments or city council, the working hours of the employees would be held to be from 9 a. m. to 4 p. m., and the time of employees outside of those hours belongs to the persons themselves, and not to the city. If work is done for the city outside of those hours compensation must if insisted upon be made. I am informed from your department that this question was heretofore passed upon by Hon. Francis Adams, late Corporation Counsel, and that the views herein expressed are in substance in accord with the views expressed by him.

Respectfully yours,

GEORGE M. HAYNES, Corporation Counsel.

April 13, 1887.

W. H. Purdy, Esq., Commissioner of Public Works.

My Dear Sir—

You have called upon this department for an opinion as to the right of the city to require permits for blasting rock or stone within the city limits. I respectfully invite your attention to Sections 948 to 953, inclusive, of Municipal Code, and will say that under the sections cited it is absolutely necessary that a permit should be obtained as therein stated, accompanied by the conditions required,

before blasting block or stone can be permitted within the city limits. I am unable to find any order or ordinance of council repealing, modifying or annulling the sections above cited, hence they should be enforced. Respectfully yours,
GEORGE M. HAYNES, Corporation Counsel.

May 20, 1887.

Hon. John A. Roche, Mayor.
Dear Sir—
I am of opinion that any person desiring to act as an "auctioneer," in the city of Chicago, must first obtain a license in which his *place of business is designated.*

No "auctioneer" is authorized to sell, or offer for sale, at public auction, personal property at any place *other* than the place designated in his license, *without* first having *obtained* from the mayor a *special permit* and paying therefor as provided in Section 943 of the Municipal Code of 1881, and the amendment thereof, passed April 23, 1883, found in supplement to said code, page 12.

This code does not apply to officers who *personally* make sales under legal process nor to mortgagees or trustees who *personally* sell under a mortgage or trust deed.
Yours respectfully,
O. H. HORTON, Corporation Counsel.

May 23, 1887.

Hon. W. J. Onahan, City Collector.
Dear Sir—
In response to your inquiry would state that I am of opinion that traveling salesmen selling wines or liquors in this city are not subject to license any more than in selling dry goods.

Also, that if a party residing or doing business here sells goods by sample, or otherwise, as a broker, he must procure a broker's license.

Also, that if wines or liquors are shipped here consigned to the order of foreign shippers to be placed in store and disposed of afterwards, such party must procure a wholesale liquor dealer's license. Yours truly,
O. H. HORTON, Corporation Counsel.

July 2, 1887.

Hon. John A. Roche, Mayor of the City of Chicago.
Sir—
In regard to the question of the right of the oil inspector to charge for the inspection of the material used by the People's Gas Light & Coke Company, I am of the opinion that the ordinances do not entitle the oil inspector to such charges, for the following reasons:

1st: Section 878 of the Municipal Code provides that when the "importers or dealer or vendor shall request the inspection," and further provides that if upon such testing and examination it shall meet the requirements, he shall brand   *   *   *   *when it shall be lawful for any dealer to sell the same.*

Section 897 provides that "if it shall not meet the requirements   *   *   *   it shall not be lawful for the owners thereof to offer the same for sale," and that, if it shall not meet the requirements, it shall not be lawful for the owners thereof *to offer the same for sale*, and "that it shall be condemned for *illuminating purposes.*"

Section 302, provides "that upon the application of any manufacturer, refiner or producer thereof."

Section 306, any manufacturers, refiners or producers of, or any dealer in.

The oil inspector calls my attention to Section 306 and cites the sentence of receiving into *his possession*. The term "his" is to be construed by referring back to the terms "manufacturers, refiners or producers."

Section 383, "or shall keep within said city for more than twenty four (24) hours any of said oils which have not been inspected," is an enumeration in the penalty clause and is to be construed in connection with the prior articles and sections.

All of the provisions of the law and the ordinances have reference to certain vocations that are engaged in the storage and sale of the article, and were enacted for the protection of the citizens and the public. If the oil inspector merely inspects the oil and permits the company to use the same for the purpose of making gas, the ordinance should have no practical application save to enable the inspector to receive the fees.

Under the provisions of the charter of the gas company they are authorized to manufacture gas from all substances, or a combination thereof, from which illuminating gas is usually obtained. It is evident that, if the oil inspector did inspect and charge for the inspection, the company, provided they complied with all police regulations, would still be entitled to use the same for making gas.

The only question involved is whether the oil inspector is authorized to charge for inspecting; in my opinion he is not.

Respectfully yours,

JOHN W. GREEN, Corporation Counsel.

July 7, 1887.

To the Honorable City Council of Chicago.

Gentlemen—

In reply to your request I herewith submit my opinion as to the legality of the ordinance submitted relative to licensing telephones.

The general incorporation law authorizes the corporate authorities of the city to license certain trades and occupations. These trades and occupations are specifically enumerated. It does not include in the enumeration telephones. It may be for the reason that the telephone as a system was not in public use at the date of the passage of the act. When the legislature in the general incorporation law declares that the corporate authority, organized under said act, shall have power to license certain occupations and kinds of business, specifically enumerating them, such declaration may be construed precisely as if the act in express terms inhibited the license of all trades and occupations not contained in the enumeration. This specific enumeration of the power implies the exclusion of all others.

Bross v. City of Cairo, 101 Ill., 475.

Applying this principle to the provisions of the ordinance submitted, the general law by necessary implication denies the right of the council to impose upon the telephone companies a license such as is proposed by the ordinance submitted, for the reason that in no clause of the general incorporation act is there any reference to the telephone system, or to any vocation or business similar in character or use.

I am of the opinion that the license cannot be imposed under the exercise of the police power of the city.

Judge Drummond in the street car cases held for the purpose of enabling the parties to take the case to the Supreme Court, that the licensing of street cars was a proper exercise of the police power and he bases his decision upon the theory that the general incorporation act provided that the city council shall have authority to license hackmen, etc., and all others pursuing like occupations, and he holds under the section specifically enumerating these occupations, "and all others pursuing like occupations." That this was intended as conferring a police power upon the city council in relation to the various classes *named in the statute.* And he accordingly held for the purpose of having the Supreme Court decide the case that street cars are of a like nature and character with omnibuses.

Judge Blodgett held that it was not a proper exercise of the police power. In the case of the Chicago Packing Co. the right to license was determined under the 81st clause of the 63d section, where the particular vocation is enumerated, and the police power was exercised for the reason that from the very nature of the business it might prove obnoxious to the health and comfort of the public. Under the exercise of the police power under legislative authority, unless such appears to have been the legislative intent, the law does not give the authority to the council to use the license as a mode of collecting revenue.

Judge Dillon, in his work on municipal law, says ordinances of this character ought not to be sustained unless the authority be *expressly or otherwise unequivocally conferred.*

Believing that the power to license is inhibited by the fact that the occupation is not directly or impliedly enumerated in the general incorporation law, and that it is not within the intent or boundaries of the police power and that it does not come within the spirit or letter of the law authorizing the exercise of that power for the protection of the lives or health of the citizens, or the preservation of good order and public morals, I am of the opinion that the ordinance submitted is illegal. This view disposes of the reasonableness of the license fees.

Respectfully submitted,

JOHN W. GREEN, Corporation Counsel.

October 31, 1887.

Hon. O. D. Wetherell, Chairman, Finance Committee.

Sir—

In reply to your request as to the construction of the act providing for the formation and disbursement of a Firemen's Pension Fund, I herewith submit the following opinion.

The act provides for three sources of revenue.

First. One per cent of all revenues collected or received from licenses.

Second. One per cent of salary of members of fire department, not to exceed $20.00 from each member.

Third. All gifts, rewards, devises, etc.

Section 4 provides that the sum of two hundred thousand dollars, which may be received and accumulated under the provisions of this act (aside from such gifts, grants, devises, or bequests) shall be when *received and accumulated* retained as a *permanent* fund, the annual income of which may be made available for the uses and purposes of such pension fund.

Section 6 provides that the interest received from any such investment of said fund after said fund shall have reached the sum of two hundred thousand dollars shall be made applicable to the payment of pensions under this act, and when such interest shall become so applicable it shall be in the power of the council of said city to diminish such annual rate of 1 per centum from licenses so that said income from interest and from licenses shall meet the requirements of the pension lists as provided by this act.

If the language of Sections 4 and 6 is to control the construction of this act then, until the fund shall reach the sum of two hundred thousand dollars, and an income is derived therefrom, the firemen can receive no benefits from the act.

Section 6 provides that when such interest shall become applicable then, if the interest is not sufficient to meet the requirement of the fund, the city council shall have the power to diminish the annual rate of 1 per cent from licenses to such a sum as will pay the deficiency between the income from interest and the amount required to be paid to those entitled to pension.

Sections 4 and 6, if construed in accordance with the strict interpretation of the words used, are susceptible of the construction that until an income is derived from the accumulated sum of two hundred thousand dollars the board is not authorized to pay any pensions whatever. But this construction is inconsistent with the general theory and other sections of the bill.

Plainly the intention of the act was that the firemen should receive. their pensions under the provisions of the act, and that when a surplus equal to the sum of two hundred thousand should yield an income from the interest, then this sum should be a limitation upon the payment of any further sum from the city or the firemen, save such a percentage of the licenses as would make up the deficiency between the income and the amount required to pay the pension due to the firemen under the act.

That this was the intention of the legislature is evidenced by the fact that Sections 7, 8 and 10 provide for monthly payments for firemen retired on account of physical or mental disability, also it is enacted that monthly payments shall be made to the widow and heirs for death occasioned while in performance of duty; also for a percentage of monthly payments in case there shall not be sufficient money to the credit of said pension fund, also for monthly payments for officers who are retired after twenty-five years service.

Your attention is respectfully called to the clause in Section 8, to-wit: "Provided that if at any time there shall not be sufficient money to the credit of said pension to pay each person entitled to the benefit thereof, the full amount per month as hereinabove stated then in that event an equal percentage of said monthly payment shall be made to each beneficiary thereof, until said fund shall be replenished.* * ."

If the construction is to be given to the act that the sum shall reach two hundred thousand dollars and when so accumulated only the income and the percentage of license necessary to make up the deficiency shall be applicable to pension, then there was no necessity for incorporating the clause in the act for the percentage of license, and the income and the assessment upon the firemen, would yield a sufficient revenue to pay the amount required for pensions.

It cannot be reasonably inferred that the legislature intended that the firemen should be deprived of the benefit to be derived from the act for at least six or seven years. If you will make a calculation based upon the percentage of licenses received from the city and the percentage of assessments upon the firemen, the accumulated sum would not reach two hundred thousand dollars for at least six years.

The act is made applicable to cities of over fifty thousand inhabitants. If the strict construction of the act is to be followed then no other city or town in the state would derive any benefits from the act, for it would be impossible ever to accumulate two hundred thousand dollars in any city or town in the state save the city of Chicago.

It is unreasonable to suppose that the legislature intended that the firemen should pay their assessments until the fund shall reach the sum of $200,000 and in the meantime derive no benefits from the act.

The evident intention of the framers of the act was, that the funds

should be used for the benefit of the firemen whenever they were entitled to pensions, and that whenever the surplus accumulated reached the sum of two hundred thousand dollars and yielded an income, then the city should only be required to pay from the license fund such a sum as would make up the deficiency between the income and the amount required to pay the pensions due under this act. If the income from this surplus of $200,000 was sufficient to pay the pension under the act then this amount was an absolute limitation as to the amount that should be paid by the city or the firemen. That this is true is evidenced by the fact that when this surplus yields an income the firemen by the provision of Section 6 are released from the payment of assessments.   Respectfully submitted,
JOHN W. GREEN, Corporation Counsel.

October 31, 1887.
To the City Council of the City of Chicago.
Gentlemen—
In reply to the following order of the council:
Ordered: That the corporation counsel be and he is hereby directed to prepare and send to this council, at its next regular meeting, an opinion as to the right of the city to erect, maintain and operate gas-works for the purpose of illuminating the streets and public buildings, and furnishing gas to private consumers; and also as to the right of the city to issue bonds to defray the cost of constructing, maintaining and operating the same.
I herewith submit the following opinion:
The city charter specifically grants to the city the right:
1st. To provide for the lighting of the streets.
2nd. The legislature has given authority to levy and collect a tax for that purpose.
Judge Drummond, in the case of Garrison v. City of Chicago, 7 Bissell, 480, held that authority to light the public streets and to levy and collect a tax for that purpose gives the power to the municipality to do this either *by the construction of gas-works of its own,* or by a valid contract with others acting within the scope of its authority.
Judge Dillon, Section 27, Dillon Municipal Corporations, says a city may be expressly authorized to erect a public wharf and charge tolls for its use, or to supply its inhabitants with water or gas, charging them therefor and making a profit thereby.
There can be no doubt that the city has the legal right to erect, maintain and operate gas works, provided it confine its expenditures within the constitutional and legislative limit. The city is limited by constitutional provisions from incurring indebtedness over a certain amount, and by legislative enactment from levying a tax beyond a specified per cent.
In my opinion the city cannot issue bonds to defray the expense

of erecting gas works until it shall be given the authority by specific legislation.

The city has the power to levy a tax for lighting purposes. The sum collected from the levy would be inadequate to successfully commence the operation of a system of gas works that would meet the demands of the city. The city has no power to issue bonds for the purpose of erecting, maintaining and operating gas works for the purpose of illuminating the streets and furnishing gas to private consumers until the legislature authorizes it so to do.

Respectfully,

JOHN W. GREEN, Corporation Counsel.

December 16, 1887.

To the City Council of the City of Chicago.

Gentlemen—

In reply to the order of the council, asking an opinion as to the validity of an ordinance providing for the establishment of a gas commission, I herewith submit the following opinion:

The city, in my opinion, would have the right to build gas works and operate the same if it were in a financial condition to do so. But the constitutional limitations as to indebtedness would deprive the city of this power, when we are advised that the present indebtedness is fully up to the constitutional limit.

It is proposed by the present ordinance that this commission, acting as agents for the city, shall issue bonds, for which the city shall not be liable. I am clearly of the opinion that the commission appointed by the city and in reality acting for the city could not issue bonds as provided for by the present ordinance. If the city is prohibited by constitutional limitations from issuing bonds, or increasing its indebtedness, it could not delegate any valid authority to a commission created by its authority so to do. The plain provisions of the constitution could not be violated by any such indirect method. The city council, that delegates the authority, having no power, it certainly could not by ordinance give to a commission created by its authority any greater legal rights than those possessed by the council.

The question has been submitted whether the commission provided for in this ordinance could, under the general incorporation act, be incorporated, issue bonds, and legally exercise the right to issue bonds.

The individuals of the commission might incorporate under the general law and erect and operate gas-works if legally authorized so to do, but their authority would be solely derived from the general law. They would act entirely independent of any control of the city. The franchises and rights would belong to the company, and not to the city. The city of Chicago cannot create a gas commission and have that commission incorporated under the general law of the state, and then issue bonds to evade the constitutional limitation. It has no power to delegate such authority.

The second proviso of the ordinance says: "Provided, the city would appropriate a liberal sum, say $150,000, as an earnest of the intention of the city to carry forward the project in good faith."

The provision is plainly at variance with the provision of the constitution which says that no city, or other municipality, shall ever become subscriber to the capital stock of any railroad, or private corporation, or make any donation to, or loan its credit in aid of such corporation.

The plan, as proposed, would, in my opinion, be illegal.

Respectfully,
JOHN W. GREEN, Corporation Counsel.

January 16, 1888.

To the City Council of the City of Chicago.

Gentlemen—

In reply to the communication of the city council, asking for an opinion of the law department as to whether, under the ordinance pending before the city council, the city has the authority to license telephones, I herewith submit the following opinion:

In a former opinion I decided as follows: "Believing that the power to license is inhibited by the fact that the occupation is not directly or impliedly enumerated in the general incorporation law, and that it is not within the intent or boundaries of the police power and that it does not come within the spirit or letter of the law authorizing the exercise of that power for the protection of the lives or health of the citizens, or the preservation of good order and public morals, I am of the opinion that the ordinance submitted is illegal."

I find no reason for changing my opinion.

The Supreme Court of Wisconsin, in the case of Wisconsin Telephone Company v. City of Oshkosh, following the opinion of the Supreme Court of Illinois in the City of Cairo v. Bross, say: "The charter having expressly stated what the common council might license, without naming telephones, has by necessary implication prohibited the exaction of such license. The mere exaction of money for revenue is not among the police powers of the city. Telephones are not named among the several things that the Common Council are expressly authorized to license."

Until the legislature gives the city the legal authority so to do, I am compelled to follow the decision of the courts upon the question at issue.

The further question is submitted that the corporation counsel report by what authority the Chicago Telephone Company occupies any of the public streets and alleys of the city of Chicago.

On the ninth day of September, 1887, an ordinance was passed authorizing the Bell Telephone Company of Boston, Mass., to operate a telephone system through and upon the streets of the city of Chicago. In a bill filed April 30, 1883, in the Circuit Court of Cook county, case No. 44632, the Chicago Telephone Company vs. The City of Chicago, the following history of the transfer of the property of the Bell Telephone Company is given:

"That thereafter in the year 1881 your orator (The Chicago Telephone Company) was organized as a corporation under the laws of the State of Illinois for the purpose of manufacturing telephones and all appurtenances connected therewith; and to construct and acquire by lease or otherwise, own and operate telephones and telephone lines and offices and to lease the same, or any portion thereof, and to do a telephone, telegraph and district telegraph business. That upon the organization your orator purchased from the American District Telegraph Company aforesaid, all its lines, plant, property and appurtenances and franchises in said city, and your orator also purchased from the Union Telegraph Company, a corporation theretofore organized under the laws of the State of Illinois, all the telegraph lines, plant and appurtenances which have been so constructed and placed in operation in said City of Chicago, as aforesaid, by said Bell Telephone Company, said Union Telephone Company, having acquired said property and plant from the said Bell Telephone Company and its assigns. And your orator alleges that by such purchase and the payment of the consideration therefor, it became not only the owner of all the telegraph and telephone property and plant, but in all respects the successor to and owner of the right and franchise granted under said patent and said ordinance to the American District Telegraph Company and the Bell Telephone Company."

In a communication to the commissioner of public works the president of the Chicago Telephone Company alleges that the Bell Telephone Company of Boston, Massachusetts, was succeeded by the Bell Telephone Company of Illinois, the Bell Telephone Company of Illinois by the Union Telephone Company, and the Union Telephone Company was succeeded by the Chicago Telephone Company in the spring of 1881. The statute provides that no company can operate its lines upon any street, alley or other highway without the consent of the corporate authorities of such city, town or village. The ordinance granting a license to the Bell Telephone Company does not extend the privilege to lessees, successors or assigns. The Chicago Telephone Company claims the right to operate its lines in the streets of the city of Chicago by virtue of a purchase of the Bell Telephone Company. The Bell Telephone Company had obtained the consent of the city of Chicago by an ordinance heretofore referred to and they conveyed its property to the Chicago Telephone Company. The Chicago Telephone Company entered into the ownership of all the property purchased, as aforesaid and claim that the right to occupy the streets of the city of Chicago comes to them indirectly as an incident or element in the property acquired. If this theory is true the consent given to the Bell Telephone Company is negotiable and capable of being passed by sale indefinitely. It would combine the consent of the city with a franchise so as to constitute easement.

But this theory is an attempt to evade the plain provision of the law. The legislature intended that there should be an immediate relation between the city and the corporation carrying on its operation in the streets. It was the evident intention that every company should apply for the consent of the city to operate its lines directly to the city council, and it was not the intention of the legislature that the company that had the consent could sell its property to another corporation and thus deprive the city of any voice or authority in determining the question as to what company should exercise the right to operate its lines upon the streets of the city.

The condition of the streets, the changes and modifications that have occurred since the passage of the ordinance, the increasing demands for public protection against monopolies, all require that when a new company desires to occupy the streets, it should directly obtain the consent of the city council.

In this case a new corporation, with amplified, additional and different powers, having purchased not only the Bell Telephone Company's property but those of several other companies, attempts by the purchase of these other companies to exercise the right to occupy the streets of Chicago. The law contemplates that the municipality is competent to pass upon the question of permission, and does not delegate that right to any private corporation. The consent of the city of Chicago is authorized because the terms on which streets may be safely allowed to be occupied can best be determined by leaving the regulation to be harmonized with all other exigencies by the authorities controlling their use.

It is a matter which should be under municipal supervision to prevent clashing among the many convenient uses to which streets must necessarily be subjected; for water, gas, drainage, and other city necessities. The law provides the method by which each corporation can use the streets of the city, to-wit, by obtaining the consent of the city. The authority is given to the Bell Telephone Company as a personal privilege and in my opinion was not transferable by that company to another without the consent of the city of Chicago. The Chicago Telephone Company claim that the city is estopped by virtue of contracts made with the heads of departments recognizing the successorship of their various companies.

If the Chicago Telephone Company has not obtained the consent of the city to operate its lines upon the streets of the city, the action of the officials cannot render valid an occupancy that has not been obtained in acordance with the provisions of the statute requiring the consent of the city council.

Respectfully,

JOHN W. GREEN, Corporation Counsel.

May 7, 1888.

Hon. O. D. Wetherell, Chairman, Finance Committee.

Sir—

In reply to your question in regard to leasing, or permitting the occupancy of any portion of the public grounds, known as the Lake Front, I respectfully call your attention to the following decision of Judge Blodgett:

"This day came * * * argued by counsel * * * proof * * * and being fully advised in the premises it is ordered by the court that the city of Chicago absolutely desist and refrain from further leasing the whole or any part of the public ground on the said Bill described, or further granting any manner of license or permit to use the same to the defendant, the Chicago Base Ball Club, or to any person or corporation whatsoever until the further order of the court in the premises, and that the said city of Chicago absolutely desist and refrain from obstructing or occupying the whole or any part of the said public ground or permitting the obstruction or occupation of the same by any building or structure of any not *now* standing thereon, until the further order of the court in the premises; and that from and after the 30th day of October next, the said Chicago Base Ball Club absolutely cease, desist and refrain from using or occupying in any manner or for any purpose the public ground aforesaid, or any part thereof, or permitting such use or occupation of the same until further order of this court in the premises; and said club shall remove all buildings, etc., and leave the ground free and open."

Chancery Record 30, United States Circuit Court.

Under the above decision the city council has no right to grant any privileges to any party, as the decree specifically prohibits the city from leasing the whole or any part of the public grounds, and enjoins the city from permitting the obstruction or occupation of the same by any building or structure, until the further orders of the court. Respectfully,

JOHN W. GREEN, Corporation Counsel.

September 10, 1888.

To the Financial Committee.

Gentlemen—

In compliance with your request I herewith submit an opinion as to the validity of an ordinance proposing to fix the annual rates to be charged for telephone.

The question involved is whether the city council is vested with power to fix the rates set forth in the ordinance submitted. The power to regulate the rates to be charged for telephones must be derived from General Incorporation Act, under which the city is incorporated. Corporate authorities, acting under its provisions, can only exercise such powers and rights as are clearly comprehended within the words of the act or derived therefrom by necessary implication.

McAllister, J. in People vs. Howard, says, "That the following summary of Judge Dillon, Section 89, page 115, is the best summary of all the decisions upon that point to be found in all the books."

"It is a general and undisputed proposition of law that a *municipal corporation possesses and can exercise the following* powers and no others: First, those granted in *express words*. Second, those *necessarily or fairly* implied in or *incident* to the powers' expressly granted. Third, those essential to the declared objects and purposes of the corporation, not simply convenient but indispensable."

The Supreme Court of the state in the case of the City of Cairo vs. Bross, 101 Ill., page 478, says: "When the legislature, by the general incorporation act, declares that the corporate authorities of cities and villages organized and acting under its provisions shall have power to license certain occupations and kinds of business, specifically enumerating them, such declaration must, by a familiar canon of construction, be construed precisely as if the act in express terms inhibited the licensing of all trades and occupations not contained in the enumeration."

The Supreme Court of the United States in Thomas vs. West Jersey Railroad Company, 101 U. S., 82, says: "Conceding the rule applicable to all statutes, that what is fairly implied is as much granted as what is expressed, it remains that the charter of a corporation is the measure of its powers, and that the enumeration of those powers implies the exclusion of all others."

Mather vs. City of Ottawa, 114 Ill., p. 659.

City of Champaign vs. Harmon, 98 Ill., p. 494.

Gaddes vs. Richland County, 92 Ill., p. 123.

Cook County vs. McCrea, 93 Ill., p. 238.

It cannot be seriously contended that the express power to regulate the rates to be charged for telephones is embraced within the expressed charter powers of the city council.

My attention has been called to the fact that the city council of the city of Cleveland passed an ordinance regulating the price of gas, but your attention is respectfully called to the fact that the power is expressly delegated by Section 2478 of the Ohio statute, to-wit:

"The Council of any city or village in which gas companies, or gas light, or coke companies may be established are hereby empowered to regulate from time to time the price which said gas or gas light and coke companies may charge for gas furnished by such companies to the citizens, public grounds and buildings, streets, lanes, alleys, avenues, wharves and landing places, and such gas light or gas light and coke companies *shall in no event charge more for any gas furnished to such corporation or individuals than the price specified by ordinance* of such Council.

The validity of the ordinance was tested in the Circuit Court of

Cuyahoga County, State of Ohio, in the case of the State of Ohio vs. The Cleveland Gaslight and Coke Company, and Upson, J. says: "It will be seen by an examination of the ordinance that it literally complies with the provisions of the section of the statute. The statute provides that the Council of the city are empowered to regulate the price which said gas or gaslight and coke companies may charge for gas. The ordinance is within the strict letter of the provisions of the statute authorizing the City Council to pass such ordinance."

In this case the power was specifically granted by the legislature.

My attention has been called to an ordinance passed by the city council of the city of St. Louis, regulating the rates to be charged for telephones. The city charter of the city of St. Louis gives to the city council the power to license, tax and regulate among many other vocations specifically enumerated, bankers, *or others corporations and institutions,* and the general power to *tax license and regulate all occupations and trades not heretofore enumerated, of whatever name or character.*

In the ordinance giving to telephone companies the right to transact business in the city of St. Louis, it is provided, "That the city of St. Louis *reserves the right to fix the rates* and charges for the use of telephones."

When the question of imposing a license fee on telegraph and telephone companies, the amount of the fee to be determined by the number of poles in use, was submitted to Judge Grinnell, then the city attorney of the city of Chicago, he decided as follows:

"By the general ordinances of the city, no additional wires can be run under ground, and no more poles erected, so, in fact, the enclosed ordinance is to compel the companies to pay a tax or license on existing poles, and unless there is a reservation in the ordinance granting the privileges to erect poles, that the company shall pay a tax or license fee in the manner suggested, the ordinance is of no force or effect, as I understand there is no such reservation."

The power not being specifically enumerated in the charter, if it exists at all, must be found in the general police power of the city, embraced in the powers granted to the City Council by Subdivision 66 of Section 63 of the General Incorporation Law. The power there given is to "regulate the police of the city and enforce all necessary police ordinances."

Justice Lacey, in the case of the Village of Chebanse vs. McPherson, 15 Bradwell, p. 313, says: "The general police power of the *state legislature* to pass laws for the benefit of the people and society generally is very comprehensive and is used in an enlarged sense, permitting the passage of laws for the protection of life, liberty, and property, or laws for the general welfare, only limited by the provision of the constitution, *but the word has a more limited and restricted sense as used in paragraph 66, Section 1, Article V, of the General Incorporation Act,* in relation to cities, towns and villages, and may be

8

regarded as restricted to those subjects pertaining to health, morals and good order of the people within the city, town or village."

Hawthorn vs. People, 109 Ill., 302.

As to the construction of the police power of the city, Justice Bailey, in the late case of the City of Chicago vs. Phoenix Insurance Company, says: "It is urged, however, that the power to license, regulate and tax the business of a fire insurance is a police power, that is embraced within the power granted to the City Council by Subdivision 66 of Section 63, of the General Incorporation Law. The power there given is to 'regulate the police of the city, and pass and enforce all necessary police ordinances.' The statute, while giving such general power, specifically sets forth a great number of subjects of municipal legislation, most of them matters of police regulation, and prescribes the manner and extent of the exercise of the police power over them respectively. Among the subjects thus specifically subjected to police regulation are various avocations and kinds of business, that of fire insurance not being of the number. In another part of the statute, however, the contribution which foreign insurance companies are required to make to the municipal government is especially prescribed, and no provision is there made for any control by the municipal authorities over such companies or their agents beyond that of collecting and receiving the tax thus imposed. Under these circumstances it is manifest that the licensing and taxing of foreign insurance companies, even if held to be proper subjects for police regulation, are not within the grant of power given to the Common Council by the general laws of the statute authorizing it to regulate the police of the city

"Judge Dillon, in his treatise on Municipal Corporations, says: 'Occasionally the charter or Incorporation Act, without any specific enumeration of the purpose for which by-laws may be made, contains a general and comprehensive grant of power to pass all such as may seem necessary to the well being and good order of the place. More frequently, however, the charter of an incorporating act authorizes the enactment of by-laws in certain specified cases and for certain purposes, and after this specific enumeration a general provision is added that the corporation may make any other by-laws or regulations necessary to its welfare, good order, etc., not inconsistent with the constitution or laws of the state.

"This difference is essential to be observed, for the power which the corporation would possess under what may, from convenience, be termed the general welfare clause, if it stood *alone*, may be limited, qualified, or, when such intent is manifest, impliedly taken away by provisions specifying the particular purposes for which by-laws may be made. 1 Dillon on Municipal Corporation, No. 315. See also State vs. Ferguson, 33 N. H., 424."

This case was appealed to the Supreme Court and they say, that it would be a difficult task to formulate a general rule which would determine definitely the character and scope of every ordinance which a city might pass under this clause of the statute. They dispose of the question that under the police power an ordinance may be passed for the purpose of raising a revenue by licenses, by saying, that it is a subject foreign to the police power conferred on incorporated towns and cities by the statute.

Under the decisions of the case by the Appellate Court of the City of Chicago vs. Phoenix Insurance Company, there would be no question that the right to fix the rates to be charged for the telephones would not come within the police power of the city council.

The Supreme Court refused to pass upon the question when it was directly presented in the argument and until the Supreme Court shall construe this question, the decision of the Appellate Court shall govern the rulings of this department.

JOHN W. GREEN, Corporation Counsel.

September 26, 1888.

Hon. A. H. Burley, Comptroller.

Dear Sir—

You ask an opinion from this office whether or not the library board has the right to withold from the city treasury moneys collected from fines, lost books, etc. In my opinion it has not the right so to do. All moneys collected by the library board from fines, or otherwise, become a part of the library fund, and as such should be deposited in the city treasury to the credit of such fund. The law provides "that all moneys received for such library shall be deposited in the treasury of said city to the credit of the Library Fund."

Respectfully yours,

CLARENCE A. KNIGHT, Asst. Corporation Counsel.

October 12, 1888.

To the Committee on Streets and Alleys, South.

Gentlemen—

The following communication was received from your Committee:

Chicago, October 1, 1888.

Sir—

The committee on streets and alleys, south, at their last meeting passed the following:

"Moved that the petition be referred to the Law Department for an opinion as to the legality of the signatures being signed by H. H. Nash as an attorney in fact, for the property owners; also if the property owners have a legal right to withdraw their consent to the ordinance of the Chicago Rapid Transit and Elevated Railroad, and to further inform the committee as to whether the names of property owners were signed conditionally and what the conditions are, and to report as soon as possible."

Please govern yourself accordingly.   Yours, etc.,

W. NICKERSON, City Clerk.

Hon. J. W. Green, Corporation Counsel.

In reply I submit the following opinion: In the matter of granting a license to the Consolidated Rapid Transit and Elevated Railroad Company of Chicago the following documents are in the possession of and filed with the council and your committee:

1.   A petition of property owners in favor of granting a license to the aforesaid Elevated Railroad Company. The petition is signed by H. H. Nash, as attorney in fact, for each individual property owner.

2.   A draft of an ordinance granting permission and authority to Consolidated Rapid Transit and Elevated Railroad Company of Chicago to locate, construct, maintain and operate with steam power a double track elevated railroad over and along the route therein specifically described.

3.   A remonstrance of property owners, accompanied by their written revocation of the authority given to H. H. Nash, their attorney in fact, to sign their names to the foregoing petition. Also a remonstrance from property owners who allege that they are the present owners of the property adjacent to the proposed route, and that they purchased the property subsequent to the date at which the party from whom they purchased signed the petition in favor of the elevated railroad.

4.   A supplemental petition of property owners favoring the granting of the privileges to the said elevated railroad.

5.   A draft of an ordinance to be substituted for the original ordinance presented.

Your committee requests an opinion. First, "as to the legality of the signatures being signed by H. H. Nash, as an attorney in fact, for the property owners."

The following is a copy of the form of signatures attached to said petition:

JOHN D. JENNINGS,

By H. H. NASH, Attorney in Fact.

(Giving a description of the property, with the frontage upon said route.)

In my opinion the property owner, as the principal, has the legal right to delegate this power to his agent, and the agent, when duly and legally authorized, has authority to sign a petition.

The Supreme Court of Arkansas, in the case of Rector v. Board of Improvements, reported in American and English Corporation Cases, Vol. 19, p. 630, in passing upon an act which provides, "If within three months after the publication of an ordinance a majority in value of the real property shall present to the Council a petition," says, "the power of the Council depends upon the assent or petition of a majority in value of the property holders owning property adjoining the locality to be affected. This fact is jurisdictional and the want of it makes a local assessment void. The petition must be signed by property holders owning real property adjoining the locality to be affected, *or their duly authorized agents*."

Parsons on Contracts, Vol. 1, Sec. 39.

Story on Agency, Chap. 2, Sec. 6.

Second, "Have the property owners a legal right to withdraw their consent to the ordinance of the Consolidated Rapid Transit and Elevated Railroad Company of Chicago?"

The Consolidated Rapid Transit and Elevated Railroad Company of Chicago has not filed with the council or the committee the authority of the attorney in fact to sign the petition in favor of granting the license. They refuse to produce the authority for inspection by this department, although I am instructed by your committee to report "Whether the names of property owners were signed conditionally, and what the conditions are." I am thus compelled to decide this question upon the documentary evidence that is before the council and the committee.

The act of June 18, 1883, provides:

"Section 1. Be it enacted by the People of the State of Illinois, represented in the general assembly, that no person or persons, corporation or corporations, shall construct or maintain any elevated railroad, or any elevated way or conveyor, to be operated by steam power, or animal power, or any other motive power, along any street or alley in any incorporated city or village, except by the permission of the City Council or Board of Trustees of such city or village, granted upon a petition of the owners of the land representing more than one-half of the frontage of the street or alley, or of so much thereof as is sought to be used for such elevated railroad or elevated way or conveyor; and the City Council, or Board of Trustees, shall have no power to grant permission to use any street or alley, or part thereof, for any of the purposes aforesaid, except upon such petition of land owners as is herein provided for."

"Sec. 2. When the street or alley, or part thereof sought to be used for any of the purposes aforesaid, shall be more than one mile in extent, no petition of land owners shall be valid for the purposes of this act, unless the same shall be signed by the owners of the land representing more than one-half of the frontage of each mile and fractional part of a mile, of such street or alley, or of the part thereof sought to be used for any of the purposes aforesaid."

And the General Incorporation Act, as amended by act March 30, 1887, provides:

"Ninetieth. The City Council or Board of Trustees shall have no power to grant the use of or the right to lay down any railroad tracks in any street of the city to any steam, dummy, electric, cable, horse or other railroad company, whether the same shall be incorporated under any general or special law of the state now or hereafter in force, except upon the petition of the owners of the land representing more than one-half of the frontage of the street, or so much thereof as is sought to be used for railroad purposes, and when the street or part thereof sought to be used shall be more than one mile in extent no petition of land owners shall be valid unless the same shall be signed by the owners of the land representing more than one-half of the frontage of each mile, and of the fraction of a mile, if any, in excess of the whole miles, measuring from the initial point named in such petition, of such street or of the part thereof sought to be used for railroad purposes."

The petition giving the consent must comply with the statutory requirements. For when this required consent has not been obtained the city is absolutely without power to grant the license and the exercise of it would be wholly without warrant and unlawful.

McCartney et al. vs. C. & E. R. R. Co., 112 Ill., 639.

It is within the power and discretion of the council to determine whether the petition complies with the statutory requirements. In determining the question as to the sufficiency of the petition in the present case, the council is undoubtedly limited to the evidence filed with the council and committee. In the decision of the question submitted. I am of the opinion that the rule laid down by the courts in cases where a petition is required from property owners for a public improvement is clearly applicable. So far as the record before the council and your committee shows, the petition of the property owner is signed by his agent and filed with the council. Subsequent to the date when the agent signed the petition and filed it with the council the property owner, by a written instrument, revokes the authority given to his agent. Under this state of facts can the owner revoke the authority given to his agent?

Judge Dillon, in note to Section 801, of his work on Municipal Corporations, says: "Until the city authorities act on the application of real estate owners to have a street improved any one of the applicants may revoke his action, and if this reduces the number to less than that which is required by the charter the power to make such improvement is thereby taken away," citing:

Irwin v. Mobile, 57 Alabama, 6.

The Supreme Court of Indiana, say: "There can be no question of the right of the appellants to dismiss the petition as to themselves, or to withdraw their names from it at any time before final action on it by the board. The written withdrawal of their names was in effect a dismissal of the petition as to them. It was an error of law in the Commissioners to deny the appellants' right to so withdraw and to regard them as petitioners afterward."

Hoard v. Elliott, 33 Ind., 222.

In the case of People v. Goodwin, 5 New York, 568, the court say: "Referees appointed by the court can hear and decide the appeal, not on the facts existing at the time of the original application for the road, but on the facts existing at the time of hearing them."

These cases are followed by an almost unbroken line of decisions in the states of Nebraska, Indiana, New Jersey and New York.

If the property owner can withdraw his consent when he has personally signed or given it, he certainly can revoke an authority given to an agent, or attorney in fact, unless for good cause shown in the nature of an estoppel he is inhibited. The record before your committee shows merely the signatures of the attorney in fact, and the written revocation. In my opinion, so far as this record shows, the property owner would have a right to revoke the authority given to his agent. Additional names can undoubtedly, under the rulings of the courts, be added to the petition up to the time that the council proceed to take final action, and the filing of the additional petition by the company with the council is an admission that the petition can be changed, prior to the time when the council takes final action upon the question of granting the license.

When property has been purchased, subsequent to the date when the petition was signed, the sale and conveyance of the land in good faith, before the council finally acts upon the petition and ordinance, is a revokal of the consent given by the prior owner. The person to whom the damages would accrue, if any, is the party that the statute contemplates should petition the council.

Third. I am required to report to your committee, "Whether the names of property owners were signed conditionally and what the conditions are?"

In pursuance of your request, I addressed communications to the attorney and general manager of the elevated railroad, requesting them to furnish me with the power of attorney and contracts. These they have refused to produce, and I, therefore, report that I am unable to furnish to your committee the information requested. The copy of their replies are hereto attached. Respectfully,

JOHN W. GREEN, Corporation Counsel.

October 24, 1888.

To the Committee on Streets and Alleys, West.

Gentlemen—

In reply to your communication, requesting an opinion on certain questions therein submitted, I herewith submit my reply:

First. Did the petition of property owners accompanying the original draft of the ordinance, apply only to the original ordinance?

Second. After the property owners have petitioned the council for an elevated railroad company, can the company, of its own motion, and without the consent of the petitioning property owners, make a radical change in that ordinance?

The original petition is as follows: "The undersigned owners of the land representing more than one-half of the frontage on Randolph Street, from a point near the southwest corner of Canal Street to the intersection of said Randolph Street with Ogden Avenue and Bryan Place."

"Also the owners of the land representing more than one-half the frontage on Ogden Avenue from Randolph Street to Crawford Avenue. Also the owners of the land representing more than one-half the frontage on Bryan Place, from Randolph Street to Lake Street. Also the owners of the land representing more than one-half of the frontage on Lake from a point twenty feet west of the east line to a point four hundred feet east of Crawford Avenue, hereby petition your Honorable Body to grant to the West Chicago Rapid Transit Company, the right to construct, maintain and operate a double track elevated railway along, upon and over said Randolph Street, Ogden Avenue, Bryan Place and Lake Street *between the points heretofore mentioned.* And your petitioner would further respectfully represent to your Honorable Body, as required to do by legislative enactment, that we have formally consented and do hereby consent in manner and form as required by law, that the said West Side Chicago Rapid Transit Company shall locate, construct, maintain and operate its proposed lines of elevated railway *along, upon and over said Randolph Street, Ogden Avenue, Bryan Place and Lake Street between the points* heretofore mentioned."

Subsequent to the filing of the original petition the West Chicago Rapid Transit Company filed with the council a petition herewith submitted:

As to the power of the petitioners to insert conditions the Supreme Court of Illinois, in the case of the People ex rel. vs. West Division Railway Company, 118 Ill., page 120, say: "It is true that the property owners might have inserted such conditions in their assent as they thought proper, and the Common Council might have been powerless to grant the railroad company permission to occupy the streets except upon the conditions specified by the property owners in their consent."

The consent of the property owners is based upon conditions named in their petition, and is specifically set forth as between the points set forth in said petition. They say, we have formally consented and do hereby consent in the manner and form as required by law that the said West Chicago Rapid Transit Company *shall* locate, construct and maintain its proposed lines of elevated railroad along, upon and over said Randolph street, Ogden avenue, Bryan place and Lake street, *between the points hereinbefore mentioned.*

If, as stated in the foregoing case, the petitioners might insert such condition in their assent as they may deem proper and "the Common Council is powerless to grant the railway company permission to occupy the streets, except upon the conditions specified by the property owners in their consent," then the petition, as pre-

sented with the condition therein contained is the basis of the jurisdiction of the Council, and the railway company would have no right
to change the route from that which is set forth in the petition
of the property owner.

It must be assumed that the route to which the property owners gave their assent is the route they wanted, and there is nothing
before your committee, or the council, to indicate their assent to any
change of route. The charter of the company defines the route to
be "from within the city of Chicago to without the said city and its
various suburbs, and on some or all of the following streets in said
city of Chicago, to-wit: Lake, Randolph, Madison and Van Buren
streets, *from as near a point to Lake Michigan as practicable, and
extending westward the entire length of said streets in said city.*"

The initial point and terminus of the said road, stated in the
petition, undoubtedly induced the property owners to give the consent
as expressed in the petition, and in my opinion it would be illegal to
permit the railway company to change the route, and have as a
basis for the changed route, a petition that assents to another different route, virtually to be determined by the company, and not along
the entire length of the street, but "upon property of not over fifty
feet in width to be acquired by purchase, or condemnation."

Second. As to the questions asked in regard to the power of
the property owners to sign by an attorney in fact, this department
gave an opinion to the committee on streets and alleys south, that
covers all that is asked, save the proposition, whether the contracts are
against public policy. Until the contracts and authority of the attorney
in fact are presented for inspection, I cannot pass upon the question
submitted.

Third. As to whether Stephen F. Gale authorized his signature
to be attached to the petition, I report that Mr. Gale files an affidavit
with the council that he never signed, or authorized his signature to
be attached to the petition.

Fourth. As to the question whether any portion of the frontage
was signed by tenants. This department has not the force at its
command to investigate the question asked.

Fifth. As to the question whether A. J. Stone and Henrietta
Snell signed the petition as owners, I have to report that upon the
face of the petition they appear as owners of the property (there being
an erasure opposite their names).

Sixth. As to whether administrators and executors have the right
to sign frontage to property owned by the heirs of an estate, I herewith
submit the decision of the supreme courts of California and Arkansas
upon the question:

"The petition must be signed by property holders owning real
property adjoining the locality to be effected, or their duly authorized
agents. An administrator is not the owner of the real property which
belonged to his intestate at the time of his death. That belongs

to his heirs. They hold the legal title to it, subject to the payment of his debts. The statute authorizing administrators to sign
for estates, cannot, so far as the heirs are concerned, give their signatures any efficacy in the face of the constitution requiring the consent
of the owners. Nor is the signature of a member of a company or
stockholder in a corporation to such petition evidence of the assent of
the company or corporation to the assessment."

Rector v. Board, etc., 19 A. and E., Corp. Cases, 635-636.

"It is also equally clear, as a conclusion of law, that executors,
administrators and agents, to whom as such, no frontage was assessed on the assessment roll, were not owners, within the meaning
and intent of the statute, who were authorized to petition for the
opening of the avenue.

"Executors and administrators are but the legal personal representatives of the decedents whom they represent. They are but
agents of their constituents, created by law, whose duties and powers are prescribed by law. Whatever they do must be done according
to law, and within the authority of the law; for the acts of an agent are
binding only when done within the scope of the authority conferred
upon him. In any transaction in which executors or administrators
pretend to act as such, they cannot create any liability on the estate
of which they are representatives. They have no power to charge
or incumber or sell and convey, the real property of the estate, unless
authorized by the law under which they are acting. In favor of such
an act there is no legal presumption. If it purports to be done by
authority, the authority should be produced. The signatures of
the executors, administrators and agents to the petition were, therefore, ineffectual as signatures of the frontage for which they signed.

"And where real property is assessed upon an assessment roll
to two or more persons, the legal presumption is that all are joint
owners. Being the common property of all, one of the joint owners or tenants in common cannot do any act in hostility to the
common title. He cannot, by his act alone, attempt to incumber
or charge the estate of his co-tenants. If he signs a petition for
the opening of a street over the common lands, which will lead
to the assessment of the lands to pay the cost of opening the street,
his signature affects only his own estate; he does not represent or
bind the estate of his co-tenant. No one can do that without special
authority."

Mulligan v. Smith, 59 Cal. 225-226.

Administrators, guardians, tenants, joint tenants in common,
are, in my opinion, not entitled to sign this petition, and executors,
unless they are vested with the power to sell and convey by will,
have no power to sign.

Sixth. Have the park commissioners the right to sign the petition under the provisions of the statute, which provides that the
city council shall have no power to grant the use or right of way to

lay down railroad track in any street of the city, except upon the petition of the owners of the land representing more than one-half of the frontage of the street to be used for railroad purposes?

The Supreme Court of Illinois, in construing the word "owner," as used in connection with real estate, say: "The word owner has been repeatedly determined to mean a fee simple interest in the land."

2 Gilman, 138.

Wright v. Bennett, 3 Scam., 258.

I. M. F. Ins. Co. vs. Manf. Co., 1 Gilman, 236.

W. Ins. Co. vs. Schueller, 60 Ill., 465.

This is the definition as uniformly given by the Supreme Court of the state as applying to realty. It is a well-known rule of construction that when words have acquired a meaning through judicial interpretation *it is to be presumed that they were used in that sense in subsequent statutes.*

98 U. S., 440.

1 Peters, 46.

There are three different questions presented in the petition as to the authority of the park commissioners:

First. Their authority to sign for Union Park.

Second. Their authority to sign for Ogden Avenue from West Twelfth Street to California Avenue.

Third. Their authority to sign for the frontage on Douglas Park and Garfield Park.

The power of the park commissioners over Union Park is exercised under the following ordinance passed by legislative authority:

"Be it ordained by the City Council of the City of Chicago:

"Section 1. Whereas, the West Chicago Park Commissioners are desirous of taking charge of and improving 'Union and Jefferson Parks' at their own charge and expense and without cost, charge or expense to the City of Chicago.

"Sec. 2. Therefore, for the purpose aforesaid authority is hereby given to the said West Chicago Park Commissioners to take charge of and improve and maintain 'Union and Jefferson Parks' under such plans and in such manner as shall be approved by them and to that end the management and control of said Parks is hereby surrendered to the said West Chicago Park Commissioners, provided the said Park Commissioners shall improve, maintain and keep in good repair said 'Union and Jefferson Parks,' otherwise the control of said 'Union and Jefferson Parks' shall revert back to the City of Chicago.

"Sec. 3. Nothing herein contained shall authorize said West Chicago Park Commissioners or any person to alter, change or use said, 'Union and Jefferson Parks' for any other or different purpose than that for which said 'Union and Jefferson Parks' were dedicated.

"Sec. 4. The said West Chicago Park Commissioners shall accept the provisions hereof within thirty days from date; otherwise this ordinance shall be null and void."

The city of Chicago hold title to Union Park by virtue of its having been dedicated to the public by its owners for park purposes. The city had no right to vest any title or ownership in any grantee. By this ordinance it did not transfer any title in and to said park. The control, given in the words of the ordinance, was to take charge and improve and maintain, and they, by the terms of the ordinance, are inhibited from altering or changing its use for any other or different purpose than that for which it was dedicated. The park commissioners have no title to the property in question, save the specific right of the "management and control" expressed in the words "to take charge of, improve and maintain." They are not owners of land, for the ordinance vested no title in and to the premises. In my opinion, the park commissioners have no authority to sign as owners of frontage for Union Park by virtue of the control given under said ordinance.

In the case of the City of Jacksonville v. I. R. W. Co., 67 Ill., 544 and 545, the Supreme Court of Illinois say: "It would hardly be contended that the city holding the property merely as trustee could divert the trust, divide the square into lots, and sell and convey them to private individuals to be appropriated to such purposes as they might desire. The conveyance would be an absolute nullity and the act would be abhorrent to every principle of right. It would be a gross perversion of the trust. If the municipality could not divert the property neither could the legislature. The power of the latter is not unlimited and cannot be exercised to interfere with trust estates. In this case the attempted use of the public square by the railroad company for the track of its road is a manifest perversion of the trust created and declared, *would operate injuriously to the public and abutting lot owners, would mar the beauty of the ground, destroy it as a place of public recreation and cannot be justified.*"

The Supreme Court of Pennsylvania, in the case of the Commonwealth vs. Ruth, say, as to a park dedicated to the public: "Their power over it is restricted and circumscribed; *it is not theirs to sell or to dispose of;* they may control it within their right and designate the use, but can go no further."

Price vs. Thompson, 48 Mo., 361.

Warren vs. Mayor of Lyons City, 22 Iowa, 351.

Second. As to the boulevard between Twelfth Street and California Avenue.

The park commissioners appear upon the face of the petition as having signed for the following frontage:

1. Ogden Avenue, between Twelfth Street and Western Avenue, 675 feet.

2. Ogden Avenue, between Western Avenue and Campbell Avenue, 585 feet.

3. Ogden Avenue, between Campbell and Maplewood Avenues, 540 feet.

4. Ogden Avenue, Maplewood to Tallman Avenue, 515 feet.
5. Ogden Avenue, Tallman Avenue to Washtenaw, 325 feet.
6. Ogden Avenue, Washentaw to California Avenue, 600 feet.

The control of the park commissioners over the street from West Twelfth Street to California Avenue, the eastern line of Douglas Park, is derived from an ordinance passed January 17, 1887, authorized by an act of the legislature passed June 27, 1883.

It will be observed that the ordinance does not give consent to the park commissioners to occupy the whole of Ogden Avenue, the power to regulate, control and improve is limited to the center seventy feet of the street. The city has delegated no right or control to the remaining portion of the street. By virtue of their control over the seventy feet in the center of Ogden Avenue the park commissioners have, as appears from the petition, signed as owners of frontage from Twelfth to California Avenue. To permit them so to sign cuts off the individual owners from being represented by petition as owners of frontage and gives this right to the park commissioners. The act which authorizes the ordinance, and the ordinance upon its face, plainly interprets who are to be considered owners of frontage. The authority given in the statute by which the park commissioners assume control of Ogden Avenue, recites that the "consent in writing of the *owners of a majority of the frontage of the lots and land abutting on such street or streets* so far as taken shall be first obtained. The property owners who own to the street line were owners of the frontage at that date, and in my opinion are the owners of the frontage at this time. These private property owners on either side of the street were recognized by the council when it passed the ordinance and by the park commissioners when they accepted the ordinance as the owners of frontage, for the preamble of the ordinance reads, "Whereas, the owners of a majority of the frontage of the lots and lands abutting on that part of West Twelfth Street and Ogden Avenue have petitioned."

The location of the elevated road in Ogden Avenue is not defined. The council might locate it on the north or south of the seventy feet, and if the theory of the petitioners is correct, and the park commissioners are owners of frontage, by virtue of the power vested in them by the ordinance and statute, then if located in Ogden Avenue north of the line of seventy feet the park commissioners would be conceded as owners of frontage on the south side of the right of way of the elevated road. If located in Ogden Avenue south of the seventy feet, they would be owners of frontage on the north side of the right of way of the elevated road. Thus if the line is located outside of the seventy feet in Ogden Avenue, if the park commissioners, by their consent, mean that they are owners of frontage on Ogden Avenue, one lot owner in addition to their frontage on either side, would be a majority in frontage. The statute plainly means that the lot owners adjoining the street line are to be considered as owners of frontage.

Have the West Chicago park commissioners the right, as the

owners of land, to petition the city council to grant the use of the streets to the Elevated Railway Company in front of Garfield and Douglas parks?

The act of June 18, 1883, provides that no person or persons, corporation or corporations, shall construct or maintain any elevated railroad along any street or alley in any incorporated city, except by the permission of the city council, granted upon a petition of the *owners of land* representing more than one-half of the frontage of the street or alley or of so much thereof as is sought to be used for such elevated railroad.

Section 90, of the amended city charter, provides, that the city council shall have no power to grant the use of, or the right to lay down any railroad tracks in any street of the city except upon a petition of the *owners of land* representing more than one-half of the frontage of street, or so much thereof as is sought to be used for railroad purposes.

The act of February 27, 1869, creates a board of commissioners for the town of West Chicago, to be known under the name of "The West Chicago Park Commissioners." The Supreme Court of the state have decided that this board is a quasi municipal corporation, and in constructing the corporate powers of this board we must apply the familiar canon of construction that the charter of a corporation is the measure of its powers and that the enumeration of those powers implies the exclusion of all others.

Thomas vs. West Insey Railroad Company, 101 U. S., 82.

Does this act and the subsequent amendments to it give the park commissioners *as owners* of frontage the right to petition for an elevated railroad in the streets of the city?

Section 5, of the act of 1869, defines the title of the park commissioners as follows:

"The said board shall have power and it is made their duty and they are hereby authorized to select and take possession of and to acquire by condemnation, control, donation or otherwise, *title forever in trust* for the inhabitants of the town of West Chicago and of the West Division of Chicago, and for such parties or persons as may succeed to the rights of said inhabitants and for the public, *as public promenade and pleasure grounds and ways*, but not without the consent of a majority by *frontage of the owners of property* fronting the same for any other purpose and without power to sell, alienate, mortgage or encumber the same."

By the specific terms of the charter the title to all property whether acquired by condemnation, contract, donation or otherwise, is held *in trust* for the inhabitants of the town of West Chicago, "without power to sell, alienate, mortgage or encumber the same." They have never been authorized by the legislature to dispose of any portion of the lands save by the act of June 16, 1887, the park commissioners having any piece or parcel of land not exceeding one acre in area, which shall no longer be deemed necessary or useful for park purposes may appy to the Circuit Court, and if the court deem the granting of said application to be for public interest, it may be sold. The park commissioners, under the provisions of their charter, are the legal representatives of the inhabitants of the town of West Chicago, they are agents of their constituents, created by law. Their duties are specifically defined by statute and as quasi corporations their powers being enumerated, the act of the legislature inhibits all powers not enumerated.

City of Cairo vs. Bross, 101 Ill., 478.

Under the judicial construction of the Supreme Court of Illinois, as cited heretofore, the word owner as applied to real estate means an estate in fee, which gives the owner the right to alienate, encumber and mortgage. The park commissioners hold the title as trustee for the public as promenade and pleasure grounds and ways, and in the statute of 1869 and amendment thereto, they have never been authorized to exercise any control over the park property, save such authority as is implied in the terms for public promenade, pleasure grounds and ways. The only provision in regard to the control over railroads under the park act is the limitation of their powers as to roads already located. It will not be contended that the elevated railroad would have the power to condemn a right of way through the park premises. This park being dedicated to a public use, the legislature would have to specifically confer the power upon the elevated railroad to enter upon and take possession of the property held and dedicated by authority of law to one public use.

The park commissioners, by authority of an ordinance, or by written consent, or resolution, could not give to an elevated railroad the right to use any portion of the park grounds proper, for in the language of the court in the case of Lohr vs. Metropolitan Elevated Railroad Company, 104 N. Y., 26, "An elevated railroad in the streets, operated by steam power, is a perversion of the use of the street from the purposes originally designated for it." It would be a use not consistent with park purposes and the Supreme Court in the case of the City of Jacksonville vs. J. R. W. Co., 67 Ill., 540, say, "the attempted use of the public square by the railroad company, is a perversion of the trust created and declared; would operate injuriously to the public and abutting lot owners; would mar the beauty of the ground, destroy it as a place of public recreation and cannot be justified." Then, if by a judicial construction, an elevated railroad is a use inconsistent with park purposes, unless specifically authorized by the legislature, by what authority are the park commissioners to be considered as owners, who are entitled by their consent to confer jurisdiction upon the city council to authorize a use inconsistent with the use of the park for the purposes set forth in the statute.

The consent required is from owners of property; the property is held in trust by the park commissioners, without power to alien- ate, sell or encumber; they are strictly limited in their power and control to uses, enumerated in the statute. The consent required is not a mere property right; the legislature refers and delegates *the matter of its own consent* to the council and the owners ·of frontage, and the concurrence of these two agencies is required that the public's rights in and to the street may be more carefully guarded.

In my opinion the park commissioners are not owners within the meaning of the statute; they hold property in trust by virtue of the act creating them, and by virtue of many deeds that appear in the abstract of their title. The property is not subject to taxation; it is trust property, held by a quasi corporation to whom the legislature has not delegated the right to consent as owners of frontage to a use of street by an elevated railroad. This same conclusion applies to Union Park and the boulevard. If a majority of frontage is obtained other than the park commissioners, the consent of the council would authorize the use of Ogden Avenue and Lake Street for an elevated railroad. Respectfully,

JOHN W. GREEN, Corporation Counsel.

December 15, 1888.

Geo. W. Hubbard, Esq., Chief of Police, City of Chicago.

Dear Sir—

In reply to your request I submit the following opinion: A parade or procession within the meaning of the terms as used in an ordinance passed July 23, 1886, is any aggregation of persons meeting or gathering for some specific purpose, and using the streets or sidewalks by marching in consecutive order, or military file. The ordinance prohibits the use of the streets by any organization or gathering of men who, in their collective capacity, shall attempt to use the streets of the city without a permit. It excludes any extraordinary assemblage of persons from using the streets by marching for show, parade or exhibiting themselves in a showy or ostentatious manner. As to numbers, any body of men marching upon the streets that would interrupt the usual public travel should be stopped, unless they have the required permit. In my opinion a large number of persons congregating at a public depot and marching from the depot in any continuous line of march along the streets of the city would plainly come within the provisions of the ordinance.

Respectfully yours,

J. W. GREEN, Corporation Counsel.

May 11, 1889.

To Hon. De Witt C. Cregier, Mayor.

Dear Sir—

You ask my opinion as to the right of the commissioner of public works to issue a permit, where directed so to do by the city council, to parties desirous of building projections upon and over the sidewalk from their buildings in the nature of storm doors, porches, porticos, windows, and other permanent structures of this character, for the personal convenience of the parties so building them, and not for the public good or convenience.

The importance of this subject at this time is greater, perhaps, to the city than at any previous period, because the encroachments upon the sidewalks of the city have already become very numerous, and the demands for further projections of this character are rapidly increasing, and the question arises whether these permits shall continue to be freely issued, with the prospect before us in the near future that many of the principal sidewalks of the city will be partially, at least, occupied by such encroachments.

It is a principle generally recognized that local corporate authorities cannot give valid permission to occupy streets without express power by charter or statute.

In Dillon on Municipal Corporations, Section 660, we find the following language: "The usual power to regulate and control streets has even been held not to authorize the municipal authorities to allow them to be encroached upon by the adjoining owner by erections made for his exclusive use and advantage, such as porches extending into the streets, or flights of stairs leading from the ground to the upper stories of buildings standing on the line of streets."

In several cases mentioned in Note 4 to this section, it was held that a purpresture or permanent encroachment by the adjoining owner is, in law, a nuisance to the public, having a remedy by indictment or in equity.

Again, in Note 1, to Section 611, Id., we find the following: "A city has exclusive jurisdiction of its streets and alleys, not for the purpose of appropriating them in perpetuity to the use of private individuals, but to keep them open and free to all." 12 Ind., 315; 1 Denio, 524, p. 213; 9 Wend., 571.

In City of Quincy vs. Jones et al., 76 Ills., p. 232, the court says: "As an incorporated town or city owns the title to its streets and alleys for the use of the public and have no rightful authority to grant them for any purpose inconsistent with the public use, it follows that an individual cannot acquire a prescriptive right therein for any private use."

Again, in Dillon, Section 669, we find the following, being a citation from the Supreme Court of Pennsylvania: "The view of the court is, in substance, this: Streets and public squares are dedicated or required for the public use, and not alone for that of the people of the city, the corporation being the mere trustee for the public; that, erection by private persons on property thus dedicated or acquired cannot be authorized by the original proprietor, nor by the city corporation, and can be authorized only by the act of the legislature."

Again in Dillon, Section 680, we find the following: "As the

9

highways of a state, including streets in cities, are under the paramount and primary control of the legislature, and as all municipal powers are derived from the legislature, it follows that the authority of municipalities over streets and the uses to which they may be put depends entirely upon their charters or legislative enactments applicable to them. It is usual in this country for the legislature to confer upon municipal corporations very extensive powers in respect to streets and public ways within their limits, and the uses to which they may be appropriated. * * * The authority to open, care for, regulate, and improve streets, taken in connection with the other powers usually granted, gives to municipal corporations all needed authority to keep the streets free from obstructions and to prevent improper use, and to obtain ordinances to this end."

"The primary object of a street is ordinary passage and travel, and the public or individuals cannot be rightfully deprived of such use. A city has no right to so obstruct its streets, or to authorize the same to be done, as to deprive property holders from free access to and from their lands abutting on the same. If the municipal authorities of a town or city authorize a structure upon a public street or other obstruction that causes injury to adjacent lot holders it will be liable for the damages sustained."

Stack vs. City of East St. Louis, 85 Ill., 377.

In numerous cases cited in American and English Corporation Cases, Section 8, p. 396, it is held that any occupation of a public street of a city for other purposes than those ordinarily incident to travel is a nuisance which is indictable unless such occupation is authorized by law.

In Bybee vs. State, 6 American and English Corporation Cases, the court says: "It has been repeatedly held by this court that a public street is a public highway. The obstruction of a public street wrongfully is, therefore, a misdemeanor. Public highways belong, from side to side, and from end to end, to the public. The permanent and exclusive use and occupancy of any public street or highway by any person by the erection or maintenance of any structure on, beneath, or above its surface, which wrongfully obstructs, or may obstruct such street or highway, is a misdemeanor within the meaning of the statute and is punishable as a public nuisance. Whether or not the particular structure so erected or maintained obstructs, or may obstruct, wrongfully the public street or highway is a question of fact in every case for the court or jury trying the case."

"Porches extending into the streets, or flights of stairs leading from the ground to the upper stories of buildings, standing on the line of the streets, were held to be nuisances."

People vs. Carpenter, 2 Doug. (Mich.), 273.

Comm. vs. Blaisdell, 107 Mass., 234.

Pettis vs. Johnson, 56 Ind., 139.

Section 1939, of the Municipal Code, now in force, is as follows:

"Hereafter no person shall construct, or place, or cause to be constructed, or placed, any portico, porch, door, window, or step which shall project into or over any street or sidewalk in such manner as to obstruct free passage along the same, under penalty," etc.

This is a valid ordinance fully authorized by the charter. There can be no question as to the power and duty of the municipality to keep its streets and sidewalks free from obstructions so that the public may have the free use thereof.

The street is the property of the city from building line to building line, and the city has, in my opinion, no authority to permit the use of any part of the same, in the manner aforesaid, for purely private purposes, especially when such use would amount to an obstruction. It is clearly the duty of the city to keep its streets (roadways and sidewalks) free from obstruction for the use of the public for whom it holds the fee thereto in trust.

There are many encroachments of the character herein mentioned upon the sidewalks of our city, which probably do not interfere with the free use thereof by the public, from which no inconvenience arises and of which no complaint can reasonably be made. Such encroachments are not termed, in the law, nuisances.

Where no injury would arise to individuals, the public or the city, in the exercise of its rights and duties, by such encroachments, and where they do not amount to obstructions, but accommodate the party desirous of making them, it is undoubtedly in the discretion of the municipality, upon the application being made for a permit, applying to it these tests, to grant or refuse it; but the municipality has no authority to allow erections of the kind herein referred to upon or over the sidewalks, which would interfere with free passage along the same, or which would interfere with the rights or privileges of the city, or any of the public. The law on this question is clear, and seems to have been thus understood and interpreted when the ordinance above recited was adopted.

Respectfully submitted,
JONAS HUTCHINSON, Corporation Counsel.

May 18, 1889.

To the Honorable, the Judiciary Committee of the City Council of the City of Chicago.

Gentlemen—

You ask my opinion as to the right of the city to deposit its money in national banks and take the bonds of such banks therefor, also what effect such depositing will have on the bond given by the city treasurer?

First: "The Treasurer may be required to keep all moneys in his hands belonging to the corporation in such place or places of deposit as may be designated by ordinance. Provided, however, no such ordinance shall be passed by which the custody of such money shall be taken from the Treasurer and deposited elsewhere than in some reg-, ularly organized bank, nor without a bond to be taken from such bank in such penal sum and with such security as the City Council, or Board of Trustees shall direct and approve, sufficient to save the corporation from any loss   *   *   *   . Article VII, Section 9, City Charter.

I think the city council has, clearly, the right to designate the place where the money of the city shall be kept under this provision of the charter. It contravenes no provisions of the constitution or bill of rights. The ordinance passed March 25, 1889, pursuant to this provision of the charter, is as follows.

"Be it ordained by the City Council of the City of Chicago,

Section 1. That the city treasurer of the city of Chicago is hereby directed and required to deposit and keep all moneys in his hands belonging to the city of Chicago, in such banks as may be designated by an ordinance of the city council of the city of Chicago, in pursuance of the provisions of Section 9 of Article VII of the city charter.

Sec. 2. The mayor, comptroller and chairman of the committee of finance are hereby authorized and directed to secure from time to time, as occasion may require, proposals from such banks as they shall recommend for the deposit therein by the city treasurer, of the moneys in his hands belonging to the city, and to submit such proposals to the city council for acceptance.

Section 3. This ordinance shall be in force and effect from and after its passage," is in my opinion, valid, and in acordance with it I think the city council has the right to proceed on the report of the mayor, comptroller and chairman of finance committee and designate the banks in which the city money shall be deposited as provided for in the ordinance introduced in the city council on the sixth day of May, 1889 (which has not yet been passed).

I see no reason why the designated banks may not be national banks, and why a valid bond may not be taken from each of them with securities as provided for in the charter and proposed ordinance. I think a national bank can enter into such a bond. It has not express authority, in terms by charter, so to do, but it is expressly empowered to make contracts, to receive deposits and exercise such incident powers as shall be necessary to carry on the business of banking. In arriving at my opinion I am governed by what I consider to be the law on this subject as laid down in many cases, some of which I call your attention to. It will be observed that if a national bank has not the implied power to execute a bond the obligators on it cannot take advantage of that fact and urge that it is ultra vires, that is a matter between the bank on the United States government.

The words "by discounting and negotiating promissory notes," etc., in Section 5136, are not to be read as limiting the mode of exercising the "incidental powers" necessary to carry on the business

of banking, but as descriptive of the kind of banking which is
authorized; and the true meaning of the provision is that the bank
may carry on banking by "discounting," etc., and may exercise "all
such incidental powers as shall be necessary" for that purpose.

Shindle vs. First Natl. Bank of Ripley, 22 Ohio, St. 516.

In Pratt's Digest of cases under National Bank Act, page 9, we
find the following: "To make contracts (this power is conferred by
Section 5136 of the act). This has been held to mean not all contracts,
but such contracts only as are natural and germane to the exercise of
the other powers granted in the section. Thus, a bank could not
legally contract to build a railroad, but it might contract to make a
loan at a future date."

In First National Bank of Charlotte vs. National Exchange Bank
of Baltimore, Parson's Natl. Bk. cases, the court say: "Authority
is thus given to transact such a banking business as is specified, and all
incidental powers necessary to carry it on are granted. These powers
are such as are required to meet all the legitimate demands of the
authorized business, and to enable a bank to conduct its affairs, within
the general scope of its charter, safely and prudently. This necessarily
implies the right of a bank to incur liabilities in the regular course
of its business, as well as to become the creditor of others. Its own
obligations must be met, and debts due to it collected or secured. The
power to adopt reasonable and appropriate measures for these purposes is an incident to the power to incur the liability or become the
creditor."

"A national bank cannot take real estate security by a conveyance
to it at the time of the loan or for future loans, but only for debts
previously contracted, although if it does take concurrent security by
trust deed, mortgage, etc., only the United States can object, and a
bank can successfully sustain a suit for foreclosure unless its sovereign
interferes, though it exceeds its powers and violates the supreme law
in taking a mortgage."

National Bank vs. Mathews, 98 U. S., 625.

"The validity of a transaction with a National bank cannot be
enquired into in an action between the parties based upon the transaction. The question of ultra vires in such a case is one between
the Federal government and the bank exclusively."

First Natl. Bank of Waterloo vs. Elmore, 9 Rep. 110. (Sup. Ct.
of Iowa.)

"The banking powers are those which are either fundamental
parts of the business or have become so linked with them as to be
identified with the exercise of the bank franchises.."

In Morse on Banks and Banking. Section 48, we find the following: "A bank may receive especial, specific and general deposits and
give security for them."

Section 63, id., provides: "So far as it is involved in receiving
deposits, borrowing is a part of banking."

"Like every other corporation a bank 'has an inherent right to borrow money whenever it is reasonably necessary in the proper conduct of its business unless specifically) restricted.

"The borrowing must be incident to the banking business, otherwise the act is ultra vires. Aside from the theory of law, as no one but a bank can judge whether a loan is reasonably necessary or not, the practical fact is that a bank can borrow whenever it wishes to, and if the money is used in its proper business no fault will be found, even if wrongfully applied it wil¹ not affect the validity of the loan, between the parties ordinarily.

"Whenever a bank may rightfully borrow on time, it can give its negotiable note on time, and a bank may secure persons who loan it money by deposit or on time by a mortgage of its property, but not of its franchise."

"Such a power is a mere incident of the right to receive deposits, which by necessary implication gives power to assign and mortgage negotiable instruments as the security for them and to do all other acts that the nature of such business involves, on principles of prudent commercial conduct."

Section 191, id., "It has generally been considered that taking an especial deposit falls within the general scope of the banking business. Although no express power is conferred by the charter of the bank, or by the organic law, so to do, it has been regarded as incident to the general functions of the institution."

Section 56, id., "A bank has power to make all such contracts as are necessary or usual as direct means to attain the objects of its incorporation and no other. In deciding whether a corporation can make a particular contract we are to consider, in the first place, whether its charter, or some statute, binding upon it forbids or permits it to make such contract, and if the charter and valid statute law are silent upon the subject. In the second place whether the power to make such a contract may not be implied on the part of the corporation as directly or incidentally necessary to enable it to fulfill the purpose of its existence, or whether the contract is entirely foreign to that purpose.

"The modern tendency is to liberal construction of corporate power to contract * * * "

"A national bank may receive deposits. By the usage of banking there is an implied agreement upon the part of the bank with the depositor that it will pay the same, or any part thereof, on demand from time to time as the depositor may require. This contract would be none the less binding on the bank if it were reduced to writing and signed and sealed by the corporation, and should any third person or persons execute an agreement with a bank as security or securities the undertaking would lose none of its validity, and as deposits from day to day are in the course of business between the banks and their customers the agreement might properly contain a provision as to future deposits, that in the event they should be made the obligation should cover them. It must be conceded that a national bank, as any other, may have recourse to the courts to force its right. For instance, it may bring replevin to recover any of its personal effects, and to that end execute the necessary bond with security. So it may proceed by attachment and give the bond required. So it may pray and effect an appeal from a lower to a higher court, giving the necessary bond. None of these acts are specifically authorized but as incident to the due transaction of its business it may be necessary and the authority for so doing is therefore implied."

"Unless restrained by law every corporation has the incident power to make any contract and evidenced by any instrument which may be necessary to advance the business for which such a corporation was created."

Strauss vs. Eagle Ins. Co., 5 Ohio St., 59.

"It is well settled that a corporation without especial authority * * * in the course of its legitimate business may make a bond, mortgage, note or draft * * * except when restrained by law; hence it may issue its bonds to secure a loan it is authorized to obtain and may therein pledge its property for the payment."

Abbot's Digest, Law of Corporations, Sec. 2, and cases there cited.

"A corporation may make contracts within the scope of legitimate purpose of its organization, although its charter has no express authority to make contracts; when the charter or act of incorporation is silent as to what contracts a corporation may make, it has power as a general rule to make all such contracts as are necessary and usual in the course of business as means to enable it to attain that for which it was created and none other."

Id., page 208, Sections 3 and 4.

"A corporation has, incidentally, authority when not especially restrained, to borrow money for any of its lawful purposes."

Id., Sections 44, 45, and 50.

In Rockwell vs. Elkhorn Bank, 13 Wis., 653, the plaintiff sued the bank as the maker of a note, given to him to secure a balance due for moneys deposited and for his salary as one of its officers. The defense was that the note was void because the bank had not authority to make an issue. Held that the bank was liable. The court says: "It is an universally accepted principle that corporations authorized generally to engage in a particular business have, as an incident to such authority, the power to contract debts in the legitimate transaction of such business, unless they are restrained by their charters or by statute. It is likewise an equally well acknowledged rule that the right to contract debts carries with it the power to give negotiable notes or bills in payment of security for such debts unless the corporations are in like manner prohibited." These positions are abundantly sustained by the authorities cited.

Where a school commissioner executed a bond for the use of the township, providing for the care of moneys, etc., the said bond was not the one required by law. It was sustained as a common law obligation and one that did not interfere with the duties of the official to give the statutory bond as well.

Todd, et al. vs. Cowell, et al., 14 Ill., 72.

If a national bank gives its bond with securities, and if this act on the part of the bank is ultra vires, the law seems to be that the parties to the bond cannot take advantage of it. This was so held in the cases above cited and this position is sustained by the following cases:

Allegheny City vs. McClurhen, 14 Pa., St., 81, as cited in Green's Brice's Ultra Vires, page 614, where municipal corporation issued bonds without any right or authority. Held that as the city received the benefit they were liable thereon.

Same note, Green's Brice, page 614, "Though a charter of the corporation may not confer the power of banking or issuing checks to pass as currency, and it may be penal offense to issue such checks or notes, yet the corporation must pay for plates and notes or checks procured to be made by the officers of such corporation.

"If a contract made by a corporation is not in violation of its charter or any statute prohibiting it, and the corporation has by its promise induced a party relying upon such promise and in execution of the contract to expend money, and perform its part of the contract, the corporation is liable."

Green's Brice, page 615, note.

"While public policy requires that corporations should be confined strictly within limits of their charter and not be allowed to exercise powers beyond those expressly conferred, that would be hurtful to public interests; yet where they have exercised powers incidental to those conferred and in furtherance of the general objects of the corporation, although the subject of the contract may not be within any express right conferred, they will be estopped from denying that they had authority to make such contracts."

Chicago Building Society vs Crowell, 65 Ill., 453.

While courts are inclined to maintain the limitation of corporate action, whether it is a question of restraining the corporation in advance, from passing beyond the boundaries of its charter, they are equally inclined, to enforce against private corporations, contracts though ultra vires, of which they have received the benefits."

Bradley vs. Ballard, 55 Ill., 413.

I conclude that a national bank can be a party to such a bond as the city proposes to take. That it is within its implied rights and franchise to enter into such a bond, and that it could not, with sureties upon it, if such a bond should be given, successfully interpose the defense in a suit thereon that this act was ultra vires, and that it had no power to give such bond.

Second. If the money of the city is thus deposited in national banks what effect will it have on the bond already given by the city treasurer. I answer no effect. The bond will remain in full force and effect; the sureties will continue, in my opinion, liable for the malfeasance and default of the city treasurer, if any, but not for loss through the designated banks of deposit.

As expressed in several decisions of our Supreme Court: "A city is a state in miniature, having executive, legislative and judicial departments and government." The people of the city are bound by and are presumed to know the enactments of the city council, the same as they are bound by and are presumed to know the acts of our state legislature. Before this bond was executed the ordinance of March 25, 1889, had passed the city council and the sureties in law before signing the bond knew of it. They were bound to know that the city treasurer pursuant to that ordinance might be compelled to deposit the city money in banks to be designated by ordinance, and I think the law is clear that if the money shall be so deposited they will remain liable on the bond for any default of the city treasurer. The logic, law and the bond are all this way.

The bond contains the following: "Now, therefore, if the said Bernard Roesing shall well and faithfully perform and discharge the duties of said office as prescribed and required by law and the orders and ordinances of said city, and shall account for and pay over all moneys received by him, as such city treasurer, in accordance with law and in accordance with orders and ordinances heretofore passed, or hereafter to be passed by the City Council of said City, and in conformity with law and deliver all books, papers and all other property belonging to said city to his successor in office, then this obligation to be void, otherwise to be and remain in full force and effect."

By the terms of the bond they shall clearly remain liable. They agree to be bound by the orders and ordinances of the council, past and future. I do not, however, think the sureties on the treasurer's bond would be liable for the default of the banks, or any of them, in which the city money shall be deposited. These sureties cannot be held for the malfeasance and default of the banks in case they, or any of them, shall fail or be in default and unable to pay or refuse to pay over the city's money. The city in such event must have recourse upon the bonds furnished by the banks.

I call your attention to certain cases which are in support of the views here expressed:

"The sureties of any officer upon his official bond conditioned for the faithful performance of the duties of the office are liable for the performance of all duties imposed upon him which come within the scope of his office, whether those duties were required by laws enacted prior or subsequent to the execution of the bond."

Governor of Illinois vs. Edward H. Ridgeway, et al., 12 Illinois, 14.

The same principle is announced in the People vs. Leake, et al., 13 Ill. On page 269 of that case the court says: This court held in the cases of the Governor vs. Ridgeway, 12 Ill., 14, and Compher vs.

The People, Id., 290, "That the sureties of an officer upon his official bond, conditioned for the faithful discharge of the duties of the office are liable for the performance of all duties imposed upon him which are within the scope of his office, whether such duties are imposed by laws passed before or after the execution of the obligation. It was said in the latter case, the power to control the revenue is one of the highest attributes of sovereignty. Without this power no government could exist, and it cannot be supposed that the General Assembly intended to part with this important prerogative, or to contract that no change should be made in the manner of collecting the revenue during the continuance in office of any of its collectors. Parties who go security on bonds of this character do so with the full knowledge and expectation that the revenue laws will be changed and the duties of collectors altered as the public interest may require. And they have no right to complain of any alteration in the laws not materially changing the character of the duties of their principal, especially when such alterations are in no wise prejudicial to their interest." The principle of those decisions is perfectly conclusive of this case. The condition of the bond was that the sheriff "shall perform all the duties required to be performed of him as collector of the said County of Henderson in the time and manner prescribed by law."

Smith vs. Peoria County, 59 Ill., 413, the courts says: "They will be presumed to have become sureties knowing that such acts could and might be done during the official term of the treasurer. Such sureties are liable for the faithful performance of all duties of such an officer, whether imposed by laws enacted previous or subsequent to the execution of the bond, only so that it comes within the scope of his official duties."   Very respectfully submitted,

JONAS HUTCHINSON, Corporation Counsel.

July 29, 1889

To the Honorable, the City Council.

Gentlemen—

Upon the 24th, ult., your honorable body requested my opinion upon certain questions propounded in the following terms:

"Whether the city charter contemplates or authorizes any agreement between the city and such banks as may be designated as depositories of the city moneys that such banks shall pay and the city shall receive interest on account of such deposits, and whether the city charter contemplates competition as to which bank or banks shall offer the highest rate of interest on such deposits."

And in conformity therewith I submit my conclusions as follows: I take the scope of the inquiry to be, whether the city can make legal contracts with banks for the payment of interest upon the money of the city deposited therein, and whether the city can properly invite competition as to the rate of interest to be paid upon such deposits, it being understood that such competition may have some effect in the manner of designating such depositories.

The only provision of the city charter directly bearing upon this question is Section 9 of Article VII, which is as follows:

"The Treasurer may be required to keep all moneys in his hands, belonging to the corporation, in such place or places of deposit as may be designated by ordinance; provided, however, no such ordinance shall be passed by which the custody of such money shall be taken from the treasury and deposited elsewhere than some regularly organized bank nor without a bond to be taken from such bank, in such penal sum and with such security as the City Council, or Board of Trustees, shall direct and approve sufficient to save the corporation from any loss; but such penal sum shall not be less than the estimated receipts for the current year from taxes and special assessments levied, or to be levied by the corporation." * * *

The power of the city council to make such designation is undisputed, but the question is presented whether the city can make any binding contract as to the terms upon which such deposits shall be made? In general terms, I should say, that as the greater includes the less, the right to designate the places of deposit, necessarily takes with it, the right to arrange the terms upon which the deposit may be made, subject, of course, to the charter provisions as to bond, etc.

The material factor in this matter is the right to indicate the places of deposit, it being understood that the funds so deposited are to be paid on demand. In my opinion, the terms, as to interest, upon which such deposits are made, are of subordinate character, and wholly incident to the right to control the place of deposit, and as such entirely the subject matter of a contract by the city. I have thus answered, as I understood it, the first branch of the inquiry, but as it may be objected that these moneys are, in some sort, a trust fund, raised by taxation to pay the expenses of the city government, and in contemplation of law should be, theoretically at least, in the vaults of the city treasury, and under the immediate control of the city treasurer to answer the demands for such expenses, and further, that the city is not in the brokerage or discount business, and has no money to loan upon any rate of interest, I deem it proper to further elucidate my views.

To the first of there objections it is sufficient to reply, that by the express terms of the charter, the city is authorized to keep its funds elsewhere than in its vaults, hence this objection has no force.

The remaining objections are substantially alike in effect, and are all based upon a misconception. There is no loan or brokerage features about the matter. In one sense every deposit in the bank is a loan to the bank, the money deposited is mingled with the money of the bank, and becomes a part of its assets; when called for, no pretense is made that the identical currency received is paid out. In case of refusing to pay the check of the depositor, the remedy is by action upon contract against the bank. Yet a deposit in a bank is not a loan in the ordinary sense of the term; it is simply a deposit, or place of safe keeping, and as such is expressly authorized by the city charter.

I have stated above that in my opinion the right to deposit the money, necessarily implied the right to contract as to the terms of deposit. Let the matter be put in another way. It must be obvious to every one that there are a multiplicity of affairs incident to the government of the city, which cannot be particularized in charter powers. For instance, the sale of worn out or useless material; the leasing of property, as in the case of the lot at the southeast corner of Adams and La Salle streets, at an annual rental of over thirty thousand dollars; the provisions for viaducts, in case of crossing of streets by railroads; the provision for bridges, when granting the use of a tunnel, and other cases of similar nature. There are no particular provisions on these subjects, and yet does any one question the right of the city to make these contracts? They are simply to the effect that for certain benefits granted certain compensation shall be made. I am unable to distinguish between the matter of compensation for deposits and instances above noted.

Second. As to the right of the city to invite competition as to the rate of interest.

I am clear as to the right of the city to negotiate for, and contract as to the compensation for its deposits. It follows from this, that the city has the right to take all practicable measures to secure the best possible terms, as much in this, as in any other matter relating to the welfare of the city. There is no obligation upon the city to accept an offer because it is the highest. The security of the principal is of vastly greater moment than the rate of interest. The city council has the right to designate the depositories; it is a matter to be disposed of in its sound discretion. The question of responsibility is to be considered, in connection with that of the rate of interest offered and in designating depositories for the public funds the city council has the same rights as an individual (subject, of course, to the charter provisions as to bond, etc.), that is to say, the city government has the right to make for the city the best contract possible. This contract may be made under competition; it may be made without competition; it may be made for the payment of interest; it may be made without the payment of interest; it is one of those matters upon which the council may decide and without other appeal than to the electors at an election. The fact that competition was invited, and apparently formed an element in the selection of the depositories, cuts no figure as to validity of any contract to pay interest.   Respectfully submitted,

JONAS HUTCHINSON, Corporation Counsel.

August 5, 1889.
To the Honorable, the City Council of the City of Chicago.
Gentlemen—
At the last meeting of the city council the opinion of this department was requested as to whether or not sewers could be legally constructed and paid for by special assessment. The occasion for this

opinion arose, as I understand, through the desire on the part of many citizens to build a sewer, to De paid for by special assessment in that part of the city of Chicago commonly known as the Town of Lake, wnere this method of paying for sewers prevailed prior to annexation, while within the corporate limits of Chicago, before enlarged by annex-ation, sewers were paid for, as now, out of a fund raised by general taxation.

It seems at first glance inconsistent, and, perhaps, illegal, that the two methods of providing and paying for sewers should obtain in the same municipality, but I can see no legal objection to it. The annexa-tion act expressly provides that where sewers have been paid for by special assessment before annexation in any of the annexed territory the same practice may be continued by the enlarged city, if it so elects, in that locality. This provision of the annexation law is unquestion-ably valid. It announces no new doctrine, neither does it clothe the city council with power which it could, not in the absence of it, ex-ercise.

The charter, Article IX, Section 1, says: "That the corporate au-thorities of cities and villages are hereby vested with power to make local improvements by special assessments, or by special taxation, or both, of contiguous property, or general taxation, or otherwise, as they shall by ordinance prescribe."

The power hereby conferred is broad and coupled with the pro-vision of the annexation law, above referred to, leaves no doubt in my mind as to the legality of the proposed proceeding.

Respectfully,
JONAS HUTCHINSON, Corporation Counsel.

October 5, 1889.
To the Honorable, the City Council of the City of Chicago.

Gentlemen—

Agreeably to a recent order passed by your honorable body I pre-sent the draft of an ordinance relating to fares and transfers on the street cars, together with my opinion thereon:

Subdivision 42, of Section 1, of Article V, of the city charter, pro-vides that the city council shall have power "to license, tax and regu-late hackmen, draymen, omnibus drivers, carters, cabmen, porters, ex-pressmen and all others pursuing like occupations, and to prescribe their compensation."

In Allerton vs. City of Chicago, 9 Biss., p. 552, Judge Drummond decided that "street railway companies pursue a like occupation with hackmen, draymen, omnibus drivers, cabmen and expressmen, and are, therefore, within the provisions of the general law of 1872, for the in-corporation of cities and villages in this state."

The Supreme Court of Pennsylvania has also held that street rail-way companies are of a like nature as omnibuses.

In Buffalo, East Side Railroad Company vs. Buffalo Street Railroad Company, 19 N. E. Rep., 63, the New York Court of Appeals held, "that the legislature could fix the fares of street railway companies as an exercise of police power."

In Ruggles vs. People, 91, Ill., 256, the court says: "It has been repeatedly held by this court the corporations created within the state are amenable to the police power of the state to the same extent as are natural persons, but to no greater extent. The legislature may require of these bodies the performance of any and all acts which they are capable of performing that it may require of natural persons. The legislature of this state has the power under the constitution to fix a maximum rate of charges by individuals as common carriers, warehousemen, or others exercising a calling, or business, public in its character, or in which the public have an interest to be protected against extortion or oppression, and it has the same lawful power in respect to corporations exercising the same business, and such regulation does not impair the obligation of the contract in their charter."

The decision in this case was affirmed by the Supreme Court of the United States.

Ruggles vs. People, 108 U. S., 526.

And the same doctrine was laid down by the same court in:

Stone vs. F. L. & T., Co., 116 U. S., 307.

I. C. R. R. Co. vs. People, 108 U. S., 541.

Stone vs. I. C. R. R. Co., 116 U. S., 347

See also the Granger decision in 94 U. S.

Clearly under the above authorities the power to fix the rates of fare to be charged is lodged in the legislative department of the state government, and the legislature may delegate that power to the city of Chicago.

The only question that in my view can be made as to the validity of the contemplated ordinance, is whether any of the different companies have, under their charters or ordinances of the city, any contract rights as to charging fares which would be thereby infringed. The rule is very familiar that such a contract, being in derogation of the governmental right of regulation cannot be implied and cannot be held to exist unless the language of the charter or ordinances imperatively so requires.

None of the charters of street railway companies of Chicago contain any agreement that the rates of fare shall not be subject to legislative control, either directly or by act of the legislature delegating the power to the city of Chicago.

One statute bearing upon this question is the act of February 6, 1865, which contains the following provisions, Municipal Code, 510: "Provided, that any contract hereafter made by the Common Council of the City of Chicago, with either of the corporations referred to in this act, for a higher rate of fare than five cents, shall be subject to modification or repeal at any regular meeting of said Common Council by a majority vote of all the aldermen elected, or by the general assembly of the State of Illinois."

There are no provisions here which would restrain the council from passing, or which would tend to invalidate the proposed ordinance. The mere fixing by the charter of a maximum fare of five cents is not a contract that the rate shall not be reduced below that limit.

In Georgia Railroad and Banking Company vs. Smith, 128 U. S. Reports, p. 174, the court says: "In order to exempt a railroad corporation from legislative interference with its rate of charges within a designated limit it must appear that the exemption was made in its charter by clear and unmistakable language, inconsistent with any reservation of power by the state to that effect.

"In almost every case which has been before this court where the power of the state to regulate the rates of charges of railroad companies for the transportation of persons or freight within its jurisdiction has been under consideration, the question discussed has not been the original power of the state over the subject, but whether that power has not been, by stipulation of the charter, or other legislation, amounting to a contract, surrendered to the company, or been in some manner qualified. It is only upon tne latter point that there has been differences of opinion."

In that case the charter provided, "That the company shall, at all times, have the exclusive right of transportation of merchandise, and of produce, over the railroad, while it sees fit to exercise the exclusive right, provided the charge of transportation shall not exceed fifty cents per hundred pounds," etc.

This was held not to constitute a contract that the company should fix its own rates free from legislative regulation within the designated limits.

The court further said: "It would require much stronger language than this to justify us in holding that notwithstanding any altered conditions of the country in the future, the legislature had, in 1833, contracted that the company might, for all time, charge rates for transportation of persons and property over its line up to the limits there designated."

In Dow vs. Beidlemann, 5 South. West. Rep., 297, the court says: "It is contended, however, that by the charter of the Memphis and Little Rock Railroad Company the exclusive power of regulating its tolls for the transportation of passengers was conceded to that corporation. The sixth section of the charter did indeed provide that the charge for transportation should not exceed five cents a mile for every passenger. This is far from being a contract on the part of the state that passenger fare should never be reduced below that rate."

The next question is, have the street railway companies any rights as to rates of fare by the ordinances under which their different lines were built which would be infringed by the proposed ordinance.

It may be remarked at the outset that it is doubtful whether if any of these various ordinances did contain provisions which, in explicit terms, purported to deprive the city of its power from time to time to regulate the fares of these companies, such provisions would be a valid contract.

In various ordinances of the street railway companies the rate of fare is fixed at not to exceed 5 cents. The language in this regard varies in different ordinances, but in no case is it stipulated that the company shall have the right to charge any specified fare. In no view can any of them be regarded as a contract by the city not to reduce the fares below 5 cents, or that the city has lost control of the subject matter, so it cannot by ordinance fix the rate of fare to be charged, unless the language of the ordinances imperatively requires such construction, and we do not think any of them are susceptible of it.

The law cited above, as to the power of the legislature, over charters granted by it, applies equally to ordinances of the character in question passed by the city council.

I see no reason why the council cannot regulate, by ordinance, the fare to be charged by the street car companies. This power, I think, is conferred by the charter, and includes the right to require transfers, as provided for in the proposed ordinance.

The only limitation upon the power of the council to fix the rates of fare to be charged is that the ordinance should be reasonable in its provisions, and in my opinion the accompanying one would be so considered.   Respectfully submitted,

JAMES HUTCHINSON, Corporation Counsel.

November 27, 1889.

To Hon. W. J. Onahan, Comptroller.

Dear Sir—

To your inquiry of the twenty-seventh inst., whether the city of Chicago is liable for the rent of the polling places in use at the late county election I beg to reply: that the election law now in force provides that the county of Cook shall pay the salaries of the election commissioners and the chief clerk of the board of election commissioners; and also that the county shall pay for the services of the judges and clerks of election and official ticket holders at all general county and state elections, which includes officers elected through the whole county, and all exclusively judicial elections, and at all special elections for county or state officer, or member of congress, or member of the legislature.

The law does not in express terms require the county to pay any other expense of election.

The law does provide that "all expense incurred by said Board of Election Commissioners shall be paid by the city." Also that "such expenditures shall be paid by the city treasurer upon the warrant of the county judge out of any money in the city treasury not otherwise appropriated."

It is made the duty of the governing authority of such cities to make provision for the prompt payment of such "expenses." It would seem to be the meaning of the law that the expenses for rent of polling places is to be provided for and paid by the city.

There is no other provision in the law for the payment of such expense than as a part of the expense incurred by said Board of Election Commissioners to be paid by the city; and the obligation under the law upon the city to pay such expense seems to be manifest.

I am of opinion, therefore, that expense for rent of polling places within the city of Chicago at the late election, and at all elections, is to be provided and paid for by the city.

.Respectfully submitted,

M. W. ROBINSON, Asst. Corporation Counsel.

January 3, 1890.

To Hon. D .J. Swenie, Fire Marshal.

Dear Sir—

In your communication of January 2, you inquire: " Is a member of the Fire Department who is under suspension entitled to his pay during such suspension, and can he, while still suspended, engage in any other position?"

To the first branch of the question I should answer, no. Suspension from service involves, as an incident, suspension of pay from the time of suspension. The person suspended has no legal right to salary, or other compensation, during the suspension. Of course it may happen that for reasons satisfactory to the fire marshal, and as an act of kindness to a party who may have been unjustly dealt with, it may be proper to recommend the granting of pay during the suspension, but this would be a pure matter of favor on the part of your department, and not a matter of right that the party suspended could demand.

To the second branch of your question it is evidently a matter of choice with the party suspended whether he shall take employ - ment during the suspension or not. He has a clear right to do so if he sees fit, and the department has no control over the matter.

Yours very truly,

M. W. ROBINSON, Asst. Corporation Counsel.

January 9, 1890.

W. B. Purdy, Esq., Commissioner of Public Works.

Dear Sir—

You ask the advice of this department in regard to the following state of facts: By ordinance of the City of Lake View, passed and and approved June 21, 1889, a corporation styled the Western Light & Power Company was authorized to erect and maintain poles, with wires stretched thereon, along streets, alleys and public highways within the territory of the then city of Lake View, and to maintain such structures for a period of five years, and the further period

10

of two years after being notified by the proper authorities to place the wires underground.

The company accepted the provisions of the ordinance, filed their bond, as required, purchased a plant, and commenced doing work under the ordinance, expending considerable money thereon, and incurring liabilities in the prosecution of their work. The ordinance prescribes the size and height of the poles, their distance apart, and general manner of construction and requires the company to obtain the permits from the proper public authorities for making excavations in the street and other matters in the prosecution of their work, and that the doing of certain things in the public streets shall be to the satisfaction of the proper public authorities.

On July 15, the territory of the former city of Lake View was annexed to the city of Chicago, and the authority of the city of Chicago extended over such territory. By the general ordinances of the city of Chicago the telegraph and electric light wires are required to be placed under ground. You ask whether those general ordinances of the city of Chicago have the effect to annul the right granted to this corporation by the Lake View ordinance in question, and whether it would be proper to now permit the erection of poles and stretching of wires above ground within the territory contemplated by that ordinance.

I am of opinion that by the passage of the ordinance in question, and its acceptance by the Western Light & Power Company, it became vested with what is equivalent to be a contract right to exercise the privileges purported to be authorized by the ordinance, and that this vested right is a property of which the company was not divested by virtue of annexation; and that its rights and privileges were not annulled by the extension of the jurisdiction of Chicago over the territory. The franchises of that company will remain substantially the same as if annexation had not taken place. The sole effect of the annexation is to substitute the city of Chicago for the city of Lake View in the contract. All such things as the authorities of the city of Lake View might have been required to perform in respect to the subject matter of the ordinance, if annexation had not taken place, must now be exercised and performed by the proper authorities of the city of Chicago.

Such permits, therefore, as the company were required to obtain from the city authorities of Lake View the company must now apply to the city of Chicago for; and the city of Chicago will be required to grant such permits in all respects as the city of Lake View was authorized and required by the terms of the contract to grant.

There is another case of a franchise granted by the village of Hyde Park of like effect and involving precisely the same question. Without fully stating the fact of that case I would add that precisely the same rule will apply in that case.

Yours very truly,
M. W. ROBINSON, Asst. Corporation Counsel.

March 22, 1890.

To the Committee on Gas, Oil & Electric Lights.

Gentlemen—

The opinion of this department has been asked as to the right of the city to regulate the price to be charged by the various gas companies, doing business in the city of Chicago, to the consumers of their product.

It has often been decided that the state legislature has the right to regulate the charges of the companies or corporations engaged in business of a public nature, or whose duty, by reason of the franchises and privileges given it, is to serve the public as well as to promote the interests of their stock-holders, unless prevented by an express provision of the charter granted to such company. This has been frequently held of railroad companies, warehouse companies, telephone companies and the like.

In support of this proposition a long line of cases might be cited, among which are:

Dow vs. Beidleman, 125 U. S., 680.

St. Louis vs. Bell Telephone Company, 98 Mo., 623.

Illinois Central Railroad Company vs. People, 108 U. S., 541.

Munn vs. The People, 69 Ill., 80; which case was affirmed in the 94 U. S., 113.

Ruggles vs. People, 91 Ill., 256; affirmed in 108 U. S., 526.

People vs. Budd, decided by the N. Y. Court of Appeals, 22 North-Western Reporter, 670.

Spring Valley Water Works vs. Schottler, et al., 110 U. S., 347.

The right of the legislature to control and regulate gas companies has been expressly upheld in:

34 Ohio State, in State vs. Gas Company, 572.

The State vs. Gas Company, 18 Ohio State, 262.

Chicago Gas Light and Coke Company, vs. Gas Company, 121 Ill., 530.

The decisions in these cases were rendered upon the theory that such business as the operation of railroads, warehouses, telephone companies, supplying gas, water and the like, were, in their nature public, and should be conducted for the public good, as well as for private gain.

In the case of the Chicago Gas Light and Coke Company vs. People's Gas Light and Coke Company, the Supreme Court, in rendering its decision, used the following language:

"The manufacture and distribution of illuminating gas, by means of pipes or conduits placed under legislative authority in the streets of a town or city, is a business of a public character. It is the exercise of the franchise belonging to the state. The services rendered, and to be rendered, for such grant, are of a public nature. Such right is conferred by legislative grant as well for the benefit of the public as of the corporation taking the same."

The question, then, for determination is, whether the power to regulate and control the price of gas has been delegated to the city council.

It is well settled that the city council has no powers except those which have been delegated to it by the legislature, or which are necessary for the purpose of carrying out the powers granted by the legislature.

This proposition has been repeatedly laid down by our Supreme Court, as well as by the courts of other states. In support of which the following cases may be cited:

Huesing vs. Rock Island, 128 Ills., 465.

Mather vs. Ottawa, 114 Ills., 660.

Chicago vs. Case, 126 Ills., 278.

St. Louis vs. Bell Telephone Company, 96 Mo., 673.

The legislature has nowhere expressly delegated to the city council the right of regulating the charges of gas companies. If the city council has any power in that question it must be under some general provision of the city charter.

The only general provisions that, in my opinion, could in any way be said to be applicable thereto, are:

First. Subdivisions 11 and 13 of Section 1, Article V, which provide, in reference to public streets, that the city council shall have power to provide for the lighting of the same, and to regulate the openings therein for the laying of gas or water mains and pipes, and the building and repairing of sewers, tunnels and drains, and erecting gas lights; provided, however, that any company heretofore organized under the general laws of this state, or any association of persons organized, or which may be hereafter organized for the purpose of manufacturing illuminating gas to supply cities or villages, or the inhabitants thereof, with the same, shall have the right, by consent of the common council, subject to existing rights, to erect gas factories, and lay down pipes in the streets or alleys of any city or village in this state, subject to such regulations as any such city or village may by ordinance impose.

The rights herewith granted are meant to be given in relation to the public streets, and while it would doubtless give the city council the power to prescribe by any ordinance giving the right to any gas company to use the public streets, terms and conditions upon which such right should be exercised, it would not, in my opinion, give the city council any power to control the charges of gas companies to private consumers where no conditions were imposed at the time of granting the right to said companies to occupy and lay their mains in streets.

If these charter provisions can be held to allow any regulation by the council after pipes have been laid, and factories built, such regulations must, in my opinion, have reference to the manner in which the pipes are laid, or the factories constructed.

Second. Under Subdivision 66, of Section 1, or Article V, which gives power to the city to regulate the police of the city or village, and pass and enforce all necessary police ordinances.

It is doubtless a question just how far a city may go under the exercise of its general police power.

The city may pass ordinances concerning vagrants, prohibiting persons from keeping open their places of business on Sunday, from cruelty to animals, and regulating many affairs and providing many regulations which conduce to the general welfare, but to say under this provision that the city would have the right to fix the compensation of gas companies, would, in my opinion, be interpreting the police powers to be broader than the courts would sustain. It seems to me clear that the legislature did not intend by the general provision granting police powers to cities to allow municipal corporations to fix the rates of gas companies.

The legislature has expressly given cities the power to license, tax and regulate hackmen, draymen, omnibus drivers, carters, cabmen, porters and expressmen, and other like occupations, and to prescribe their compensation, from which it seems that the legislature did not consider that the general police powers would be sufficiently broad to provide for the regulation of these occupations. Had the legislature intended that gas companies should be regulated as provided in the occupations above enumerated, it seems to me they would have been included with the rest.

In the language of the Missouri court, in the case of St. Louis vs. Shuebrush, 95 Mo., 618, I would say: "With this specific enumeration of cases where the city may regulate the compensation to be charged, it impliedly appears that such was not intended to be given in other cases."

The Supreme Court of Illinois has, substantially, affirmed this doctrine to be the law in the case of City of Cairo vs. Bross, 101 Ills., 495.

It may at least be said that the right of the city council to regulate charges of gas companies is so exceedingly doubtful, and the way to obtain such right by appeal to the legislature is so plain, that it would be ill-advised to attempt the exercise of such powers without the express authority of the legislature. Respectfully submitted,

C. S. DARROW, Asst. Corporation Counsel.

March 24, 1890.

To the Honorable the City Council.

Gentlemen—

The opinion of this department has been asked as to the right of the city to regulate the charges of the telephone companies doing business in the city of Chicago. Practically the same questions arise in this case as in that of the right of the city to regulate the price of gas. Upon that question I have already submitted an opinion to the committee on gas, oil and electric lights.

In my opinion the legislature has the right to regulate the charges of all companies engaged in a public business, or whose business partakes of the nature of a monopoly. This position is supported by numerous authorities. That the telephone business falls in this class, and is subject to control by the legislature has been held by the Supreme Court of Indiana, in the case of Hockett vs. The State, 103 Ind., 250; also in the case of the City of St. Louis vs. The Bell Telephone Company, 96 Mo., 622. It must also be obvious from the nature of the business itself. However, the doctrine is well established that municipal corporations have only such powers and rights as have been delegated to them by the state legislature.

The legislature has not expressly given to the city of Chicago the power to regulate the charges of telephone companies. It could only be argued that this power exists in connection with the general police powers granted to the city. In my opinion the legislature did not intend to give the city the power to regulate the rates to be charged by telephone companies under the general police powers granted to municipal corporations. Such an interpretation of the police powers would doubtless be broader than our courts would sustain.

In the case of St. Louis vs. Bell, above cited, the Supreme Court of Missouri expressly held that the city of St. Louis, under charter rights substantially like our own, had no power to regulate the charges of telephone companies.

If the city desires to regulate the charges of the telephone companies the safest course, at least, is to apply to the legislature to so amend the city charter as to give it that power.

Respectfully submitted,
C. S. DARROW, Asst. Corporation Counsel.

April 3, 1890.

Hon. D. C. Cregier, Mayor.

Sir—

You ask the opinion of this department: (1) Whether the city council can provide for dredging or deepening of the channel of the Chicago river by special assessment and, if so, (2) whether the ordinance authorizing such assessment may provide that one-third of the cost of the work shall be borne by the property on one side of the river, one-third by the property on the opposite side of the river and the remaining third by the city.

1. The constitution provides (Art. IX, Sec. 9.) that "The General Assembly may vest the corporate authorities of cities, towns and villages with power to make local improvements by special assessment and by special taxation of contiguous property, or otherwise."

The charter provides (Art.. IX, Sec. 1): "That the corporate authorities of cities and villages are hereby vested with power to make local improvements by special assessment or by special taxation, or both, of contiguous property, or general taxation, or otherwise, as they shall by ordinance prescribe."

By clause 30 of Section 1 of Article V of the charter, the council is given power "To deepen, widen, dock, cover, wall, alter, or change channel of water courses."

Under these various provisions I think the council can pass an ordinance to deepen the channel of the river (i. e., to dredge it) and can provide that the cost thereof shall be met by special assessments.

This same question was before our Supreme Court in 1858, when the city was operating under the old charter (Wright vs. City of Chicago, 20 Ills., 252), and the court, upon a construction of the then charter, held that the city did not have authority to levy a special assessment for deepening the river.

In that charter no authority was conferred to make local improvements generally by special assessment and only certain enumerated improvements. Express power was given to *widen* but not to *deepen* the river by special assessment, and the court held as it did because of the absence of such express authority.

The court, however, upon the general question say, "That there is as much propriety in requiring the owners of property benefited by the deepening of the harbor to pay the expense of the improvement as there is in requiring those benefited by widening it, or improving a street, would seem to be self-evident. To say that the owner of a dock which is useless, because of the want of water to bring vessels to it, shall not pay the expense of deepening the harbor in front so as to make it valuable, while the owner of the lot shall be compelled to pay for paving the street in its neighborhood we cannot doubt is unjust, and had we the making of the laws we could not hesitate to affirm this judgment."

Under our present charter I think the right to dredge or deepen the channel of the river falls within the provision authorizing the council to make local improvements by special assessment.

2. I do not think the council can undertake in the ordinance for the assessment, to apportion the cost of improvements.

Respectfully yours,
MORRIS ST. P. THOMAS, Asst. Corporation Counsel.

April 15, 1890.

To the Hon. De Witt C. Cregier.

Dear Sir—

In reply to your question as to your right to license the carrying of concealed weapons I would say: The statutes make it an offense to carry concealed weapons. The city has no authority to license anything which the state prohibits.

The section of the Municipal Code which provides that the mayor may give a license to carry concealed weapons, in my opinion, contemplates that this license should be given to those connected with the police department, or, at least, for the purposes of the police protection of the city. For this purpose I have no doubt that you would have the right to grant a license to carry a concealed weapon, but you would have no right to do it except for police purposes.

Respectfully yours,

C. S. DARROW, Asst. Corporation Counsel.

April 21, 1890.

To Honorable William J. Onahan, Comptroller.

Dear Sir—

You request an opinion as to the liability of the city for lighting and maintaining the lamps in the parks and along the boulevards and streets under the control and jurisdiction of the various boards of park commissioners.

The question, as I understand it, refers only to such parks, streets and boulevards as have been duly surrendered to the park boards.

First. By an act of the general assembly, entitled "An Act to enable Park Commissioners, or corporate authorities, to take, regulate, control and improve public streets leading to public parks; to pay for the improvement thereof, and in that behalf, to make and collect a special assessment, or special tax, on contiguous property," approved and in force April 9, 1879. Every board of park commissioners is authorized to connect any public park, boulevard or driveway, under its contract, with any part of any corporated city, town or village by selecting and taking any connecting street or streets, or part thereof, leading to such park; and to accept and add to such park any street or part thereof which adjoins and runs parallel with any boundary line of the same, provided such street or streets shall lie within the district of territory taxable for park purposes; and provided the consent of the corporate authorities having control of such street or streets, and of the owners of a majority of the frontage, be first obtained.

Section 3, of the act, gives such park boards the same power and control over the streets so taken "as are, or may be by law, vested in them, of and concerning the parks, boulevards or driveways under their control," and Section 5 authorizes any city, town or village to invest any of such park boards with the right to control, improve and maintain any of the streets of such city, town or village.

Second. By an act of the general assembly, entitled "An Act to enable Park Commissioners having control of parks to take, regulate, control and improve parks now under the control of incorporated cities, villages or towns," approved and in force April 11, 1885, boards of park commissioners are given substantially the same powers as to acquiring, controlling, improving, and maintaining public parks under the control of cities, towns and villages, as are conferred upon them in relation to streets under the act first above referred to.

Third. By Section 13 of the act creating the South Park commissioners, the board is given full and exclusive power to govern, man-

age and direct the park contemplated by the act, and to pass ordinances
for the regulation and government thereof; to appoint a police force
and generally it is given all the power and authority then by law conferred upon or possessed by the common council of the city of Chicago
in respect to the public squares and places in said city.

The acts creating the Lincoln Park Commissioners and the West
Chicago Park Commissioners invest those boards with like powers.

Fourth. Pursuant to these various legislative enactments the different park boards with the consent of the city council and the trustees
of Hyde Park, Lake and Lake View, have taken under their jurisdiction certain of the public parks and streets of the city, and of the other
municipalities now included within the city.

The various ordinances surrendering these streets and parks to the
park boards are substantially alike and authorize the park commissioners to take, regulate, control, improve and maintain the parks, or
streets, so taken, reserving, however, the right to build sewers and to
lay water and gas mains.

The effect of these various legislative acts and ordinances is virtually to surrender the designated streets and parks to the park boards.
They control the streets, make police regulations concerning them, improve and maintain them, pave, repair and clean the streets, and I see
no reason why they should not bear the expense of lighting them and
maintaining the lamps. They are provided with the power of taxation
for park purposes, and, therefore, have the necessary means of revenue.

I am, therefore, of the opinion that it is not incumbent on the city
to pay for lighting or maintaining said lamps.

Respectfully submitted,

MORRIS ST.' P. THOMAS, Asst. Corporation Counsel.

July 18, 1890.

To the Committee on Streets and Alleys, W. D.

Gentlemen—

Your committee refers to this department for an opinion on the
following questions, with the statement of facts accompanying the
same:

"First. Where the owner of property fronting on Milwaukee
avenue signed a petition to the City Council of the City of Chicago to
grant to the Chicago & Cook County Passenger Dummy Railway
Company the privilege of constructing and operating an elevated railway on Milwaukeee avenue.

"And afterwards, *but before the said company, or any one else,
had presented said petition to said city council,* said owner signed and
presented to the City Council his revocation and protest, wherein, after
reciting above statement, he used the following language:

"Now, therefore, I, by these presents do revoke, countermand,
annul and declare void, the said written petition, whether signed by
myself or by any one for me, and any and all consents or petitions of

whatever nature, and by whomsoever signed for me, and all power and
authority heretofore given, or which may be construed to have been
given to said company, or its officers, or to said City Council, and I do
hereby enter my protest against the granting of permission by the
proper authorities to the said named company, to construct and operate
an elevated railroad in or along any portion of the said Milwaukee
avenue and in front of the premises above described."

"*Query.* Does the first petition stand, notwithstanding it was annulled and declared void by an instrument in writing, signed by the
owner of the property and presented to the City Council before the said
first petition was presented to the City Council?

"Second. Where the owner or owners of property fronting on
Milwaukee avenue, signed a petition to the City Council of the City of
Chicago, to grant to the Chicago & Cook County Passenger Dummy
Railway Company the privilege of constructing and operating an ele-
vated railway on Milwaukee avenue.

"And afterwards, *but before the said company, or any one else,
had presented said petition to said city council, said owner sold and
conveyed said said property to another party, who has not signed said petition* (the deed of conveyance being of record in the Recorder's office
of Cook County). So that at the time of the presentation of said petition to the City Council, the person who signed said petition was *not
in fact* the owner of the property for which he had signed.

"*Query.* Can said petition be counted in favor of the construction and operation of an elevated railway on Milwaukee avenue?"

In reply to the first question I answer no. I do not think the
petition for the privilege of constructing and operating a railway on
Milwaukee avenue ought to be considered by the council when the
revocation was presented to the council before any action had been
taken by the council upon the petition.

In this case, according to the statement submitted to me, the revocation was received by the city council before the petition was,
and, therefore, when the petition was presented to the council, the
council had before it the revocation of the property owners, or some
of them, and as to them, the property they represented should not,
in my judgment, be considered in estimating frontage.

In answer to the second question I say no. I do not think
"the petition should be counted in favor of the construction and
operation of the road," when the owner of the property who had
signed the petition, conveyed said property to another party, who
did not sign it, the deed being of record before the petition had been
presented to the city council. The person who signed the petition
for the property, was not the owner of it at the time the petition was
presented to the council.

This is a question of jurisdiction and when the city council takes
up for consideration the petition of the property owners, if there
is at that time before the council any revocations which were before

the council before the petition was presented, or at the same time, I do not think, the property signed for in the petition and included in the revocation, should be counted in estimating the frontage, and if any of the property represented in the petition has been sold, and the deed of it is of record, before the time, or at the time when the said petition comes before the city council for action, I do not think the property thus conveyed should be considered in estimating the frontage.

It is essential to the validity of the ordinance on this subject, in my opinion, that there shall be before the council when it considers this question the necessary frontage, and if it is found that this is wanting because it was never originally in the petition, or has been withdrawn before the petition is filed or acted upon, then I think the council has no jurisdiction as to such property.

Respectfully submitted,
JONAS HUTCHINSON, Corporation Counsel.

August 4, 1890.

To Hon. B. Roesing, City Treasurer.

Dear Sir—

You ask if you can legally make a transfer of fifty thousand ($50,000.00) dollars from the special assessment fund to the water fund on request of the comptroller.

I am informed by the comptroller that this transfer is simply for a temporary loan to the water fund, which will soon be returned to the special assessment fund, and that this is in conformity with the former practice of the department.

The object, I understand, is to accumulate a fund that temporarily needs assistance by borrowing from a fund which can spare the money as well as not, thereby obviating an enforced sale of bonds held by the city. If this be the case I think you are justified in making the transfer. ` Yours very respectfully,
JONAS HUTCHINSON, Corporation Counsel.

November 17, 1890.

To the Honorable, the City Council of the City of Chicago.

Gentlemen—

In obedience to the resolution of your honorable body, I herewith submit an opinion as to the right of the city council to regulate fares and transfers on street railways within the limits of the city of Chicago:

It is a well established doctrine that the legislature has the right to regulate the rates of common carriers, such as railroad companies, and to exercise control over business of a public nature.

In Ruggles vs. People, 91 Ill., 256, the court say that it has been repeatedly held by this court that corporations created within the state are amenable to the police power of the state to the same extent as are natural persons, but to no greater extent. The legislature may require of these bodies the performance of any and all acts which they are capable of performing, that they may require of natural persons. The legislature of this state has the power, under the constitution, to fix a maximum rate of charges by individuals as common carriers, warehousemen, or others exercising a calling or business public in its character, or in which the public have an interest to be protected against extortion or oppression. And it has the same lawful power in respect to corporations exercising the same business, and such regulation does not impair the obligation of the contract in their charter.

The decision in this case was affirmed by the Supreme Court of the United States in

Ruggles vs. People, 108, U. S., 526.

And the same doctrine is laid down by the same court in

Stone vs. F. L. & T. Co., 166 U. S., 307.

I. C. R. R. Co., vs. People, 108 U. S., 547.

Stone vs. I. C. R. R. Co., 116 U. S., 347.

Also in Granger's decision in the 94 U. S. Many other cases might be cited sustaining this proposition.

The doctrine, that the power to fix the rates of fare to be charged by common carriers and individuals and corporations pursuing business public in its nature, is lodged in the legislative department of the government, is too well established to be seriously controverted.

It is also a well established principle of law that the city council has only such powers and rights as are delegated to it by the legislature of the state, and that the legislature of the state has the power to give the city council the right to control and regulate business of a public nature, such as the state has the right to control.

The question then arises as to whether the legislature of the State of Illinois has given the city of Chicago the right to regulate fares of street railroad companies within the city.

Sibdivision 42, of Section 1, of Article V, of the city charter provides "that the city council shall have power to license, tax, and regulate hackmen, draymen, omnibus drivers, cabmen, porters, expressmen, and all others pursuing a like occupation, and to prescribe their compensation." Under this section the city of Chicago does license and tax and otherwise regulate the occupations mentioned in said section. If the business of operating a street railroad is a like occupation with those herein enumerated within the meaning of the law, then the city council has the right to regulate such business, and to prescribe the compensation of such companies; provided, of course, such regulation and such compensation so fixed by said city council shall be reasonable and just.

In Allerton vs. City of Chicago, 9 Biss., 552, which was a proceeding to determine whether the city of Chicago, under this section, had the right to fix a tax or license fee upon each street car operated by street railroad companies, Judge Drummond, decided "that street railway companies pursue a like occupation with hackmen, draymen, omnibus drivers, cabmen and expressmen, and are, therefore, within the provisions of the general law of 1872, for the incorporation of cities and villages in this state."

It is under this power that a tax is now collected on the street cars of many of the lines within the city of Chicago.

The Supreme Court of Pennsylvania has also held that street railway companies are of a like nature with omnibuses, etc.

While there has been no decision by the Supreme Court of this state upon this question, yet whatever authority can be found seems to hold that street railroads are of a like character with omnibuses, etc.

Unless the clause contained in the city charter "and all others pursuing like occupations" includes street railroad companies, it is difficult to determine what it does include. All are engaged in substantially the same business, all are peculiarly matters which the city ought to have the power to regulate, and, in my opinion, the court would hold that the operation of a street railway is a like occupation to that of omnibus, drayman, etc., and that, therefore, its business and compensation are subject to the regulation of the city council.

It might be that the various ordinances granting street railroads the right to lay their tracks and fixing the rate of fare could deprive the city council of any such power, but these ordinances seem to provide only for the maximum to be charged by the company, and it is by no means certain that even if they did provide for a certain rate of fare, it would deprive other councils from exercising control over said companies.

I see no reason why the council cannot regulate, by ordinance, the fare charged by the street car companies. This power, I think, is conferred by the charter, and includes the right to require transfers as has been provided by ordinance. The only limitation upon the power of the council to fix the rate of fare to be charged is that the ordinance should be reasonable in its conditions and provisions.

Respectfully submitted,
JONAS HUTCHINSON, Corporation Counsel.

December 15, 1890.
To the Judiciary Committee:
Gentlemen—
The villages of Washington Heights and West Roseland were annexed pursuant to the provisions of an act in force April 25, 1889, commonly called the annexation act. Neither of these villages has the square mileage or population requisite to a ward, but taken together they contain 4.6 square miles which is in excess of the minimum square mileage essential to a ward.

The question arises must the council combine the two villages into one ward, or annex them to the adjacent wards.

Section 19 of said act, under which this annexation took place, does not provide for joining the territory of the two villages into one parcel and making a ward of them, but it says:

"Whenever the whole or a part of any city, village or incorporated town is annexed to a city having thirty thousand inhabitants or more and such annexed territory is three or more square miles in extent, or contains 15,000 inhabitants and not more than 25,000 inhabitants, then such annexed territory shall constitute a ward of the city to which it is annexed, and the city council of such city shall authorize the legal voters of such annexed territory to elect two aldermen from such ward in such annexed territory, which said aldermen from such annexed territory shall be additional aldermen to the number theretofore required in such city, and shall possess all the qualifications of and be elected at the time and in the manner provided by law; provided, that if said annexed territory shall contain more than 25,000 inhabitants, then the city council shall authorize the legal voters of such annexed territory to elect two aldermen for every 25,000 inhabitants thereof, and two additional aldermen for a fraction of 15,000 inhabitants or more, the number of inhabitants to be determined by the last preceding national, state or school census of such annexed territory, and if any such annexed territory has less than 15,000 inhabitants, and is less than three square miles in extent, then the city council shall annex it to any ward or wards which it adjoins; provided further, that nothing herein shall prevent the city council from re-districting such city according to law."

If the legislature intended two or more parcels of territory or villages should be united in order to secure the population or square mileage necessary to wardship it would so appear by the act. It so happens that these villages are adjacent not only to each other, but to established wards, and that they were annexed at the same time, but I do not think these facts should change the manner of dealing with them. Each came in independently of the other. Suppose one of these villages was adjacent to the twenty-fifth ward would it be contended that they should be united into the thirty-fifth ward? The reasoning that unites two adjacent villages into one ward in order to get the necessary population or mileage for a ward would put into the same ward villages many miles asunder. I cannot think the legislature intended such a union as that, and to guard against such a condition of things, each city, village and incorporated town, or part thereof, is treated singly, and the act plainly says, if any one of them has not the population or mileage essential to a ward, it shall be annexed to any ward or wards which it adjoins.

I do not think Section 2, of Article III, of Chapter XXIV, Revised Statutes, is in conflict with the views herein expressed.

The part of Section 2 material to this question is as follows:

"Provided, however, that in cities of over 350,000 inhabitants there shall be elected forty-eight aldermen and no more, unless additional territory shall be annexed to such city, after such city shall have been divided into wards on the basis of forty-eight aldermen, in which case and as often as new territory shall be annexed to such city, as aforesaid, containing three or more square miles of territory, or 15,000 inhabitants, and not exceeding 25,000 inhabitants, such annexed territory shall constitute a ward of such city."

It will be seen that the language here is substantially the same as in Section 19 of the annexation act. The word "territory" is used instead of the words "incorporated city, village or town." The provisions of Section 2 went into effect after the annexation act, and I think these expressions are not inharmonious, and that it was not the intention of the legislature by this later act to modify Section 19 of the annexation act.

This view is strengthened when we consider the fact that the annexation act, under the emergency clause, went into effect April 25, 1889, while the other act was passed June 4, 1889, at the same session, and by its title was expressed to be an amendment of Section 2, Article III, of an act entitled "An act to provide for the incorporation of cities and villages," approved April 10, 1872, and not as designed to amend in any manner the act of April 25, 1889, under which this annexation took place.

I am of opinion that these villages should be annexed to adjoining wards. Respectfully submitted,
JONAS HUTCHINSON, Corporation Counsel.

February 4, 1891.

Hon. De Witt C. Cregier, Mayor, etc.
Dear Sir—

You have asked this department to advise you as to your rights and duties in the manner of issuing licenses to persons who desire to establish dram shops within two hundred (200) feet of a public or other school building.

Section 1850, of the Municipal Code of 1881, as amended February 18, 1884, provides "That the Mayor of the City of Chicago shall, from time to time, grant licenses for the keeping of dram-shops within the city of Chicago, to any person who shall apply to him in writing, upon said person furnishing sufficient evidence that he or she is a person of good character and upon such person executing to the city of Chicago a bond with at least two sureties, to be approved by the Mayor, etc."

Under this ordinance the mayor is given no discretion, except in so far as the character of the applicant and the sufficiency of the bonds presented to him are concerned. Undoubtedly the council has power to provide by ordinance that no license shall be issued to keep a dram-shop in the vicinity of a school building, but not having passed such an ordinance the mayor is not vested with authority to impose any condition or restrictions not contained in the ordinance.

In the case of the People, ex. rel. Jacob Moser vs. The Mayor, recently decided by Judge Baker, of the Circuit Court of this county, it was squarely decided that the fact that the applicant for a license desired to establish a saloon within two hundred (200) feet of a school building in this city, was no reason for withholding the license. . I have no doubt that this decision was correct, and in my opinion it should be acquiesced in, and unless the character of the applicant, or the bonds furnished by him, are not satisfactory, the license should issue in all cases.   Respectfully yours,

MORRIS P. ST. THOMAS, Asst. Corporation Counsel.

February 4, 1891.

Hon. De Witt C. Cregier, Mayor, etc.

Dear Sir—

Your communication of the 4th inst. requests the opinion of this department as to the authority of the city to grant what are called transfers of saloon· licenses from one location to another, and from one person to another.

The city of Chicago has undertaken to regulate the manner of the so-called transfer of licenses by the various provisions in Article XXXVI, of the Municipal Code, entitled "Licenses."

Section 1568 provides, "That no license granted under this ordinance shall be assignable or transferable without permission of the mayor, nor shall any such license authorize any person to do business, or act under it but the person named therein, except as is in this ordinance otherwise provided."

Section 1573 provides, "That any person or persons to whom any license may have been issued under any ordinance of the City Council, may, with the permission of the Mayor, assign and transfer the same to any other person or persons, and the person or persons to whom such license is issued or the assignee or assignees of such license may, with the permission of the Mayor, surrender such license, and have a new license issued for the unexpired term of the old license, authorizing the person or persons so surrendering such license to carry on the same business or occupation at such place as may be named in such new license; provided, that in all cases the party applying for such new license shall give a bond, with sureties, which shall conform as near as may be to the bond upon which such surrendered license was issued."

We are of opinion that those provisions of the ordinance are valid and a reasonable exercise of the power granted to the city to license and regulate the selling of intoxicating liquors, and those provisions do not conflict with any law of this state.

Strictly speaking. one person to whom license is granted may not by mere arrangement with the purchaser, assign or transfer his license, so as to authorize that purchaser to continue business under the same license. A license is not assignable in that sense, but its transfer may be effected by the consent of the mayor in the manner pointed out in the ordinance quoted, and the arrangement will then be in effect that the person desiring the transfer surrenders his license and the transferee is granted in his own name a license for the unexpired term without being required to pay for the license fee. In effect, there is rebated to the transferer the unaccrued portion of his license fee, and that is immediately paid over to the city again for the unexpired portion of the term granted to the transferee.

As to exercising the privilege under the license in a different place to that named in the license, there seems to be nothing in the ordinances specifically permitting such change of place, except so far as it may be implied in the language of Section 1573, which provides that the new license shall authorize the person so surrendering such license to carry on the same business at such place as may be named in such new license. It would seem to be within the reasons of the regulation that the person licensed to carry on a saloon at a given place might by permission of the mayor, and upon giving a new bond, have a new license, issued for carrying on the same business at the new place, to be named in the new license, although such an arrangement is not specifically provided for by any ordinance.

And in our opinion such a regulation would not be in conflict with any law of this state, but would be a reasonable exercise of the powers conferred on the city to regulate this business.

Respectfully submitted,

M. W. ROBINSON, Asst. Corporation Counsel.
I concur in the above.   C. S. DARROW.

June 8, 1891.

To the Hon. Hempstead Washburne, Mayor, etc.

Dear Sir—

The matter submitted to this department for an opinion as to whether the mayor, under the existing ordinances relating to junk shops, has the power to revoke licenses to keep junk shops, and if so, under what circumstances such licenses may be revoked, I find that under Section 2561, of the Laws and Ordinances of Chicago (Ed. 1890), which is now in force, the mayor may revoke any license granted to a second-hand dealer, or keeper of a junk shop, "on satisfactory cause appearing to him for so doing."

As to what constitutes satisfactory cause is a question addressed to the sound discretion and judgment of the mayor, and while it is presumed that he will exercise a reasonable discretion, any circumstances which seem to him sufficient to afford cause to revoke a license will justify his action in so doing.   Respectfully yours,

ARTHUR H. CHETLAIN, Asst. Corporation Counsel.

11

J. Frank Aldrich, Esq., Commissioner of Public Works.

Dear Sir—

You ask my opinion as to your duties and powers in the matter of requiring the removal of obstructions in the streets in the city of Chicago.

The city council is empowered, by the charter, to regulate the use of the streets, and to prevent and remove encroachments or obstructions upon the same, and to regulate the use of sidewalks and all structures thereunder; and to regulate and prevent the use of streets, sidewalks and public grounds for signs, sign-posts, awnings, etc.; and to regulate and prevent the hanging of flags, banners or signs across the streets or from houses; and to regulate traffic and sales upon the streets, sidewalks and public places.

By the ordinances of the city it is provided that the commissioner of public works may direct the removal of any article or thing whatsoever which may encroach or obstruct any street, alley or avenue in the city of Chicago; and it is made his duty, subject to the ordinances of the city, to take special charge and superintendence of all streets, alleys, lanes and highways.

The obstructions upon the streets of the city are divisible into these classes:

First: Cases where the fronts of buildings abutting upon the street have been extended so as to encroach upon or enclose portions of the streets.

Second: Porticos, steps, railings, awnings, signs, etc., placed upon or over the streets.

Third. The occupation of the sidewalk or roadway to the exclusion or obstruction of public travel by piling or placing goods or articles on the walk; by receiving or shipping merchandise into or from stores; or by keeping drays, wagons, and other vehicles standing upon the streets.

The first class of obstructions referred to, even if authorized by the order or permit of the city council, are illegal. The city of Chicago has no power to authorize or permit portions of its streets to be enclosed within abutting buildings, occupied for private uses, to the exclusion of the public use to which the streets are devoted. It is a well settled legal proposition that the city cannot invest private parties with any rights in the public streets, inconsistent with the public right, to use the same for the purposes for which they were dedicated, and it could not, therefore, give to the owner or occupant of a store abutting upon the street the right to extend the wall or windows of his buildings so as to enclose any portion of the street, and exclude the right of the public to the use of the portion so enclosed.

Second. It has been held that under the power of exclusive control over its streets, which is given to the city by its charter, the city may allow any use of the streets which is consistent with the public purpose for which they are held. But the occupation of portions of the streets by private persons for private business or benefit, with signs or other things, is not, in any case, of right. When such occupation is by municipal authority, such permission is a mere license. It creates no right to, or easement in the streets as against the city; and is, therefore, subject to revocation. And such authority or permission is always subject to the condition that the public use be not seriously interfered with by such permitted use. When the public use of the streets is, or becomes so, interfered with, the obstruction is not authorized. When such obstructions are erected without municipal authority, they are nuisances. While their interference with the public use of the streets is the main reason for their abatement, it is not the only one. The legal duty is imposed upon the city, which cannot be evaded or laid off, of keeping its streets reasonably safe for travel. This may make the city responsible for the due care of such structures in the streets when they are authorized and liable from injuries resulting from want of such care. And when they are placed in or over the streets without authority from the city, but are suffered by the city to remain unabated, the degree of its liability for injuries therefore may be even greater. The rule is applied that a municipal corporation is liable for injuries resulting from nuisances, or unauthorized obstructions suffered to remain in its streets, whether due care is exercised in keeping the obstruction in safe condition or not.

The city council has, by ordinances, provided for and regulated the use of portions of the street by projections, such as porticos, awnings and signs, with which ordinances you are familiar. They forbid the placing of any article that shall project more than three feet from the building or street line, except awnings, for which there is a different provision. Porticos, porches, doors, windows, or steps which shall project into the street or sidewalk, so as to obstruct free passage along the same, are, however, forbidden. The ordinances provide that streets, alleys and sidewalks shall be kept free and clear from all obstructions, incumbrances and encroachment for the use of the public, and shall not be used or occupied in any other way than provided for in the odinances. In all this there is room for considerable judgment and discretion.

Structures or projections upon or over the street, that come within the permission of the ordinances, are still subject to the limitation that they do not materially interfere with the public use of the street. For instance, if a sign projecting from a building, not to exceed three feet, should substantially interfere with the public use of the street, it would be unauthorized, and may be abated and removed. Permission to occupy the public streets in such a way is subject to the paramount use of the street by the public and must give way to the necessities of the public use.

Third. The same considerations which govern such projections as signs would govern the use of the three feet of street and of sidewalk next to the building for the storage of goods. Even where that is permitted, or not forbidden, by the ordinances, it is only authorized in cases where it does not seriously obstruct public travel. Where the public use is so interfered with such encroachments should be removed.

As to the obstructions upon the sidewalk by the loading and unloading of merchandise, I beg to say: The primary purpose of the street is for passage and travel. That primary purpose, however, is subject to *reasonable* and *necessary* limitations. The owner or occupant of private property abutting upon the street has, as an incident thereto, the right of access to and egress from the street, and the exercise of such right may, in a measure, temporarily obstruct passage and travel on the street. It has been held in other states that this right of access includes the right of receiving and shipping merchandise. It is not, however, clear, in my opinion, that in a city like ours, where alleys are commonly provided, such right to receive or ship merchandise over the sidewalk exists, as it might be held to exist in cities having no such system of alleys. The right in such case where it exists is *ex necessitate* and is measured by the *necessity*. Where it has been held to be a property right, thus to use the street to the interference with travel, it was held that such obstruction could be justified only when and so far as it was reasonably *necessary*, and that anything which impeded free passage, without necessity was a nuisance. The use of the streets for storage, or for carrying on any other business operations, carried on in the abutting premises, is clearly not an incident to the private ownership of the abutting property. The movement of merchandise over the sidewalk where permitted should be carried on in all cases with dispatch and only when and where it is necessary, and so as to interfere as little as possible with travel. If the street is obstructed by the merchant, because he has not, within his own private premises, the requisite room or conveniences, such obstruction would be unreasonable. The necessity, which justifies such temporary interference with travel, cannot arise from the fact that the premises of the merchant are inadequate for his requirements. Where the obstruction partakes, in any degree, of the character of an appropriation or occupancy of the street for the purpose of a private business, such as a merchant carries on upon the abutting premises, it is without right. He should either enlarge his own premises, or remove to some more convenient place. It is no more legitimate to use the sidewalk for a shipping room than for a store room or office. Of course all of this would depend upon circumstances, and permits of no fixed line that I could lay down. Upon that question judgment and discretion would have to be exercised. It is plain, however, I think, that the greater part of the inconvenience that travelers upon the streets of the city experience from these causes is unjustifiable. If the right or privilege of receiving and shipping goods over the sidewalk is recognized as existing from necessity, I think regard may be had in applying the rule to individual cases, to the character of the street in question, and the amount of travel thereon. For instance, streets which are thoroughfares, streets connecting the different divisions of the city by bridges, over which there is a great deal of travel, would, in my opinion, require a more stringent rule than streets where travel is less frequent. The public necessities might indeed, I think, reasonably require in the case of some streets so stringent a rule that classes of business now carried on there might find it necessary or desirable to remove to other streets.

The same observations may be made as to obstructions to travel upon the roadway of the streets. These roadways are for travel and passage and not for a standing place for drays, wagons, buggies or other vehicles to the prevention or obstruction of travel. Most of the obstruction met with from this cause is unjustifiable and may be abated.

I think in this matter you have, and, in the proper exercise of your official duty may have to exercise, discretion and judgment. From some of these encroachments upon the public streets, the public suffers great, and from others less or little inconvenience. It is not likely that every one can be abated or prevented by you. Some may cause no public inconvenience, and be a plain public benefit. The streets are held in trust for the public use and benefit. You are here seeing that this trust is carried out. To subserve the public use and to best promote the public good therein, is the main purpose, which, under the charter and ordinances, is imposed upon you in this work. Yours truly,

JOHN S. MILLER, Corporation Counsel.

June 23, 1891.

R. M. McClaughrey, Esq., Chief of Police.

Dear Sir—

You inquire whether or not persons who are receiving a pension from the Police Pension Fund may be employed upon the police force and receive pay therefor in addition to their pension, such persons having been retired upon pensions from former service upon said force.

I am of the opinion that your question admits only of a negative answer.

The law upon the subject is found in an act of the General Assembly, approved April 29, 1887. This law provides for two classes of pensions upon said fund: First, those members of the police force who voluntarily retired at or after the age of fifty years, upon the completion of twenty years' service, and,

Second. Those who may be retired by the board on account of physical disability arising from injuries received in the actual discharge of their duties.

Section 3 of said act, relating to the first class, provides:

"Whenever any person, at the time of the taking effect of this act or thereafter, shall have been duly appointed and sworn, and have served for the period of twenty years or more, upon the regularly constituted police force of any such city, village or town of this state, which now is, or hereafter may be, subject to the provisions of this act, said board shall order and direct that such person shall, after becoming fifty years of age, and his service upon such police force shall have ceased, be paid from such fund a yearly pension equal to one-half the amount of the salary attached to the rank which he may have held on said police force for one year next preceding the expiration of said term of twenty years."

Section 4, relating to the second class, provides: "Whenever any person, while serving as a policeman in any such city, village or town, shall become physically disabled while in, and in consequence of, the performance of his duty as such policeman, said board shall, upon his written request, or without such request if it deem it for the good of said police force, retire such person from active service, and order and direct that he be paid from said fund a yearly pension, not exceeding one-half the amount of the salary attached to the rank whicn he may have held on said police force for one year next preceding such retirement; Provided, that whenever such disability shall cease such pension shall cease."

It will thus be seen that Section 3 in express terms relates only to persons whose "service upon such police force shall have ceased." A member of the police force who has served twenty years may or may not retire on a pension upon reaching the age of fifty years, as he sees fit. If he prefers, he may retire and the board must pension him; but he may remain on the force if he prefers, and is physically able, in which case he can have no pension. I am, therefore, of the opinion that it is clearly against the spirit of the law that such a one, having a pension, should be again employed while still drawing his pension.

In regard to the second class of persons, viz., those who have been disabled, the law is more explicit. Section 7 of the act provides: "Any person retired for disability, under this act, may be summoned to appear before the board, herein provided for, at any time thereafter, and shall submit himself thereto for examination as to his fitness for duty, and shall abide the decision and order of said board with reference thereto And all members of the police force who may be retired under the provisions of this act, except those who voluntarily retire after twenty years' service, shall report to the Chief of Police of the city. village or town where so retired on the second Tuesday of each and every month, and, in cases of emergency, may be assigned to and shall perform such duty as said Chief of Police may direct, and such persons shall have no claim against the city, village or town, for payment for such duty so performed."

To employ this class of pensioned persons on the force for pay other than their pension, and except in case of such emergency, would render it impossible for them to comply with the provisions of this section, and would be in direct conflict with the law.

Respectfully submitted,

GEORGE A. DUPUY, Asst. Corporation Counsel.

Approved: JOHN S. MILLER, Corporation Counsel.

July 11, 1891.

J. Frank Aldrich, Esq., Commissioner of Public Works.

Dear Sir—

You ask my opinion as to whether the property owners upon State street, in the south side business district, are entitled to a five-foot space next to the building line, for the exhibition of goods, or for other business purposes.

I do not find that they have any such right. If the buildings are upon the building line, then I do not think that the street space upon that street stands in any different situation than that in other streets, or that the property owners have any other or different rights than the property owners upon other streets. And even if the buildings were set back five feet within the building line, still if that five feet were, by the property owners opened and thrown into the public street without any reservation of private use, then I think such five feet would become a portion of the public street and devoted to the uses of such.

If, on the other hand, the property owners setting back the building within the building line, did, by deed or plat reserve for private use said five feet, then said five feet would be subject to such reserve use. But I have not been able to find any such reservation. I assume that the buildings along the street are upon and not within the building line. That fact, however, could only be determined by survey, which, if there is any question about it, your department can have made.

In my opinion, as I understand the facts and situation of the buildings, the entire space up to the buildings is a portion of the public street, and that the same is subject to the same public rights as are the other streets of the city.

The rights of occupants of premises abutting upon the street to use the three feet next the building line, under what is claimed to be a provision of the ordinances of the city, is involved in the suit of Leah Ritter and others vs. the City of Chicago, which will come up before Judge Tuley upon the application for an injunction as soon as we can get it up, probably the fore part of next week.

Yours truly,

JOHN S. MILLER, Corporation Counsel.

July 13, 1891.

To William R. Kerr, Esq., Member of Committee on Licenses.

Dear Sir—

Your communication of the 2d of July, asking this department for an opinion as to whether the city of Chicago has the power to require and exact licenses from insurance agents, solicitors and brokers, has been duly considered.

Although the question has not been directly decided by the Supreme Court of this state, I am of the opinion that Sections 9 and 10, of Article IX, of the Constitution of 1870, regulating and conferring the taxing power, and clause 91, Section 65, Chapter XXIV, of the Revised Statutes of this state, empowering the city council to license brokers and others, are comprehensive enough to warrant the council in imposing, by ordinance, a license on insurance agents, with a penalty for a violation thereof.

A broker is defined to be one who is engaged for others in negotiating contracts relative to property, with the custody of which they have no concern, or one employed to make contracts relative to property between other persons for compensation.

An insurance agent or solicitor is one who effects a contract of insurance between other persons upon property for a commission, and as such should be, and is, justly known as an insurance broker, and falls within said clause 91, above referred to, which applies to and includes all kinds of brokers. However, there is one restriction to be observed, which applies to all licenses, namely, that the provisions of any ordinance must be uniform and operate alike upon all persons of the same class within the city limits.   Respectfully yours,

ARTHUR H. CHETLAIN, Asst. Corporation Counsel.

August 21, 1891.

Hon. J. Frank Aldrich, Commissioner of Public Works, City.

Dear Sir—

Replying to your communication requesting to know whether the city council could order a stone sidewalk to be placed at the expense of the owner in front of lots where a wooden sidewalk had been recently built, which wooden sidewalk is still in fair condition, I am of the opinion that the same may be done. I am of the further opinion that should the owner refuse or neglect to comply with the ordinance requiring such improvement, the city council might levy a special tax for the cost of such improvement upon such lots, in proportion to their frontage, or otherwise, as the statute permits, and such tax would be valid and could be collected by the sale of the lots. It might be difficult to collect the cost of such improvement by special assessment, as in that case the owner would have the right to have submitted to a jury the question as to whether or not the property would be benefited by the proposed improvement to the extent that it would be assessed; but if the city council should levy a special tax upon the property this question cannot ordinarily arise. It has been many times decided by our Supreme Court that the city council is the sole judge of the necessity and expediency of the improvement to be made by a special tax to be so levied and collected, and that the question as to whether or not the owner will be benefited and the extent of such benefit cannot be submitted to a jury, or in any way called in question in the process of collecting such special tax.

I, therefore, think that the city council may, in its discretion, order and compel a new improvement of the character indicated, notwithstanding the old or former improvement or sidewalk may be in substantially fairly good condition. Respectfully submitted,

GEO. A. DUPUY, Asst. Corporation Counsel.

August 22, 1891.

Hon. J. Frank Aldrich, Commissioner of Public Works, City.

Dear Sir—

Replying to your communication asking whether you may properly refuse a permit for the erection of a boiler shop in a purely residence district, I would say that it is a matter of some doubt whether you may refuse such permit. The general statute laws of the state confer upon city councils the right to locate foundries and to prohibit any offensive business or establishment within the limits of any city. I have no doubt whatever that it would be competent for the city council to declare such boiler shop when located or proposed to be located in a purely residence district a public nuisance, and provide for the abatement thereof; but I don't find that the city council has ever exercised this power, unless by the enactment of Section 1639 (2242) of the Laws and Ordinances of 1890, which provides that any factory, building, or structure of any kind kept, permitted, or suffered to remain for twenty-four hours in such condition as to be offensive to the neighborhood, is declared a public nuisance. It is my opinion that this clause relates more particularly to such kinds of business as rendering, soap factories, etc., which may become offensive and unhealthy by reason of offensive animal and vegetable matter collecting in and about the same. At the same time no reason is perceived why it might not apply to manufacturing establishments that become offensive to the neighborhood in which they are located on account of the excessive amount of noise incident to the carrying on of the business, such as that of boiler making.

Since it seems doubtful whether a proposed boiler factory to be located in a residence district is entitled to a permit, I would suggest that the doubt might properly be resolved in favor of the neighborhood, and that you, under the circumstances, would be warranted in refusing the permit. Respectfully submitted,

GEO. A. DUPUY, Asst. Corporation Counsel.

September 30, 1891.

To J. Frank Aldrich, Esq., Commissioner of Public Works.

Dear Sir—

The mayor has referred the laborers, whose names appear in the notice submitted herewith, to this department to ascertain what rights they have, and whether the city cán afford them relief.

It appears that the laborers in question are common day laborers, and have been working for Lyons & McNichol, who have a contract for laying the sewer between Kedzie avenue and Grant avenue. These men have not been paid for two weeks, and have asked the mayor to intervene in their behalf.

I am of the opinion that under Section 576, of the Municipal Code (Section 1069 of Laws and Ordinances of Chicago, 1890), they are entitled to the relief, and that you may, in your discretion, under Sections 575 and 576, cause notice to be served on Lyons & McNichol that no vouchers or estimates will be issued, or payments made on their contract, until these men have been paid, as provided by the terms of Section 576. If, after the expiration of ten days, they have not been paid, it may be lawful for the city to apply money, due or to become due under the contract, to the payment of the men, and to retain the moneys so paid from the contractor, as provided in said section. I enclose a form of notice.

Respectfully yours,
ARTHUR H. CHETLAIN, Asst. Corporation Counsel.

October 22, 1891.

To the Committee of Public Buildings.

Gentlemen—

In response to your request for my opinion as to the power of the city council, by ordinance, to limit the height of buildings in the city, I beg to say:

In my opinion, the council has such power within the limitations which I shall mention. Among the powers vested by the charter in the council are these:

To prescribe the thickness, strength and manner of constructing stone, brick and other buildings and construction of fire escapes therein;

To pass and enforce all necessary police ordinances;

To declare what shall be a nuisance and to abate the same;

To do all acts and make all regulations which may be necessary or expedient for the promotion of health, or the suppression of disease.

I think the above provisions confer adequate powers in the premises. The above powers are police powers. It is beyond question that the regulation of the use of land, when and as the common good requires, is within the police power. The prevention of wooden buildings within specified limits is one of the common instances of the exercise of police power. While that power is expressly given by the charter of the city it would be included in the general police power granted, if it were not so specifically provided for. This power, however, is not an absolute or arbitrary one, and the validity of its exercise in a particular case depends upon the circumstances calling for it. The owner of private property has a right to a reasonable use only of his property; he can lawfully use it only in such a manner that he will not thereby injure others. He has the right to erect on his own lands whatever kind of buildings or structures he may please, provided he does not, in doing so, threaten or do harm to others. He has no greater right than his neighbor. His neighbor may build upon his land as high as he; and if all the buildings upon the street were of a certain height, and the public health or safety or good was thereby interfered with, it would be in the power of the city council to prohibit the construction of buildings of that height. I think it is beyond question that there is a limit of height beyond which the construction of buildings would plainly interfere with the public good. The city council is, in the first instance, the judge. Within certain limits its judgment would be held conclusive, and would not be interfered with by the courts. But this judgment is subject to review by the courts. If the ordinance was clearly unreasonable it would be invalid. If the limit of the height of buildings fixed were say two stories, it would be plain that an ordinance prohibiting higher buildings would interfere with the right of the property owner to make a reasonable use of his property. If the ordinance declared that to be a nuisance which plainly was not, the ordinance would be invalid. But within the limits of what is reasonable, and in cases whereupon a consideration of all the circumstances the judgment of persons may reasonably differ, the legislative judgment and discretion of the city council would be respected by the courts and held to be final.

The city council may take into consideration all of the circumstances bearing upon the question of the public good. The public upon the streets are entitled to light and pure air, and to travel the streets with safety. It is a matter of public concern that buildings should be safe to the occupants. If the health of the occupants of the buildings or public is affected by the question in hand of the height of the buildings, that may be considered. The question of congestion of travel upon the streets produced by the prevalence of high buildings may be considered. The width of the streets may be considered. And I think that in connection with all the other facts bearing upon the question of the public good, the question of the sightly or unsightly appearance of the city may be taken into consideration. In fact, every circumstance and consideration in connection with the matter affecting the common good may be taken into consideration. And if upon a consideration of them by the city council it should pass an ordinance limiting the height of buildings in the business district of the

city to eight, ten or twelve stories, or to a corresponding number of feet, such ordinance would be valid.   Respectfully submitted,
                JOHN S. MILLER, Corporation Counsel.

                                    December 7, 1891.
To the Honorable, the City Council.
     Gentlemen—
     You ask my opinion as to the power of the city council to pass and enforce an ordinance forbidding pool selling within race track enclosures within the city, and as to the validity of the ordinance on that subject published on page 889 of your proceedings.
     In my opinion the city council has such power.   I think the powers conferred by the charter "To suppress gaming and gambling houses, lotteries, and all fraudulent devices and practices for the purpose of gaming or obtaining money, or property;" "to declare what shall be a nuisance and to abate the same;" and to "pass and enforce all necessary police ordinances," are sufficient for this purpose. And I do not think the pool selling act of 1887 (if it should be held not to be unconstitutional, and whatever its proper construction may be held by the courts to be), limits or affects the power of the city council in the premises.   And in my opinion the pending ordinance in question would, if passed, be valid.
                Truly yours,
                JOHN S. MILLER, Corporation Counsel.

                                    December 8, 1891.
To the Honorable Hempstead Washburne, Mayor.
     Dear Sir—
     . I have been informed that the so-called races at Garfield Park are a mere cover for the main purpose of pool selling and gambling; that the parties in charge are continuing pretended races in the snow and mud.
     I do not think such racing is a meeting of race track associations within the meaning of the pool selling act of 1887. I do not think the proviso of the act in question, which excludes from its prohibition "the enclosure of fair or race track associations that are incorporated under the laws of this state, during the actual time of the meetings of said associations, or within twenty-four hours before any such meeting" was intended to include, as the actual time of meeting, racing continuously during the year, or continuously from one season into another, or pretended meetings where the real purpose is pool selling for the benefit of the association, and not racing, and where the racing in the enclosure is mere incident, shift or cover for the selling of pools; and very clearly does not include sham races in deep snow or mud.   Very truly yours,
                JOHN S. MILLER, Corporation Counsel.

December 21, 1891.

To James R. B. Van Cleave, Esq., City Clerk.
Dear Sir—

In reply to your communication requesting to know whether or not the publication of the ordinances of the city, as passed from time time by the council, in the printed minutes of the proceedings of the council, is a sufficient publication of the same, to meet the requirements of Sections 64 and 65 of Chapter XXIV of the Revised Statutes, I would say:

That I think if the form of the minutes of the meetings of the city council, as heretofore published,was amended by inserting directly after the words "official record" the following, "published by authority of the city council," publication of the ordinances in such minutes would be sufficient publication. Very truly yours,
JOHN S. MILLER, Corporation Counsel.

December 28, 1891.

To the Honorable the City Council of the City of Chicago.
Gentlemen—

In response to your request for my opinion as to the power of the city to compel street railway companies, operating their railway along the streets of the city, to construct proper waiting rooms for the accommodation of passengers, I beg to say that, in my opinion, the city council, in the exercise of the police power conferred by the charter and recognized in the act of March 19, 1874, in regard to horse and dummy railroads, has such power where the public necessity and convenience reasonably call for and justify its exercise. The validity of its exercise would, in a particular case, depend upon the circumstances. The ordinances of the council would be valid only in case it was reasonable. I think the action on the part of the council, if any is taken, should be by ordinance, and not by order of the council.

I am also asked as to the right of such companies to construct such waiting rooms within the area of the street. If they were placed upon streets of sufficient width, and where public travel was not so great that it would be seriously interfered with, I think the council might authorize such structures within the street. But by the act of 1874, above referred to, the company is given the power to acquire by purchase or condemnation, any property for that purpose. I do not think it would be within the power of the council to give up any portion of the street for that purpose in case it would seriously interfere with the convenience of public travel thereon.
Very truly yours,
JOHN S. MILLER, Corporation Counsel.

January 11, 1892.

To the Honorable the City Council of the City of Chicago.

Gentlemen—

In obedience to your order of December 7, 1891, asking for my opinion whether the ordinance passed July 30, 1883, extending the time of operating street railways twenty years, granted to the companies named in said ordinance any special privileges which are not revokable by the city council before the expiration of said twenty years, and whether said ordinance is not within the meaning of Section 14, Article II of the constitution of 1870, I beg to say that my opinion is, that the provision in question in the ordinance of 1883 is not revocable and is not within the section of the constitution referred to.

The section of the constitution referred to provides that "no *ex post facto* law, or law impairing the obligation of contracts, or making any irrevocable grant of special privileges or immunities shall be passed."

The charters of these companies, which were passed prior to the adoption of the constitution of 1870, authorize them to construct and operate their railroad in the city of Chicago, over and along such street or streets as the common council might by contract prescribe. It is settled that such a charter constitutes a contract, which, under the constitution of the United States, cannot be impaired by subsequent state constitutions or legislation.

In the case of Chicago City R. R. Co. vs. People, 73 Ill., 348, the question was involved whether a street railway ordinance passed by the common council after the adoption of the constitution of 1870 was in violation of the provision of that constitution prohibiting special legislation granting any special or exclusive privilege, immunity or franchise; and the Supreme Court held in effect, that the charter of the railway company, and not the ordinance, was the grant; and that an ordinance of the common council, under such charter of the railway, authorizing the company to lay down and operate its railroad on prescribed streets, was not such a grant of special privileges as the constitution referred to. The court said:

"It is a misconception of the law to suppose the railway company derives any power to construct a railroad from any ordinance of the city. All its authority is from the state, and is conferred by its charter. The city has delegated to it the power to say in what manner and on what conditions the company may exercise the franchises conferred by the state, but nothing more. The authority of the city in this regard is not affected by the provisions of the constitution which inhibit the granting by the General Assembly of any special or exclusive privilege, immunity or franchise. Whether it is in the power of the state to revoke that authority is a question that does not arise for decision, and upon which we refrain from expressing any opinion. It is sufficient it has not been done by any provision of the constitution, nor by any general law enacted by the legislature."

This case was decided by a divided court. But it should control my opinion so long as it stands not overruled.

It holds in effect that the part which, under the charters by these companies, the city council takes, in respect to the granting of the privilege of operating the street railway in the streets of the city, is, not the granting of the privilege, but only the power to say in what manner and upon what condition the company may exercise the privilege granted by the charter. I think under that decision, the provision in the ordinance of July 30, 1883, extending the times limited for the operation of such railroads, is not a law making a grant of special privileges within the meaning of the constitution.

Truly yours,
JOHN S. MILLER, Corporation Counsel.

June 4, 1892.

James R. B. Van Cleave, Esq., City Clerk.

Dear Sir—

Your communication has been received, asking for an opinion as to the powers of the council to hear and determine contests of election of aldermen; the right of the committee to summon and compel the attendance of witnesses, and for instructions as to the mode of procedure to be followed in the contested cases of election now pending before the court.

Section 34 of Chapter XXIV, Hurds, Rev. Stats. 1891.

Sec. 35, Laws and Ordinances, 1890 provides that: "The City Council shall be judge of the election and qualification of its own members."

Under the above section it has been held by the Supreme Court of this state, in several well considered cases, that the city council has *exclusive* jurisdiction of contests of election of aldermen.

Keating vs. Stack, 116 Ill., 191.

Winter vs. Thistlewood, 101 Ill., 450.

Jennings vs. Joyce, 116, Ill., 179.

Linegar vs. Rittenhouse, 94 Ill., 208.

The Supreme Court of California, under a similar grant, has held that the council of municipalities has exclusive authority to pass upon such contests.

People vs. Metzker, 47 Cal., 524.

And such is the construction put upon the law by the council, as evidenced by Section 1776, Laws and Ordinances of 1890, which is as follows:

"1776. The City Council shall be the tribunal before which such contests shall be heard, and their decision shall be final."

Since the last decision of the supreme court, *Ketaing vs. Stack, supra,* two election laws have been passed by the legislature—one entitled "An act regulating the holding of elections and the canvassing the result thereof in cities, villages and incorporated towns in this state," approved June 19, 1895, in force July 1, 1895, which created the Board of Election Commissioners, gave them the charge of the registration and conduct of all municipal and other elections, established a canvassing board and provided for the canvassing of votes; the other entitled, "An act to provide for the printing and distribution of ballots at the public expense and for the nomination of candidates for public offices, and to regulate the manner of holding elections and to enforce the secrecy of the ballot," approved June 22, 1891, in force july 1, 1891, commonly known as the "Australian Ballot Law."

Hurd's Rev. Stats., 1891, Chap. XLVIII, Secs. 155 to 287.

Hurd's Rev. Stats., 1891, Chap. XLVI, Secs. 288 to 324.

I am of the opinion that none of the provisions of these acts can be construed to change the law affecting election contests of aldermen, as announced above, and one provision in Section 314 reads as follows:

"In all cases of contested elections the parties contesting the same shall have the right to have said ballots opened and to have all errors of the judges in counting or refusing any ballot corrected by the court or body trying such contests; but such ballots shall be opened only in open court or in open session of such body, and in the presence of the officer having the custody thereof," which would seem by the term "body" to contemplate a hearing of the contest by the council.

It being shown that the council has the power to hear contests of election of its members, the question arises as to the extent of its powers and how the proceedings shall be conducted. The provisions of the statute above referred to relating to contests of election and especially by Sections 112 to 124, of Chapter XLVI, Hurd's Revised Statutes, were evidently not intended to authorize a review of the action of the board of canvassers, but to show that the proceedings are so prescribed for the purpose of permitting the proper court or body hearing the contest to go behind the returns, inquire into all the facts, decide how many votes were legally cast for the different candidates, and ascertained who was elected. Such in effect is the decision in—

County of Lawrence vs. Schmaulhausen, 123 Ill., 321.

State vs. Rahway, 33 N. J. L., 111.

Touching the manner of conducting election contests, Section 57, Chapter XXIV, Hurd's Revised Statutes, 1891 (Section 60, Laws and Ordinances of 1890), provides as follows:

"The manner of conducting and voting at elections to be held under this act and contesting the same, the keeping of poll lists and canvassing the votes shall be the same, as nearly as may be, as in the case of the election of county officers under the general laws of this state." (The laws referred to herein being Sections 94 to 124, Chapter XLVI, Hurd's Revised Statutes, 1891.)

The jurisdiction as to the mode of trial and the whole contest is purely statutory, and is governed by the rules of chancery practice.

The same evidence is admitted and like principles control as in chancery cases.

McKinnon vs. People, 110 Ill., 306.
Kingery vs. Berry, 94 Ill., 518.
Dale vs. Irwin, 78 Ill., 171.
Tallington vs. Turner, 71 Ill., 234.
County of Lawrence vs. Schmaulhausen, 123 Ill., 321, with such changes as may be necessary to apply to the council or body which tries the same, as in the present cases.

Linegar vs. Rittenhouse, 94 Ill., 211.

The council under the powers conferred upon it by clause 96, Section 65, Laws and Ordinances of 1890 (Clause 96, Section 62, Chapter XXIV, Hurd's Revised Statutes, 1891), and Section 35 of Laws and Ordinances, 1890 (Section 35, Chapter XXIV, Hurd's Revised Statutes, 1891), and by virtue of the inherent implied power to pass such ordinances as are necessary to carry into effect the powers conferred and to determine its own proceedings, have passed ordinances which regulate the mode and prescribe the manner in which contests before the council shall be conducted.

Sections 1775 to 1784, inclusive, Laws and Ordinances of 1890.

These provisions of the ordinances, so far as the contests in question are concerned, although not altogether in harmony, are not materially inconsistent with the provisions of the statutes and they may be followed and are sufficient to justify the action of the council under them.

It is not necessary that the witnesses shall appear before the council so that the evidence shall be taken or proofs be presented to it, in the first instance. While it is the duty of the council and it has the power to determine contests, and that duty and power cannot be delegated, it is nevertheless competent for the council, should it deem it advisable, to refer the matter to an appropriate committee to take the testimony and report their conclusions and submit the testimony to the council for its adjudication. If, therefore, the council should not desire to follow the method of procedure provided by Section 1775 to 1785, Laws and Ordinances of 1890, it may by ordinance, resolution or order refer the matter of taking testimony to the committee on elections or other appropriate committee with instructions to take testimony, report their conclusions, and submit and return the same with all the evidence in the cases, to the council for determination. Such is the well-known course of proceeding of every legislative body having power to judge of the election of its own members in cases of election contests.

Salmon vs. Haynes, 50 N. J. L., 100.

The council has the power to compel the attendance of witnesses and their answer to all proper questions; also the production of all papers and proper proofs, and punish witnesses for contempt for refusing to comply. This is a power inherent in all legislative bodies

12

and is necessary for their preservation, but it should be exercised only in matters clearly within the jurisdiction of such bodies. This can be done in the same manner and by the use of the same means that courts of justice use in like cases.

Kilburn vs. Thompson, 103 U. S., 168.

If the council shall deem it advisable to proceed in the manner provided by the ordinances now in force, relating to contested elections, cited above, testimony may be taken before any judge, justice of the peace, master in chancery or notary public, at the time and place fixed by the council, and should witnesses refuse to testify the officers taking such depositions can certify the facts to the council, where the witnesses may upon proper notice be dealt with for contempt or they may possibly be proceeded against under Section 108, Chapter XLVI, Hurd's Revised Statutes of 1891, which gives the officer taking testimony the power to compel the production of papers and attendance of witnesses, and provides for enforcing obedience to the orders of such officer as provided in cases of taking depositions, to be used in courts of law and equity. If, however, the council should see fit to refer the taking of testimony to a committee, such committee can compel the attendance of witnesses and the production of papers and answers to all proper questions, and in the event of the refusal of witnesses to comply, the committee can certify the facts constituting the disobedience to the council, where recalcitrant witnesses may, upon notice, be dealt with for such contempt. From what precedes, it follows that the council has itself the right to have the witnesses appear before it, the testimony taken and the case tried in open session.   Respectfully submitted,

ARTHUR H. CHETLAIN, Assistant Corporation Counsel.

June, 1892.

To the Joint Committee on Judiciary and Streets and Alleys, North.

Gentlemen—

In answer to your inquiry as to whether or not the city council has the power to pass an ordinance providing for cleaning and sprinkling streets by special assessment, I beg to say that, in my judgment, the city council has such power.

The councils of cities have no power to impose taxes or assessments, except such as are directly or by necessary implication conferred upon them, either by constitution or by act of the legislature.

Section 9 of Article IX of the constitution provides that "the General Assembly may vest the corporate authorities of cities, towns and villages with power to make local improvements by special assessment."

Accordingly the legislature provided (Section 1, Article IX, of the general act for the incorporation of cities, etc.) that "the corporate authorities of cities and villages are hereby vested with power to make local improvement by special assessment." The whole question is, therefore, involved in the inquiry as to what is meant by *"local improvement,"* within the meaning of the foregoing legislation.

An improvement is defined in Bouvier's Law Dictionary to be "an amelioration in the condition of real or personal property effected by the expenditure of labor or money for the purpose of rendering it useful for other purposes than those for which it was originally used, or more useful for the same purposes." Anderson's Law Dictionary—"Amelioration in the condition of property by the outlay of labor or money."

The word "property" may mean the *corpus* of things personal or real, or it may have the meaning given it by our Supreme Court in the case of Rigney vs, The City of Chicago, where it was said: "Property in its appropriate sense means that dominion or indefinite right of user and disposition which one may lawfully exercise over particular things." Thus in one sense land is property; in another sense the land is not the property, but its susceptibility and fitness to be put to certain uses advantageous to the owner is the property. Every one knows that the property interest of the owner in land is not measured by acres or feet, but by its susceptibility to uses and purposes advantageous to him."

If, therefore, special assessments may be levied for "local improvements" and an improvement is an "amelioration in the condition of property," that is to say, an enhancement of its susceptibility to be devoted to useful and beneficial purposes, it would seem to follow that the cost of such enhancement might be raised by special assessment. To have the streets adjacent to property clean and wholesome and free of dust and dirt, would surely ameliorate its condition and increase its fitness for almost any use to which it might be put.

The question above considered has not, so far as I have been able to find by considerable inquiry, been passed upon by the courts, and many lawyers hold views contrary to those above expressed. It must indeed be admitted that the question is not free from doubt, but upon the whole I am of the opinion that the power of the city to levy such assessment would be sustained by the courts.

Respectfully submitted,
GEORGE A. DUPUY, Asst. Corporation Counsel.

August 3, 1892.

R. W. McClaughrey, Superintendent of Police.
Dear Sir—

In reply to inquiry as to whether persons who are not registered can be considered "legal voters," within the meaning of the ordinances, which, in some localities, require a petition signed by certain proportion of the "legal voters" of the town or district to accompany an application for a saloon license, I quote the provision of the constitution of this state (Art. VII, Sec. 1), which prescribes the qualification of voters, to wit:

"Every person having resided in this state one year, in the county ninety days, and in the election district thirty days next preceding any election therein, who shall be a male citizen of the United States above the age of twenty-one years, shall be entitled to vote at such election."

Registration, required by the election law, is not a qualification; it is merely the way provided by law to ascertain and determine whether a man has the necessary qualifications.

If a citizen of the United States has lived in this state one year, in the county three months and in the election district thirty days, he has the right of suffrage, which he may or may not exercise at will. *Although not registered*, he possesses the qualifications of a "legal voter." While I am aware that a contrary rule would be highly desirable, and that an inspection of the registration would be a quick, safe and practicable way to determine the question, the words *"legal voter"* have a well-defined meaning in law which should not be departed from, and which the applicant has the right to insist should be respected. The question in each case is: Did the signers of the petition possess the necessary qualifications of *legal voters* on the day of the presentation of the petition?

In determining *who are "legal voters,"* the registry list cannot be depended upon, for there are deaths and removals from the election districts. The only way to determine who the "legal voters" in a given district are is to canvass the district to verify the registry list and the signatures of the petition. Where the officers of your department do not find the names on the registry list, which are signed to the petition, the applicant should be required to furnish satisfactory evidence by affidavit of the alleged voter, or affidavits of one or more householders who are acquainted with such voter, or both, as to his qualifications, or, if demanded, the petitioner should also compel the personal attendance of the person whose vote is questioned for examination as to his qualifications.

Very respectfully,
ARTHUR H. CHETLAIN, Asst. Corporation Counsel

April 29, 1893.

Frank X. Brandecker, Esq., City Collector.

Dear Sir—

In response to your inquiry as to what the rights of the city are in relation to demanding that the owners of boats plying between Van Buren street and the grounds of the World's Columbian Exposition, on which liquors are sold, to take out a license from the city for the sale of such liquors, I beg to say:

That in my opinion the city may properly require such persons to take out a license from the city for the sale of liquors upon such boats. The boundary of the state of Illinois extends eastward to the center of Lake Michigan (Article I, constitution of 1870).

The boundary of Cook county extends eastward to the center of Lake Michigan (Séction 3, Chapter XXXIV, Hurd's Revised Statutes). The jurisdiction of the city of Chicago extends eastward three miles from the shore of the lake (Section 71, Chapter XXIV, Hurd's Revised Statutes). The laws of the state absolutely prohibit the sale of intoxicating liquors at retail without a license.

It, therefore, clearly follows that the only source from which a license could be received by the owners of these boats is the city of Chicago, or the county of Cook, but the laws of the state prohibit the issuing of any license by the county authorities for the sale of liquor within two miles of the incorporated city or village.

The ordinances of Hyde Park prohibit the sale of liquors between 39th and 54th streets east of Cottage Grove Avenue (see Section 150 of the Municipal Code of Hyde Park, 1887).

These ordinances are still in full force and effect, notwithstanding annexation (see Section 228, Chapter XXIV, Hurd's Revised Statutes).

If the ordinances of the city of Chicago apply on the water east of that part of the city north of 39th Street, as I think they do, then it may be a question whether the provisions of the Hyde Park prohibition ordinance do not apply on the waters of Lake Michigan lying east of the shore between 39th and 54th Streets extended.

On the whole, I am of the opinion that the owners of these boats clearly have no right to sell liquors without a license, and that the city may issue licenses for the sale of liquors at the Van Buren Street landing and on these boats plying between that point and the World's Columbian Exposition grounds, but that such licenses should, however, state that nothing therein contained is to authorize any sales of liquor forbidden by any laws or ordinances of Hyde Park.   Respectfully submitted,

     GEORGE A. DUPUY, Asst. Corporation Counsel.
  Approved:
ADOLPH KRAUS, Corporation Counsel.

                                        May 16, 1893.
To the Honorable Judiciary Committee.
  Gentlemen—
     In response to your request for an opinion as to the legal authority of the city council to authorize the construction of public urinals in the streets and alleys of the city, I beg to say:

     That in my opinion the city council has such authority. The 9th clause of Section 1, Article V, of the incorporation act of cities and villages authorizes the city council to "regulate the use of" streets and alleys. It is the universal rule that the proper and legitimate use of streets and alleys includes the laying of pipes, conduits, sewers and many other things therein below the surface, as well as the erection of lamp posts, telegraph and telephone poles, fire hydrants and other erections that in a limited measure obstruct the surface of the streets and necessarily interfere, to a limited extent, with the ordinary uses of streets and alleys as highways. All such uses must, however, be public uses, and primarily beneficial to the public, although private individuals or corporations may receive financial, profit from such use.

I am, therefore, of the opinion that a public urinal of limited size and so constructed as not to materially interfere with the use of streets and alleys for highway purposes, would, when authorized by the city council, be a legal structure. I am inclined to think that the courts would find no difficulty in sustaining an use, in a case where like this the advantage derived would be wholly to the public with no element of private or individual profit or financial advantage involved.

Respectfully submitted,
ADOLPH KRAUS, Corporation Counsel.

May 22, 1893.

Oscar D. Wetherell, Esq., City Comptroller.

Dear Sir—

I have carefully considered the questions submitted by you to this department as to whether the ordinance passed on· May 2, 1893, providing for the issue of new bonds of the city of Chicago to the amount of five hundred thousand dollars to retire a like amount of river improvement bonds, is obnoxious to the requirement of the Constitution and of the City Charter, which prescribes that a municipal corporation shall, before or at the time of incurring an indebtedness, provide for the collection of a direct annual tax sufficient to pay the interest on such debt as it falls due, and also to pay and discharge the principal thereof within twenty years from the time of contracting the same.

From an examination of the law I am of the opinion that the constitutional provision above mentioned does not prescribe a condition precedent to the validity of the ordinance or to the validity of the bonds which may be issued in accordance with said ordinance. The Supreme Court of Illinois, in the case of City of East St. Louis vs. People, 124 Ill. 655, declared the constitutional provision under consideration to be self-executing, which means that said provision "supplies a sufficient rule by means of which the right given might be enjoyed and protected, or the duties imposed may be enforced" (Cooley's Constitutional Limitations, 5th Ed., page 100).

The Supreme Court in said case further declared that pursuant to said constitutional provision every debt incurred by municipal corporations under authority of law carries with it "the constitutional obligation of a municipality to levy and collect all the necessary taxes required for its payment." Following out this principle the Supreme Court in said case affirmed the decision of the lower court granting a writ of mandamus against the city of East St. Louis, compelling it to levy a tax for the payment of judgment recovered upon a bond of said city.

It seems to me that even if no ordinance should be passed by the city of Chicago, providing for the collection of a tax to pay the interest on the bonds in question and the principal when it becomes due, such failure would not in the least affect the validity of the bonds. And that the holders of those bonds could by mandamus proceedings compel the city of Chicago to levy such a tax if the interest or principal were not paid.

I may say, however, that in my opinion no indebtedness is created at the time of the passage of the ordinance; the ordinance simply provides for the incurring of indebtedness. The indebtedness is incurred at the time when the bonds are issued. The ordinance in question provides that the bonds are to bear date July 1, 1893, and there is ample time between now and July 1 to provide for the collection of a direct annual tax such as is required by the constitutional provision above mentioned.

As regards your question as to the proper publication of the ordinance in question I find that Section 67 of the Laws and Ordinances of the City of Chicago, as revised and in force April 2, 1890, provides as follows:

"All ordinances of cities and villages imposing any fine, penalty, imprisonment or forfeiture, or making any appropriation, shall, within one month after they are passed, be published at least once in a newspaper published in the city or village, or, if no such newspaper is published therein, by posting copies of the same in three public places in the city or village; and no such ordinance shall take effect until ten days after it is so published. And all other ordinances, orders and resolutions shall take effect from and after their passage unless otherwise provided therein."

As the ordinance in question does not impose a fine, penalty, imprisonment or forfeiture, and is not one making an appropriation, and inasmuch as said ordinance does not otherwise provide, it took effect from and after its passage. Respectfully submitted,

SIGMUND ZEISLER, Asst. Corporation Counsel.

May 22, 1893.

To the Commissioner of Public Works.

Sir—

I have your communication of May 20th, in which you submit certain questions, as follows:

1. Has the city council power and authority to stay proceedings for a public improvement, after the contract for such improvement is duly executed?

2. If such stay is ordered, is the city liable to the contractor for damages?

3. In case the city council orders such stay of proceedings with-

out making provision for damages, if any, what course should be pursued?

I am not sure whether the orders of the council to which you refer are orders directing the suspension of work upon improvement, or are directions to suspend proceedings in court for the confirmation and collection of the assessment.

If the latter, the city, as a party litigant, can take such orders in court for the continuance, postponement or stay of such proceedings, as the court will sanction, and in this modified sense may suspend the legal proceedings for a definite period.

So far as the right of the city council or the city to suspend a public work, after a contract therefor has been duly executed is concerned, this depends, of course, upon the terms of the contract; the city, as a contracting party, being bound to the same extent as an individual could be.

I have before me a blank form of contract used by your department in cases where the contract price is to be paid only out of a particular special assessment, and will assume that such a contract has been executed in the cases to which you refer.

This contract provides that the work shall be commenced on or before a specified date and be fully completed on or before a certain other specified date; the time of commencement, rate of progress, and time of completion of the work being declared to be essential conditions of the contract.

Under this contract it is the right of the contractor to proceed to its execution so as to perform within the time limited, and to have the moneys for which to pay him collected without injurious delay.

The effect of any action of the city which should place it out of the power of the contractor to proceed with the work for a fixed period, such as one year, or which should deprive the city of the power to collect the money due him for such a long and fixed period, would undoubtedly release the contractor and his sureties from all obligations under the contract, and might be treated by him as a rescission thereof.

The contractor being ready and willing and offering to perform the contract on his part, might treat it as still subsisting and recover damages from the city for its breach; what the measure of such damages would be depends upon the particular circumstances of each case.

I am informed that my predecessors in this department have uniformly advised the commissioner of public works that he could not safely obey the orders of the council directing a suspension of public work after the contract thereof has been duly executed. I concur in this view, and suggest that in such cases you should call the attention of the mayor and through him the city council to the legal liability of the city for damages if the order is carried into effect, so that it may be deliberately decided by the proper authority whether under all the circumstances such liability ought to be incurred.

JOHN MAYO PALMER, Asst. Corporation Counsel.

May 24, 1893.

To His Honor, the Mayor—

By your direction I have carefully investigated the following questions:

1. Whether that branch of the city government established by the ordinance of March 13, 1893, and to which is entrusted the general duty of cleaning the streets and alleys of the city, is an independent executive department, or is a mere bureau or division of the department of public works.

2. Whether the superintendent of street and alley cleaning can let a contract for any public work, where the expense thereof exceeds the sum of $500, otherwise than to the lowest responsible bidder, after inviting public competition.

OPINION.

The first question is no doubt suggested to you by the peculiar and apparently conflicting language of the ordinance under consideration, which in some of its sections refers to this branch of the government as a "department," and in other sections describes it as a 'division' or "bureau" of the department of public works.

The title of the ordinance is, "To establish a division of the department of public works," and the effective words which create it, and give it a legal name, describe it as a division of the department of public works, to be known and designated as "The Bureau of Street and Alley Cleaning."

The language creating the office of superintendent of street and alley cleaning, is that usually adopted in creating offices within recognized executive departments.

In all the instances in which the word "department" is used, it appears by the context that reference is made to the branch of government created by the first section of the ordinance, and no purpose is shown to vary its legal destination.

The language defining the powers of this officer is no broader than that generally used in conferring special and exclusive duties upon officers, in other executive departments.

Every officer whose powers and duties are specifically defined by ordinances, must be held to have adequate authority, and as responsible for the discharge of those duties; but when his office is attached to, or made part of an executive department, he is subject to such supervision of the head of that department as is not expressly excluded by the ordinance specially defining his powers.

I am of the opinion that the branch of the government created by the ordinance referred to is properly a division or bureau of the department of public works.

Upon the second question there is, in my opinion, no difficulty whatever. By Section 8 of the ordinance under consideration the provision of the statute requiring competitive bids for all public work, is repeated in express terms; and although it is certain that no ordinance, whether passed unanimously or otherwise, could dispense with the statute, or otherwise any contract involving the expenditure of over $500.00, without the requisite two-thirds vote of the council upon such particular contract, no such action is attempted by this ordinance.

It is, therefore, quite clear that the superintendent of street and alley cleaning can make no contract for work in charge of his bureau which would cost over $500.00, without competitive bids as required by law, and no contract made by him under such circumstances, unless all of its terms had been previously approved by a two-thirds vote of all the members elected to the city council, would be in any manner binding upon the city.

JOHN MAYO PALMER, Asst. Corporation Counsel.
Approved:
ADOLPH KRAUS, Corporation Counsel.

June 29, 1893.

O. D. Wetherell, Esq., City Comptroller.

Dear Sir—

The opinion of this department is asked upon the question of the right of the Washingtonian Home to compel the city of Chicago to pay that institution $20,000 per annum, in accordance with an act of the legislature passed June 29th, 1883. The city of Chicago is a corporation under the general laws of the state, and its powers, as a municipal corporation, are such as are conferred upon the city by the legislature. Among these powers are the power "to appropriate money for corporate purposes only, and to provide for payment of debts and expenses of the corporation; to fix the amount, terms, and manner of issuing and revoking licenses; to license, regulate and prohibit the selling or giving away of any intoxicant, malt and vinous or other liquor."

The power to license or sell intoxicating liquors is conferred by the legislature upon the city of Chicago and the city exercises this power both for the purpose of police protection and for the purpose of obtaining revenue for the public needs of the city. The city charter gives these powers to the city of Chicago without making any reservations in the charter as to what is to be done with the moneys thus obtained, except that it is "to appropriate money for corporate purposes only, and to provide for payment of debts and expenses of the corporation."

The Washingtonian Home was incorporated by special act of the legislature, approved February 16, 1867. This act gives this institution in general terms the right to build and operate a home for the care, cure and reformation of inebriates, also conferring upon them the power necessary to carry out the provisions of their charter. The act also provides that, "it shall be the duty of the Treasurer of the County of Cook and the Treasurer of the City of Chicago, or of the officers of either into whose hands the same may come or be paid, to pay over to said corporation in quarterly installments, for the support and maintenance of said institution, ten per cent. of all moneys received from all licenses granted by said county or city for the right or privilege to vend or sell spirituous, vinous or fermented liquors within the County of Cook or City of Chicago."

This charter creates a corporation known as the Washingtonian Home of Chicago, which is purely and solely a private corporation. Whatever may be the object of those connected with the institution, or whatever may be the result of the work of this institution so far as the law is concerned, it is purely a private corporation, and has substantially no different standing than that of any other corporation organized for pecuniary profit. Since the passage of this act of the legislature, creating this corporation, an act was passed which limited the amount to be paid to this institution to $20,000 per annum, this amount has been paid to and received by the Washingtonian Home in lieu of the amount that was originally fixed by the terms of their charter.

I am of the opinion that the legislature has not the power to direct that the funds of the city of Chicago, either raised by general taxation or by license, shall be paid to a private corporation, or shall be expended in any way except for public purposes. If the legislature has the right to direct that a certain amount of funds shall be paid to the Washingtonian Home, they have the same right to direct that funds should be paid to any other private corporation or institution. Whatever may be the object of this institution, or whether the funds are wisely appropriated or not, is a matter of no consequence. There are, no doubt, very many worthy institutions in the city of Chicago that are incorporated and managed purely for philanthropic purposes, and if the legislature had the power to divert the public funds, there is no reason why all the money collected in this manner might not be paid out to these various institutions, provided the legislature supposed them sufficiently worthy and important. This is not, in the meaning of the law, a public institution· it is purely a private corporation, and I am of the opinion that the city of Chicago cannot be compelled to contribute to its support.

Respectfully submitted,

C. S. DARROW. Asst. Corporation Counsel.

Approved:

ADOLPH KRAUS, Corporation Counsel.

July 15, 1893.

O. D. Wetherell, Esq., City Comptroller.

Dear Sir—

I have examined the question submitted by you to the corporation counsel, whether the city of Chicago should, out of its general fund, pay vouchers for work done under special assessments by the village of Rogers Park, where the installment of the assessment for which the voucher issued has been collected, but where the money thus collected has been illegally used by the village treasurer for the payment of a voucher issued for a later installment, which has not yet been collected.

That such action by the village treasurer, as supposed in your question, is clearly illegal and constitutes an unauthorized payment by the treasurer, clearly appears from Section 193 of Myers' Laws and Ordinances of 1890. If in making such unauthorized payment the treasurer can be considered to have acted as an agent of the city, acting within the lines of his duties, then the city would be liable to the holder of the voucher for the misapplication by the treasurer of the money collected for its payment.

From an examination of the law I am of the opinion that in the collection and disbursement of special assessments a city or village treasurer does not act as the agent of the city, and that, therefore, the remedy of the holder of the voucher is a suit against the treasurer and his sureties upon his official bond, and not against the municipal corporation. If, however, the city is not liable to the holder of the voucher, then there is no justification for the city paying the voucher out of its general fund.

Article VII, Section 12 of the city charter, provides: "All moneys received on any special assessment shall be held by the treasurer as a special fund to be applied to the payment of the improvement for which the assessment was made, and said money shall be used for no other purpose whatever, unless to reimburse such corporation for money expended for such improvement."

It will be seen that the section just quoted charges the city treasurer with the duty to properly apply special assessment moneys collected by him. This, of course, means that the treasurer must follow the law in disbursing the special assessment funds. If he uses money collected by virtue of one special assessment to the payment of a voucher for work done under another special assessment, or if he uses money collected on one installment to pay a voucher for a different installment, he simply diverts the moneys in question from uses to which the law directs him to put the same, just the same as if he embezzled that money.

Money collected by the city treasurer on any particular installment of a special assessment is a trust fund in his hands for the payment of the voucher issued for that installment. For a misapplication of that fund, as well as an embezzlement of the same, the treasurer is liable to the holder of the voucher.

The law expressly provides that the holder of the voucher shall have no claim or lien upon the city except from the collection of the installment for which it is issued. The city is powerless to pay the voucher except from the collection of the particular installment. If the treasurer misapplies or embezzles this special fund he cannot be regarded as acting as the agent of the city.

Suppose the city council or village trustees should expressly order the city treasurer to apply moneys collected upon one installment for the payment of a voucher for another installment, or for the payment of a voucher on an entirely different assessment. Would the treasurer be obliged to obey such order? Could he lawfully obey it? Could he, if he carried it out, shield himself behind the order of the corporation? Certainly not, because such an order made by the corporation would be absolutely illegal and void. In other words, even if the council made such an order, the treasurer, if he carried it out, could not claim to act as the agent of the corporation, because there can be no agency in an action which involves a clear violation of the law and because the treasurer is under no obligation to carry out any illegal order of the council. How, then, can the treasurer be regarded as the agent of the corporation, if he does the illegal act without any order or authority from the council?

"A municipal corporation is not liable for the misfeasance or non-performance of one of its officers in respect to the duty imposed on such officer."

Lorillard vs. Monroe, 11 N. Y., 396.

The general rule is that a municipal corporation is not responsible for acts of its officers which are unauthorized or unlawful.

Mitchell vs. Rockland, 41 Me., 368.

Where a tax collector embezzles an amount of money paid to him under an illegal tax no action can be maintained against the town, the town not being liable for his misfeasance.

Bank vs. Mayor of New York, 43 N. Y., 189-190.

Moneys collected by the city treasurer on special assessments are not in any sense of the word a part of the revenue of the city. They cannot be used for the purpose of defraying the expense of the city government. They are held by the treasurer for the specific purpose of paying the vouchers drawn for the work. Therefore, the position of the treasurer in respect to special assessment funds seems to me analogous to that of a town collector towards the city. As regards the latter, the Appellate Court of this state holds: "The position which a collector occupies in respect to moneys collected by him for city taxes is that of a mere trustee, and in no proper sense that of an agent of the city."

Chicago vs. Fidelity Bank, 11 Brad., 169.

"Where a warrant or order, payable from a specific appropriation, of a tax levied but not yet collected, is accepted in exchange for services rendered or to be rendered, or for materials furnished or to be furnished, so that there is, in fact, but the exchange of one thing for another, the duty remains for the proper officers to collect and pay over the tax in accordance with the appropriation—but, obviously, for any failure in that regard the remedy must be against the officer and not against the corporation, for, otherwise, a contingent debt would, in this way, be incurred by the corporation."

Springfield vs. Edwards, 84 Ill., 633.

A municipal corporation cannot be held liable for the acts of its officers and agents which are wholly ultra vires and beyond the power of the corporation to perform, nor for the illegal or unlawful acts of its officers, though done colore officii, unless they were previously authorized or subsequently ratified.

19 Am. and Engl. Encyl. of Law, 559.

My conclusion, therefore, is that the city should not pay the vouchers in question out of the general fund. The owners of the vouchers can either sue the late treasurer of Rogers Park upon his bond, or they will have to wait until the installments, the vouchers for which the treasurer has illegally paid, are collected, so as to provide moneys with which to reimburse the funds which the treasurer has illegally applied. Very truly yours,

SIGMUND ZEISLER, Asst. Corporation Counsel.

Approved:

ADOLPH KRAUS, Corporation Counsel.

July 14, 1893.

Hon. James R. Mann, Chairman Judiciary Committee:

Dear Sir—

I have examined the law recently passed for the division of special assessments and the issuing of bonds in anticipation of collection of deferred installments.

I have also examined the draft of an ordinance providing for the issuance of bonds submitted by you to the corporation counsel.

It appears to me that while the law contemplates the passing of an ordinance covering special assessments heretofore levied but upon which the collection has not commenced, it does not contemplate the passing of an ordinance providing in advance that bonds shall be issued in all cases of special asesssments at any time in the future to be levied.

I believe that the passage of an ordinance once for all fixing upon a bond issue for all the future special assessments is neither within the contemplation of the statute nor advisable. Cases may arise in which the city might find it more convenient to follow the course heretofore observed in the payment of contractors, in which case the city would be hampered by such a general ordinance as that submitted.

I believe that the law contemplates that from time to time as special assessments will be levied, the ordinance shall fix the number of installments and shall, if it is deemed advisable in that particular case, provide for an issue of bonds pursuant to the provisions of the act in question.

It seems to me, however, proper that an ordinance should be passed prescribing which officers of the city shall sign improvement bonds when issued.

The draft of the ordinance as submitted contains a number of provisions which seem to be superfluous, inasmuch as they are mere repetitions of what the act in question clearly provides.

I cannot pass upon the question as to whether it is desirable that an ordinance be passed providing for the issuance of improvement bonds in all cases of special assessments heretofore levied upon which collection has not commenced, because I am not sufficiently familiar with the details and nature of all such pending assessments. In the event, however, that your committee may think the passage of such ordinance advisable, I herewith submit a draft of such a one.

I also submit to you a draft of an ordinance containing provisions as to the manner and method of the execution of improvement bonds whenever their issuance should be ordered in the future.

Respectfully yours,
SIGMUND ZEISLER, Asst. Corporation Counsel.

Aug. 4, 1893.

To the Commissioner of Health:

Sir—

In response to your communication of recent date I submit the following:

The questions asked by you are, whether under what is known as "the sweat shop law" the prohibition against the employment of children under the age of fourteen years, and the employment of females for more than eight hours a day, or forty-eight hours in a week, applies to all places where any *goods or products* are manufactured, repaired, cleaned or sorted in whole or in part, for sale or for wages; or applies only to places where the articles mentioned in the first section of the act are made or repaired.

If a construction of this statute in those particulars is necessary to enable you to properly discharge your official duties, I am bound to give you my opinion upon these questions; otherwise I must decline to do so.

From a very careful examination of the act referred to me, it seems to me that all the duties and powers conferred upon the Board of Health by its terms are wholly disconnected with the provisions relating to child or female labor, the enforcement of those provisions being apparently vested in the state inspectors appointed under the act.

By Section 1 the Board of Health is entitled to notice of the location, the nature of the work carried on, and the number of persons employed in workshops of the particular kind described therein.

Under Section 2 the Board of Health is authorized to investigate workshops with a view of ascertaining the existence of infection and contagion, and to destroy infectious and contagious articles. By Section 3 the Board of Health is authorized under certain circumstances to destroy certain specifically enumerated articles which are being transported into the state, and Section 7, the Board of Health, or any of its officers, are authorized to inspect the list workshops of a particular kind and possibly to inspect such workshops.

In the sections relating to child labor and the employment of females, which are Sections 4, 5 and 6 of the act, no reference whatever is made to the Board of Health; nor can anything be found elsewhere in the act imposing upon it the general duty of enforcing its provisions; on the contrary, Section 9 concludes with these words: "It shall be the duty of said inspector to enforce the provisions of this act, and to prosecute all violations of the same before any magistrate or court of competent jurisdiction in the state."

It seems to me, therefore, that while this act has recognized and perhaps to some extent enlarged the powers of the Board of Health to take all proper steps for the preservation of the public health, the general assembly has not seen fit to entrust that Board with the supervision of the contracts of any persons with respect to their labor.

Under existing laws and ordinances, the Board of Health may make, and possibly has made regulations based upon sanitary considerations which have special reference to the employment of females and children, and the force of such regulations is in no way impaired by the act under consideration.

But as the Board of Health has no concern with the enforcement of the provisions of this act in relation to female and child labor, an opinion upon its construction in the particulars mentioned could not aid you in the discharge of your official duties, and is therefore respectfully declined.

     JOHN MAYO PALMER, Asst. Corporation. Counsel.
    Approved:
ADOLPH KRAUS, Corporation Counsel.

                      November 4, 1893.
To the Honorable, the City Council of the City of Chicago.

Several members of your honorable body have requested that I render an opinion upon the power of the city council to elect a presiding officer of its body, who shall at the same time be temporary or acting mayor of the city, until the vacancy created by the death of Mayor Harrison can be filled by a special election. I reply as follows:

The general act of the state of Illinois providing for the incorporation of cities and villages, which in 1875 was by a vote of the people of the city of Chicago adopted as the charter of the city, contains no provision covering the present case, as may be readily seen from the following sections of that act:

Article II, Section 2: "Whenever a vacancy shall happen in the office of the mayor, when the unexpired term shall be one year or over from the date when the vacancy occurs, it shall be filled by an election."

Section 3: "If the vacancy is less than one year, the city council shall elect one of its number to act as mayor, who shall possess all the rights and powers of the mayor until the next annual election, and until his successor is elected and qualified."

Section 4: "During a temporary absence or disability of the mayor, the city council shall elect one of its number to act as mayor pro tem, who, during such absence or disability, shall possess the powers of mayor."

The above embrace all of the provisions of that charter which have reference to the present inquiry. It will be observed that Section 2 specifically provides, that in the present case, the unexpired term of office being more than a year, the vacancy caused by tne death of Mayor Harrison must be filled by special election.

Section 3 relates to vacancies where the unexpired term is less than one year, and, therefore, has clearly no application to the present vacancy.

Section 4 is likewise inapplicable, inasmuch as it provides only for the case of a temporary absence or disability of the mayor. If, therefore, the power of the city council to elect a temporary mayor depends solely upon the present general charter of the city, such power clearly does not exist and cannot be exercised. The old or former charter, as amended in 1875, contained the following provision: "In case of a vacancy in the office of mayor, or his being unable to perform the duties of his office, by reason of absence or sickness, the common council shall appoint, by ballot, one of their members to preside over their meetings, whose official designation shall be 'acting mayor.' And the alderman so appointed shall be vested with all the powers and perform all the duties of mayor until the mayor shall resume his office or the vacancy be filled by a new election."

It would seem that the provision of the former charter of the city of Chicago just quoted still remains in force by virtue of the saving clause in Article I, Section 6, of the general charter, which reads as follows:

"But all laws or parts of laws, not inconsistent with the provisions of this act, shall continue in force and applicable to any such city or village, the same as if such change of organization had not taken place."

While I have, upon mature reflection, reached this conclusion, I deem it my duty to advise you, that counsel of eminent standing in this city, who have given careful thought to the subject, entertain a different opinion upon the question under consideration.

They argue with considerable force that the words "laws or parts of laws" in the saving clause above quoted, refer only to laws of general application and, therefore, not to special charters; that the Supreme Court of this state has held, in the case of City of Cairo vs.

13

Bross, 101 Ill., page 475, "that it was the object of the legislature in adopting the general incorporation law, to place the cities, towns and villages organized under it, and of the same rate, upon a uniform and common footing with respect to their corporate powers and in the manner of exercising them," and that, to keep in force provisions of special charters, might lead to a result in conflict with the object of the legislature in adopting the general city incorporation law, thus declared by the Supreme Court.

It is also contended that the new charter, by providing how vacancies shall be filled and what the powers of the city council in the premises are, by implication excludes the exercise of such powers in all other cases.

It is also argued that the adoption of the general charter implies an abandonment of the special charter, and there is some support for the view in certain language of the Supreme Court of Illinois.

While these arguments are entitled to respect, yet I am of the opinion that the old charter provision governs. In acting upon the same, you will have to be strictly guided by all the requirements thereof.

I deem it my duty, however, to advise you that in view of the doubt expressed by eminent lawyers as to your powers in the premises and as to the extent of the powers of such an acting mayor as you might select, you should confine yourselves, during the interval until the filling of the vacancy by popular election, to such legislation only as is absolutely urgent and necessary.

In compliance with a request of Aldermen Hepburn, Sexton, Mann, Campbell and others, I herewith submit an order calling a special election. The old charter, which in this respect governs also, provides that the election must be called within ten days after the vacancy occurs. Notice of the election must be given of not less than twenty days, and no more than is reasonably necessary under the circumstances. Respectfully submitted,

ADOLPH KRAUS, Corporation Counsel.

November 17, 1893.

Hon Edward Marrener, Chairman, Committee on Printing.

Sir—

In reference to your request for an opinion on the question whether the council has the legal power to prohibit grocers and butchers from keeping open their places of business on Sunday, I have to say:

The council has the power by ordinance to prohibit the exercise of all the ordinary business avocations on Sunday.

It has not the power to single out trades and pursuits of the same character, and forbid the exercise of one, and permit the exercise of the other on Sunday.

An ordinance which should prohibit butchers and grocers from keeping open their places of business on Sunday, while at the same time, and in the same locality, bakers, confectioners, and dry goods merchants are permitted to carry on their business on that day, would be illegal as discriminating between persons engaged in like pursuits under like circumstances, without any reasonable ground for such discrimination.

JOHN MAYO PALMER, Asst. Corporation Counsel.

December 15, 1893.

Arthur R. Reynolds, M. D., Commissioner of Health, City.

My Dear Sir—

You have asked the corporation counsel for an opinion upon the following question:

1st. Whether you have authority to force people to be vaccinated against their will.

2nd. Whether you have authority to forcibly enter a man's house and remove a member of his family to the smallpox hospital if suffering from smallpox.

I answer your first question in the negative. All you can do in regard to the matter of vaccination is to issue an order, pursuant to Section 1190 of the Revised Ordinances, requiring persons to be vaccinated within such time as you may prescribe. Refusal or neglect to obey such order is visited with punishment by fine of not less than $3.00 nor more than $25.00. Your second question I answer in the affirmative. Very truly yours,

SIGMUND ZEISLER, Asst. Corporation Counsel.

January 27, 1894.

John W. Hepburn, Esq., Chairman of Sub-committee of the Council Committee on Wharves and Public Grounds.

Dear Sir—

In reply to your question relative to the project of moving the Manufactures building from Jackson Park to the Lake Front, namely, (1) What, if any, legal objections exist to the use of the Lake Front between Madison and Randolph streets, west of the Illinois Central right of way, as a site for said building? And (2) whether the city would accept said building in whole or in part of the amount of money to which it is entitled from the World's Columbian Exposition? We herewith beg to give you the following opinion:

(1) So much of the Lake Front between the south line of Randolph street and the center line of Madison street east of Michigan avenue as was not then covered by water, formed a portion of an irregularly shaped piece of ground, which, upon the plat of a subdivision made by authority of the United States Secretary of War, known as "Fort Dearborn Addition to Chicago," acknowledged on June 7, 1839, was marked "Public ground forever to remain vacant of buildings."

The acknowledgment and recording of said plat amounted to a statutory dedication to the city of Chicago of those portions of the premises platted as were marked thereon as granted to the public. This dedication has been judicially declared to have vested in the city of Chicago the fee simple title to the public grounds in question in trust for the public uses and purposes as indicated on the plat (the Lake Front cases, 33 Fed. Rep. 730, 754, affirmed in the United States Supreme Court, 146 U. S., 387).

The same effect must be given to this dedication with reference to the land reclaimed from the waters of Lake Michigan east of what marked the shore line at the time of the dedication.

The question arises whether the direction on the plat that this ground should forever remain vacant of buildings is a condition subsequent annexed to the estate, or merely imposes trust to use or not to use the land in the manner directed. The difference between the two interpretations is very material. If it is a condition subsequent, then a breach of the same would work a forfeiture and entitle the original grantor to re-entry. If, on the other hand, this limitation is to be regarded as a regulation to guide the trustee, the municipal corporation of the city of Chicago, and explanatory of the object and purpose of the dedication, then it imposes merely a trust, a violation of which would entitle those affected by it to relief in a court of equity, but would not operate to determine the estate. Conditions subsequent are not favored in law. A deed will not be construed to create an estate on condition, unless language is used which, according to the rules of law, imports a condition, or the intent of the grantor to make a conditional estate is otherwise clearly and unequivocally indicated. If it be doubtful whether a clause in a deed be a covenant or a condition, courts will always lean against the latter construction. (*Greene* vs. *O'Connor*, Supreme Court of Rhode Island, 25 Atl. Rep., 692.) And "Although a deed contain a clause declaring the purpose for which it is intended the granted premises shall be used, if such purpose will not inure specially to the benefit of the grantor, but is in its nature general and public, and if there are no other words in the grant indicating an intent that the grant is to be void if the declared purpose is not fulfilled, such a clause is not a condition subsequent." (*Horner* vs. *C., M. & St. P. Ry. Co.*, 38 Wis., 165. 175; *Greene* vs. *O'Connor*, 25 Atl. Rep., 692; *Rawson* vs. *Inhabitants*, 7 Allen, 125.)

Where the words of limitation in a grant do not contain a provision for re-entry for condition broken, and there is nothing in the instrument indicating an intention on the part of the grantor that the appropriation of the premises to any other purpose than the one indicated should have the effect of defeating the estate granted, the limitation will not be treated as a condition. (*Tinker* vs. *Forbes*. 136 Ill., 221.)

The words of limitation in a grant will be construed as imposing a trust and not a condition where it is clear that the grantor intends to impose a duty in favor of others, and has no interest in, or reason for, having the premises used solely in the way indicated. (*Gabert* vs. *Olcott*, 22 S. W. Rep., 286, decided by the Court of Civil Appeals of Texas, March 2, 1893; *Neely* vs. *Hoskins*, 84 Me., 386.)

In the case before us it seems clear that the United States can have no interest directly or indirectly in the observance of the limitation that this public ground should remain vacant of buildings. This requirement was evidently intended for the benefit of abutting land owners and perhaps for the benefit of the general public. Moreover, the clause in question is solely a declaration of the purpose for which the dedicated land was to be used and improved, but contains no language which imports that the grant should be void in case the purpose of the dedication is not carried out, nor does it reserve to the United States the right to re-enter in that event. We are, therefore, as well as for the reason that the United States have no constitutional capacity to exercise municipal jurisdiction, sovereignty or eminent domain within the limits of a state, except in the case in which it is expressly granted, of the opinion that the United States have no control over the public ground in question, and that no congressional legislation is required to make the same available as a site for the Manufactures or any other building.

The direction upon the plat, however, that this ground should forever remain vacant of buildings creates an easement in the abutting property owners, of which, unless they consent, they cannot be deprived without compensation to be made pursuant to law. As a matter of fact, there is at the present time in force a preliminary injunction issued by the Superior Court of Cook County in the case of Montgomery Ward et. al. vs. City, restraining the city of Chicago and all other persons from in any manner obstructing and encroaching upon the land in question. What, if any, damages the abutting property owners would be entitled to, if their easement of light and view were appropriated under the right of eminent domain, it is not now necessary to consider. In our opinion such damages would propably be of a nominal character. At the time of the original dedication all the residences of the city were immediately contiguous to the Fort Dearborn Reservation. These conditions have long since ceased to exist. There are no residences fronting on this ground and it has no longer any value as a mere public square. It is now, and has for many years been, a barren waste, and it may be that all the abutting property owners would be glad to give their consent to a proper improvement of the ground, even to the extent of the erection of a permanent building upon the same.

The city of Chicago, however, cannot in the absence of express legislative authority alienate this public ground or divert it from the uses and purposes for which it was dedicated. (Kreigh vs. Chicago, 86 Ill.. 407.) The fee to that ground is in the city as the agent or representative of the public, it holds the fee for the use of the public, not the citizens of the city alone, but the entire public, of which the legislature is the representative. (*Chicago* vs. *Rumsey*, 87 Ill., 348, 355; *People* vs. *Walsh*, 96 Ill.. 232, 248.)I

The general assembly, however, undoubtedly has the power to direct or authorize the municipal corporation of the city of Chicago to change the use of the ground in question. "The legislature repre- sents the public. So far as concerns the public, it may authorize one use to-day and another and different use to-morrow. If the new use affects private rights, proceedings for condemnation may have to be invoked, but so far as it affects the public alone its representative, in the absence of constitutional restraint, may do as it pleases." (*People* vs. *Walsh*, 96 Ill., 232, 250.) There being no restraint in that re- gard arising from either the United States constitution or the consti- tution of the state of Illinois, all property held for the public is under the uncontrolled power of the assembly. (*Harris* vs. *Board of Super- visors*, 105 Ill., 445, 451.)

Our conclusion upon this branch of the question is, that to make the lake front property available as a site for tne Manufactures building, the legislature of the state of Illinois will have to authorize the use of said ground for the purpose suggested; the city of Chicago, by its common council, will have to pass an ordinance for the same purpose; and the consent of the abutting property owners will have to be obtained, or else their right of easement will have to be con- demned pursuant to the statute of eminent domain.

(2.) As to the second branch of the question we find that the amendment to the constitution adopted at the election in November, 1890, contained the provision, "That said corporate authorities may take, in whole or in part of the sum coming to them, any permanent improvements placed on land or controlled by them."

In pursuance of the authority conferred by that constitutional amendment, the city of Chicago on December 4, 1890, passed an ordinance for the issuance of bonds to the amount of five million dol- lars, which ordinance is absolutely silent as to the taking of improve- ments instead of money, but on the contrary contains the provision "That said bonds shall be issued and the proceeds thereof are directed to be paid to the Treasurer of said World's Columbian Exposition *upon the express condition and agreement* that the city of Chicago shall be repaid as large a proportionate amount of the proceeds of said bonds as is paid to the stockholders of said World's Columbian Expo- sition on the sums subscribed and paid by them, and the money so re- paid to the city of Chicago *shall be used in the redemption of the bonds issued as aforesaid."* Section 3 of the ordinance provides for the right of the city to redeem any of the said bonds before maturity at five per cent. above par.

As the World's Fair bonds were issued and the money raised and expended under the ordinance just referred to, there can in law be no doubt that the said ordinance constitutes a valid and binding contract between the holders of said bonds and the city of Chicago. (Fazende vs. City of Houston, 34 Fed. Rep., 95.) This ordinance provides that the city is to receive from the World's Columbian Exposition, not buildings or other improvements, but money, and those moneys to which the city should be entitled are pledged to the bondholders as a special fund for the redemption of the bonds *pro tanto*.

It is true that at the time of the passage of that ordinance the city had, by virtue of the constitutional amendment, the right to elect whether it would avail itself of the authority to make an arrangement with the World's Columbian Exposition whereby it might take improvements instead of moneys. By omitting to provide in the ordinance for such substitution of improvements, the city, as against the bond holders, must be held to have elected not to avail itself of that authority.

It cannot be contended that the constitutional amendment in question can be the source of authority for the city of Chicago to elect *at this time* to take buildings instead of money. Such election at this time would have the effect of diverting the special fund above mentioned from the use prescribed by the ordinance, namely, the redemption of bonds issued pursuant to the ordinance, and that ordinance constituting the contract between the city and the bond holders, it cannot be modified without the consent of the bond holders.

There is another reason why the city should not accept in lieu of the moneys coming to it, any building which might in the future be erected upon the lake front. Admittedly, the city could not first take money from the World's Columbian Exposition and then use it for the expense of the erection of a building, or for any other purpose than the redemption of bonds. But it is proposed to avoid this obstacle by having the World's Fair expend the money to which the city is entitled, in the removal and re-erection of the Manufactures building upon the lake front, and then turn it over to the city. The World's Columbian Exposition has never obtained any authority to use the lake front *north* of Madison street. The consummation of the above plan would, therefore, necessitate an ordinance by the city of Chicago authorizing the Exposition to use the ground in question for the purpose of re-erecting thereon the Manufactures building. Apart from the fact that in our opinion the city would have no authority to grant to the World's Columbian Exposition the use of said ground for that purpose, now that the Exposition is closed, what would be the possible object of the ordinance? It could be none other than to make an arrangement for the sole purpose of evading the provision of the law that the moneys which the city is entitled to receive from the World's Columbian Exposition shall be used for the redemption of bonds. This would be a mere shift, device, trick or artifice to evade the law. It is a principle of universal application that that cannot be done indirectly which the law forbids to be done directly.

If the Manufactures building, after its removal to the lake front, were to be used for corporate purposes, then it would be lawful for the city council to pass an ordinance making a direct appropriation for the expense of its removal and re-erection. But from a careful investigation of the law we are of the opinion that the city is obliged to receive in money from the World's Columbian Exposition whatever it is entitled to, and to use that money for the redemption of World's Fair bonds and for no other purpose. Respectfully submitted,

HARRY RUBENS, Corporation Counsel.
SIGMUND ZEISLER, Asst. Corporation Counsel.

I have carefully examined the foregoing opinion and concur in the conclusions therein stated.   JOHN P. WILSON.

February 5, 1894.

To the City Comptroller.

Sir—

I have your communication in which you submit to me for an opinion the question, whether the comptroller has the legal right to procure loans of a temporary character in anticipation of the tax levy of 1893, which is now in process of collection to meet the demands due from the city for labor, materials, etc., and to pay interest on such loans.

By Section 12, Article IX, of the present constitution of this state it is provided that "No * * * city * * * shall be allowed to become indebted in any manner, or for any purpose, to an amount including existing indebtedness in the aggregate exceeding five per centum on the value of the taxable property therein, to be ascertained by the last assessment for state and county taxes previous to the incurring of such indebtedness."

The city of Chicago having reached the constitutional limit of indebtedness it can do nothing which would in legal effect be the creation of a new indebtedness. The question arises then whether any proposed temporary loan would or would not be the creation of indebtedness. If such would be its legal effect it would be illegal, otherwise it may lawfully be done. The Supreme Court of Illinois has had occasion in a number of cases to consider methods adopted by cities, which had reached the constitutional limit of indebtedness, to relieve themselves from embarrassment by temporary loans, and has with great precision prescribed the methods which may be lawfully employed. The result of these decisions may be briefly stated thus:

First: No promise of the city to pay a sum in excess of the constitutional limit absolutely either on demand or at a specified future day would be valid, but the legal effect of the contract must be the mere appropriation or assignment of taxes in process of collection.

Second: The city may, after a specified appropriation of a tax already levied and in process of collection is made, draw a voucher or order upon such appropriation for temporary loans to meet just demands upon it, but the payment of such warrant must be specifically limited to the proceeds of the taxes levied for the payment of the appropriation against which it is charged, and must be accepted by the person to whom issued in complete satisfaction of claim.

This subject is fully discussed in the following cases:

City of Springfield vs. Edwards, 84 Ill., 626.

Law vs. The People, 87 Ill., 385.

Fuller vs. City of Chicago, 89 Ill., 282.

Fuller vs. Heath, 89 Ill., 296.

Since these cases have been decided the doctrine therein announced has been embodied in the following statute, passed in 1879, which is still in force:

"That whenever there is no money in the treasury of any municipal corporation to meet and defray the ordinary and * * * necessary expenses thereof, it shall be lawful for the proper authorities of any * * * municipal corporation to provide that warrants may be drawn and issued against and in anticipation of the collection of any taxes already levied by said authorities for the payment of the ordinary and necessary expenses of any such municipal corporation, to the extent of seventy-five per centum of the total amount of any said tax levied: Provided, that warrants drawn and issued under the provisions of this section shall show upon the face that they are payable solely from said taxes when collected, and not otherwise, and shall be received by any collector of taxes in payment of the taxes against which they are issued, and which taxes, against which said warrants are drawn, shall be set apart and held for their payment.

Inasmuch as the city may lawfully agree to pay interest upon demands, for materials, supplies, etc., it may also insert in the warrants drawn upon taxes in process of collection to meet these demands provision for the payment of interest, provided the payment of such interest is also to be made by way of assignment of taxes levied and in process of collection and covered by an appropriation for such interest. Respectfully,

HARRY RUBENS, Corporation Counsel.

February 17, 1894.

To the Superintendent of the Bureau of Street and Alley Cleaning.

Sir—

In response to your inquiry as to the duty of property-owners to remove snow from sidewalks abutting upon their premises, I have to say that they are under no legal obligation to do so.

While Section 2636 of our Municipal Code attempts to impose this duty upon property-owners, the Supreme Court of the state has held such an ordinance to be void.

City of Chicago vs. Crosby, 111 Ill., 532.

JOHN MAYO PALMER, Asst. Corporation Counsel.

Approved:

HARRY RUBENS, Corporation Counsel.

March 19, 1894.

To the City Comptroller.

Sir—

I have your request for an opinion as to the validity of the 4 per cent. gold bonds of the city of Chicago, which were recently issued in place of, and to retire, prior issues of municipal and water bonds.

By the "Act to provide for the incorporation of cities and villages," in force July 1, 1872, under which the city is organized, it is provided in Article V, Section 1, that the city council shall have power—

"Sixth: To issue bonds in place of or to supply means to meet maturing bonds, or for the consolidation or funding of the same."

By Section 38 of the former charter of the city, passed in 1863, it is provided that "whenever any of the bonds of the city which may have been heretofore, or hereafter may be carefully issued, shall become due, the Common Council may authorize the Mayor and Comptroller to issue new bonds to an amount sufficient to retire and satisfy the same, running either ten or twenty years, bearing interest at a rate not exceeding 7 per cent. per annum, payable semi-annually, and payable, principal and interest, in the City of New York."

By an act of the general assembly passed March 26, 1872, and amended April 14, 1875, entitled "An Act to enable counties, cities, townships, school districts and other municipal corporations to take up and cancel outstanding bonds and other evidences of indebtedness and fund the same," the general rule prescribed is that no such funding shall take place except upon a vote of the people and municipality; but the same act provides that "Nothing in this act, or in the act to which this is an amendment, shall be held to repeal or in any wise affect the power of the City of Chicago to issue new bonds to an amount sufficient to retire and satisfy maturing bonds of said city, conferred by Section 38 of an act of the General Assembly approved February 13, 1863, amending the charter of said city."

The prior issues of municipal and water bonds referred to having unquestionably been lawfully issued, ample power in the city to issue new bonds in their stead is found in both the special charter and the general incorporation law. That the new bonds are the valid obligations of the city admits of no question.

JOHN MAYO PALMER, Asst. Corporation Counsel.

Approved:

HARRY RUBENS, Corporation Counsel.

May 16, 1894.

Hon. James R. Mann, Chairman of Committee on Judiciary.

Sir—

I have your communication of May 14, enclosing a communication from the Central Labor Union of Chicago concerning the abolition of labor agencies, and note your request for an opinion as to the powers of the city council in the premises.

It seems to be well settled by repeated judicial decisions that the city has not the power to prohibit, license, tax or specially regulate lawful occupations, except where the legislature has in express terms granted authority for that purpose.

It has been decided that employment agencies are not the subject of regulation by the city.

The complaint made of certain employment agencies within the city is that they obtain money from persons seeking employment under circumstances which constitute, practically, the criminal offense of obtaining money under false pretenses.

Attempts have been made to convict certain persons conducting employment agencies of this criminal offense, but without success, owing to their methods of conducting their business. At the instance of the police department I have had under consideration the question whether it might not be possible to place this business under police control or scrutiny, but became satisfied that no power exists in the council to regulate this business by special rules, which would not be applicable to all other lawful occupations, and certainly the council has no power to prescribe or change the rules of evidence.

I am regretfully forced to the conclusion that any relief for the evils complained of in the resolutions which you hand me must be sought from the general assembly, and not from the city council.

Respectfully, etc.,
JOHN MAYO PALMER, Asst. Corporation Counsel.

May 17, 1894.

Hon. John P. Hopkins, Mayor of Chicago.
Dear Sir—

At your request I have carefully examined the report of the commissioner of health on the sanitary condition of the county building, as well as the question of the power of the city of Chicago in the premises, and beg leave to herewith submit to you my opinion thereon.

The powers of counties and county boards are expressly enumerated and defined by statute. There is no power given to them to make or enforce health regulations. It is, however, a principle of universal application that municipal corporations and quasi municipal corporations cannot exercise any powers except those which are expressly conferred by law or arise by necessary implication. The power to make and enforce health regulations is, therefore, denied to the board.

On the other hand, the general city incorporation act of the state of Illinois, under which the city of Chicago is organized, in Article V, Section 1, gives the city council the following powers: To declare what shall be a nuisance and to abate the same (clause 75); to appoint a board of health and prescribe its powers and duties (clause 76); to do all acts and make all regulations which may be necessary or expedient for the promotion of health or the suppression of disease (clause 78). Article III, Section 16, of the same act even extends the territorial jurisdiction of the city council for the purpose of enforcing health ordinances and regulations to all places within one-half mile of the city limits.

In the exercise of police power, which includes the making and enforcing of health regulations, the city is regarded as an agent of the state government; and in matters of this kind, whenever a power is conferred, it carries with it a corresponding duty to exercise that power. This power being vested in the city and denied to the county, I am of the opinion that the city may and should exercise it with reference to the county building in exactly the same manner as with reference to any building within the city devoted to purely private purposes.

It remains to be seen what specific provisions are contained in the city ordinances applicable to the reported condition of the county building.

By Section 2238 of the compiled laws and ordinances, any building which shall become nauseous, foul or offensive is declared a nuisance, and the same declaration is made by Section 2242 with reference to any building which is suffered to remain for twenty-four hours in such a condition as to be dangerous or prejudicial to the health or safety of the occupants or other persons. Under the provisions just cited the county building, if the report of the commissioner of health is correct, is now a nuisance.

Under Sections 1185 and 2251 it is the duty of the commissioner of health to give twenty-four hours' notice to those owning or controlling a building in which a nuisance may be found to abate or remove the same in such manner as he shall prescribe. If such nuisance is not promptly abated or removed in accordance with such notice the commissioner may cause it to be abated, and expense of such abatement shall be collected by suit or otherwise, in addition to the fine or penalty prescribed by the ordinances, from those who have created, continued or suffered such nuisance to exist.

Under Section 2056 no building used for any purpose whatever shall be used, kept or maintained in the city, if the use, keeping or maintenance of the same shall be the occasion of any nuisance or dangerous or detrimental to health. And under Section 1931, whenever it shall be decided by the commissioner of health that any building or part thereof is unfit for human habitation, by reason of its being so infected with disease, *or from other causes*, as to be likely to cause sickness among the occupants, and notice of such decision shall have been affixed conspicuously on the building or part thereof so decided to be unfit for human habitation, and personally served upon the owner, agent or lessee, requiring all persons therein to vacate such building or part thereof for the reasons to be stated therein, such building or part thereof shall within ten days thereafter be vacated, or within such shorter time, not less than twenty-four hours, as in said notice may be specified.

Under the provisions last cited I am of the opinion that if the sanitary condition of the county building is such as to justify the commissioner of health in the conclusion that it is likely to cause sickness among the occupants, and, therefore, unfit for human habitation, the commmissioner could compel the vacation of the building or parts thereof.

Under Section 1189 the commissioner of health is given discretionary power to take such measures and order and cause to be done such acts for the preservation of the public health as he may in good faith declare the public safety and health to demand, whenever the city is visited with a pestilence or epidemic disease, or in case the sanitary condition of the city should be of such a character as to warrant such measures.

By Section 1255 the superintendent of police is charged with the duty of causing to be executed all orders of the commissioner of health so far as they may relate to the preservation of the health of the city.   Respectfully submitted,
              SIGMUND ZEISLER, Asst. Corporation Counsel.

                                                      May 25, 1894.
M. B. Madden, Esq., Chairman Finance Committee.
   Dear Sir—
   You have asked for an opinoin, first, as to whether a contract for more than one year, involving no expenditure of money on the part of the city, can legally be made; second, whether in the contemplated contract for the removal of dead animals the city can insure to the contractor all dead animals within the city. In other words, whether the city can prevent the owners of dead animals from removing or disposing of them.

   There is nothing in the statutes of the state to prevent the city from entering into a contract for more than one year which does not involve the expenditure of money on the part of the city.

   As to the second question, Section 2024, page 597, of the laws and ordinances of 1890, provides:

   "Section 2024. That no person other than the inspectors or officers of the department of health, or department of police, or persons thereto authorized by contract or otherwise, shall, in any way, interfere with such dead, sick or injured animal in any street or place, and no person shall skin or wound such animal in such street or public place, unless to terminate its life as herein authorized; except that the owner or person having control of such animal may terminate the life thereof in the presence and by the consent of a policeman, or an inspector or officer of said department."

   This ordinance is based upon the police power and the police power in such cases depends entirely upon the law of overruling necessities. A dead animal is not *per se* a nuisance. The owner may still put it to useful purposes. This ordinance cannot be literally construed, else it would, without proper authority, empower a city officer or contractor to seize upon the property of private citizens, even though such property be not a nuisance, and even though the circumstances of the case did not justify the exercise of police power. In most cases, it is true, the owner of an animal which dies in the streets is unwilling or unable to remove the animal in time to prevent its being a nuisance. In such cases the city certainly has the power to order its removal. But the ordinance can only be construed to apply to such dead animals as are nuisances or are dangerous or deleterious to public health. Very respectfully,

T. E. GUERIN, Asst. Corporation Counsel.

Approved:
HARRY RUBENS, Corporation Counsel.

July 20, 1894.

To the City Comptroller.

Sir—

I have yours of June 21, 1894, enclosing form of contracts of police justices, and requesting an opinion upon the question as to who is entitled to the fees for the approval of special bail bonds on Sundays and holidays.

While by the literal terms of the contract the city might possibly be entitled to such fees, yet when it is considered that the police justices are not required by their contracts to attend in their courts on these days, to deny them the right to this compensation for extra official services might be productive of great injury to private citizens entitled to bail. The true spirit is that the city shall have the fees for official services rendered during ordinary office hours, but not for those which are extra official or rendered at night or on Sundays, and in this view, I am of opinion that the fees in question should be allowed to the justices.

JOHN MAYO PALMER, Asst. Corporation Counsel.

Approved:
HARRY RUBENS, Corporation Counsel.

July 31, 1894.

Wm. K. Ackerman, Esq., City Comptroller.

Dear Sir—

Referring to the correspondence between yourself and Mr. C. B. Farwell regarding the lease of the wharfing privileges at the foot of Monroe street, east of the river, I beg to inform you that the city has the right to lease the wharfing privileges of the river at the ends of streets, upon such terms and conditions as may be usual in the leasing of other real estate, reserving such rents as may be agreed upon. But no building shall be erected on such street ends nor shall a lease be made for a longer period than three years.

This power is contained in the first clause of Section 8 of Chapter IV of the former charter of the city of Chicago. Inasmuch as there is no provision in the city and villages act (which was adopted by the city of Chicago as its charter in 1875) with which the above quoted provision of the former charter is inconsistent or in conflict, that provision is still in full force.

The power to make such lease is, however, vested only in the common council, which of course can only act by ordinance. I am, therefore, of the opinion that a lease of wharfing privileges executed by the mayor and comptroller without special authority conferred upon them for that purpose by the city council is invalid and would certainly not bind the city. This view is strengthened by the provision of Section 2070 of the Municipal Code of Chicago (Section 2782 of Myers' Laws and Ordinances of 1890) by which the occupation of street ends without special authority and permission from the city council is made an offense punishable by a fine of $20 for each day or part of a day any such street end is occupied by any building, wharf, lumber, stone or other substance or material.

The Archer Avenue case referred to by Mr. Farwell has no application to the question under consideration. I presume the case Mr. Farwell means is that of Ligare vs. City of Chicago, 139 Ill., p. 46, wherein it was held that the city has no power to give to a steam railroad company the exclusive use of a street.

Very respectfully yours,
SIGMUND ZEISLER, Asst. Corporation Counsel.
Approved:
HARRY RUBENS, Corporation Counsel.

September 11, 1894.

To the City Comptroller.
Sir—

I have yours of recent date in which you inform me that applications are frequently made to you for the return of moneys paid as fines for impounding horses and dogs, and note your request for an opinion as to whether you have authority to return moneys received by you on this account.

I find no authority for the return of *fines* paid for the violation of the ordinance in relation to horses or dogs. The only circumstances under which you are required to make any special disposition of funds arising from the impounding of animals are those mentioned in Section 2442 of the compiled ordinances of 1890, which are as follows:

"When the proceeds of the sale of any animal or animals shall exceed the amount of judgment and costs and the expense of sustenance which shall have accrued subsequently to the rendition of the judgment, and such excess shall have been paid to the comptroller, the owner or owners of such animal or animals shall be entitled to a warrant on the city treasurer for such excess, upon presenting to the city comptroller satisfactory evidence of his right thereto."

JOHN MAYO PALMER, Asst. Corporation Counsel.

September 20, 1894

Hon. Michael Brennan, General Supt. of Police.

Sir—

In answer to your inquiry whether you are legally authorized to execute certain warrants for the searching of places alleged to be kept as public gambling houses and for the seizure of the gambling apparatus which may be found therein, placed in your hands for execution by officers of the Civic Federation, I beg to advise you as follows: The apparent authority for the issuing of search warrants in such cases and the seizure and destruction of gambling apparatus is found in Division VIII of the Criminal Code of this state, and Section 2 of said Division VIII authorizes the issuing of a search warrant "to search for and seize gaming apparatus or implements used or kept and provided to be used in unlawful gaming in any gaming house, or in any building, apartment or place resorted to for the purpose of unlawful gaming."

Section 7 of said Division VIII provides:

"When an officer in the execution of a search warrant finds stolen or embezzled property or seizes any of the other things for which a search is allowed by this act, all the property and things so seized shall be safely kept by direction of the judge, justice or court, so long as necessary for the purpose of being produced or used as evidence at any trial. As soon as may be afterwards all such stolen and embezzled property shall be restored to the owner thereof and all other things seized by virtue of such warrants shall be burned or otherwise destroyed under the direction of the judge, justice or court."

While the law authorizes the summary destruction of all property which constitutes a nuisance per se, irrespective of the use to which the property is put, such destruction does not seem to be authorized in cases where the nuisance consists merely in the use to which the property is put. In other words, where property may be devoted to a lawful as well as to an unlawful use the destruction thereof in cases of unlawful use can only take place *"By due process of law."*

Whether the provision of the statute of our state authorizing the searching of gambling house premises and the seizure and destruction of the apparatus which may be found therein, is in violation of the constitutional provision that, "No person shall be deprived of * * * property without due process of law" has been the subject of judicial investigation in this county as in the case of People vs. Copely, in a decision by Judge Rogers, of the Circuit Court, the statute has been declared to be unconstitutional and void as far as it relates to the seizure of gambling implements and the property seized has been or--

dered to be returned. In applying the constitutional test to the
statute in question, the court said in that case:

"The proceedings by search warrant, seizure, * * * of property or things used or kept to be used as gaming apparatus, arrest of
the person found in possession of it, its destruction by fire or otherwise, is a summary one, consisting only of complaint, warrant, seizure,
bringing of property and the possessor before the magistrate so long
as necessary for the purpose of being produced as evidence on any
trial, and then the burning or destroying it otherwise, under the direction of the Judge or Justice. There is no trial by jury, nor, in fact,
by the Judge or Justice, required. The only evidence required in
any part of the proceeding is a complainant shall state his belief only of
the facts set forth, upon which the Judge is required to issue the warrant, and upon seizure the property is brought before the Judge, who
is to direct its safe keeping for a time, and then direct its destruction.

"It is true that persons and property are subject to many re-
straints and burdens in order to secure the general comfort, health
and prosperity of the state. Of the rights and powers of the legislature
to impose them, 'no question ever was, or, upon acknowledged general
principles, ever can be made, so far as natural powers are concerned.'
But the power and right of the legislature to establish reasonable
laws and ordinances is subject to the limitations imposed by the
constitution of the United States and of the several states. The
destruction of property summarily, without process of law, has been
recognized as a proper exercise of police power in case of nuisance
per se. This was instanced in the ordinance to protect against calamities of fire. This is unquestionably within the competency of legislative power, and in all such cases 'formal legal proceedings and trial
by jury are not appropriate to, and have never been used in such
cases.' These tables, etc., were not, and are not. in and of themselves, a
nuisance. It is the gaming contrary to the law and good morals which
is the nuisance, and then the remedy is by indictment, and not by the
destruction of the implements. The articles used in gaming are
property, notwithstanding their use is illegal, immoral and criminal
practices. The statutes of this state provide penalties for all offenses and crimes, and prescribe the mode of procedure according to
the due course of the law. The legislature has attempted to change
those wise principles and modes of procedure, but in attempting to do
so it has departed so widely that no court of last resort can do otherwise than declare its action a violation of the constitution, and therefore void. The order of the court is that the warrant is dismissed,
and the officers holding the property seized are directed to return it
to the owners."

The same conclusion has been reached by the Supreme Court of
the state of Missouri in the case of Lowry vs. Rainwater (70 Mo. Supreme Court Reports, p. 152), in the case of a statute which substan-
14

tially differs from our statute only in the provision that the warrant is issued by the president of the board of police commissioners and the destruction directed by him, while under our statute the warrant is issued and the destruction of the property directed by a judge or justice of the peace. The court, in deciding that case, make use of the following language:

"An act which, under the pretense of preserving public morals provides for the seizure of private property should also provide a summary mode of judicial proceedings for the determining whether it is the kind of property and was used or held for purposes condemned by the Act. Even to authorize the property to be seized and held until, in an ordinary action at law for the recovery of his property, the claimant should negative the allegation in the warrant of seizure, would be oppressive and unjust, and not in harmony with the spirit of our constitution, hence a statute which authorizes a seizure of private property under a warrant issued in pursuance of provisions such as are contained in Section 7, should also afford a speedy trial to ascertain whether the property is of the character and is used or held for the purposes condemned by the act, and making provision for duly notifying the owner and giving him his day in court. The constitutional safeguards thrown around the rights of property are not to be demolished in order to suppress gambling or gambling houses. The vices which acts authorizing these summary proceedings propose to eradicate are inconsiderable in comparison with the value of the constitutional guarantees which secure to the citizen his liberty and his property. We recognize the right of the state to adopt, and the propriety of the rigorous enforcement of laws for the suppression of gambling and gambling houses, but these laws may be so framed as to harmonize with those constitutional provisions, and hasty and inconsiderate legislation which disregards them cannot be upheld."

The principles upon which Judge Rogers based his decision of the Circuit Court of Cook County are the same as those which govern the courts to hold similar statutes to be unconstitutional in Massachusetts (1st Gray, p. 1), in Michigan (4th Mich., 126), and Vermont (27 Vt., 325).

I am, therefore, of opinion that in view of the decision of the Circuit Court of this county and the apparently unbroken current of authority in other states in which similar statutes have received judicial construction, you are not justified in executing search warrants issued under the provisions of the statute above quoted, and that in all probability you and your subordinate officers would be held liable in the courts as trespassers for all the damage done in the execution of the warrants and a consequent destruction of the property.

It is unfortunate that, as far as I could ascertain in the very limited time at my disposal, the validity of the statute has never been tested by the Supreme Court of Illinois, but in the absence of a decision by .

our court of last resort I advise you to be bound by the decision of the Circuit Court, and by what seems to be the opinion of all the courts of last resort in which similar statutes have received judicial construction.

I beg to call your attention to the fact, however, that irrespective of the statute quoted the keeping of public gaming houses is an offense under statutes and ordinances admittedly valid, and that the keepers of such gaming houses are liable to arrest, indictment and conviction upon proper proof.   Respectfully,   .
                         HENRY RUBENS, Corporation Counsel.

                                        October 18, 1894.
Hon. John P. Hopkins Mayor.
   Dear Sir—
   Some time ago I reported to you verbally on the question whether the concealed carrying of an unloaded pistol constituted an offense under the ordinances of Chicago and the statute of this state against the carrying of concealed weapons. Upon your instructions I now report to you in writing, that both the ordinance and statute are violated if a person carries concealed about his person a pistol or revolver, although such pistol or revolver may not be loaded. I have examined all the decisions which I could find upon the subject, and wherever similar statutes or ordinances have been in force the courts have held that the question whether the pistol is loaded or unloaded or whether it is out of repair so that it could not be shot off, is entirely immaterial. The exact question was presented to the Supreme Court of Indiana and it was held by that court, that "whether the pistol was loaded and what the defendant's intentions were in having the pistol in his possession were both immaterial questions in that cause." (Ridennour vs. State, 65 Ind., 411.)
   The Supreme Court of Mississippi decided, that an indictment was sufficient without averring that the pistol was loaded. (Gamblin vs. State, 45 Miss., 658.)
   The Supreme Court of Arkansas, in a case right in point, used the following language:
   "The statute does not require that the pistol shall be loaded. If it did, its value would be seriously impaired, for that is a fact which can hardly ever be ascertained beyond peradventure, until somebody is shot."
   State vs. Wardlaw, 43 Ark., 73.
   In Alabama the Supreme Court decided that a pistol with the tubes imperfect and battered up and the lock so much out of order that it could not be discharged by the trigger comes within the prohibition. (Atwood vs. State, 53 Ala., 508.)
   And the same court in a later case decided that a party is guilty of carrying concealed weapons if he carries about his person all the pieces of a pistol which could readily be put together so as to make an

effective weapon, though at the time he carried them the pieces were separate and incapable of use as a firearm. (Hutchinson vs. State, 62 Ala., 3.)

The Supreme Court of Georgia, in the case of Williams vs. State, 61 Ga., 417, also decided, that a pistol with its main spring broken so that it could not be discharged was prohibited by a statute similar in language to our ordinances.

It is, therefore, too clear to admit of question, both upon principle and authority, that the carrying concealed upon the person of anything which answers the popular description of a pistol or revolver, whether loaded or unloaded, is a violation of both the city ordinances and the statute concerning the carrying of concealed weapons. I return the letter of Inspector Shea, and other documents submitted to me in connection with this matter. Respectfully,

HARRY RUBENS, Corporation Counsel.

October 24, 1894.

To the Commissioner of Health.

Sir—

I have your communication of October 22d, in which you inquire whether you have authority to prevent the sale of a proprietary medicine where it can be proven that it is dangerous to the general health and well being of at least some of those who use it.

No special duty is imposed upon or authority given to the commissioner of health, either by any law or ordinance, with respect to the sale of proprietary medicines, and in a proper sense it may be said that you have no *authority* to interfere with their sale.

You should, however, if you think the public interests require it, cause prosecutions to be instituted by the proper officers for violations of the state laws, which fully regulate the subject.

JOHN MAYO PALMER, Asst. Corporation Counsel.

November 10, 1894.

To the City Comptroller.

Sir—

We have your communication of recent date in which you inform us that as a result of special investigation of the methods employed for the assessment and collection of water rates, made by direction of the mayor, the revenues from the water works have been increased more than $100,000, and note your request for an opinion whether you can lawfully pay the cost of this investigation.

It is provided by the charter that no department "shall add to the corporation expenditures in any one year anything over and above the amount provided for in the annual appropriation bill of that year"; and you inform us that the cost of this investigation is not included in the appropriation ordinance of 1894.

In determining whether the payment of the cost of this investigation would add to the corporation expenditures within the meaning of the law, the relation of the city to the water works, and the effect of the investigation upon its revenues, must be considered.

It is held by our Supreme Court that the city, in carrying on the business of supplying water to consumers, acts in its capacity of a private corporation, and not in the exercise of its powers of local sovereignty; it would seem, therefore, that the expense of making and collecting assessments, and remedying defects therein, so as to make the water works most productive of profit, is properly chargeable to the receipts thereof, and that only the net revenues are available for appropriation for corporation expenditures.

If this view be correct then the cost of an investigation necessary to the proper collection of rates, and which actually produces a large increase in revenue, could neither be regarded as an appropriation of the corporate funds, nor as adding to the corporation expenditures, within the meaning of the law.

If the annual appropriation ordinance had made no provision whatever for carrying on the water works as was the practice prevailing until quite recently, no one would doubt but that all the expenses of producing revenue would be properly chargeable to the water rates collected.

If the present appropriation ordinance provided for the payment of all the expenses of the water works system, it might be implied that an omission to mention a particular object of expense prohibited the use of the proceeds of water rates for that purpose, but it is matter of common knowledge that the very large expenses of extending water mains, the construction of tunnels, and many other methods of improving the system and increasing the revenues, and which are not referred to in the annual appropriation ordinance are habitually paid out of the proceeds of water rates.

Under these circumstances, and in view of the fact that the duty of managing the water works and of assessing and collecting water rates is imposed upon the commissioner of public works in general terms, without any special directions as to the methods to be employed, or limitation as to the expenses which may be incurred in producing revenue, the omission of any reference to such expenses in the appropriation ordinance cannot be treated as prohibiting such expenses.

It is the duty of the mayor "to take care that all the laws and ordinances of the City are faithfully executed"; it was, therefore, clearly in his power to cause the investigation to be made. This having been done with such satisfactory results, it seems quite clear that the cost thereof should be paid from the proceeds of water rates.

JOHN MAYO PALMER, Asst. Corporation Counsel.
Approved:
HARRY RUBENS, Corporation Counsel.

December 18, 1894.

To the Commissioner of Health.

Sir—

I had occasion recently to give you my opinion that the commissioner of health had no special duty to perform in preventing the sale of proprietary medicines, which, when administered contrary to the directions given by the manufacturer, are productive of injurious consequences.

This opinion was based upon the absence of any ordinance imposing that duty upon the commissioner of health, but it contained a suggestion that it would be entirely proper for you to see to the enforcement of such ordinances of the city as relate to the general subject, and to invite the attention of the state officers whose duty it is to enforce them, to any violations of its laws in this particular.

It is now suggested that the council by ordinance prohibit the sale of patent or proprietary medicines containing cocaine or other poisons without a special permit from the health department of the city; and that no such permit shall be issued until the manufacturer shall file with the commissioner of health an affidavit setting forth the exact formula by which such medicine is prepared, nor unless the commissioner shall be satisfied that such medicine is not injurious to public health.

You desire my opinion as to whether such an ordinance can be lawfully passed and enforced by the council.

If the city council has this authority it must arise from two clauses in the charter, by one of which it is vested with power "to appoint a Board of Health and prescribe its powers and duties," and by the other "to do all acts, and make all regulations which may be necessary or expedient for the promotion of health or the suppression of disease."

While these powers are exceedingly broad and are granted in the most comprehensive terms, the language employed must be limited by and construed in connection with other legislation of the state, and with reference to the established usages of society, which constitute our common law upon the subject.

In considering a question of this kind it is always to be kept in mind that the city council possesses such legislative powers only as are expressly conferred upon it by the state, and such as can be reasonably and fairly implied from the express powers conferred.

Under our system the lawmaking power is vested primarily in the general assembly of the state, and upon subjects, which, in the nature of things, affect all the people of the state alike, the legislation of the state must be deemed adequate and exclusive, unless express power is given to municipal bodies to legislate upon the same subject.

And when it appears that a city has been authorized in general terms to legislate upon a subject, which in its widest definition might include a matter which the state has itself fully regulated, the grant of power to the city must be limited in its scope so as not to trench upon the power thus impliedly reserved to the state itself; and even in cases where a city is allowed to legislate upon the same subject, it can neither authorize that which is forbidden nor prohibit that which is permitted by the state.

Now, while the practice of medicine and surgery and the conduct of the business of the druggist and pharmacist are so intimately connected with the health of the community that laws or ordinances governing these avocations might in a broad sense be properly characterized as regulations "For the promotion of the public health and the suppression of disease," yet it would hardly be contended, especially when the state has fully legislated upon the subjects, that a city could properly prescribe the qualifications of physicians and druggists.

In view of these principles, before we consider what the city council may do, let us see what the state and the city have done in that behalf.

By the criminal code of the state which has been in force for at least forty years, the sale of any substance usually denominated as poisonous, without having the word "Poison" placed upon the package containing it; and the sale and delivery of *any* drug or medicine otherwise, than upon the prescription of a physician, *without having the name of the drug or medicine placed upon the package containing it,* is forbidden.

By other criminal laws the adulteration of drugs and medicines, the sale of them under false names, and other practices by which the purchaser may be deceived, as to the purity, quantity or potency thereof, are prohibited. By more recent legislation the qualifications of physicians, surgeons and pharmacists are prescribed, and by the act regulating the practice of pharmacy passed in 1881, no persons other than registered pharmacists, and registered assistants, are permitted to compound or dispense prescriptions, or vend drugs, medicines, or poisons; but that act, which regulates in the most precise manner the whole subject of the sale of drugs and poisons, contains this proviso, "That nothing in this Act shall apply to nor in any manner interfere with the business of any physician, or prevent him from supplying to his patients such articles as may seem to him proper, *nor with the making or vending of patent or proprietary medicines, or medicines placed in sealed packages, with the name of the contents and of the pharmacist or physician by whom prepared or compounded.*"

This act also forbids the sale of articles commonly recognized as poisons, without a label bearing the name of the article, the word "poison," and the name and place of business of the seller, who must not deliver any such article to a person under the age of fifteen years, nor shall he deliver such poison to any person without satisfying himself that it is to be used for a legitimate purpose.

By the ordinances of the city which have been in force for a great many years it is provided that "no person shall make, sell, put up, prepare or administer any prescription, decoction or medicine under any deceptive or fraudulent name, direction or pretense," and it is further provided that "no poisonous medicine, decoction or substance shall be held for sale or sold, except for lawful purposes and with proper motives, and by persons competent to give the proper directions and precautions as to the use of the same; nor shall any bottle, box, parcel or receptacle thereof be delivered to any person unless the same is marked "Poison"; nor to any person to whom the party delivering the same has reason to think intends it for any illegal purpose."

It is significant that the state, which possesses all legislative power, when establishing a Board of Health in 1877, did not vest that board with the power to control the sale of drugs, medicines and poisons, but that the substance of all prior legislation upon these subjects, and much that was new, was reserved for and embodied in an act entitled "An Act to regulate the practice of pharmacy in the State of Illinois."

In view of the provision of our constitution that the subject of an act shall be expressed in its title, this cannot be regarded as less or other than an authoritative declaration by the legislature that the vending of drugs, medicines and poisons is to be controlled under the specific power to regulate the practice of pharmacy, rather than under the power to establish a board of health and prescribe its duties, or the more general power to adopt regulations for the promotion of health and the suppression of disease.

But without regard to the circumstance that the general assembly has deemed it proper to treat the sale of medicines and poisons as a matter to be regulated by an act relating to the practice of pharmacy, applicable uniformly throughout the state, and assuming that the city may, under any of its powers, also legislate upon the same subject, it will not be claimed, I think, that the city may impose any restrictions upon the sale of these articles, by druggists, inconsistent with the theory of the state laws.

So far as my limited knowledge of the subject extends, there is no destructive agent known to science under the name of poison which may not have its beneficial or at least harmless uses, either alone or in combination with other agents; at least this is the theory of the law, if not an accurate statement of the medical or chemical view of the matter.

Recognizing this theory, the law only requires that these destructive agencies shall not be put in motion otherwise than by those who have furnished the legal evidence of their knowledge of their properties, and of their skill to apply them under proper circumstances, that is, circumstances proper as judged by the laws of the great profession whose province it is to administer them, and not as judged by the law of courts and lawyers.

That cocaine, for example, may be lawfully used, either alone or in combination with other substances by medical men themselves in their practice, and that it may lawfully be sold by druggists upon a physician's prescription, cannot be doubted, for "so the law is written."

The law also recognizes the fact that many things called medicines, which contain elements proper to be applied in disease, but which might be harmful if used by persons in health, are prepared in large quantities by manufacturing chemists or pharmacists, and are sold by druggists throughout the entire country and are freely used by the medical profession.

Such preparations as these, if labeled with the name of the physician or pharmacist by whom prepared, and the name of the article or its component parts, so that no deception can be practiced upon the purchaser, are treated in precisely the same manner as if they were compounded, in each instance, upon the prescription of a physician.

That proprietary medicines thus labeled may be used by individuals contrary to the directions given by the manufacturer, or in attempted treatment of maladies for which they are not recommended, and when so used would be productive of disease or death, may be assumed to have been known to the general assembly when the pharmacy act was passed; but that these same consequences might follow the improper or unauthorized use of medicines compounded upon the prescription of a physician was equally well known.

If, then, the general assembly in the exercise of its plenary power of legislation upon a subject of equal importance in all portions of the state, has chosen to place proprietary medicines and those compounded upon the prescriptions of physicians upon the same plane, and has authorized the sale of both by pharmacists throughout the state, no legislation of a single city can forbid such sales by pharmacists absolutely; nor can a pharmacist be required as a condition precedent to the exercise of a legal right to sell a proprietary medicine to disclose the formula by which it is prepared, which might have the effect to deprive him of his property in a valuable trade secret, nor can he be required to refrain from exercising a right recognized by the laws of the state, because, in the opinion of the commissioner of health of a single city, the article sold might under some circumstances be injurious to health.

In my opinion, the city council has no legal power to pass or enforce an ordinance of the kind suggested.

JOHN MAYO PALMER, Corporation Counsel.

December 21, 1894.

City Collector, Chicago, Ill.

Dear Sir—

Replying to your request for advice as to whether or not a license should be granted to a corporation, which is seeking to conduct a business as a pawnbroker, we advise you that Chapter 74, paragraph 14, of Starr & Curtis' Statutes, provides, "That every person or company engaged in the business of receiving property in pledge or security for money, or other things advanced to the pawner or pledger, shall be held, and is hereby declared and defined to be a pawnbroker."

It has been held by the Supreme Court of this state that cities incorporated under the general law have power to license, regulate, etc., hawkers, peddlers and pawnbrokers, but they have no power whatever to determine who is, or who may be, a pawnbroker; that question has already been determined by the legislature of this state in the above act.

The legislature having provided that every person or company engaged in receiving property in pledge, etc., is a pawnbroker, and the legislature recognizing that a company or a corporation may conduct a pawnbroking business, any interpretation of an ordinance of the city of Chicago contrary to the above definition would not be proper.

An ordinance of this city provides, Section 2311, "That the Mayor may from time to time grant licenses to such persons as shall produce to him satisfactory evidence of their good character to exercise or carry on the business of a pawnbroker," but this cannot be interpreted as meaning that a corporation cannot conduct a pawn business.

Corporations have the same standing as to fitness for the pursuit of business in which they are engaged as individuals, and if they abuse the charter rights conferred upon them, the statute has provided means for revoking these privileges. Again, a corporation acts only through its executive officer, and is responsible for the acts of the officer, and the executive officer is responsible for his acts irrespective of the fact that such are carried on for the corporation, and particularly in any penal action which may be instituted for a violation of any ordinance. Therefore, in granting a license to a corporation, it is necessary that the executive officer's character and fitness for the work should be taken into consideration, and if the executive officer's character is not good, then a license should not be granted.

We therefore advise you that, in the case of Frank's Collateral Loan Bank, which is a corporation seeking to do business as a pawnbroker, if the Mayor is satisfied as to the good character of the executive officer of this corporation, who we understand is Jacob Frank, a license should be granted to it, bearing in mind, however, that in this particular case Frank's Collateral Loan Bank does business in three different places in the city. It should pay a license fee for each and every place of business it conducts. Respectfully submitted,

WALTER W. ROSS, Asst. Corporation Counsel.
Approved:
JOHN MAYO PALMER, Corporation Counsel.

December 27, 1894.
To the Honorable, the City Council.
Gentlemen—
The council recently declared, in substance, that within the past six months the price of wheat has been reduced more than one-half;

that the price paid by bakers for flour has been correspondingly reduced; but that in consequence of a trust or combination among the bakers of the city, no reduction in the price of bread has been made by them.

In view of these facts, the Corporation Counsel was directed to submit "an opinion as to whether or not some action cannot be taken by the council, by the passage of a proper ordinance, or otherwise, to compel bakers to reduce the price of bread to the consumers to a figure proportionate to the reduction made to them by the manufacturers and producers of flour."

By the charter of the city, the council is authorized "to regulate the sale of bread within the city, and to prescribe the weight and quality of the bread in the loaf."

In the exercise of this power the council has, by ordinance, passed many years ago, and still in force, prescribed:

That all bread baked and exposed for sale in the city shall be made of good and wholesome flour or meal; that it shall be sold only by avoirdupois weight; that it shall be made into loaves of certain specified weights; that each loaf shall be marked with numbers indicating its weight, and that each loaf shall be marked with the name of the baker thereof.

The making, sale or offer for sale by any person of any bread not conforming in all respects to these requirements is visited with a penalty of $10.00 for each offense.

As a means for the enforcement of these requirements, it is further prescribed that it shall not be lawful for any person to engage in the business of a baker without a permit from the mayor for that purpose, and paying a fee of $5.00 therefor, and having his name and place of business recorded in a book kept for that purpose in the city clerk's office, under a penalty of $25.00 for each offense, and $10.00 for each day the same shall be continued.

Any alderman, the superintendent of police, or any policeman, may in the day time, enter any place where bread is baked, stored or offered for sale, and may stop, detain and examine any person or vehicle carrying bread, and search for, view, try or weigh any bread, and if any be found made in violation of the ordinance, seize it, and enter a complaint before any justice of the peace, against the person guilty of such violation.

Bread thus seized shall be deposited with the superintendent of police and kept for use as evidence on the trial. If the person charged is convicted, the seized bread shall be retained till the fine and costs are paid; unwholesome bread shall not in any case be returned to the owner, but shall be destroyed.

The sale or offer for sale of any bread which has been seized for violation of the ordinance is prohibited under a penalty of $50.00 for each offense.

To this extent only has the council, by legislative action, exercised its power to regulate the sale of bread within the city.

It has been suggested that if the city council should go a step further in legislative regulation of the sale of bread, and by ordinance fix the price at which it should be sold, a complete remedy for the evils of which complaint is made would be furnished.

The remedy thus proposed is so attractive in its simplicity and directness that I have devoted much time to a study of the question whether the council has the legal power to employ it. In this study I have had the benefit of an exceedingly able brief prepared by distinguished counsel, and while I agree with them that the state has not authorized the council to fix the price of bread, this conclusion is a mere incident in the search for a remedy for the evil alleged to exist.

It by no means follows that, because one remedy which seems to be the most direct cannot be employed that our laws afford the people of Chicago no relief from the evils of which they complain.

As the propriety and adequacy of any suggested remedy must be tested by the nature of the right invaded or wrong inflicted, it is of the first importance in the further consideration of this subject that we should clearly understand the rights of the people of Chicago in respect to the price of bread, and know in what manner and to what extent those rights have been invaded.

The people of Chicago have not a legal right to demand bread at a price which would deprive the manufacturer of such a profit upon the capital and labor invested in its production as he could realize from its sale under the operation of the ordinary laws of fair and honest trade; and if the council were invested with power to fix the price of bread, he could not be deprived of such profit.

But the people of Chicago do have the legal right to demand bread at a price which is not influenced by any unlawful restrictions upon free competition in its sale, or by any unlawful device, combination or arrangement by which it is enhanced.

This legal right of all the people of Chicago, it is alleged, is invaded by a combination among the bakers of the city, and it is for this wrong that a remedy is sought.

If it be true that in the city of Chicago there exists a combination between persons and corporations to create or carry out restrictions upon the trade in bread; or to increase the price of bread; or to fix any standard whereby the price of bread to the public shall be in any manner controlled or established; or by which they agree not to sell or dispose of bread below a certain common standard or list price; or by which they agree to keep the price of bread at a fixed or graduated price or by which they, in any manner establish the price of bread among themselves, or between themselves and others to preclude free and unrestricted competition among themselves and others in the sale of bread, or by which they agree to pool, combine or unite any interest they may have in connection with the sale of bread, so that its price may be in any manner affected; then a criminal conspiracy against trade exists, and all persons who take part in such combination, or aid or advise the same, or do any act in pursuance thereof, are liable to the most severe penalties.

If any of the parties to this conspiracy be a corporation organized under the laws of the state of Illinois, it thereby forfeits its corporate existence, and if it be a foreign corporation it is thereby deprived of any right to do business in this state.

If there is reasonable cause to believe that this wrong exists, the remedy is not far to seek. Every agency which the law supplies should be vigorously and intelligently employed, to ascertain whether this criminal conspiracy exists in fact, and if it does, to detect the offenders, procure the legal evidence of their guilt, cause them to be punished to the utmost limit of the law, and to utterly destroy the combination by which the evils complained of are produced and perpetuated.

This being the wrong, and this the remedy afforded by the law, we have yet to ascertain what the city council may do to make the remedy effectual.

Whether any further legislative action by the council, under its express power to regulate the sale of bread, would add anything to the effectiveness or simplicity of the remedy now provided by the laws of the state punishing conspiracies against trade, is exceedingly doubtful.

The question whether an unlawful combination or conspiracy against the trade in bread exists in fact, is one which can only be determined by the judicial tribunals of the state, and for the punishment of offenders and the destruction of the combination, resort must be had to these same tribunals, whose machinery can be set in motion only in the orderly and regulated manner prescribed by the laws of the state.

Courts and juries may be confidently relied upon to convict and punish all those who are proven to be guilty of a violation of our criminal laws, but detection must precede prosecution, and convincing evidence of guilt must precede conviction and punishment.

The practical work, and the difficult task before those who would remedy the evils of which complaint is made, is to detect the offenders and procure the legal evidence of their guilt. Once this is done, all real difficulties vanish.

The question then really is, what steps may the council take to aid in procuring legal evidence of the guilt of persons charged with a conspiracy against the trade in bread.

The circumstance that private individuals may or the attorney general and the state's attorney should institute prosecutions for the violation of this law, does not make the power and consequent duty of the city government in the premises greater or less.

A city so frequently exercises its governmental powers by the passage of ordinances for the regulation of matters of local concern, that we sometimes overlook the fact that it is vested by law with every large and important administrative function.

The primary object for which a city government is created is to act as an agency of the state, as the representative of organized society, to enforce within a densely populated territory all those laws of the state which are designed to protect the citizen in the exercise of every absolute and relative right, especially those laws which denounce and punish offenses against the person and property of the citizen.

To this end the city is vested with the power and charged with the duty of regulating the police, and of prescribing the powers and duties of a superintendent of police and policemen, which implies, at the very least, that it must cause to be enforced within the limits of the city all those laws designed to preserve and protect the peace and good order of society. It may also undoubtedly employ all officers and agents of its own creation in such manner as to it may seem most conducive to this end.

While it is not common for a city government to directly interpose for the enforcement of the criminal laws of this state, this is so only because, fortunately, the necessity for such interposition does not often arise; but when crime has assumed such proportion as to seriously threaten the persons or property of a considerable number of citizens, or where for any reason the ordinary methods of detection and prosecution seem ineffectual, the city of Chicago has never declined to act.

Instances, fresh within the recollection of all, are not wanting where the whole power of all branches of the city government was brought into operation for the protection of the property rights of persons and corporations, alleged to be threatened with danger from combinations similar to the one now alleged to exist, which were violative of the laws of the state.

This was done with the approval of all classes of society, and no doubt was ever suggested as to the power and duty of the city government to vigorously aid in the enforcement of these laws, although for the ultimate punishment of the offenders the co-operation of other agencies of the state must be secured.

It was not supposed that the city government could lawfully decline to exercise all its powers for the protection of property, because its owners were rich and powerful and possessed the means of enforcing the laws of the state in their own behalf, against alleged offenders who were poor and feeble.

Nor can the city government now be excused from exercising all its powers to enforce the laws of the state, if a combination and conspiracy against those laws exists, when the conspirators and oppressors are rich, strong and powerful, and the victims and sufferers are poor, weak and humble. If the municipal government may and should interfere to punish a conspiracy against property, surely it must interfere to suppress a conspiracy which vitally affects the rights of many to live.

If a conspiracy exists in our midst by which burdens upon ill requited labor, now almost too heavy to be borne, are unlawfully increased, and by which the awful pain and bitterness of grinding poverty are heightened, where the voices of the sufferers are too weak to make their complaints heard in the courts of justice; if organized municipal society has any value; if its power and influence may ever be employed to vindicate the right and subdue the wrong; then, unless municipal government is to abdicate its most vital functions, surely it may act under these circumstances.

The constitution of the council and the circumstances that its functions are mainly of a legislative character, forbid that it should itself enter upon the work of detecting and prosecuting offenders against the criminal laws of the state, but it may in the exercise of its undoubted powers authorize the proper executive departments of the city government to engage in that work, and furnish them with the requisite funds for that purpose.

I have prepared and submit herewith the drafts of an order which if passed by your honorable body will probably bring about the desired result.   Respectfully submitted,

JOHN MAYO PALMER, Corporation Counsel.

January 3, 1895.
Joseph Schofield, Esq., Superintendent of Bureau of Street and Alley Cleaning.

Dear Sir—

Your communication of this date to Mr. Palmer asking if the power to abate nuisances comprehends forcible destruction of garbage boxes upon a failure of the owner to remove the same from the street or alley in compliance with a notice from your bureau ordering their removal, has been referred to me.

In my opinion any garbage box left upon the street or alley, after notice to remove the same, may be destroyed as provided in Sections 2682, 2683, Myers' Laws and Ordinances. Very respectfully,

JESSE B. BARTON, Assistant Corporation Counsel.
I would advise that your notice be ten instead of five days.

J. B. B.

January 28, 1895.
To the Common Council of the City of Chicago.

Gentlemen—

In compliance with request of your honorable body at its last meeting, we herewith submit to you an answer to the following question:

Is it necessary for a corporation seeking a railroad franchise to secure merely a majority of the frontage in a mile, where the mile in question embraces several different streets, or must a majority of the frontage of each of the several streets in question be obtained?

The charter of the city of Chicago was amended by the act of March 30, 1887, and provides that the city council shall have no power to grant the right to lay down any railroad tracks in any street of the city to any steam, dummy, electric, cable, horse or other railroad company, except upon the petition of the owners of the land representing more than one-half of the frontage of the street, or so much thereof as is sought to be used for railroad purposes, and when the street or part thereof sought to be used shall be more than one mile in extent, no petition of land owners shall be valid unless the same shall be signed by the owners of the land representing more than one-half of the frontage of each mile, and of the fraction of a mile, if any, in excess of the whole miles, measuring from the initial point named in such petition to such street or the part thereof sought to be used for railroad purposes.

We are clearly of the opinion that it is absolutely necessary to give validity to the grant of the city council to a railroad company that the petitions upon which the council acts must show a majority of all private property in each street within the mile and fraction thereof, petitioning for the construction of the railroad. We fail to see how the frontage law admits of any other construction in this regard.

In this connection, we desire to call the attention of the council to a matter of very grave moment.

The control of the streets and alleys of the city is vested in the city council for the public interest, and also it is the council's duty to protect owners of lots fronting on the streets and alleys in the employment of their rights incident to such frontage. If ultimately it should be determined by the Supreme Court of this state that the city council is to be the sole judge of the sufficiency of the petition, and that the council having once found that there was a sufficient frontage signed, its action is conclusive upon all parties, there will necessarily then be placed within the council a power, that if not exercised with the greatest caution, citizens owning property fronting on the proposed right of way may suffer irreparable damage, and in many instances by inadvertence upon the part of the council in regard to the necessary amount of frontage and the genuineness of the signatures to the petition its action might be tantamount to a denial of justice to the citizen.

Citizens have lately, in many instances, appealed to the courts of this county for protection against what they allege is an unauthorized invasion of the street by a railroad company under the frontage law. Many injunctions have been sought and granted, and suits are now pending in which ultimately will be decided the question as to whether the determination and finding of the council upon the matter of frontage and necessary signatures to the petition shall be final upon all parties.

In view of the unsettled condition of this pending litigation, and in view of the fact that at the present time so much complaint is made that grants are given to various corporations to lay their tracks in our streets upon petitions lacking necessary frontage and containing signatures which are alleged to be unauthorized and forged, we deem it our duty to suggest to the council the feasibility of at once devising some simple yet efficient method by which it can intelligently have investigated and determined not only whether the petitions contain the necessary frontage, but also whether the signatures to the petition are genuine.   Respectfully submitted,

W. S. JOHNSON, Asst. Corporation Counsel.

Approved:
JOHN MAYO PALMER, Corporation Counsel.

March 18, 1895.

To the Mayor—

You furnished me a copy of a resolution passed by the city council on March 11, 1895, as follows:

"Ordered, That the mayor and commissioner of public works be and they are hereby directed to make such additions to the pumping capacity of the several pumping stations in the city of Chicago of pumping engines and boilers as in their judgment may be necessary to furnish the inhabitants of the city with an abundance of water, and that cne hundred and fifty thousand ($150,000) dollars be and hereby is appropriated from the water fund of the city of Chicago for the commencement and continuance of this work during the year 1895."

You desire my opinion as to whether the mayor and commissioner of public works may, by virtue of the charter and the general ordinances of the city, in connection with the order of the council, make contracts involving the necessary expenditures from the water fund to secure such additions to the pumping capacity of the several pumping stations of the city as in their judgment may be necessary to furnish the inhabitants of the city with an abundance of water, or whether your power to contract is limited to such arrangements as will involve an expenditure of no more than $150,000.

In my opinion the power of the commissioner of public works, who is vested by the ordinance with the supervision and control of the water works system in conjunction with the mayor as the executive head of the city council, to make such improvements in and additions to the water works system as shall be necessary from time to time to meet the just demands of the public and of private consumers, is complete. The only limitation upon this power is that contained in the requirement of the ordinances that contracts for work and materials payable out of the water fund shall be let by competitive bidding. In the present case this has been done and the council duly informed of that fact by the mayor. The resolution under consideration must, therefore, be deemed only as expressive of the approval of the council

15

of the efforts of the mayor and commissioner of public works toward the improvement of our water works system, although not expressly referred to in the resolution. The reference to an appropriation of $150,000 for the water fund "For the commencement and continuance of this work during the year 1895" is no limitation upon the right and duty of the commissioner of public works to make the necessary expenditures to accomplish the general result desired, but is simply to be regarded as an expression of opinion by the council that the sum mentioned would be sufficient to meet the demands of the year 1895 in that behalf.

In my opinion the mayor and commissioner of public works have ample authority to make any contracts for the improvement of the water works system, which have been awarded in pursuance of a competitive bidding.

JOHN MAYO PALMER, Corporation Counsel.

March 18, 1895.

To the Honorable, the City Council.

Gentlemen—

On March 11, 1895, your honorable body passed a preamble and resolution as follows:

"Whereas, by an agreement entered into on the 17th day of June, A. D. 1891, between the Chicago Gas Light & Coke Company, the People's Gas Light & Coke Company, the Consumers' Gas Company, the Equitable Gas Light & Fuel Company, the Suburban Gas Company, the Hyde Park Gas Company and the Lake Gas Company, parties of the first part, and the city of Chicago, party of the second part, it was provided that the net price of gas for the year 1894 should not exceed $1.15 per thousand cubic feet of gas of 24 candle power, and during the year 1895 should not exceed $1.10 per thousand cubic feet of gas of 24 candle power, and other provisions were made in said contract for the price of gas to be furnished to the city, both for street lamps and in public buildings and places, based upon gas of 24 candle power; and

"Whereas, The various reports of the gas inspector show that for many months past the gas supplied by the different companies above named is of a quality of much less than 24 candle power, thereby entitling both the city and the citizens under the aforesaid agreement to a considerable rebate on account of the poorer quality of gas furnished; therefore, be it

"Resolved, That the Corporation Counsel be and he is hereby requested to report to this council at its next regular meeting what redress the city and citizens of Chicago have on account of the failure of the said gas companies to comply with the terms of the said contract."

I desire before submitting an opinion as requested, to inform you that the gas companies referred to in your resolution have furnished me with a copy of an opinion of their counsel, Messrs. Winston & Meagher, upon this subject, and in connection with this opinion they have handed me sworn statements from their officers having special knowledge of the facts asserting that the gas furnished by them to the city and private consumers during the years 1894 and 1895 has at all times exceeded 24 candle power in illuminating capacity or quality.

While I have been greatly aided in the discharge of my duty to answer the questions of law involved in your resolution by the opinion of the distinguished counsel for the gas companies, I have informed them that it is not within my province to pass upon the question of the fact referred to in the statements as to the actual quality of gas furnished by the companies.

I, therefore, submit the opinion of counsel and the statements of the officers of the gas companies, as to the quality of gas furnished, to be considered by you in connection with my opinion.

It is also necessary that your honorable body should consider in arriving at a proper conclusion upon the questions of law and fact involved in the present inquiry, the opinion of my predecessor, Mr. Rubens, furnished to you on May 2, 1894, and published in the council proceedings for the present year at pages 282-283, in which he stated the legal effect of the gas contract of June 17, 1891.

By reference to this opinion, and that of the counsel for the gas companies, it will be apparent that there is but little if any difference between the city and the companies as to the legal effect and proper construction of the gas contract of 1891.

The substance of the situation in my opinion is this: That since the close of the year 1891, the city, not being bound by the contract of June 17, 1891, had, from time to time, accepted the continuing offer of the gas companies to furnish gas of a particular quality and at a specified price, and has annually, with full knowledge of all the facts, settled the account for gas furnished, either by payment therefor in money, or by permitting judgment to be rendered for unpaid balances claimed on the basis of the quality and price specified in the contract of 1891.

So far as the city is concerned it is thus conclusively estopped from asserting that the gas furnished up to February 1, 1895, is not satisfactory in quality.

The same principle must apply with equal if not greater force to the dealings between private persons and the gas companies.

Assuming, without undertaking to decide, that the contract of 1891 was a continuing offer by the gas companies to furnish, after the year 1891, to each individual consumer, gas at 24 candle power, such consumer must be deemed to have been satisfied with the quality of the gas furnished up to the time of each monthly payment therefor by him, unless at the time of payment he at least made some objection on that account. In view of the monopoly possessed by gas companies and the practical compulsion imposed upon the consumer to deal with them, I must not be understood as holding that he waives his right to complain of the quality of gas simply because he continues to use it; but he must, in fairness, before paying his gas bill and adjusting the account, indicate in some way that it is unsatisfactory and call for its correction. If he does not do at least this much he cannot escape the just implication of law and facts arising from his payment of the bill without objection, that no ground of complaint in respect to the quality of the gas in fact exists.

The precise question submitted by your resolution for my opinion is "What redress the city and citizens of Chicago have on account of the failure of the said gas companies to comply with the terms of said contract." (The contract of June 17, 1891).

To which I answer:

First: This contract is not now in force either as to the city or the gas companies; the city is now, and since the close of the year 1891 has been, receiving gas from the gas companies upon an implied promise to pay therefor "So much as the gas received is reasonably worth," and no more. The obligation of the companies to the city, and the rights of the city against the companies, are in no way dependent upon the contract of 1891, and therefore there is no redress for the city merely "On account of the failure of said gas companies to comply with the terms of said contract." The city has a right to demand, and the company is impliedly bound to furnish, gas of a sound quality for a sound price. If, during the present year the city has received gas for which no payment or adjustment has been made, and the price demanded for such gas is more than it is reasonably worth because of defects in quality or otherwise, then the city may properly decline to pay such price, and may discharge its obligation to the gas companies by paying the actual value of the gas received.

Second: The "redress" of the citizen is similar to that of the city. But neither his right nor his remedy is affected by the gas contract of June 17, 1891.

In conclusion I venture to suggest, as I have before suggested, that the remedy for the city as well as for the citizen against the furnishing by the gas company of gas of inferior quality or at an unreasonable price, is by the execution of proper contract between the city and the gas companies, by which the rights and obligations of all concerned shall be accurately fixed. In such contracts a high standard for gas may be prescribed, proper tests of the quality of gas may be made under public supervision which will conclusively bind all parties, and by such contract the price of gas may be scaled and limited in proportion to its actual illuminating capacity and value. Until such contracts are made the city and its citizens can have no definite or fixed rule for ascertaining their rights; but the transactions of each month or quarter will be opened to dispute with the gas companies, and must be determined by the application of the rules of abstract justice in each particular case.

Under present conditions the city and its citizens must either submit to the demands of the gas companies without question, or involve themselves in endless litigation. While, on account of the absence of competition, it cannot be expected that by awarding contracts as required by law, the price of gas can be greatly reduced below that at present paid by the city and private consumers, yet the great public and private benefits which will certainly result from having a fixed standard of quality and a scale of prices based thereon, with simple but effective methods of determining all disputes arising between the gas companies and the city or private consumers, all unmistakably point to the execution of proper contracts as the only remedy or means of redress for the conditions complained of in the resolutions under consideration.

Believing that the passage of the ordinance submitted to you by me on January 7, 1895, at the instance of the city comptroller, is a necessary preliminary to the awarding of a proper contract for gas, I again venture to advise its adoption. Respectfully submitted,
JOHN MAYO PALMER, Corporation Counsel.

March 22, 1895.
To the Honorable City Council of the City of Chicago.
Gentlemen—
In pursuance of an order passed by your honorable body March 11th inst., asking an opinion on the authority of the council to pass an ordinance, requiring electric light companies to furnish meters so constructed that the customers can read the same, I have examined into the question, and am of the opinion, that if there are devices which will measure the electricity used, upon which a schedule of charges can be based, the city council can compel the light companies to use the same, when they charge by measurement, and if it be possible to construct such devices so that they may be read by customers, the council can require them to be so constructed.
Very respectfully,
JESSE B. BARTON, Asst. Corporation Counsel
Approved:
JOHN MAYO PALMER, Corporation Counsel.

April 3, 1895.
To the Honorable, the City Council of the City of Chicago.
Gentlemen—
At a recent meeting of your honorable body, the following order was passed: "Ordered, That the Corporation Counsel be and he is hereby directed to report to this council his opinion as to the authority of this council to pass an ordinance requiring street car companies to make proper provision for the protection of gripmen and other employes from undue exposure to severely cold weather."

In my opinion street car companies are subject to supervision of the city in exercising their functions as common carriers on the streets of the city and can be compelled to furnish proper protection to their employes if such protection will tend toward increasing the efficiency of the service to be rendered the public by the companies through such employes.

Whether any, and if any, what device can be adopted which by enclosing or protecting gripmen and other employes will promote the interests of the public, are matters of fact rather than law. But any ordinance upon the subject which is reasonable would be legal.

Respectfully submitted,

JOHN MAYO PALMER, Corporation Counsel.

May 3, 1895.

To the Commissioner of Public Works.

Dear Sir—

I have your communication of April 18th in which you call my attention to an order passed by the city council on April 15th, as follows:

"*Ordered*, That the Commissioner of Public Works be and he is hereby directed to cancel all contracts made in each and every case for sewers under the first letting, where said contracts have not been let to the lowest responsible bidder or bidders."

You informed me that work under some of these contracts has already been commenced, and that contractors are now prosecuting work under them, and upon this statement of facts, you call upon me for an opinion "as to the legal status of the various contracts that you may take proper action."

The order of the council seems to impose upon you the duty of determining, as a matter of fact and law, what, if any, contracts have been let in violation of law for the construction of sewers.

As a matter of law you are not bound to assume this responsibility, but on the contrary you may, if you choose, cause the facts in each particular case to be ascertained and require the Corporation Counsel to take the responsibility of advising you specifically upon the necessary legal steps to be taken for the protection of the interests of the city.

Should you think proper to pass upon the question of law and fact in these cases, I advise you as matter of law:

First. That the award of a contract for public work by the commissioner of public works is a determination by the proper officer that the person to whom it is awarded is the lowest responsible bidder, and this determination is binding upon the city and the contractor in the absence of fraud participated in by the officer and the contractor.

Second. A mere change in the incumbent of the office of commissioner of public works does not authorize a review of the action of a predecessor in that position, but the contractor is entitled to the benefit of the same presumptions in favor of the honesty and fairness of the acts of your predecessor, as he would be entitled to with respect to your own official acts.

JOHN MAYO PALMER. Corporation Counsel.

May 15, 1895.

James R. Mann., Esq., Chairman Judiciary Committee.

Dear Sir—

At your request, I return herewith a draft of an order directing the Corporation Counsel to prepare an opinion as to the validity of an ordinance to establish a system of sewers ten feet in diameter, to be used, the lower half for drainage, and the upper half to be rented out by the city to private parties or corporations, or to be used by the city for lighting, heating and power purposes, and the furnishing of water, the cost of the same to be paid one-half by the abutting property-owners, by special assessment, and one-half by the city of Chicago, same to be constructed in the downtown portion of the city; also your communication of May 13th inst., expressing the desire of your committee that the Corporation Counsel submit to it his opinion as to the right of the City Council to pass such an ordinance to be paid for in part by special assessment.

The city is authorized by Section 1 of Article IX of its charter "to make local improvements by special assessment, or by special taxation or both, of contiguous property, or general taxation or otherwise, as they shall by ordinance prescribe."

The city is authorized to construct a system of sewers, and for that purpose it may levy special assessments upon the property benefited, or a special tax upon specified property, but the system of sewers contemplated in the ordinance referred to is a combination of a sewer and a conduit; that part which is conduit, in my opinion, is in no sense a local improvement, and consequently no part of it can be paid for by a special assessment. In my opinion also, it will be absolutely impossible to separate the cost of the sewer from the cost of the conduit, and that therefore a special assessment for the part which is a sewer, or which is to be a sewer, would be defeated in the courts.

I would respectfully refer you to the case of Chicago vs. Law, 144 Ill., p. 569, for a discussion of the question of what is a local improvement. Very respectfully,

JESSE B. BARTON, Asst. Corporation Counsel

Approved:
WM. G. BEALE, Corporation counsel.

May 15, 1895.

James R. Mann, Esq., Chairman Judiciary Committee.

Dear Sir—

I return herewith your communication of the 13th inst., with accompanying draft of ordinance prohibiting the further opening or erection of brick-yards within the city of Chicago. In accordance with your request, I have examined into the authority of the city council in regard to this matter, and as to the validity of such an ordinance if passed.

I find the 75th clause of Section 63, of the city charter, empowers the city council "To declare what shall be a nuisance and to abate the same," and the 83d clause of the same section gives it the further power "to prohibit any offensive or unwholesome business or establishment within or within one mile of the limits of the corporation."

The city council has no authority to declare that to be a nuisance which is not in fact a nuisance, nor has it a right to declare a business offensive or unwholesome, which is not in fact offensive or unwholesome. It is a mere question of fact, then, whether or not a brickyard is in itself a nuisance or an unoffensive or unwholesome establishment. I am not sufficiently advised as to be able to pass upon this question, and have no access to such statistics as would justify me in deciding the same. It, however, does seem to me extremely doubtful if a jury could be made to believe that a brickyard is in itself a nuisance or is unwholesome or offensive in the sense that would make it a subject of prohibition on the part of the city.

Very respectfully,

JESSE B. BARTON, Asst. Corporation Counsel.

Approved:
WM. G. BEALE, Corporation Counsel.

May 17, 1895.

James R. Mann, Esq., Chairman Judiciary Committee.

Dear Sir—

I return herewith your communication of May 13th inst., with the accompanying documents, viz: A communication from the Horse-Shoers, Teamsters, Harness, Carriage and Wagon Workers, Allied Council, an ordinance prohibiting the letting of any horse-shoeing, harness work, or carriage or wagon work for the city, to those not employing union labor, and an ordinance requiring drivers of police patrol wagons, to be members of the Teamsters' Union.

You ask an opinion as to the authority and right of the city council in the premises. The ordinance first mentioned seeks to limit the officers of the city when they order certain repairs or purchase certain new articles to deal only with those who employ union labor. Of course, these matters are outside of the class required by the charter to be let to the lowest responsible bidder; and therefore relate to minor expenditures only. The city in the management of its business affairs is as free to deal where it pleases as a private corporation, or a private individual is, and may be actuated by just the same motives as they, but it is also a trustee of a fund to be expended in such an economical and proper manner as would characterize a reasonably prudent individual. -If then, this freedom to trade at will, can be exercised without a breach of such trust, under the ordinance in question, the same would be valid. In my opinion the ordinance should be changed so as to give free exercise to the naturally economical tendency of city employes, and I submit herewith a draft of an ordinance in accordance with that suggestion.

The second ordinance above mentioned deals with a class of city employees who come under the provisions of what is known as the civil service bill, and would therefore be inoperative and void.

Very respectfully,

JESSE B. BARTON, Assistant Corporation Counsel.

Approved:

WM. G. BEALE, Corporation Counsel.

May 17, 1895.

James R. Mann., Esq., Chairman Judiciary Committee.

Dear Sir—

I return herewith your communication of May 13th inst., passed by the executive board of the Hotel and Restaurant Employees National Alliance.

An opinion is asked by your committee of this department as to the right and authority of the city council to prohibit by ordinance, the employment of any female, except the wife or daughter of the proprietor in any place or places where intoxicants are sold. I have been unable to find any provision of the city charter which expressly, or by implication, empowers the city council to pass a valid ordinance in the nature of the one suggested by the resolutions before mentioned.

Very respectfully yours,

JESSE B. BARTON, Asst. Corporation Counsel.

Approved:

WM. G. BEALE, Corporation Counsel.

May 23, 1895.

O. D. Wetherell, Esq., City Comptroller.

Dear Sir—

A number of discharged police officers have, at different times during the past week, complained at this office that their pay was being held under assignments of the same which they had made to clothiers, and asking if this department could not give them relief. Your assistants have verbally repeated the statements made by the officers, and I take the liberty of submitting my opinion on the matter in question.

I have examined a bill filed in the circuit court by Sawyer, Manning & Co., in the nature of a creditor's bill, claiming the amount due from a number of officers. I am satisfied that the bill will be dismissed on demurrer, and I have inquired whether any statement was made by the court which would have the effect of staying payment to the men, and find that none was made nor was any injunction taken out, or even ordered by the court, or recommended by a master in chancery. I therefore think that we are not bound by the pendency of this suit to withhold these salaries, if they are not legally assigned, and upon a careful investigation of the subject, I believe the law to be that the salary of a public officer which is unearned at the time of an attempted assignment is not the subject of assignment, and that therefore when any of these assignments or pretended assignments antedate the earning of the salaries, you are justified in ignoring them, and paying the amounts severally due to the men.

Very respectfully,

JESSE B. BARTON, Assistant Corporation Counsel.

Approved:

WM. G. BEALE, Corporation Counsel.

May 28, 1895.

Honorable George B. Swift, Mayor, etc.

Dear Sir—

I have carefully considered the application heretofore referred to me of Mr. F. W. Klein for a license to keep a saloon at No. 5015 Cottage Grove avenue; have heard arguments and read written briefs and other papers submitted in the matter, and will now state my conclusions thereon somewhat in detail but as briefly as practicable.

I understand that until recently the applicant has been keeping a saloon at the above place for something over two months, a license issued to him for a different location having been transferred; that upon the expiration of such license he applied for a new license on or about the second day of May; that you supposing the case to be governed by the ordinary saloon licenses of the city of Chicago and seeing no substantial reason to the contrary granted such new license; that your attention was almost immediately thereafter called to certain material saloon ordinances passed by the village of Hyde Park, prior to the annexation of Hyde Park to Chicago, which ordinances were alleged to be in force and to govern this case; and that thereupon you promptly revoked the license thus granted. I understand further that Mr. Klein acknowledged the applicability of the Hyde Park ordinances and proceeded to obtain signatures to a new application, which was presented on or about the 6th day of May, and that it is this new application which is now pending and has been referred to me for my examination and opinion.

The decision of the Supreme Court of this state in People, ex rel. Morrison vs. Cregier, 138 Ill., 401, seems to establish conclusively that this case is governed by the ordinances of the village of Hyde Park, which were in force at the time of annexation and which by a city ordinance and by a state statute have been expressly kept in force in the territory concerned. This view, I believe, is conceded by both sides in this earnestly contested matter.

Section I of the Hyde Park ordinance under which, therefore, applicant must seek his license is as follows:

"Any person who shall desire to obtain a license to keep a saloon or dram-shop shall, in addition to the requirement now provided by ordinance, present his application in writing to the village comptroller for such license, in which shall be stated the name of the person or firm to whom the license is to be issued, and the place where such saloon or dram-shop is to be kept, which application shall be signed by a majority of the property owners, according to frontage, on *both* sides of the street in the block in which such dram-shop is to be kept, and shall also be signed by a majority of the bona fide householders and persons or firms living in or doing business on *each* side of the street, in the block upon which said dram-shop shall have its main entrance," etc.

The language of the foregoing section is not all that could be desired. in the matter of clearness and certainty, but I entertain no reasonable doubt as to' its meaning. I interpret the section precisely as if it had read that the application must be signed by a majority of the property owners, according to frontage on both sides taken together, of that part of the adjacent street in or along the block in which the dram-shop is to be kept, and must be signed also by a majority of the householders living on and the majority of the persons or firms doing business on the same portion of the street upon each side taken separately.

Number 5014 Cottage Grove Avenue is situated upon the west side of the street between 50th Street and 50th Court. 50th Court is a street running westerly for several blocks from Cottage Grove Avenue between 50th Street and 51st Street and parallel to them. On the east side of Cottage Grove Avenue there is no street corresponding to 50th Court, and the distance from 50th Street to 51st Street on the east side is not broken save by an alley opposite 50th Court. The existence of this alley has not been put forward as having any material bearing in the case.

Mr. Klein's application, as presented on or about May 6th, was supported by the signatures of a number of property owners, householders and business persons and firms claimed by him to be sufficient. The remonstrants who are opposing the issuance of the license, contend that the signatures should be, as they confessedly are not, of a majority of the property owners, householders and persons or firms engaged in business between 50th Street and 51st Street on both sides of Cottage Grove Avenue. or at least on the east side of that street. I do not think this contention is well founded. Whatever meaning we give to the word "block" as used in the above ordinance I feel no doubt that the block in which the proposed saloon is to be kept lies between 50th Street and 50th Court on the west side of Cottage Grove Avenue, and as I interpret the ordinance it is immaterial for the purpose of this case what particular territory or distance comprises a block on the east side of the street, only the block in which the saloon is to be kept is required to be considered. In my view the ordinance has regard, for the purposes of this case, only to the property owners, householders and persons or firms doing business between 50th Street and 50th Court on the west side of Cottage Grove Avenue, and between 50th Street and a point (in this instance an alley) opposite 50th Court on the east side of the street. This view seems to me to be in strict accord with the language of the ordinance, and I understand that a like view of the ordinance was taken by Mr. John S. Miller when Corporation Counsel, in a similar case which came before him, and that this interpretation of the ordinance has since been acted upon by this department and others.

A large number of papers now accompany the application. They represent recommendations, remonstrances, explanations or qualifications of signatures, revocations of consent, confirmations of consent, etc. The signatures to the application have also been investigated by the police department for purposes of verification, and through the police department and otherwise the frontages, the householders and the other proper persons to sign have been ascertained. It is established to my satisfaction that the applicant has presented the favoring signatures of the requisite majority of property owners on both sides of the street and the requisite majority of householders and business people upon the west side of the street. About the householders and business people on the east side of the street I am not so clear. The only building upon the east side of the street is an apartment house containing four stores and a large number of apartments. The lessee or head of any one of the different series of apartments comes within the legal definition of a householder. There is some doubt in my mind as to the sufficiency of certain of the signatures from this apartment building, and consequently as to the presence of a sufficient number of signatures, but I am inclined to the opinion that the applicant presented with his application on or about May 5th the requisite majority. Since then there have been several attempted revocations of the signatures or consents from the householders in this building. These attempted revocations, if taken into account, would destroy the requisite majority, and it is insisted by the remonstrants that the revocation should be upheld. Upon this point I am constrained to a different conclusion. The ordinance does not base the granting of license upon *consents* at the time of issuing the license or of passing upon the application. It merely calls for the presentation of an application bearing required number of actual bona fide *signatures*. After such an application with the requisite signatures has been presented it seems to me the requirements of the ordinance have been fully complied with and the right of the applicant to his license must be decided with reference to that state of facts. Revocations appear to me to be neither material nor permissible, and obviously to tolerate them opens the door to grave confusion and embarrassment. The present case furnishes apt illustration of the difficulty. There are before me two papers, both dated May 9, 1895, one in favor of the application, the other against it, each having several signatures, and the names of three of those "householders" appear on both of the contradictory papers. One man has signed four papers, two in favor of the applicant, and two against him. I think the rule should be, under this ordinance, that the matter is closed in respect to the cancelling of signatures upon presentation of the application; that a signature properly upon the application which has been presented must stand there and be counted. It follows that I hold the application sufficient in this case.

One further point remains to be considered and in my judgment it is the most important of all because its application is not confined to this particular case. It is the question whether you as the officer charged with the power to issue licenses have any discretion to grant or refuse a license under the Hyde park ordinance.

Another existing ordinance, passed by the village of Hyde Park contains the following question:

"The President and Board of Trustees may by resolution grant licenses to keep so many dram shops, saloons, or beer wagons in the village of Hyde Park, outside of prohibited districts, as they may think the public good requires, but they expressly reserve the power to revoke any license at their discretion."

It will be understood, of course, that Number 5014 Cottage Grove Avenue is not within a district in which saloons have been prohibited.

In the Morrison case already referred to, which was decided in October, 1891, the Supreme Court passed upon the saloon ordinances of Hyde Park at the time of its annexation to Chicago and the above provision came under consideration. Respecting it Mr. Justice Bailey, who delivered the opinion of the court, said:

"By passing a general ordinance on the subject the municipal authorities may determine when, to whom and under what circumstances licenses may be granted, and if such ordinance is not unreasonable, the power of the executive officers of the municipality to issue licenses will thereafter be controlled and measured by its terms. If no discretion is reserved in relation to the number or location of the dram-shops to be licensed, then none can be exercised, and the duty becomes mandatory upon the executive officer to issue licenses to all applicants who comply with the prescribed terms. If, on the other hands, a discretion is reserved as to the number or location of the dram-shops to be licensed, such discretion may be exercised by the officers charged with the duty of issuing the licenses, and if the ordinance restricts the location of dram-shops to certain portions of the municipal territory, said officers have no power to issue licenses except in obedience to said restrictions.

"The ordinance of the City of Chicago set out in the relator's petition provides, in substance, that the Mayor of the City shall grant licenses to all persons applying therefor, upon their furnishing sufficient evidence that they are persons of good character and offering to give the required bonds and to pay the prescribed license fee.' It may be admitted that where such an ordinance is in force the Mayor has no discretion to refuse a license to any applicant who is able to comply with the terms of the ordinance. In this respect, however, the ordinance of the village of Hyde Park set out in the defendant's answer is essentially different. In the first place that ordinance gave no power to issue licenses except in certain portions of the territory of the village and prohibited their issue in the other portions of said territory, and secondly, it was not mandatory in respect to issuing licenses outside of the prohibited districts, but merely authorized the village authorities to grant licenses to keep as many dram-shops in those portions of the village as they might think the public good required. * * * There is no evidence pending to show that in the opinion of the village authorities before the annexation, *or in the opinion of the Mayor of the City of Chicago to whom their functions in this respect were transfered by the annexation* there were not already in the annexed territory as many dram-shops as the public good required. There can be no doubt that said reservation by the ordinance of the discretion as to the number of licenses to be granted was valid, as it was clearly a reasonable exercise of the power over the subject given to the village board by the statute."

It must I think be admitted that much of what is said in the above quoted language of Mr. Justice Bailey was unnecessary to the decision of the real issue in the Morrison case and is, "therefore, to be regarded an *obiter dictum* and so not authoritative, but it still remains as a significant expression by one of the justices of the court in a formal and apparently carefully considered opinion and it suggests a grave question whether, as stated by him, the function of the President and Board of Trustees of the Village of Hyde Park as administrative officers to determine how many licenses shall be issued in any given portion of territory, have not passed to you. The language of Mr. Justice Bailey is: "There is no evidence tending to show that in the opinion of the village authorities before the annexation, *or in the opinion of the Mayor of the City of Chicago to whom their functions in this respect were transferrsd by the annexation*, there were not already in the annexed territory as many dram-shops as the public good required."

I do not believe that Justice Bailey used thoughtlessly the above words respecting the transfer to you of the functions of the president and board of trustees of Hyde Park in issuing licenses, and while the question is a doubtful one I feel impelled by many strong reasons to take the same view of it myself.

This question was also raised in a case before Judge Windes in the Circuit Court of Cook county (People, ex rel. Spittal, vs. Hopkins, 25 Chicago Legal News 388) in July, 1894, but was not distinctly decided, although some expressions of Judge Windes upon it seems to indicate that he took the same view previously expressed by Mr. Justice Bailey. In the face of these expressions of able judges I should not feel like advising you that you already had no authority to determine whether the public good requires more saloons in the particular territory involved. Moreover, my opinion leans toward the idea that you have such authority or discretion. Of course this discretion is something different from a capricious or arbitrary determination to allow a license to one man and to refuse a license to another upon grounds not contemplated by the ordinance. Whether the public good in your opinion requires a saloon in any given territory must under this ordinance be the basis of your decision.

In this particular instance the residents of the locality concerned are in the main greatly opposed to this saloon. They are emphatic in their view that there are sufficient saloons already in that neighborhood and that the public good does not require another there. In this view I concur and under the circumstances I think the doubtful question of law should be resolved against the applicant and that the license should be refused.

I, therefore, advise and report that, in my opinion, you may properly undertake to determine whether the public good requires license for another saloon in the locality where Mr. Klein desires to keep one, and if you decide that the public good does not require that, you may then refuse his application for a license, and I further advise and report that in my judgment, the granting of this license is not required by the public good and that it should be refused.

I am brought to this ultimate conclusion the more readily because I think this case is not unlikely to furnish a precedent. If the view to which I incline is wrong upon the legal question, the effect of the error can readily be corrected through a mandamus proceeding on the part of the applicant. If the lower court should decide in his favor in such a proceeding it would then be proper and wise to issue a license to him pending an appeal if any appeal should be thought desirable. If the remonstrating residents wish to do so it can readily be arranged to allow them to contest the questions from their standpoint in the name of the city, in case any such mandamus proceedings should be instituted.   Very respectfully yours,

WM. G. BEALE, Corporation Counsel.

I return to you the pending application, retaining in this office the other papers.   W. G. B.

June 11, 1895.

John J. Badenoch, Esq., General Supt. of Police.
Dear Sir—
In reply to your request to be furnished with the opinion of this department respecting the meaning of the section of the saloon ordinance providing that "No person shall *keep open* any saloon, barroom, or tippling house during the night time between the hours

of 12 o'clock midnight and 5 o'clock a. m.," and inquiring particularly whether a closing of the outer doors, the shutters, etc., of any place where liquors are sold would be a compliance with this section of the ordinance, I beg to say, that I have given the matter very careful consideration. In this state I do not find any reported cases tending to throw light upon the meaning of this section, but cases have arisen in other states, and the highest courts of New Hampshire, Rhode Island and Tennessee have declared that similar language used in a closing ordinance requires the establishment to be completely closed for business purposes; that is, to cease doing business, and is not complied with by a mere closing of doors, windows, etc. In my judgment the above section has the same meaning, and was intended to compel the complete cessation of the business of selling liquors in the places mentioned within the hours specified and that it is not a compliance with the ordinance merely to close doors, shutters, etc. For your information I refer briefly to the above mentioned cases.

In the Rhode Island case, Hudson vs. Gary, Fourth Rhode Island, 485, an ordinance prohibited the opening of places of trade or entertainment on Sundays, or late at night. Upon the evidence introduced the defendant requested the court to instruct the jury "that where the front door and front window shutters and the back door, the entrances of the shop, are all closed after 11 o'clock at night and before daylight in the morning, and no one is seen going into the shop after or at that hour, but only seen coming out, and there is no proof of any selling or trade being carried on at that hour, then, and in that case, there has been no keeping open under the ordinance."

The case went off upon other points, but concerning this request the court said: "Without finding it necessary to define with precision what an opening or keeping open of a shop, etc., within the terms of this ordinance is, such a construction is quite too latitudinarian to meet the obvious purpose for which the ordinance was passed."

In the Tennessee case, Smith & Lackey vs. The Mayor and Aldermen of Knoxville, 3rd Head, 246, an action had been brought against Smith & Lackey in the lower court to recover a penalty for the violation of an ordinance providing that houses retailing spirituous liquors should be closed at 9 o'clock. They contended that the ordinance was complied with by the closing of the door of their establishment, concerning which the court said: "On the other side it is contended that the only sensible construction is, that it means, that not only the door, but the business, must be suspended at the hour designated. This certainly must be so, or the law would be nugatory."

The New Hampshire case plainly shows what the court understood to be the "keeping open" of any place required to be closed. In that case the establishment was a restaurant. The ordinance provided that "no persons should keep open any restaurant after 10 o'clock." At that hour the lights in the place were extinguished and the outside door was closed but a customer remained in a back room of the place where a light was kept burning. A customer paid for and ate an oyster stew. Upon the specific point now under consideration the court said: "No question is made in the argument that the place * * * was a restaurant within the meaning of the ordinance, nor that it was kept open notwithstanding the shutting of the outer door. * * * * It does not seem to us that any question could seriously made as to either." Very respectfully yours,

WM. G. BEALE, Corporation Counsel.

June 13, 1895.

W. D. Kent, Esq., Commissioner of Public Works.

Dear Sir—

In answer to your inquiry of June 10th inst., I beg to say that there is an ordinance (Section 2675 of the Municipal Code), "which provides that streets, alleys and sidewalks in the City of Chicago shall be kept free and clear of all obstructions, encumbrances and encroachments for the use of the public, and shall not be used or occupied in any other way than herein provided in this article." It is by other ordinances made your duty to keep the streets and sidewalks clear from obstructions. I therefore think that you have authority to prevent peddlers and venders of all sorts from obstructing streets or sidewalks with articles offered for sale whether the same be fruit, flowers, or other commodities. There is, however, an ordinance (2621 of the Municipal Code) which allows owners to occupy a space, not exceeding three feet, next to the building, for the storage of articles of merchandise. This ordinance has been in force a long time, and I understand has been upheld by legal adjudication.

Very respectfully,

GEORGE A. DUPUY, Asst. Corporation Counsel.

June 19, 1895.

O. D. Wetherell, Esq., Comptroller.

Dear Sir—

I am requested by Mr. Mark Crawford, superintendent of the House of Correction, and Mr. Harper of your office, to furnish you an opinion in regard to whether or not said superintendent may cause prisoners in his custody to do work outside of the House of Correction. Mr. Crawford states that it has been proposed to employ some of the prisoners in doing calcimining and other repair work in and about the police stations and other public buildings of the city.

Section 7 of Article 5, Chap. XXIV, Revised Statutes, being the so-called city and village act under which the city of Chicago is organized as a municipal corporation, provides: "The City Council or Board of Trustees shall have power to provide by ordinance that every person so committed shall be required to work for the corporation at such labor as his or her strength will permit, within and without such

16

prison, work-house, House of Correction, and other places provided
for the incarceration of such offenders, not exceeding ten hours each
working day."

This provision makes it plainly within the power of the city council to provide by a proper ordinance that persons confined in the
House of Correction for violation of city ordinances may, under the
direction of the superintendent, be employed "without such House of
Correction." However, I find no ordinance on the subject and before
the superintendent will be authorized to act it would be necessary that
the city council should provide by ordinance for the employment of
such persons outside of the House of Correction.

Respectfully submitted,

GEORGE A. DUPUY, Asst. Corporation Counsel.

June 24, 1895.

Joseph Downey, Esq., Commissioner of Buildings.

Dear Sir—

In your communications of June 19th and 21st, respectively,
you ask:

First: Your power to compel the removal of large canvas signs
placed on buildings covering windows?

Second: If your department has control over signs placed on
buildings?

Third: Has your department control over bill-boards on vacant
lots?

Fourth: Has your department any control over show-cases
placed outside of buildings extending on the sidewalk?

I find no authority anywhere vested in the department of buildings
giving it control exclusively, or otherwise, of any of the matters which
you have referred to. It is my opinion that it is primarily the duty of
the police department to see to the enforcement of all ordinances of
the city, and that members of each department are charged with the
duty of reporting to the heads of departments all violations of ordinances coming within their purview, and from the peculiar nature of the
duties of the inspectors in your department they should not only report
violations of ordinances relating to or connected with buildings, but
lend all the assistance in their power to prosecute the violators of the
ordinance.

The matter of signs seems by, Section 1970 of the Municipal
Code of 1881, to be especially under the supervision of the police department.

I find nothing making the placing of signs made of canvas below
the third story and within three feet of the building unlawful.

I do not know the existence of any ordinance which controls the
placing of bill-boards on vacant lots. There was an ordinance under
consideration last winter, but I do not find that it passed.

Sections 1960 and 1940 of the Municipal Code have been construed by Judge Tuley, of the Circuit Court, and possibly by some of the other judges, to grant rights affirmatively to the adjoining property owners to use the three feet of sidewalk space next adjoining the lots occupied by them respectively, for all sorts of commercial purposes and that judge has held that these sections of the code having been in force substantially as they are now, since the very earliest year of the municipality, having carried with them rights which have become vested and are beyond the control of the city to annul or cancel, except perhaps, where a general and sweeping order should annul matters or where peculiar circumstances might arise making their enjoyment inconsistent with the public good and Judge Tuley has gone so far as to enjoin the city and the police officers from interfering with a fruit vendor, who occupied the three feet of the sidewalk under a lease from the owner or lessee of the adjoining building.   Very respectfully,

JESSE B. BARTON, Asst. Corporation Counsel.

July 1st, 1895.

Martin B. Madden, Esq., Chairman Finance Committee.

Dear Sir—

The corporation counsel has referred to me an ordinance entitled "An ordinance providing for compensation to members of the City Council for attendance at meetings of the committees," and Alderman Manierre, of your committee, has stated to me that an opinion is requested first, as to the legality of this ordinance, and, second, whether or not a legal ordinance can be passed now providing for an increase in the salaries of aldermen.

Section 14, Article VI, Chapter XXIV, of the Revised Statutes, which is the organic act of the city, provides as follows:

"The aldermen and trustees may receive such compensation for their services as shall be fixed by ordinance: Provided, however, such compensation shall not exceed three dollars to each alderman or trustee for each meeting of the City Council, or Board of Trustees, actually attended by him, and no other compensation than for attendance upon such meetings shall be allowed to any alderman or trustee for any services whatsoever.   Such compensation shall not be changed, after it has been once established, so as to take effect as to any alderman or trustee voting for such change, during his term of office."

It is clear from the provisions of this section that no alderman of any city is entitled to any other pay for any services whatever rendered to the city than a sum not to exceed $3.00 for each meeting of the city council actually attended by him.   Therefore, in my opinion, the ordinance in question is absolutely void; and I am further of the opinion that no ordinance would be legal which provided for any greater compensation to an alderman than the sum of $3.00 for each council meeting actually attended by him.   Therefore, the question submitted orally by Alderman Manierre, which was, "Can the City Council by ordinance

provide for payment to each alderman a fixed annual salary of $5,000.00.
or any other sum legal?" must be answered in the negative.
Very respectfully,
JESSE B. BARTON, Asst. Corporation Counsel.

July 12, 1895.
W. D. Kent, Esq., Commissioner of Public Works.
Dear Sir—
Mr. Beale has referred to me your communication to him of date
July 10th, as follows:
"Please advise me if, under Sections 1434 and 1441, whether the
loading of garbage and ashes in the portion of the city therein designated can be prevented during the hours of seven o'clock a. m., and
six o'clock p. m."
I presume the sections referred to are of the Municipal Code of
1881. You will find that Section 7 of an ordinance passed May 29,
1893, gives to the superintendent of street and alley cleaning the power,
under the supervision of the commissioner of public works, to determine the times and manner in which garbage, ashes, etc., shall be
removed, and Section 11 of the same ordinance provides, "In contracts executed on behalf of the City, the right shall be reserved to the
Commissioner and Superintendent to finally decide all questions arising as to the proper performance of the work of garbage removal and
street and alley cleaning."
In my opinion these sections vest in the commissioner and superintendent the power to designate the hours mentioned in your communication between which all garbage and ashes in the portion of the
city designated in Section 1434, shall be removed, and that that supervision or control extends over contractors, whose contracts were made,
as all of them were, subsequent to the passage of the ordinance of
May 29, 1893.   Very respectfully,
Approved: JESSE B. BARTON.
WM. G. BEALE, Corporation Counsel.

July 12, 1895.
Joseph Downey, Esq., Commissioner of Buildings.
Dear Sir—
Your communication of July 6th inst., in which you ask if you
are compelled, under the ordinances, to have a building taken down
which has become damaged by fire to the extent of about eighty per
cent. of its value, and yet not dangerous to life or limb, has been referred to me for answer, together with your verbal inquiries on the
general subject of such damaged buildings.
The city council is empowered, by ordinance, to *direct* "That all
and any buildings within the fire limits when the same shall have been
damaged by fire, decay or otherwise to the extent of fifty per cent. of

the value, shall be torn down or removed, and to prescribe the manner of ascertaining such damage."

Sections 11, 34 and 236 of the Building Ordinance, now in force, are the only ones which, upon a rather cursory examination, I have found attempting to carry out this charter power.

Section 34 undertakes to lay down the course of procedure under which the extent to which a building has been damaged can be ascertained, creating the building commissioner an officer with somewhat judicial functions from whose decision an appeal may be taken to the board of arbitration. Assuming that the ordinance is valid, you should follow strictly the conditions of Section 34, giving in every instance the owner of the building reasonable notice of any intended action, and only upon the final determination that the building was dangerous, or had otherwise become a nuisance, would you be authorized to employ force to remove it. Such course would completely exonerate you from all blame, and shield you from any claim for damages by the owner, if the ordinance is valid, and if it be invalid you would nevertheless be protected by the city. But by assuming the duties of a public office the incumbent undertakes to exercise his best judgment in ascertaining what his duties are in a particular case, and to act promptly and thoroughly in the matter. Upon investigating the condition of buildings, to ascertain whether they are safe or dangerous to the public, you find a building, or walls of a building, unsafe, you must act so as to avert threatened danger. If the danger be, in your opinion, imminent, you must act promptly and summarily, and by force, if necessary, and use such means as are within your reach, namely, the men in your department, the members of the fire and police departments, the appliances owned by the city and subject to your control, or to your requisition, and voluntary assistance from outside, together with the expenditure of such moneys as may be subject to your order for such purpose. You must assume the liability that would result from your mistake, or other improper action; you will be protected when you act rightfully and with reasonable care.

Very respectfully,

JESSE B. BARTON, Asst. Corporation Counsel.

Approved :

WM. G. BEALE, Corporation Counsel.

You are not compelled to have such a building as you mention taken down. W. G. B.

July 15, 1895.

John J. Badenoch, Esq., Superintendent of Police.

Dear Sir—

In response to your inquiry as to whether or not the police authority of the City of Chicago extends over that portion of territory adjacent to the harbor usually known as the North Pier, and territory adjacent thereto, I beg to say, that in my opinion, such territory is subject to the police power of the city.

The jurisdiction of the State of Illinois extends to the middle of Lake Michigan. (See Article 1 of Constitution of 1870.)

The jurisdiction of Cook County, extends eastwardly over the lake to the east line of the state, namely, to the center of Lake Michigan. (See Section 3 of Chapter XXXIV Revised Statutes.)

In regard to the jurisdiction of the city, Section 71 of Chapter XXIV of the Revised Statutes provides: "The City * * * government shall have jurisdiction upon all waters within, or bordering upon, the same, to tne extent of three miles beyond the limits of the city or village, but not to exceed the limits of the State." It thus clearly appears that the jurisdiction of the city extends over the territory named.

I have not considered what authority the United States has, or may exercise over the harbor, or territory adjacent thereto, as I understand that the United States authorities are entirely in accord with your purpose to extend the police protection to this territory, if the same can be done under municipal authority. Very respectfully yours,

GEORGE A. DUPUY, Asst. Corporation Counsel.

July 23, 1895.

Philip Maas, Esq., City Collector.

Dear Sir—

Your verbal request of recent date for the opinion of this department as to what classes of persons and business are within the provisions of the ordinance of June 11, 1883, entitled, "Brokers" (L. & O. 1890, Secs. 1499 to 1504) has been referred to me by the Corporation Counsel."

The authority of the city with respect to the subject matter of said ordinance is derived solely from clause 91, Section 1, Article V, of the city charter. By that clause the city council was empowered "To tax, license and regulate * * * money changers and brokers."

Sections 1 and 5 of said ordinance are as follows:

"Section 1: It shall not be lawful for any person to exercise within this city the business of a money changer, or banker, broker, or commission merchant, including that of merchandise, produce or grain broker, real estate broker and insurance broker without a license therefor."

Section 5: There shall be collected annually for every license granted for any banker the sum of one hundred dollars, and there shall be collected annually for every license granted for any broker, including any merchandise, produce or grain broker, or commission merchant, or money changer or broker, the sum of twenty-five dollars, and there shall be collected annually for any license granted any real estate broker, the sum of twenty-five dollars, and there shall be collected annually for every license granted for any insurance broker the sum of twenty-five dollars."

This ordinance goes beyond the power of the city council in several important particulars:

First: A commission merchant is a factor, an agent for the sale of goods in his possession or consigned to him. He is neither a money changer nor a broker, and therefore cannot be regulated or licensed by the city council.

Second: The city council has no power to determine who are money changers within the meaning of the charter.

Third: The city council has no power to regulate or license bankers as such; nor has it the right to classify money changers as bankers and other money changers and to then impose a license fee of $100.00 upon the former, and a license fee of $25.00 upon the latter, for the license fee must be uniform and equal with respect to all persons of the same class—that is, all money changers—within the city.

I am therefore of opinion that Section 1 of said ordinance, so far as it attempts to regulate commission merchants as such; Sections 2, 3 and 4, which attempt to define different classes of brokers, and the first clause of Section 5, which provides that "There shall be collected annually for every license granted for any banker the sum of $100.00;" must be considered as invalid, and of no effect. This limits the application of the ordinance to money changers and brokers by those general terms, and the question now is, who are money changers and who are brokers?

MONEY CHANGER.

Webster defines a money changer to be "A broker who deals in money or exchanges;" and the Supreme Court of Illinois in Hinckley vs. City of Belleville, 43rd Ill. 183, said that one who buys and sells exchange and uncurrent funds, or exchanges one kind of money for another, is a money changer. While it may perhaps be doubted that the legislature intended by the use of the word money changers to authorize the city council to license the business of banking, yet, as I understand that business to be conducted in this city, those engaged in it are certainly within the definitions above given. In the case just cited bankers were held to be money changers within the meaning of the word as used in an ordinance similar to the one in question. I am therefore of opinion, that under this ordinance all persons or corporations engaged in a general banking business, except national banks—which are not subject to municipal regulations—must procure a money changer's license and pay therefor the sum of $25.00. Of course, all other money changers, not bankers—if there are such—are also subject to the same requirement.

BROKER.

Strictly speaking, a broker is "one who is engaged for others in negotiating contracts relative to property with the custody of which he has no concern;" and his contracts are usually made in the names of his principals. Those engaged in negotiating contracts relative to real estate, the placing of loans, the chartering of ships, the sale of bonds, and the placing of insurance, known respectively as real estate brokers, loan or money brokers, ship brokers, bond brokers, and insurance brokers are clearly within the definition above given. With respect to insurance brokers, however, it should be observed that they are not brokers who are the acknowledged agents or representatives of particular insurance companies. An insurance broker usually acts for both parties representing no particular company, and is employed for a specific purpose upon particular occasions.

The term broker has been extended by common usage to include all those members of the Board of Trade and of the Stock Exchange, who are engaged in the business of buying and selling grain, provisions or stocks for others upon a commission, and who are variously known as commission men, grain brokers and stock brokers, etc. In my opinion, these persons, as well as those previously named, are brokers within the intent of the ordinance, and should pay the license fee of $25. Yours very truly,

GILBERT E. PORTER, Asst. Corporation Counsel.

August 15, 1895.

Phillip Maas, Esq., City Collector.

Dear Sir—

In reply to your verbal request for an opinion in reply to inquiry of John C. Durgin & Co., as per letter attached, I have the honor to reply as follows: After a careful investigation of the authorities I am of the opinion that the city council exceeded its authority in attempting to regulate or license commission merchants.

The council has the authority to tax, license and regulate, etc., money changers and brokers. There is, however, no authority whatever to tax, license and regulate commission merchants. By legal definition, a commission merchant is defined as being a factor or agent for the sale of goods in his possession and consigned to him. He is one who receives goods, chattels or merchandise for sale, exchange or other disposition, and who is to receive a compensation for his services, to be paid by the owners or derived from the sale of the goods.

A broker, strictly speaking, is an agent who negotiates sales between parties for a commission.

For the above reasons, therefore, I am of the opinion that merchants engaged in the lumber business, to whom cargoes are consigned on commission, do not come within the power conveyed upon the city by statute to tax, license or regulate. There has been unquestionably an attempt upon the part of the council to exercise this power, but I am of the opinion that it has no authority to do so and is in excess of the power vested in it by the terms of the statute.

Yours very truly,

FRANK HAMLIN, Asst. Corporation Counsel.

August 16, 1895.

Philip Maas, Esq., City Collector.

Dear Sir—

In reference to your inquiry of yesterday as to whether or not a person may be licensed to sell liquors in the course of a retail grocery trade within the so-called prohibition district of Hyde Park, where such liquors are sold in pint, quart or larger packages, and not to be drunk on the premises, I beg to say: That the saloon ordinances of Hyde Park existing prior to annexation are, as you are aware, still in force. (See case of People ex rel. vs. Cregier, 138 Ill. Supreme Court Reports, p. 411).

Section 2 of Chapter XV of the ordinances of said village defines a dram shop or saloon, and said section is as follows:

"A dram shop or saloon is a place where spirituous or vinous or malt liquors are retailed in less quantities than one gallon, and intoxicating liquor shall be deemed to include all such liquors within the meaning of this ordinance."

Section 3 provides—

"No person without a license to keep a dram shop or saloon, shall, by himself or another, either as principal, agent, clerk or servant, directly or indirectly, sell or give away any intoxicating liquor in any less quantity than one gallon, or in any quantity to be drunk upon the premises or in or upon any adjacent room, building, yard, premises, or upon any highway, park, public water or place of public resort."

Section 20-21 specifies certain territories in which "Hereafter no license shall be issued to keep a saloon or dram shop." If, therefore, a grocery store in which liquors are sold in packages and not to be drunk on the premises comes within the meaning of a dram shop or saloon, as defined in this ordinance, and if saloons and dram shops as thus defined are prohibited in certain districts, then it necessarily follows that such sales of liquor cannot be made within such district. It is apparent from a reading of Section 2 that a grocery store or liquor store in which liquors are sold in packages of less than one gallon do come within the definition of dramshop or saloon, as used in this ordinance.

I am, therefore, of the opinion that within the prohibition district as defined in Section 21 of this ordinance, the city of Chicago, has no authority to issue any license for the sale of liquors in packages less than one gallon, although the same are not to be drunk on the premises. If sales are to be made only in packages of more than one gallon and not to be drunk upon the premises then the general or-

dinances of the city of Chicago apply without regard to the ordinances
of the former village of Hyde Park, to which I have hereinbefore referred in this communication.
Very respectfully yours,
GEO. A. DUPUY, Asst. Corporation Counsel.

August 17, 1895.

Inspector Fitzpatrick, City.
    Dear Sir—
    In response to your inquiry as to whether or not a bill poster's
license is required by persons exclusively in the employment of theaters or other similar places, and who post bills on bill boards owned
or controlled them, i. e., the theater company, I am of the opinion
that such persons are not required to have a license unless they do
a general bill posting business. The language of the ordinance is
(Sec. 2214):
    "Section 1. No person, firm or corporation shall carry on the
business of bill posting within the city of Chicago without first obtaining a license therefor, under a penalty of not less than $100.00,
nor more than $200.00."
    "Section 2. Every person, firm or corporation carrying on the
business of bill posting within the city of Chicago shall pay an annual
license fee of $100.00; provided, however, that any person carrying on
the business of bill posting who does not use a horse or wagon or a
cart in his said business shall be charged for license only the amount of
$25.00 per annum."
    These ordinances repeatedly use the expression "carrying on the
business of bill posting." A theater is not properly carrying on the
business of bill posting, although it might hire a man who is not a
bill poster to post bills for it. In such case the bill posting is not the
carrying on of the business of bill posting, but is merely an incident to
the carrying on of the theater business. It is my opinion that no court
would hold that a party who is not engaged regularly in the business
of bill posting for others for hire, but who is employed by a theater or
similar company to put up bills on boards owned or controlled by it, is
required to have a license under this ordinance.
Very respectfully yours,
GEO. A. DUPUY, Asst. Corporation Counsel.

August 22, 1895.

Hon. O. D. Wetherell, City Comptroller.
    Dear Sir—
    You ask my opinion as to the legality of the time warrants now
being issued by the city of Chicago.
    Your inquiry involves three principal questions:
    1. Is the city of Chicago authorized to issue warrants against

uncollected taxes, which have already been levied, to meet its current expenses?

2. Are these warrants issued by the proper municipal authorities?

3. Are the warrants in proper legal form as required by the statutes of the state?

There can be no possible doubt that the city of Chicago possesses power to issue warrants to meet current municipal expenses whenever there is no money in the treasury for that purpose. The only doubt cast upon this power arises from the provisions contained in Article IX, Section 12, of the present constitution of the State of Illinois, which provides:

"No city * * * shall be allowed to become indebted in any manner or for any purpose to an amount including existing indebtedness, in the aggregate exceeding five per centum of the value of the taxable property therein to be ascertained by the last assessment for state and county taxes, previous to the incurring of such indebtedness."

The city of Chicago being already indebted to the extent of this constitutional limit, no further municipal indebtedness can be incurred because of the inhibition of the foregoing constitutional provision. If, therefore, these warrants constitute a liability against the city of Chicago they are not only unauthorized by law, but are directly prohibited by the constitution, and, therefore, clearly and unquestionably void. An inspection of the language of these warrants and an examination of the laws under which they are issued, make it very plain that they neither create any liability on the part of the city of Chicago, nor even purport to create any such liability. Their language to the city treasurer is " pay from the tax levy of the year 1895 when received by you"; also, "this warrant is payable solely from the taxes levied for the year 1895, and not otherwise."

A person of ordinary intelligence could hardly fail to understand this language, and to recognize the fact that the city of Chicago, by the issuance of these warrants, enters into no general undertaking to pay the amount named in these warrants in any other manner or from any other fund, except that as therein specified, viz: From the moneys collected for the taxes of the year 1895. The holder of one of these warrants could not sue the city and compel the payment of the same generally from any other fund which the city might then or thereafter have in its treasury. Such being the fact, these warrants, in consequence of such fact, do not constitute any liability against the city of Chicago within the meaning of the foregoing constitutional provision. These warrants in substance amount merely to an assignment of so much of the uncollected taxes of the year 1895 to the holder of the warrant. This fund, when collected, and this only, the holder of the warrant, by virtue of the same, becomes entitled to receive. The city having the power to levy taxes for municipal purposes and having levied such taxes, and the same being now in process of collection, the city may transfer or assign the right to receive a portion of such taxes when collected, and yet in so doing create no indebtedness against the city either directly or indirectly. This point was expressly determined by the Supreme Court of Illinois in the case of Fuller vs. Heath in 1878. (See 89 Ill. Reports, page 307). The court there used this language in regard to warrants which were in substance exactly like the present ones:

"These warrants, under the law, have no legal effect except as an assignment without recourse on the city made by the city to the holder of the warrant of the part of the uncollected taxes mentioned in the warrant. This is the legal effect and the only legal effect of these instruments."

It was accordingly decided that they were legal and valid, and that they were not forbidden by the above quoted constitutional provision. Subsequently (in 1879) an act of the general assembly embodied in express legislation, the substance of the decision of the Supreme Court in the above case. This statute is now in force, is the law under which these warrants are issued, and reads as follows:

"Whenever there is no money in the treasury of any county, township, city, school district or other municipal corporation to meet and defray the ordinary and necessary expenses thereof, it shall be lawful for the proper authorities of any county, township, city, school district or other municipal corporation, to provide that warrants may be drawn and issued, against and in anticipation of the collection of any taxes, already levied by said authorities for the payment of the ordinary and necessary expenses of any such municipal corporation to the extent of seventy-five per centum of the total amount of any said tax levy: Provided, that warrants drawn and issued under the provisions of this section, shall show upon their face that they are payable solely from said taxes when collected, and not otherwise, and shall be received by any collector of taxes in payment of the taxes against which they are issued, and which taxes, against which said warrants are drawn, shall be set apart and held for their payment."

The interest accruing on the amount named in such warrants is provided for by an act of the general assembly approved June 15, 1895. This act is as follows:

"Whenever any warrants shall hereafter be lawfully drawn by the proper officers of any city, village or town for the payment of money out of any particular fund in anticipation of the collection of a tax heretofore levied for such fund, such warrants shall, unless paid within thirty days after their issuance, bear interest, payable out of such fund and tax levy, at the rate of five per centum per annum from their respective dates until paid, or until notice shall be given by publication in a newspaper or otherwise, to their holders, that the money for their payment is available and that they will be paid on presentation."

If therefore there is no money in the treasury of the city to meet the ordinary and necessary expenses thereof, it seems unquestionable that the proper municipal authorities have the power to issue such warrants as those under consideration.

Who are the authorities contemplated by the statute above quoted which says that these warrants shall be issued by the "proper authorities?" It will be observed that this expression—proper authorities—in said statute refers to the authorities of townships, counties, school districts and cities. These proper authorities in the case of cities are undoubtedly the mayor and city council. They are the repository of all the legislative authority of the city and it is expressly provided in the charter of the city of Chicago (the same being the general incorporation act of cities and villages) that the city council has the following powers:

1. "To control the finances and property of the corporation.

2. "To provide for payment of debts and expenses of the corporation.

3. "To levy and collect taxes for general and special purposes on real and personal property."

Accordingly, the city council on the first day of July, 1895, passed the following resolution:

"Resolved, that the Mayor and Comptroller be and are hereby authorized to issue warrants against and in anticipation of the taxes already levied by the city of Chicago for the payment of ordinary and necessary expenses of said city for the year 1895, to the extent of sixty (60) per centum of the total amount of said tax levy; such warrants to be issued only in conformity with Section 2, of an act of the General Assembly of the State of Illinois, entitled, 'An Act to provide for the manner of issuing warrants upon the treasurer of any county, township, city, school district, or other municipal corporation and jurors certificates,' approved May 31, 1879, and in conformity with an act entitled, 'An Act to provide for payment of interest on warrants of municipal corporations,' approved June 15, 1895; provided, no such warrants shall be drawn, except against a specific fund mentioned in the annual appropriation bill, and each warrant shall state upon its face against which fund it is drawn."

Acting under this resolution, the mayor and comptroller are now proceeding to issue these warrants and such issuance by them is strictly in conformity with the law.

In regard to the form of the warrants—neither the statutes of the state nor the ordinances of the city requires any special form of warrant. The only provision of the statute is contained in the statute above quoted, which requires that the warrants "shall show upon their face that they are payable solely from said taxes when collected and not otherwise." As will be be seen by inspection the form of warrant used complies literally with this requirement of the statute.

In conclusion, I beg to say, that in my opinion, the city has full authority to issue these warrants; that the same do not in any way conflict with the laws of the state or the provisions of the constitution; that they are legal and valid for the purposes intended; that they are issued by the proper municipal authorities, and that in form they contain all that the law requires.

Of interest in this connection is the opinion of Mr. James L. High, an eminent authority of our bar, who in an opinion which is before me, and which was furnished to some banking interests of this city as a basis for their action in relation to some prior warrants of the same character, says:

"Under this act (referring to the Act of the General Assembly hereinbefore referred to) if the city has no money in its treasury to meet its ordinary and necessary expenses, the City Council may lawfully provide by ordinance for issuing warrants in anticipation of taxes already levied for the ordinary and necessary expenses of the city, to the extent of seventy-five per centum of such levy. Money loaned or advanced to the city upon such warrants, are thus secured by a pledge of the uncollected taxes already levied and appropriated by the city to the particular fund against which the warrant is drawn. The power of the City Council to thus effect temporary loans to the extent indicated clearly exists, and in view of the decisions of the Supreme Court and of the Act of 1879, it cannot be successfully challenged. Such warrants, however, are payable solely from the taxes against which they are drawn, and are in no sense an indebtedness of the city, and can be lawfully paid in no other manner than by the appropriation of such taxes when collected." Respectfully submitted,

GEO. A. DUPUY, First Asst. Corporation Counsel.
Concurred in by Mr. Beale.

September 11, 1895.
Hon. John M. Clark, President of Civil Service Commission, Chicago.
Dear Sir—

I beg to acknowledge the receipt of your letter of the 10th inst., asking my opinion for the Civil Service Commission respecting the City Treasurer, the City Clerk, the City Attorney, the Board of Directors of the Public Library, the Board of Election Commissioners and the Board of Education.

I have heretofore considered with some care the questions submitted by you, and I therefore feel able to express myself about them without delay.

In my judgment the law plainly covers the officers of the City Treasurer, the City Clerk, the City Attorney and the Board of Directors of the Public Library and applies to the subordinates and employes in those offices respectively, except as to specified exceptions under the 11th Section of the law. Under the provisions of that section the treasurer, the clerk and the library directors are not included in the classified service of the city, subject to the jurisdiction of the commission, but the exemption does not extend to the subordinates and employes under those officers, and I am, therefore, of the opinion that such subordinates and employes come under the jurisdiction of the commission. The 11th Section further excepts "members of the Law Department" (which department includes the office of the City Attorney), and question therefore arises as to who are members of the law department within the meaning of this exception, in addition to the City Attorney himself, who is specifically exempt as an elective officer. In my opinion it was intended to except from the classified service all persons connected with the law department whose duties called for some professional training in law, and only such. This would exclude from the operation of this law all assistants and law clerks in the law department engaged in work of a legal character as distinct from general clerks, stenographers, messengers and similar employ.es, whose duties would require no special legal knowledge or training. It seems a fair construction of the law to hold that these latter should be included within the classified service, and it is my opinion, and I believe it is also the opinion of the City Attorney, that they are so included.

Whether the civil service law applies to the employes of the Board of Election Commissioners and of the Board of Education depends largely, if not wholly, upon the relations of those two bodies to the municipal government. Clearly the law upon its face applies only to the civil service of the city of Chicago, of which the Civil Service Commission constitutes a department. I think it is clear that the Election Commissioners are not a part of the municipal government of Chicago, but are a distinct organization subject to the jurisdiction of the county court, and not governed by the civil service law. I am aware that the law discloses some indications of an intention to have it apply to the office of the Election Commissioners, but I do not think there can fairly be any serious question upon the whole law that it is not so applicable.

The relations of the Chicago Board of Education to the city of Chicago, I think, may fairly be said to be involved in some doubt. I know that good lawyers hold differing views upon the question. In the town of Lake annexation case of McGurn vs. Board of Education, 133 Ill., 134, Mr. Justice Bailey, speaking for the Supreme Court of the state, said that the Board of Education "in some points of view is to be regarded as a subordinate department of the city government, and in others as an independent municipal corporation." Whether any of the employes of the Board of Education come under this law is a doubtful question which ought to be promptly passed upon by the courts and put finally at rest. I should personally be glad to take such steps agreeable to the Commission as would secure a thorough presentation to the courts of all the considerations which may be urged upon either side of the question. It is not unlikely that a decision of the Supreme Court of the state could be obtained at an early date. Until a proper judicial decision is had, or at least until further advised to the contrary, I advise that the Commission refrain

from asserting any jurisdiction over the employes of the Board of Education.
Very truly yours,
WM. G. BEALE, Corporation Counsel.

September 17, 1895.
Hon. John M. Clark, President of Civil Service Commission, Chicago.

Dear Sir—

. I beg o acknowledge the receipt of your communication of yesterday requesting my opinion upon the correctness of the positions taken by the Civil Service Commission as therein set forth upon the subject of the limitations for civil service examinations, and particularly the maximum age limitation. You are particularly desirous, as I understand you, of knowing whether the Commission is correct in supposing that the law appears to give the ·Commission no right to discriminate in favor of veterans of the civil war by exempting them from the maximum age limitation while imposing such limit upon others.

In a general way I have heretofore expressed to you and to the Commission during our numerous discussions upon the subject, the opinion that the positions of the Commission are legally sound and correct. My first impression, as you know, was the other way, and my ultimate conclusions were somewhat unwillingly reached; but reflection and further investigation convinced my judgment and the informal opinion thereupon expressed I now repeat. The law plainly provides for an age limitation as well as others. In the absence of specific instructions in the law it clearly became the duty of the Commission to fix such such age limitation as it should think reasonable and just having in view the object intended to be accomplished. Had the Commission fixed ten years as the minimum limit and seventy years as the maximum limit one would hardly suppose there would have been any question raised as to the lawfulness of the restriction— that is, as to the authority of the Commission in the premises. But if the Commission would have been authorized to prescribe a maximum age limit of seventy years it must obviously have authority to prescribe some other maximum age limit, if in its judgment such other limit would be more reasonable and just, the law having specified no limit, but provided merely that the Commission should prescribe one. In this view the Commission has acted and it seems to me that the only question under the law is whether the age limit designated by the Commission is reasonable and just, or the contrary. Upon that question it is hardly my province to express an opinion here, but it may not be improper for me to say that a leading consideration to support the action of the Commission is found in a requirement of the law that original appointments as far as practicable shall be made to the lowest grades of the public service in order that there may be growth and promotion therein.

I have been and am wholly unable to see upon what basis it can be contended that the Commission possesses authority to discriminate in favor of any class of citizens, however meritorious. As you say, there is an important principle involved in this element of the matter. The fundamental purpose of the law was to do away with discriminations and to put applicants for positions purely upon their merits. Doubtless the legislature might have authorized the Commission to give some preference to veterans of the civil war, but plainly it has not done so, and it is equally plain to me that the Commission would not be justified legally in attempting to give any such preference. The Federal Civil Service Law is often referred to in this connection, but it is my impression that the Federal law does not discriminate in favor of veterans, generally, but merely provides that persons honorably discharged from the military or naval service of the United States by reason of disability, resulting from wounds or sickness incurred in the line of duty, shall be preferred for appointment to the Federal Civil Service. The Illinois law contains no corresponding provision and without some such provision it seems entirely clear that the Commission has no authority whatever to discriminate in favor of the surviving union soldiers and sailors of the late war, even if it desired to do so. I consider the position of the Commission upon that point entirely correct. Very respectfully yours,

WM. G. BEALE, Corporation Counsel.

October 18, 1895.

Hon. John M. Clark, President Civil Service Commission.

Dear Sir—

I beg to acknowledge the receipt of your letter of the 17th inst., asking my opinion as to whether city officers and employes in certain offices supported by fees collected, are included in the classified service of the city as defined by the Civil Service law and you instance such offices as that of the Boiler Inspector, the Inspector of Weights and Measures and the Inspector of Fish.

In my opinion the officers and employes in the offices above mentioned and others of the same class are as distinctly city officers and employes as if they were paid by salaries alone. The essential point is to determine for whom they are working. If they are engaged in an independent business a part of which is performing work for the city of Chicago then they are not city officers or employes. Such would be the case of a blacksmith having his own place of business, pursuing his own vocation and shoeing city horses, although he received business enough from the city to take up his entire time. The method of payment alone is not a test of the real relation in which an individual stands to the municipal corporation. The officers and employes in the offices referred to seem to me clearly to be within the classified service of the city of Chicago, and I know of no reason why the officers at the head of those offices should not respond to your request for a list of their employes and a statement of salaries paid.

Very truly yours,

WM. G. BEALE, Corporation Counsel.

October 18, 1895.

Hon. John M. Clark, President Civil Service Commission.

Dear Sir—

I beg to acknowledge the receipt of your letter of the 16th inst., requesting my opinion in respect to the seeming conflict in the laws applicable to the examination of mechanical engineers as candidates for positions in the service of the city and to their appointment.

I find that a statute enacted by the General Assembly in 1889 authorized the city council to adopt ordinances providing for the examination, licensing and regulation of persons having charge of steam boilers under steam pressure, fixing the amount, terms and manner of issuing and revoking licenses to such persons; making it unlawful for any person to exercise the business of operating a steam boiler without a license, and establishing an examining board to examine applicants for licenses. Under this statute several appropriate ordinances have been passed by the city council to carry out its terms and a board of examiners has been created, which is at present engaged in the exercise of its functions under the statute and the ordinances. The last ordinance upon the subject was passed July 6, 1892.

At the last session of the General Assembly the so-called civil service statute was passed and it went into effect March 20, 1895. Under it the commissioners therein provided for are required to classify all the offices and places of employment in the city government, with certain exceptions not material here, and to cause all applicants for offices or places in such classified service to be subjected to examination, which examination is required to be public, competitive, and free to all citizens of the United States, with specified limitations as to residence, ~ce, habits, health and moral character. A register of the result of such examination is required to be kept by the Civil Service Commission and to the person standing highest upon the register for any particular grade of the service is required to be kept appointed or to be promoted whenever an appropriate vacancy is to be filled. Appointments to the classified service cannot lawfully be made under the civil service law in any other manner than through examination by the commission and certification to the appointing board. The qualifications of a candidate are lawfully such as are determined by the civil service examination and only by such examination, no outside license being required or permitted under that law.

It will be observed the early statute and the later one seen to conflict with regard to the appointment of engineers for the city service, for apparently examinations to be held by the commission must be open to any person presumably qualified to take them within the limits laid down by the law, without regard to whether such persons are licensed by another local authority or not. There can be no reasonable question about this. Some reasonable restriction upon applicants for examination may undoubtedly be prescribed by the commission, for such restriction is hardly more than a preliminary examination, but beyond this the law does not authorize the commission to go. I am of the opinion that if a man claiming to be a mechanical engineer by vocation applies for examination to the commission and presents to the commission reasonable evidence that he is such mechanical engineer and not instead a lawyer or physician or a person pursuing some other vocation, that in such cases the commission would have no right to require that applicant must be provided with a license from the city board of examiners.

The question then arises what becomes of the provisions of the early statute and of the ordinances forbidding any person to act as an engineer without a license from the city board of examiners. The answer to this question is settled. Those provisions seem to be inconsistent with the provisions of the civil service law and must give way. The civil service law expressly provides that "All laws or parts of laws which are inconsistent with this act, or any of the provisions thereof, are hereby repealed."

So far therefore as relates to engineers in the service of the city or seeking to enter that service the statute of 1889 must be regarded as repealed by the provisions of the civil service law and the like applicable provisions of the city ordinances fall with that portion of the statute because they are not in harmony with the existing law, but are to that extent contrary to law. The operation and effect of the city ordinances must now be limited to persons outside of the city service.

Very truly yours,
WM. G. BEALE, Corporation Counsel.

October 23, 1895.
J. J. Badenoch, Esq., General Superintendent of Police.
Dear Sir—

Your communication dated October 18th in which you request an opinion from this department as to your right to interfere with persons selling or furnishing liquor with meals, said persons not having a license, has been referred to me by the corporation counsel.

Under the ordinances of this city there cannot be the slightest doubt as to your right to interfere with persons who dispense liquors without a license in the manner stated in your communication. Section 2506, Laws and Ordinances of Chicago, 1890, covers this question fully, and is as follows:

"Any person who shall hereafter have or keep any tavern, grocery, ordinary, victualing, or other house or place, within the City of Chicago, for selling, giving away, or in any manner dealing in intoxicating liquors in quantities less than one gallon, or who by himself, his agents, or servants shall sell, give away, or in any manner deal in intoxicating liquors in quantities less than one gallon, or who by himself, his agents, or servants, shall keep a dram shop for the sale of liquors in quantities less than one gallon without a license therefor, in pursuance of this ordinance and other ordinances of the City of

Chicago, shall, upon conviction, be subject to a fine of not less than $20.00 nor more than $100.00 for each and every offense."

The provisions of our state law in regard to the liquor traffic are clear and certain, and it is readily perceived from a perusal of them that it is considered a business which motives of public policy and good government require should be regulated. In order to properly regulate this traffic, it is important that the city officials should know definitely all persons engaged in it, and the places in which it is carried on. Under the license system this information is easily obtained from the records, and the officers entrusted with the duty of seeing that the requirements of the law in regard to sales of liquor to minors, habitual drunkards, etc., are faithfully carried out, are thus enabled to efficiently discharge those duties.

Again, the license system has been devised as a method of raising funds to pay the expenses of the municipal government, and it is enacted that all persons engaged in the sale of liquors should pay a certain amount for the privilege of so doing. Hence, no discrimination can, or should be made between persons engaged in this business, no matter under what guise. Were it to be permitted that restaurants sell or furnish liquors with meals without requiring a license to be paid, a wide door would be open for all manner of frauds and evasions of the law, and it would be well nigh impossible to properly enforce the laws regarding the liquor traffic. It would also be unjust to persons conducting a legitimate liquor business and who have paid a heavy license fee for the privilege of so doing, in that, it would place them in competition with irresponsible persons who would be under no expense for license, and this would tend to a diminution of the revenue of the city collector from such license fees.

In my opinion, under the law as set out in our city ordinances, and in the statutes of this state, no person by himself or agent (except druggists, for whom an express provision is made), can, without a license, directly, or indirectly, engage in the distribution of liquor by selling, giving away or otherwise disposing of it to the public, without being made liable to the penalty imposed by law and the ordinances for selling liquor without a license.

Very truly,
WILLIAM H. ARTHUR, Assistant Corporation Counsel.

October 30, 1895.

Wm. R. Kerr, Esq., Commissioner of Health.

Dear Sir—

Mr. Beale has referred to me your communication of the 23rd inst., asking to be advised as to "whether the ordinance passed by the city council May 29, 1893, creating the bureau of street and alley cleaning (Secs. 4,593 to 4,608 inclusive) annuls or repeals or otherwise modifies Section 1959 of Article XXVII, Law and Ordinances, 1890."

A mere similarity between two ordinances, even where it is such as might cause inconvenience and confusion, is not enough to create a repeal by implication of the first ordinance by the latter.

Sedgwick on Stat. & Const. Law, second Ed. says, page 106:

"Laws are presumed to be passed with deliberation, and with full knowledge of all existing ones on the same subject, and it is therefore but reasonable to conclude that the legislature in passing a statute did not intend to interfere with or abrogate any prior law relating to the same matter, unless the repugnancy between the two is irreconcilable, and hence a repeal by implication is not favored. On the contrary the courts are bound to uphold the prior law if the two acts may well subsist together."

Justice Fields says in Woods vs. United States, 16 Peters, 342:

"When there are two acts or provisions of law relating to the same subject, effect is to be given to both if that is practicable. If the two are repugnant, the latter will operate as a repeal of the former to the extent of the repugnancy, but the second act will not operate as such repeal merely because it may repeat some of the provisions of the first one, and omit others or add new provisions. In such cases the latter act will operate as a repeal only where it plainly appears that it was intended as a substitute for the first act. As Mr. Justice Story says, 'It may be merely affirmative or cumulative or auxilary.'"

It is my opinion that Section 1959, Article XXVII, is not repealed or modified in any particular by the passage of the later ordinance creating the bureau of street and alley cleaning. The two ordinances are not necessarily in conflict. It seems to me to be a reasonable interpretation of the two (so far as concerns the present inquiry), that nothing detrimental to the public health can be deposited upon any street or alley or upon any vacant lot of ground within the city limits without the written permission of the commissioner of health; that the commissioner of health can, in giving a permit, insert provisions for disinfecting and deodorizing, and impose other safeguards to the public health as he see fit; that whether garbage, etc., should, at any time for reasons connected with the public health, be removed from vacant lots by the superintendent of street and alley cleaning would depend upon whether it was deposited upon such lots in conformity with a permit from the commissioner of health; and that if it had been so deposited under permit, it would not be subject to removal by the superintendent of street and alley cleaning merely because thought by him to be objectionable on the score of health, for the permit of the commissioner of health would seem to bind him as to that element of the matter and the garbage could be removed only if objectionable for some other reason.

I am authorized to say that Mr. Beale concurs with me in this opinion.   Very truly yours,

B. BOYDEN, Asst. Corporation Counsel.

November 1, 1895.

W. D. Kent, Esq., Commissioner of Public Works.

Dear Sir—

Your question as to the ownership of old paving blocks where the street is being torn up for the purpose of repairing has been referred to me by Mr. Beale.

1. The old blocks do not belong to the contractor who paved the street formerly as he was paid for them upon the finishing of his contract.

2. They do not belong to the contractor who has the present contract for the repaving of the street unless it is so specifically set out in his contract by the city.

3. The abutting owners have no personal ownership in the paving blocks in a street any more than the citizens of the city of Chicago own any bridge spanning the Chicago river. The paving is done by special assessment and the bridges are constructed with moneys received by general taxation. In both cases the improvement is paid for by taxes although levied in a different way. The result is the same. The city receives the money and expends it on public improvements.

The title to the streets is in the city, in trust for the public and no one can have any private ownership in the street or in the material forming the pavement whether such material has been discarded and replaced by new or not, and it makes no difference if such pavement was placed in the street by private contract or by special assessment.

It is my opinion that the city owns the old blocks and can dispose of them in any way the commissioner of public works sees fit. Mr. Beale concurs with me. Very truly yours,

B. BOYDEN, Asst. Corporation Counsel.

November 2, 1895.

Hon. John M. Clark, President Civil Service Commission.

Dear Sir—

It would seem from statements in the public press that I failed to make clear to you, in the conversation we had on the day before yesterday, my ideas of certain questions arising under the civil service law about which you spoke to me.

I did not hold, and do not mean to be understood as holding, that no person in the classified civil service, could be a member of any political club; there is no such provision anywhere in the law. I am clearly of the opinion that any employe in the classified civil service of the city may voluntarily join and retain his membership in a political club.

The question as to whether such an employe can be required to pay any political assessment or contributions is best answered by the statute, Section 21 of which provides:

"No officer or employe of such city shall solicit, orally or by letter, or receive or pay, or be in any manner concerned in soliciting, receiving or paying, any assessment, subscription, or contribution for any party or political purpose whatever."

I am of the opinion that the payment of the usual dues of members in political clubs, which shall be not more than each member's fair share of the cost and expenses of maintaining the club, is not prohibited by the law, and is not a payment of any "assessment, subscription or contribution" within the meaning of Section 21, as above quoted. To hold otherwise, would be to hold that a man might belong to any association, but could not bear his share of the cost of supporting the same. It would not be logical to say that a man employed by a mercantile house may belong to a club and may pay his share of its expense while a man in the civil service may belong to the same association, but may not pay any of its expenses. I think, however, that a city employe cannot be coerced into the involuntary payment of any dues or contributions of any sort, for club dues or for general political purposes. This would be an attempt to do indirectly what may not be done directly, and in my opinion would be a palpable violation of the law.　　　Respectfully submitted,

　　　　　　GEO. A. DUPUY, First Asst. Corporation Counsel.

　　　　　　　　　　　　　　　　　　　November 11, 1895.
W. D. Kent, Esq., Commissioner of Public Works.

　Dear Sir—

　You ask to be advised by the Corporation Counsel on the following questions:

　First. Can the receiver of a firm having a contract with the city of Chicago, entered into before the appointment of the receiver, be required to fulfil the provisions of the contract without an order of the court?

　Second. Can the court issue instructions to the receiver affecting in any way the terms of the contract?

　Third: What is the effect and the provisions of the new lien law as to liens upon work contracted for with the city?

　A receiver, regularly appointed by a court of competent jurisdiction, is an officer of the court and holds his office for the benefit of all persons interested. He acts under the orders of the court and can legally do no act beyond such order.

　If the city of Chicago has entered into a contract with a person or corporation for any public improvement or for any material or supplies, and the affairs of the person or corporation are afterwards tied up in court and a receiver appointed by the court for the purpose of settling the estate the receiver could not proceed with the contract unless he was ordered to do so by the court, the proceeds to be used for the benefit of all parties interested.

　Where a person or corporation has contracted with the city to do certain work, or furnish certain material or supplies, and subsequently the business of the person or corporation is placed, by proper legal proceedings, in the hands of a receiver, the most prudent course for the city to take would be to file an intervening petition in the case setting up the facts; or where by reason of the appointment of a receiver the city has been compelled to forfeit a contract for non-performance of its conditions and had been compelled to let the contract to another person for a greater sum of money, the city should file a claim against the estate of the contractor asking the court to allow the difference between the former price and the new contract price.

The action of the court in the appointment of a receiver of a person or corporation and the diverse instructions and orders of the court issued to him from time to time, cannot affect the terms of a contract theretofore entered into by the person or corporation, but the fact that the business of a contractor with whom the city has a contract has been put in the hands of a receiver might compel the city to declare the contract forfeited because the contractor, by reason of the proceedings, was unable to carry out its provisions. In this event the court, through the receiver, should be notified of the intended action of the city, and the city should file a claim as above stated.

Section 24 of an act passed by the last legislature approved June 6, 1895, is as follows:

"Any person who shall furnish material, apparatus, fixtures, machinery or other labor to any contractor for a public improvement, in this state, shall have a lien on the money, bonds or warrants due or to become due such contractor for such improvements; provided, such person shall, before any payment or delivery thereof is made to such contractor, notify the officials of this state, county, township, city or municipality whose duty it is to pay such contractor, of his claim in a written notice and the full particulars thereof. It shall be the duty of such officials so notified to withold a sufficient amount to pay such claim until it is admitted or by law established, and thereupon to pay the amount thereof to such person, and said payment shall be a credit on the contract price to be paid to such contractor. Any officer violating the duty hereby imposed upon him shall be liable on his official bond to the person serving such notice for the damages resulting from such violation, which may be recovered in an action at law in any court of competent jurisdiction. There shall be no preference between the persons serving such notice, but all shall be paid pro rata in proportion to the amount due under their respective contracts."

The above section relates to the public improvements and provides that any person who furnishes material, etc., or labor on a public improvement in the state of Illinois shall have a lien upon the warrants due the contractor for such improvement, and provides that the person shall, before the contractor is paid, notify the officials of the city whose duty it is to pay such contractor for his claim by a written notice. Upon the receipt of this written notice it is the duty of the officials of the city to withhold a sufficient amount from the said warrant to pay the said claim, and hold the said amount until the matter is settled. Any officer violating the duty hereby imposed is made liable on his official bond to the person serving such notice. This is the only section in said law which relates to cities or to public improvements and the law does not state on whom the above notice shall be served.

A sub-contractor, material man or laborer must serve a written notice on the city, presumably on the commissioner of public works or the comptroller, before he can take advantage of this law. It would be the safer way until the courts construe the law to hold strictly to the language of this section of the statutes, and call the comptroller's attention to it, and request him, on receipt of a written notice in conformity therewith, to withhold from the contractor a sufficient amount of money to cover the sum mentioned in the notice.

Very truly yours,

B. BOYDEN, Asst. Corporation Counsel.

November 14, 1895.

E. W. Stanwood, Esq., Chairman, Committee on Health and County Relations.

Dear Sir—

In compliance with your request that I examine the two ordinances now pending before your committee, one for the prohibition and the other for the regulation of the sale of horse meat, and report to you my conclusions on the same I beg to say, that in my opinion the ordinance proposed to absolutely prohibit the sale of horse meat would not be valid if passed by the council. In other words I think the city council has the power to regulate but not to prohibit the sale of horse flesh. The other ordinance I have examined with care. Several minor changes not affecting substantially the general scope of the ordinance occurred to me as desirable. I therefore took the liberty of preparing with some care an ordinance in its general provisions very much like the one you handed me, which I respectfully return with these and suggest that the draft I have made is an improvement on the copy you gave me. This ordinance I am inclined to think would be free from legal objections if passed, except that possibly the license fee is excessively high. I am of the opinion that a smaller fee would make a safer ordinance. Very respectfully yours,

GEO. A. DUPUY. Asst. Corporation Counsel.

November 22, 1895.

Joseph Downey, Esq., Commissioner of Buildings.

Dear Sir—

In reply to your inquiry of the 21st inst., which has been referred to me, in regard to whether you have the power to suspend employes for a limited time without their losing their places on pay-rolls of the city under the civil service law, I beg to say that in my opinion you have

such authority. I think this authority is recognized in Section 12 of
the civil service act, which provides that any officer shall have the
power to suspend a subordinate for a reasonable period, not exceeding thirty days. I think as a practical method of dealing with the question and in order to avoid having subordinates feel that they are suspended, a good plan would be for them to ask for a voluntary leave of
absence for a period not exceeding thirty days without pay. This you
can readily grant, and during such time the subordinate will not feel
that he is suspended. Of course this reaches the same practical result and seems to me to be a better form of attaining the desired end.

Very respectfully yours,

GEO. A. DUPUY, Asst. Corporation Counsel.

December 4, 1895.

J. J. Badenoch, Esq., Superintendent of Police.

Dear Sir—

Your request that this department furnish you with an opinion
as to the liability of the city of Chicago for negligent, wrongful or
illegal acts committed by its police officers, has been referred to me.

A letter dated November 30, 1895, from Detwiler & Bary, attor-
neys-at-law, to yourself, in reference to the alleged shooting of Michael
McGeoghagan by a policeman, has been turned over to me, and I am
informed that your aforesaid request is made with particular reference
to the matter contained in that letter.

A criticism of the statements of law contained in said letter as to
the civil liabilities of the city for the acts therein complained of might
be out of place here, but I will say in passing, that taking the *ex parte*
statements made in said letter to be true, I am clearly of the opinion,
that the city of Chicago is in no way liable for the acts therein alleged
to have been done. It is well settled by the decisions of almost every
state in the Union, and by none more strongly than our own state,
that police officers and firemen are not agents or servants of the corporation appointing them so as to make the corporation responsible
for their acts. They are held to be officers of the city charged with a
public service for whose negligence in the discharge of their official
duties, no action will lie against the city unless expressly given by statute.

See Arms vs. City of Knoxville, 32 Ill., App. 610, and Butterick
vs. City of Lowell, 1st Allen, Mass., 172.

The reason of this rule is based on grounds of sound public
policy.

See Wilcox vs. City of Chicago, 107 Ill., 328.

In the case of Culver vs. City of Streator, 130 Ill., 238, the court
says:

"An incorporated city is not responsible to a person who receives a personal injury from one of its officers or agents in enforcing
an ordinance prohibiting the running at large of unlicensed and un-

muzzled dogs, as, where, in attempting to kill a dog, through negligence and carelessness the officer shoots and wounds such person.

"Police officers appointed or employed by a city are not its agents or servants so as to render the city responsible for their unlawful or negligent acts in the discharge of their duties, or in executing or enforcing police ordinances and regulations."

Dillon on Municipal Corporations, Vol. 2, Sec. 975, 4th Ed., covers this question very thoroughly, and supports his statement with abundant authority. He says in part:

"Police officers appointed by a city are not its agents or servants, so as to render it responsible for their unlawful or negligent acts in the discharge of their duties; and, accordingly, a city is not liable for an assault and battery committed by its police officers, though done in an attempt to enforce an ordinance of the city, or for an arrest made by them which is illegal for want of a warrant, or for other cause; or for their unlawful acts of violence. The municipal corporation in all these and the like cases represents the state or the public; the police officers are not the servants of the corporation; the principle of *respondeat superior* does not apply, and the corporation is not liable unless by virtue of the statute expressly creating the liability."

In the absence of such a statute in our state, and from a reading of the decisions and text books on this subject, there cannot be the slightest doubt that the city of Chicago is not liable in any way for the tortious or negligent acts of its police officers, and it is in consonance with sound public policy that such should be the case. Policemen are appointed to do their duty and not to do anything more than the law requires. The appointing power expects them to do no more than that, and if they do, it is their own individual act, and *they* only are responsible. Very truly yours,

WILLIAM H. ARTHUR, Asst. Corporation Counsel.

December 4, 1895.

Hon. O. D. Wetherell, Comptroller.

Dear Sir—

As requested by you, I beg to confirm the verbal opinion expressed by me a few days ago upon the three questions you ask, namely:

First. Can the comptroller lawfully transfer moneys from one fund in the city treasury to another, and particularly can he lawfully direct such transfers from the so-called general fund to a particular fund and vice versa?

Second. Can one warrant be lawfully drawn for the payment of moneys to a number of different persons, as, for example, to the head of a department for the entire pay-roll of this department?

Third. Does the comptroller's warrant fully protect the city treasurer in paying out moneys thereunder?

I have no difficulty in answering each of these questions in the affirmative, with the qualification that the treasurer would, of course, not be justified in paying out moneys upon a warrant known by him, either from its face, or otherwise, to be drawn by a comptroller for some clearly unlawful purpose, such, for example, as the payment of a personal bill. Very truly yours.

WM. G. BEALE, Corporation Counsel.

December 12, 1895.

W. Guthrie, Esq., Secy. Board of Examining Engineers.

Dear Sir—

Replying now to your letter of November 23, the subject matter of which we have discussed somewhat, I beg to say that in my opinion there is a clear conflict between the civil service act and the act under which the City passed an ordinance creating the Board of Examining Engineers, and a further conflict between that ordinance and the civil service act. The civil service act seeems to me clearly to have stripped the Board of Examining Engineers of jurisdiction or authority in respect to the examination or licensing engineers, boiler tenders, etc., in the service of the city. If this were not so it would necessarily follow that the Board of Examining Engineers would possess the power to nullify a civil service examination and a subsequent appointment following such examination by refusing a license to the appointee. The Board of Examining Engineers would not have authority to issue a license without an examination of its own, and it might happen that a successful candidate in a civil service examination would fail in an examination before the examining engineers, in which event it would be the duty of the latter board to refuse a license. The effect would be to make the civil service examination subject and subordinate to an examination of the Board of Examining Engineers, which, in my judgment, is clearly not in contemplation of the laws in force.

The serious question in my mind is whether the civil service act has not operated in legal effect to repeal the entire statute relating to the Board of Examining Engineers, but this question is not before me and I do not feel it necessary to attempt to decide it. It would be unfortunate if I should be obliged to hold that this entire law with reference to licensing engineers has been repealed, but I hope not to be called upon to pass upon the question. The Board can reasonably assume that it is still in force except as to engineers, etc., in the service of the city. Very truly yours,

WM. G. BEALE, Corporation Counsel.

December 27, 1895.

Hon. John M. Clark, Prest. Civil Service Commission, City of Chicago.

Dear Sir—

I beg to acknowledge the receipt of your letter of December 18, requesting my opinion upon certain questions arising under Section 12 of the civil service law.

In my opinion the disciplinary power of the commission outside of its own office is confined exclusively to the matter of approving or disapproving the discharge of employes from the public service. The functions of the commission under the civil service law have to do with appointments, promotions and removals; but the work and discipline of an executive department are properly left where other laws and the city ordinances have placed them, *subject to a limitation* upon the power of the ordinary authority (spoken of in the law as "the appointing officer") to discharge an unsatisfactory employe without the approval of the commission, or to suspend him for a period longer than thirty days. The provisions of Section 12 clearly constitute such a limitation of power and except in cases of laborers or persons having the custody of public money, for the safe keeping of which another has given bond, they require that the discharge of an employe who has been appointed under the civil service law must be approved by the commission, directly or indirectly, to be effective. It thus becomes the duty of the commission to investigate charges under which it is sought to discharge an employe previously appointed under the law, and this duty is expressly imposed upon it by Section 14 of the law. The provisions of Section 12 apply only to officers and employes appointed under the civil service law. The accused is entitled to be heard before the commission, or before the board or officer designated by the commission to investigate the charges made. Only one such hearing is required, and when the commission reviews the finding of any such board or officer, it need not hear the accused again, but, of course, may do so.

I have no doubt that the charges referred to should be presented by the person whose authority to discharge an employe is thus limited by Section 12, and that the commission should not take cognizance of charges presented by others. Any other course might place the commission in the anomalous position of approving charges against an employe whom the appointing officer would not desire to discharge, and would not discharge, and whom, therefore, the commission could not discharge. If an employe appointed under the civil service law is performing his duties to the satisfaction of the appointing officer, and such appointing officer makes no complaint to the commission, the law has not conferred upon the commission any disciplinary jurisdiction whatever over such employe. Until the appointing officer complains to the commission the disclipinary jurisdiction of the commission does not attach. The plain underlying purpose of the civil service law in respect to removals is not to effect proper removals, but to prevent improper ones. Desirable removals are left to be brought about by responsible superiors. Very Respectfully yours,

WM. G. BEALE, Corporation Counsel.

December 27, 1895.

Hon. John M. Clark, President of the Civil Service Commission, City of Chicago.

Dear Sir—

I have examined with some care the questions submitted by you in your letter of the 3d inst., requesting my opinion thereon.

The civil service law nowhere defines the terms "officer" and "employe," nor furnishes any basis for distinguishing between them, so far as I can discover. It recognizes that such distinction exists, but in nearly all its provisions it uses collectively the expression "offices and places of employment." Our state constitution contains a definition which distinguishes between "an office" and "an employment," but this definition is seemingly not applicable to the question under consideration, for it appears to use the word "employment" in reference to a special *agency* for a temporary purpose as distinct from any fixed and regular position in the administration of government, and it would probably be construed as referring only to state offices and employments. The state constitution and the civil service law, therefore, do not appear to help us in determining who are technically officers of the city of Chicago as distinguished from employes. It should be understood that I am referring to officers in the executive service of the city, for in a broader and more general sense the word "officer" would, of course, include a member of the legislative department, about which I understand no legal question arises.

Upon turning to the general city incorporation law under which this city is organized, an answer to the question under consideration will be found. The first three sections of Article VI, of the city incorporation law provide in substance that there shall be elected in all cities organized under the act, certain specified officers; that the city council may, in its discretion from time to time, by ordinance passed by a vote of two-thirds of all the aldermen elected, provide for the election by the legal voters of the city, or for the appointment by the mayor, with the approval of the city council, of certain other specified officers and such other officers as may by the council be deemed necessary or expedient; and that all officers of any city so organized shall, except as otherwise in that law provided, be appointed by the mayor, by and with the advice and consent of the city council. This general incorporation law has been amended in many particulars, either expressly or by acts operating legally as amendments; but I do not find that the foregoing fundamental provisions have been in any way modified except that the legislature has itself specified some additional offices which a city may have, as, for example, a civil service commission. The city incorporation law and its amendments constitute a city charter, and are a grant of power without which a city has no authority to act. Bearing this in mind, it will be seen from the foregoing charter provisions that the city of Chicago can create a city office only in the manner and with the qualities or incidents therein prescribed. Apart from the offices specially created by law, the city can have only such offices, created by ordinance, as conform to the requirements of the city charter. It is an inseparable incident of a city office, created by the council under the charter, that it be filled either through popular election, or appointment by the mayor with the concurrence of the council. If a position in the city government is, under an ordinance, to be filled in any other way, it is not an office within the meaning of the city charter, and its occupant would not be an officer. All occupants of fixed and regular positions under the city government, as distinguished from independent contractors, are either officers or employes, and it follows necessarily that the holder of such a position who is not an officer is an employe.

This method of determining who are strictly city officers and who are city employes is in harmony with numerous decisions of the Supreme Court of the United States determining who are officers of the United States within the meaning of the federal constitution. That instrument affords a definition of federal offices strikingly analogous to the definition of city offices afforded by the city charter.

Under the above view it will be noted that the number of "officers" in the executive department of the city of Chicago is now comparatively limited. Each of such officers is required by law to take an official oath and to give an official bond, and is entitled to be formally commissioned by warrant. All of them are excepted from the classified service under Section 11, of the civil service law. A city employe is not required to take an oath or give a bond, although either of these requirements can in any case be imposed by ordinance. Nor is a city employe entitled by law to receive a formal commission.

The civil service law seems to use the word "officer" in a broader and more popular sense than does the city charter. It speaks collectively of officers and employes in the classified service, although, as already pointed out, the classified service does not appear to include any city office, strictly speaking. There is nothing extraordinary in this different use of the same word. It is not unusual for a word to be used in one sense in one law and in a different sense in another law. In certain of the above mentioned decisions of the Supreme Court of the United States, that court took special note of the fact that the word "officer" was used in different senses in different federal enactments. In using the word "official" to designate one branch of the classified service, the commission has merely followed the language of the civil service law. The word has no relation to the technical and legal distinction between officers and employes under the charter, but is manifestly used in a general and popular sense, precisely as policemen are often, or perhaps commonly, called police officers. There is nothing objectionable, inappropriate or incorrect in this use of the word "official" by the commission, although, in fact, under Section

11 of the civil service law, it seems to include only employes, within the meaning of the city charter. The classification made by the commission and its designation of the two classes in the classified service seemed to be entirely logical, and consistent with existing laws.

I have discussed the distinction between officers and employes in the executive departments under the charter at some length, because there is apparently some confusion surrounding it, and it ought to be better understood. Perhaps I ought to add that undoubtedly some incongruity exists in the city ordinances on this subject. Ordinances have from time to time created positions which from their importance were probably intended to be regarded as "offices," but which, legally speaking, are not offices; while other positions of minor importance have been similarly created and made offices without any such intention. For example, a pound-keeper is a city officer within the meaning of the city charter, while the city engineer is not an officer at all, but is an employe. This incongruous and illogical arrangement in exercising the power conferred by the law cannot, of course, change the plain effect of the law.

The remaining question in your letter can be more briefly answered. The civil service law requires the commission to classify all offices and places of employment under the city government, with specified exceptions, and provides that the offices and places so classified shall constitute the classified service of the city. It seems to be clear that all persons holding any of such classified places of employment or offices (in the broad sense in which the civil service law and the rules of the commission use the latter word) are in the classified civil service of the city, whether they have obtained their positions through civil service examinations since the civil service law went into effect, or previously obtained them by direct appointment. It is the positions which have been classified, and not the occupants, and a holder of a classified position is in the classified service, whether he was appointed thereto and held the position when it was classified, or has since obtained it through civil service examination. All employes in the classified service seem to stand upon the same footing, except that employes who have been appointed through civil service examination cannot be discharged without the approval of the commission, while the others who have previously been appointed and were holding their respective positions when the law and classification went into effect can be discharged without such approval, precisely as they could be if the civil service law were not in force. In examinations for promotions, all employes in any particular grade of the service are alike entitled to be examined whether they have obtained their places in such grade through civil service examinations or through appointment before the law went into effect. In this respect it does not matter how a man got into the classified service. The essential fact is that he is there. Very respectfully yours,

WM. G. BEALE, Corporation Counsel.

January 3, 1896.

Hon. W. D. Kent, Commissioner of Public Works.

Dear Sir—

Your letter of December 27, 1895, to the corporation counsel, in which you request an opinion from this department as to whether or not your department can take any action toward preventing the gas companies from emptying refuse and inflammable matter into the Ogden slip, has been referred to me.

It is my opinion that the ordinances of the city of Chicago cover this question fully, and that your department can certainly take appropriate action in the case referred to in your letter and the correspondence accompanying it. There are two ordinances now in force which will afford a means of doing away with the nuisance complained of in Mr. Nelson's letter, which I find attached to your letter, and to which you no doubt had reference when you wrote. The first is Section 1957, Myers' Laws and Ordinances of the City of Chicago, Edition of 1890, and is as follows:

"That no person or company being a manufacturer of gas, or engaged about the manufacture thereof, shall throw or deposit or allow to run, or having the right or power to prevent the same, shall permit to be thrown or deposited in any public *waters, river, canal, slip, or into any sewer therewith connected,* or into any street or public place, *any gas, tar or any refuse matter* of or from any gas house, works or manufactory; nor shall any such person or company allow any substance or odor to escape from such house, works or manufactory, or make any gas of such ingredients or quality that any substance shall escape therefrom or be formed in the process of burning any gas, which shall be offensive or dangerous or prejudicial to life or health. Nor shall any such person or company fail to use the most approved or all reasonable means for preventing the escape of odors."

This is one of the sections of the health ordinance, and Section 2058 of the same ordinance, same edition above referred to, provides a penalty for the violation of said section, and is as follows:

"That any person who violates, disobeys, omits, neglects or refuses to comply with, or who resists any of the provisions of this article, or who refuses or neglects to obey any of the rules, orders, or sanitary regulations of the Department of Health, or who omits, neglects or refuses to comply with, or who resists any officer or order or special regulation of said Department of Health, shall, upon conviction, be subject to a fine not exceeding two hundred dollars nor less than ten dollars for each offense."

This appears to be a very appropriate section of the ordinance under which to grapple with this matter, and an enforcement of it would no doubt result in abating the nuisance complained of. The other section referred to is the one relating to the harbor. Section

18

5040, Myers' 1894 Supplement to Laws and Ordinances of the City of Chicago, defines what the harbor is, and reads as follows:

"The harbor shall consist of such portion of the Chicago River and its branches to their respective sources, including that portion known as *the Ogden Canal, and all slips adjacent to* and connecting with the Chicago River, the piers and basins, including the waters of the government breakwater, which lie adjoining to and extending three miles into the lake between the north and south lines of the city, and all the territory embraced between the limits of said survey as aforesaid, shall be a portion of the harbor of the City of Chicago and shall be subject to the control of the Harbor Master and to all the rules, and regulations of this chapter, or which shall be hereafter provided by the City Council."

Section 5038, same ordinance, same edition above referred to, relates to the befouling of the stream, and is in part as follows:

"No persons shall cast or deposit, or suffer to be cast or deposited, in the harbor of the City of Chicago, or within five miles of the harbor, any earth, ashes or other heavy substance or substances, filth, logs or floating matter or any obstruction."

This last ordinance goes more to show the jurisdiction of the city of Chicago over the river and harbor than to provide an appropriate remedy in the case referred to in your letter, but it being first shown that the city has full control and jurisdiction over the river, slips and entire harbor, and, secondly, that the section of the health ordinance first referred to covers this question fully, it is my opinion that your department can, by calling the attention of the offending gas company to this ordinance, and notifying it of your intention to enforce the same, put an effectual stop to the depositing of refuse and inflammable matter in the river, or any part of it.

Very truly yours,

W. H. ARTHUR, Asst. Corporation Counsel.

January 8, 1896.

O. D. Wetherell, Esq., City Comptroller.

Dear Sir—

Your request for an opinion from this department as to the right of a police officer of the city of Chicago to act as a constable for the purpose of serving summons in civil cases in which the city is plaintiff has been referred to me.

After a diligent search I have been unable to find any decisions of the courts of this state, or indeed of any other state, on this question, so I am forced to take it up as a case of first impression.

First: **What is a policeman?** He is primarily a conservator of the peace, and as such has the power to arrest, or cause to be arrested, any person breaking the peace, or violating any of the criminal laws of the state, and by our statutes he is empowered to arrest all persons violating any such ordinance.

Paragraph 84, Chapter XXIV, Starr & Curtis' Statutes of Illinois, further gives a policeman all the common law and statutory powers of a constable, for the purpose of serving and executing warrants for the violation of city ordinances, but policemen are nowhere given the right to serve civil process—that is to say, a summons notifying a defendant to appear and answer the plaint of the plaintiff.

It appears to me to be wholly outside of a policeman's duty, and entirely beyond the scope of his authority, to act as a constable for the serving of a summons in a civil case before a justice of the peace. A constable is the only officer authorized to do that; a constable is an officer elected by the people; he is required to furnish a bond in the sum of ten thousand dollars, and is responsible for a false return. What remedy would a defendant have against a policeman for a false return? No bond is furnished by him. The city would not be liable for any act of negligence or fraud on his part, and all safeguards provided by law for the purpose of enforcing the proper conduct of officers authorized to serve judicial process would be set at naught.

Again, the legislature of the state of Illinois has prescribed the form of summons to be used in civil cases before a justice of the peace, and this form must be followed in order to give jurisdiction. The form is as follows:

State of Illinois, County of ...., ss.

The People of the State of Illinois to any constable of said county.

Greeting:

You are hereby commanded to summon, etc.

Now a policeman certainly cannot be said to be a constable, and in my opinion, he would have no more authority to serve such a sumsoms on a defendant than any citizen of the city of Chicago. A service by him would confer no jurisdiction whatever, and a judgment rendered against the defendant on such a summons would, in my opinion, be null and void.   Yours very truly,

W. H. ARTHUR, Asst. Corporation Counsel.

January 11, 1896.

Philip Maas, Esq., City Collector.

Dear Sir—

The Corporation Counsel has referred to me your request for an opinion from this department as to the right of a person having but one saloon license to carry on the business of selling liquor in two or more bar-rooms or apartments. I am also informed that your request has been made with particular reference to the bar rooms being conducted in the Great Northern Hotel.

The question of the Great Northern Hotel bar rooms has been considered by this department before. On April 10, 1894, Assistant Corporation Counsel John Mayo Palmer rendered an opinion to the city collector, in which I concur, and will therefore set it out in full:

"April 10, 1894.

"To the City Collector.

"Sir—

"I have your communication detailing the methods pursued by the management of the Great Northern Hotel in retailing liquors under a single license issued by the city, and note your request for an opinion as to whether such methods are justified by the license.

"Under our system a saloon license authorizes the carrying on of the business of a retail dealer in liquors at one place; but the license fee paid is not dependent upon the amount of business transacted, or the methods employed at such place in disposing of such liquors.

"It seems that the Great Northern Hotel is conducted as a single enterprise, all its various departments being located in one building, and under a single management. That the different places in the building where liquors are dispensed are mere conveniences for the accommodation of its own customers, and are not designed to enable the management to run several dram shops.

"Under the circumstances, a single license is all that can be required.   (Signed)

"JOHN MAYO PALMER, Asst. Corporation Counsel."

The general question raised in your request as to persons having but one saloon license, selling liquor in two or more bar rooms or apartments, presents a problem much more difficult to solve. It must be largely a question of fact, to be governed and determined by the particular circumstances of each case. For illustration I will cite the saloon in the Ashland Block, run by T. P. O'Connor. This is a large "L" shaped apartment, having an entrance on Randolph street, and an entrance on Clark street, with a bar at each end of the room. The bars are separated by some considerable space, and neither one is visible from the other. Now these two bars being under the same roof, and conducted by the same person under the same name, and being one general enterprise, I am clearly of the opinion, that under our ordinance governing the sale of liquors, they do not constitute two dram shops, and that they can be conducted under one saloon license. If, however, O'Connor should sub-rent one or the other end of his apartment to some person, and that person should endeavor to operate a bar without procuring a license, that, to my mind, would be a clear violation of the law, although we would there have two bars in the one room. So you see, the question of the bars being in one room, or in different rooms of the same building, will not furnish a conclusive test as to whether or not one dram shop or two is being conducted. Unless the saloon license specifically states the limit of the space in which the business may be carried on under a particular license, it must always be a question of fact to be considered and determined by the particular circumstances of each case whether or not a party is conducting one or more dram shops under one license. Very truly yours,

W. H. ARTHUR, Asst. Corporation Counsel.

January 20, 1896.

O. D. Wetherell, Esq., City Comptroller.

Dear Sir—

I herewith return the letter of R. S. Critchell, and in answer to your question in relation thereto, would say that the city may grant permits and regulate the building of vaults under the sidewalks and require such compensation for the privilege as it may deem reasonable and just, when such permits relate solely to such use of the sidewalk space as in nowise inconsistent with their use by the public.

The permit should not be in the form of a lease, but simply issue a permit and have the grantee sign an agreement in which all the conditions could be incorporated. These permits could only be issued to the owner or occupants of the building abutting upon the part of the street desired.

I call your attention to Sections 2609 to 2612, Laws and Ordinances, 1890, (Myers' Ed.)

In the Gregsten case, decided by the Supreme Court in 1893, the city granted a permit to Gregsten to build a vault under an alley and took from him a bond by which the city reserved the right to revoke the permit and re-enter whenever the public interest should require it, and also upon the failure of the holder or his heirs to keep and perform the conditions and covenants of his bond. The court rightfully held that unless the *public interest* required the abandonment of the vault and the resumption of the alley by the city, or the holder of the permit had failed to perform his covenants, the city could not revoke such permit for the benefit and private use of some other individual who asked for a similar permit. From reading this case it can be readily seen that great care should be taken in the language used in both the permit and the agreement, if the city cares to derive a revenue from this source.

The following quotation from the case of Gregsten vs. Chicago, 145 Ill., 451, will be of interest in connection with this subject:

"By the amendment to the charter of the city of Chicago, passed in 1863, the Board of Public Works was given the power 'to regulate the placing or building of vaults under the streets, alleys and sidewalks, and require such compensation for the privilege as they shall deem reasonable and just, subject to the approval of the Common Council.' Under the authority thus conferred, as well as in execution of the power of exclusive control over the streets and alleys of the city by the city authorities, the Board of Public Works executed a permit to appellant, Gregsten, to excavate for and construct a vault under the alley running north and south through block 142, school section addition to said city, in the rear of an adjoining lot 16 in

said block, and to maintain and use such vault 'in connection with
the building erected, or to be erected, upon said lot,' etc. As will
be seen from the foregoing statement, said permit is, by its terms, subject to all the restrictions, limitations and conditions of the bond of
said Gregsten, of even date, executed to the city. * * *

"It is the general doctrine that municipalities, under the power
of exclusive control of their streets, may allow any use of them consistent with the public objects for which they are held." Nelson vs.
Godfrey, 12 Ill., 20; City of Quincy vs. Bull, 106 Id., 337; Gridley
vs. Bloomington, 68 Id., 47; C. & N. W. Ry. Co. vs. Elgin, 91 Id., 251;
Chicago Mun. Gas. L. Co. vs. Town of Lake, 130 Id., 42; Dillon on
Mun. Corp., 541-551.

In this case, however, special power has been conferred, by the
act amendatory of the charter, to make the grant, upon such consideration as the city authorities might deem reasonable and just.
* * * The city, through its constituted authorities, in granting
the permit upon the covenants, conditions and limitations contained
in the bond taken by the city from Gregsten, was, therefore, acting
in its private corporate capacity, as distinguished from its public
and political, or govern mental capacity, and the doctrine applicable
to the exercise of its public political powers does not apply. * * *

So in the previous case of Nelson vs. Godfrey, supra, it is held
that, as the privilege of excavating under sidewalks, etc., for vaults
is a great convenience, and may with proper care be exercised with
little or no inconvenience to the public, authority to make the same
will be inferred in the absence of any action of the corporate authorities to the contrary, they having knowledge of the progress of the
work. See also Dillon on Mun. Corp., Sec. 554. * * * And
especially will this be so when it is shown, as it is here, that the occupancy under the permit inured to the benefit of the city, which it
received with knowledge of the right claimed by the complainant.

As we have seen, the city authorities were authorized to regulate
the placing of vaults under sidewalks, streets and alleys of the city,
and required compensation for the same."

Very truly yours,

B. BOYDEN, Asst. Corporation Counsel.

January 20, 1896.
To the Honorable, The City Council of the City of Chicago.

Gentlemen—

In compliance with an order of your honorable body, passed on
the 6th day of January, requiring an opinion from this office "as to
whether or not the ordinance in force December 16, 1895, requiring a
license for the business of selling, dealing in, storing or cutting ice
is invalid for want of any penalty for a violation thereof, and for being
limited to ice merchants alone, or for either of such reasons," said

order having been referred to me for reply. I beg to say, that I have given the matter consideration, and would report as follows:

First. An ordinance is not invalid by reason of having no penalty provided therein for its violation. The authorities of the city are not obliged to rely solely on the infliction of penalties in order to compel obedience to proper police regulations. For example, an ordinance that prohibited the operation of a place of amusement without a license, and provided a penalty, might be enforced either by suit for the penalty, or by the actual closing of the place by the police department. Further, it has been held by the Supreme Court in the case of Schwuchow vs. City of Chicago, 68 Ill., 444,) that the liquor license ordinance might be enforced either by the infliction of the penalty, or by the revocation of the license. But while this is true, it is also true that in many cases it is practically impossible to enforce the provisions of an ordinance except by imposing fines or penalties. Accordingly, a standard writer on municipal law says: "That by-laws or ordinances may not be inoperative or useless, it is necessary that some penalty should be annexed to the breach of them." "Since an ordinance or by-law without a penalty would be nugatory, municipal corporations have an implied power to provide for their enforcement by reasonable and proper fines against those who break them." Dillon on Municipal Corporations, Vol. I., Secs. 270-272.

I am therefore of the opinion that this ordinance, if it had a penalty clause, would be a perfectly valid ordinance. I am of the further opinion that without the penalty clause, it is a valid ordinance if proper means for its enforcement can be found. As to those who take out licenses, the revocation of the license in case of any violation of the ordinance might be found a sufficient means of enforcing the ordinance.

Second. In regard to the second point of inquiry, as to whether or not said ordinance is invalid "for being limited to the ice merchants alone," I do not find that the ordinance is so limited. The first section provides: "It shall not be lawful for any person, firm, company, or corporation to engage or to continue in the business of selling, dealing in or storing ice in the City of Chicago, or of cutting ice for use in said city without a license therefor." I think no objection can be made to the ordinance for any reason growing out of the number or class of persons upon whom it is to operate.

Respectfully submitted,

GEO. A. DUPUY, Asst. Corporation Counsel.

January 29, 1896.

Philip Maas, Esq., City Collector.

Dear Sir—

I am in receipt of a letter from you, dated January 25, 1896, in which you ask for an opinion as to whether or not a porters' and runners' license gives the holder thereof the right to solicit customers or travelers for carriages, hacks, coupes, etc., for which he has no license as owner or driver.—No.

To my mind a reading of the ordinances now in force in regard to the occupations of porter and runner, and coaches, cabs and carts would furnish a sufficient answer to this question.

Section 1679, Myers' Laws and Ordinances of Chicago, 1890, and the following sections show clearly that the business of operating cabs, hacks, etc., for hire, is considered one which it is necessary to surround with salutary rules and regulations in order to protect the traveling public from extortion and robbery. The name of the owner and the number of his license must be plainly painted on the outside of the vehicle. (See Section 1684).

No person, except a licensed owner, is allowed to drive a hack, cab, or such vehicle, without procuring a license as driver, and no such driver can drive any other hack or cab, save the one for which he has a license. (See Section 1687.)

The prices or rates of fare to be demanded or asked by the owners or drivers of hacks, cabs, etc., are also provided for. (See Section 1694.)

It will be seen from the reading of the section referred to, and of the sections following the same, that it is not contemplated that any one but a licensed owner or driver of a hack, cab, or vehicle, shall have anything to do with the fixing of the rate of fare, making any of the necessary arrangements for the carrying of passengers, or in any way engaging in the business of carrying passengers in hacks, cabs, etc. If a porter or runner were to be permitted to make all or any of the preliminary arrangements, such as fixing rate of fare, etc., and he should be guilty of extortion, or other offense, I cannot see how he could be dealt with under the ordinance regulating porters and runners, for it nowhere gives him the right to do such work, nor does it provide any penalty for offense against the cab, hack and coach ordinance. If a porter or runner were to be arrested for charging an excessive fare for the use of a hack or cab he would have a perfect defense by showing that he was neither a licensed driver nor owner, and therefore the provisions of the ordinance relating to such did not apply to him.

It is clear to my mind that the license issued to a porter and runner is intended to allow the pursuit of those avocations only, viz.: soliciting customers for hotels, boarding houses, steamboats, omnibuses, etc., and for the transportation of baggage, and that the solicitation of passengers for hacks, cabs, etc., is not allowed by any person except he have a license as driver or owner. I will therefore answer your question in the negative.   Very truly yours,

WM. H. ARTHUR, Asst. Corporation Counsel.

January 31, 1896.

Philip Maas, Esq., City Collector.
Dear Sir—

A paper containing several questions asked by you has been referred to me with a request to answer the same. Your questions are three in number, and I will take them up in turn.

First you ask, "Can the bottling and peddling of malt liquors be carried on under a dram shop license?"

In answer to this question I will say, that in my opinion the business of bottling and peddling malt liquors cannot be carried on under a dram shop license.

Section 2496, Myers' Laws and Ordinances (1890), provides for the granting of a license, etc., and Section 2498, immediately following, provides for a bond, and sets out the substance of what the license shall authorize the holder thereof to do. This is the language of Section 2498:

"Every person, on compliance with the aforesaid requirements, and the payment in advance to the City Collector at the rate of five hundred ($500.00) dollars per annum, shall receive a license under the corporate seal, * * * which shall authorize the person or persons therein named to keep a dram shop to sell, give away, or barter intoxicating liquors in quantities less than one gallon *in the place designated in the license.*'

The clause therein inserted, "in the place designated in the license," would appear to prohibit selling, bartering or giving away intoxicating liquors in any other place than that actually named in the license, and so would prohibit the peddling of bottled malt liquors throughout the city.

But the ordinance passed by the city council on January 6, 1896, which you will find on page 1617 of the current council proceedings, seems to cover this question thoroughly, and appears to me to prohibit all persons, firms or corporations from bottling or peddling malt liquors without first obtaining a license therefor. It prohibits all persons, except licensed brewers, from engaging in that business, and they can only run five wagons without an express license to run more, for which they must pay.

I will therefore answer your first question in the negative.

Second, you ask, "Can vendor of wholesale malt liquors conduct his business under dram shop license?"

In answer to this I will again refer you to Section 2498, which specifically states that the dram shop license "shall authorize the person or persons therein named to keep a dram shop to sell, give away or barter intoxicating liquors *in quantities less than one gallon.*'' Therefore, a dram shop keeper having a dram shop license only, and not a license as wholesale vendor of malt liquors, cannot sell malt or any other intoxicating liquor, in quantities larger than one gallon, and Section 2785, Myers' Laws and Ordinances (1890) makes a specific provision for vendor of malt liquor in quantities larger than one gallon, in the following words:

"No person, firm or corporation shall sell or deliver within the City of Chicago, any ale, beer or other malt liquor in quantities larger than one gallon at one time, without first obtaining a license therefor as hereinafter contained."

It is my opinion that the business of dram shop keeper and that of wholesale vendor of malt liquors are entirely distinct from each other, and cannot be carried on under one license.

Therefore I answer your second question also in the negative.

Third, you ask, "Will a wholesale liquor license cover the business of bottling and peddling of malt liquors?"

Were it not for the ordinance passed January 6, 1896, and hereinbefore referred to, I believe this would present a more difficult question than either of the former.

Section 2786, Myers' Laws and Ordinances (1890) gives a wholesale vendor of malt liquor, upon the payment of a $500 license fee, the right to "sell or deliver *within the City of Chicago*, ale, beer or other malt liquors in quantities *larger than one gallon at a time.*"

The question which would arise here would be whether this section gives the right to sell or deliver the malt liquors in bottles containing less than one gallon, where the aggregate number of bottles delivered at one time, say in one case, would contain more than one gallon. I believe that each bottle would be considered a separate and distinct quantity, and that this section last referred to would not allow a wholesale vendor of malt liquors to peddle the same in bottles containing less than one gallon each, but the ordinance of January 6, 1896, seems to me to set at rest all doubts which might have arisen under Section 2786. The new ordinance says distinctly, "No person, firm or corporation shall carry on, engage in or conduct the business of peddling or bottling any malt liquors without first obtaining a license therefor," and in Section 2 of said ordinance it is provided that "the provisions of the foregoing section shall not apply to any person, firm or corporation who is engaged in the business of brewer, and who pays the license fee provided by the city of Chicago for brewers."

This, as you will see, absolutely prohibits all persons, firms and corporations, except those having a brewers' license, from engaging in the business of peddling or bottling malt liquors, unless they obtain a license for that express purpose. It does not allow a dram shop keeper, or a wholesale vendor of malt liquors, under their license as such, to engage in bottling or peddling malt liquors, and if either of such desire to do so, they must obtain a license for that express purpose. If it were intended that the provisions of this ordinance should not apply to them, they would have been exempted in terms similar to that in which persons having a brewers' license are exempted.

Again, if it should be considered that any of the old ordinances in force give the dram shop keeper, or the wholesaler of malt liquors, the right to peddle or bottle malt liquors, under their respective license as such, that right is certainly taken away by Section 10 of the new ordinance, in the following words: "All ordinances, or parts of ordinances, in conflict with provisions of this ordinance, are hereby repealed." This leaves the new ordinance herein referred to the governing ordinance on the question of bottling or peddling malt liquors, and any person, firm or corporation desiring to engage in such business must comply with the terms of this ordinance, or be subject to the penalty of the same.   Very truly yours,

WM. H. ARTHUR, Asst. Corporation Counsel.

February 5, 1896.

Hon. O. D. Wetherell, Comptroller.

Dear Sir—

In response to your request for a memorandum confirming the verbal opinion expressed by me yesterday to you and to the city treasurer and to the chairman of the finance committee upon the questions submitted to me, I beg to say that in my judgment the city treasurer is required by law to pay an honest appearing warrant drawn upon him, signed by the mayor and countersigned by you as comptroller, stating the particular fund or appropriation to which such warrant is chargeable, and naming the person to whom such warrant is payable, that in the absence of suspicious circumstances tending to put him upon inquiry it is not his duty to inquire into or to concern himself with the ultimate disposition of the money to be drawn out upon such a warrant, and that the payment of such a warrant in good faith by the city treasurer absolves him from responsibility in respect to the money paid thereon. The law does not require a warrant to run to the person who is ultimately to receive its proceeds, but merely requires that the warrant shall state upon its face to whom the warrant itself is payable. An injured payee could doubtless maintain an action in the name of the city (see City of East St. Louis for the use of Griswold vs. Flannigan, Treasurer, et al., 26 Ill. App. Court, 449) against the sureties upon the treasurer's bond for refusal on the part of the treasurer to pay a warrant properly drawn as I have indicated.   Very truly yours,

WM. G. BEALE, Corporation Counsel

February 8, 1896.

Joseph Downey, Esq., Commissioner of Buildings.

Dear Sir—

Your letter of February 6, asking for asking for an opinion upon Section 231 of the building ordinance has been referred to me.

The parts of that section material to the present question are as follows:

"All buildings, lodging houses and hotels of four or more stories in height * * * shall be provided with ladders, etc. * * * provided the provisions of this section shall not apply to private residences, flats and apartment buildings of four stories in height or less."

The question is whether an apartment building of four stories and a basement is included within the enacting clause of this ordinance or the proviso—in other words, whether the proprietor of such a building can be compelled to place thereon fire escapes. I assume that the basement rises above the level of the ground.

In construing this ordinance it is to be remembered that it is one of the rules of construction that a *proviso* is to be strictly construed, and nothing is to be regarded as included within it except where the meaning is unmistakable.

The ordinance is to secure the safety of the occupants of buildings. The higher the building the greater the danger. The danger is as great where the additional height is caused by a basement as by another story. The enacting part of the ordinance requires fire escapes on all buildings of four or more stories for whatever purpose used. This building, therefore, is strictly within the enacting clause. Then the proviso restrains the general words by excepting apartment buildings of "four stories or less." Thus the *highest* building excepted is one of four stories. Construing this strictly, as must be done in case of a proviso, any building higher than one of four stories is not within the proviso.

In the only case I have found on the subject, a building of two stories and a basement was held to be properly described by these words: "May be identified by house standing thereon, the first two stories being of stone and the third story of wood." In a proceeding to enforce a mechanic lien, Knowlton, J., said: "The description of the house was not inaccurate nor misleading. If the lower part of it was properly called a basement it was according to the definition of lexicographers, and the common understanding of the word, a story of the building." Cleverly vs. Moseley, 148 Mass., 280.

If this be followed here and the basement be called a story, very clearly this building is a building of five stories, and not a building of "four stories or less." But conceding for the purpose of the argument that a basement is not a "story," and that a building of four stories and a basement has only four stories, properly so-called, still the basement makes it a building higher than one of four stories. It is to be noticed that the ordinance says "four stories or less in height." The term "stories" is used as a measurement of height. Any building having anything more than four stories, whether it be an additional story, an attic, or a basement, is a higher building than one of "four stories or less," and therefore not within the proviso. Looking at this *proviso* in another light, it is clear that a building of four stories and a basement is not a building of "four stories or less." It is to be remembered that these words are to be strictly construed.

The proviso does not say that this ordinance shall apply only to buildings having more stories than four. Those are not the words. In that case a building, to be out of the proviso, would have to have at least five stories. Instead it says that an enacting clause which would otherwise include all buildings of "four stories or more in height" shall not apply to apartment buildings of "four stories or less in height." To come within the *proviso* a building must be strictly within the proviso. But it means only two classes, viz.: Buildings of four stories and buildings of less than four. Now, the present building is not accurately described as either one. It is not a building of four stories, neither is it a building of less than four stories. It is either a building of five stories, or of four stories and a basement. In neither case is it within the description.

Therefore, I am decidedly of the opinion that the owner of the apartment building in question can be compelled to conform to the requirement of the ordinance.   Very truly yours,

EDWARD B. BURLING, Asst. Corporation Counsel.

February 25, 1896.

Hon. Joseph Downey, Commissioner of Buildings.

Dear Sir—

In response to your letter of this date inquiring in regard to your authority to inspect buildings of Class IV, especially when occupied by the public, the same having been referred to me for reply, I beg to say.

That inasmuch as it is your duty to enforce the provisions of this ordinance, especially provisions of Section 196, in relation to crowding of places where the public assemble, it is clearly within the scope of your authority to use such means as will enable you to make such inspection. I therefore advise you that it would be entirely legal, and within the scope of your duty, to employ such members of the police force as will enable you to discharge your duty; that it would be competent for you to cause the immediate arrest and transportation to the police station of all persons who interfere with your authority in the discharge of your duties, and that it is your duty to see that no more persons are admitted into such places of public assemblage than can be accommodated and taken care of, according to the provisions of the ordinance. In general, I would say that your authority in the premises is ample, and I do not think you should hesitate to make use of the same in discharging the duties clearly imposed upon you by the ordinance, even to the extent of closing the theater. This matter has been referred by me to the corporation counsel, and he concurs in the views herein expressed.

Very truly yours,

GEO. A. DUPUY, Asst. Corporation Counsel.

March 7, 1896.

Hon. Geo. B. Swift, Mayor of the City of Chicago.

Dear Sir—

I beg to submit to you my conclusions in the Evert & Jaeger saloon matter, which was referred to me by you for an opinion.

For the reasons hereinafter stated it is my judgment that this saloon does not fall within the prohibitory provision contained in the charter of the Northwestern University, and there is no reason apparent to me why the license for its maintenance should be revoked.

The act of February 14, 1855, amending a previous act incorporating the Northwestern University, contains the following section:

"Section 2—No spirituous, vinous or fermented liquor shall be sold, under license or otherwise, within four miles of the location of said University, except for medicinal, mechanical or sacramental purposes, under the penalty of $25.00 for each offense, to be recovered before any justice of the peace in said county, in an action for debt, in the name of the County of Cook; Provided, that so much of this act as relates to the sale of intoxicating drink within four miles may be repealed by the General Assembly whenever they think proper."

This saloon appears to have been established in an honest belief that its location was outside the four-mile limit created by the foregoing act, and after honest investigation to ascertain the fact. A survey was made over the shortest traveled route between it and the main building of the university, and the intervening distance was found to be considerably over four miles. Application for a license was made to the proper department of the city government on that basis. The usual conditions for a license being complied with, the application was granted without hesitation, upon the supposition that the location was shown to be beyond the four-mile limit, both by said survey and by the fact that there were existing saloons nearer the university. An expenditure exceeding $10,000 is claimed to have been made upon this place of business in the belief that the saloon was outside of the four-mile limit, and in reliance upon the license from the city. No complaints are shown as to the manner in which the saloon is conducted, nor are there any complaints at all from the university authorities. The complaints against the saloon come entirely from residents near it, who demand the revocation of the license on the ground that the saloon is within the four-mile limit, *measured by an air line.* They contend that the air-line measurement is the proper one. The proprietors of the saloon, on the other hand, insist that, having located their saloon and made their expenditure in good faith, and largely in reliance upon the action of the city in issuing a license, they should not now be forced by the city to close the saloon and to suffer the consequent loss of the substantial portion of the investment, whatever method of measurement be adopted; and further insist that the distance should be measured by the shortest traveled road, and not by an air line.

It must, I think, be admitted that there is some equity in favor of the contention of these proprietors. A city ought to act, and ought to be required to act, justly and fairly, as much as a citizen. If erroneous attitude or conduct, honestly undertaken on the part of a city, has induced action by individuals from which they cannot readily recede, and on account of which they will suffer loss if the city shift its position, the city ought to be bound by its error, unless under extraordinary circumstances. In any such case, to justify a city in abandoning an erroneous position upon the faith of which others have acted, there ought to be no question as to the error. If reasonable doubt exists, the city ought, under ordinary circumstances, to stand by its original action. The contention in this case is over the method of measuring the distance of four miles, and if the facts are as above stated, and there is any reasonable doubt about the method of measurement, it seems to me that the above principles ought to be applied; that there would be no fair basis upon which the city could now reverse its previous ruling and revoke the license heretofore issued, and that the complaining residents of the neighborhood should be left to seek relief in some other way.

But in my opinion the city did not make any error in issuing this license. It will be observed that Section 2 of the above amendatory act does not prescribe any rule of measurement, nor, indeed, does it indicate just where the measurement should begin. The actual location of the Northwestern University is not confined to a single point, and just how far the four-mile limit extends must obviously depend upon the initial point of measurement. It seems to be quite generally conceded that the proper initial point is the main or administration building of the university. We must next ascertain how the distance of four miles is to be measured.

In considering this question I have found no help from judicial decisions bearing directly upon it, for I have been unable to find any such decisions which have seemed to me quite in point touching the measurement of distances. There are a few English cases having a more or less remote application, and there is one American case which is equally valueless as an authority. It cannot be said that there is any fixed rule applicable to the measurement of the distance in this case, and a decision of this question must rest primarily upon the statute itself, interpreted with reference to the object sought to be accomplished.

Numerous rules for the interpretation of statutes have been laid down by the courts, and among them the following is fundamental:

"Every statute should be construed with reference to its object and the will of the law makers is best promoted by such a construction as secures the object and excludes all others."

Castner vs. Walrod, 83 Ill., 179.

This Section 2 was before the Supreme Court of Illinois in O'Leary vs. County of Cook, 28 Ill., 534. The case involved the question whether this prohibitory legislation was void, because not referred to in the title of the act. The court held that the single design of the law was to promote the wellbeing of the university, and that it was not the intention of the general assembly, in passing the act, to legislate for the benefit of the people who might reside in the territory covered by the prohibition. It was upon this view that the court upheld the constitutionality of the section. I quote a few words from the decision (p. 538):

"The object of the charter was to create an institution for the education of young men, and it was competent for the legislature to embrace within it everything which was designed to facilitate that object. Every provision which was intended to promote the wellbeing of the institution or its students was within the proper subject-matter of the law. We cannot doubt that such was the *single design* of this law. Its purpose was to keep far away from the members of the institution the temptation to intemperance and its attendant vices. Although this provision might incidentally tend to protect others residing in the vicinity from the corrupting and demoralizing influences of the grog-shop, yet that was not the primary object of the law, but its *sole purpose* was to protect the students and faculty from such influence. It was designed for the benefit and wellbeing of the institution, and this is the touch-stone of the constitutionality of the enactment. If its design was foreign from the subject of the law, which was the creation of, and to provide for the wellbeing of, an institution of learning; if the design was to protect the community generally from the bad influences of a particular temptation, without a particular reference to the institution, then it might be said, with much propriety, that it was foreign and not germane to the subject of the law."

Now, if we exclude consideration of the effect of this law upon that portion of the general community residing in the four-mile zone surrounding the university, and confine our view to the sole object of its enactment, it is plain that the legislature was alone contemplating possible communication between the university and the outlying saloon—contemplating that the members of the educational institution would or might pass to and fro between the two places. In view of the fact that human beings cannot pass through the air "as the crow flies," that they cannot lawfully trespass upon private lands for paths of travel, and that public highways are provided for public use, the legislature must, I think, be supposed to have fixed this four-mile limit in contemplation of the existence and use of such highways. The attention of the legislature was distinctly directed to the subject of travel and intercommunication between two places, and it must have had in mind the ordinary and lawful routes of travel. Its declaration, in substance, that no saloon shall be located within four miles of the university seems naturally and reasonably to mean that the distance is to be measured by the shortest public road. In this view it follows that Evert & Jaeger's saloon is shown to be outside of the four-mile limit.   Very respectfully yours,

WM. G. BEALE, Corporation Counsel.

March 11, 1896.

John D. Murphy, Esq., City Boiler Inspector.

Dear Sir—

In answer to your questions concerning inspection of steam boilers, I would say, that under the ordinances in force relating to this subject, no class of boilers are exempt from inspection. Also, that it makes no difference whether or not an owner receives a certificate that his boiler has been inspected before payment of the fee; if he refuses to pay the fee prescribed by the ordinance, he is liable under the penalty for a violation of one of the provisions of the ordinance.

The ordinance passed by the city council on July 9, 1890, is the last legislation on the subject of the inspection of steam boilers.

Very truly yours,

B. BOYDEN, Asst. Corporation Counsel.

March 17, 1896.

Hon. Wm. D. Kent, Commissioner of Public Works, City of Chicago.

Dear Sir—

The application made to your department by the Ogden Gas Company, under date of March 11, 1896, for a permit to open streets and alleys for the purpose of laying gas mains and pipes therein under an ordinance passed February 25, 1895, (which application has, in accordance with the usual course in such matters, been referred to this office for advice in respect to any legal questions involved) ought not to be granted for the primary reason that said ordinance was repealed by the city council April 10, 1895, by an ordinance passed and approved on that date.

Question has been made as to the validity or effectiveness of this repealing ordinance. That question you need not undertake to decide or to consider. It is not your duty to do so. Had this repealing ordinance not been passed you would have been required to issue the permit under the granting ordinance, although the validity of that ordinance has been similarly questioned. The rule is that a ministerial or administrative officer cannot ordinarily refuse obedience to an apparently formal enactment of the legislative authority above him— in this case the city council. This rule or principle has just been applied by Judge Baker, of the circuit court of Cook county, to a case where a mandamus was sought and granted against the mayor to compel him to approve the sureties upon a bond presented to him under an ordinance believed by him to be invalid. Judge Baker held, and as I think correctly, that in such a manner the mayor would act merely in his ministerial capacity, entirely distinct and apart from his legislative capacity as a member of the city council.

19

As this principle is one of frequent application and of importance in the administration of your department, I refer to some further decisions illustrating it.

In the case of People, ex rel. vs. Salomon, 54 Ill., 39, the supreme court of this state punished the county clerk of this county for contempt in failing to obey a writ of *mandamus* commanding him to extend a certain additional tax pursuant to a then recently enacted law. The clerk sought to justify or excuse his failure on the ground that, acting upon legal advice, he had treated the law as unconstitutional and had delivered his tax books to the collectors, thereby rendering himself powerless to obey the command of the court. In passing judgment upon the clerk the court said to him:

"The law under which this additional tax was imposed, had passed the legislature under all the forms of the constitution, and had received executive sanction, and became, by its own intrinsic force, the law to you, to every other public officer in the state, and to all the people. You assume the responsibility of declaring the law unconstitutional, and at once determine to disregard it, to set up your own judgment as superior to the express will of the legislature, asserting, in fact, an entire independence thereof. . . . To allow a ministerial officer to decide upon the validity of a law would be subversive of the great objects and purposes of government, for if one such officer may assume infallibility, all other like officers may do the same, and thus an end be put to civil government, one of whose cardinal principles is, subjection to the laws.

"Being a ministerial officer, the path of duty was plain before you. You strayed from it, and became a volunteer in the effort to arrest the law, and it was successful. Had the property owners, who were subjected to this additional tax, considered the law unconstitutional, they could, in the proper courts, have tested the question, and it was their undoubted right so to do. Your only duty was obedience."

In Houston vs. The People, ex rel. 55 Ill., 398, the same court again enunciated the principle, which was presented to it by the refusal of a town clerk to countersign certain bonds. The clerk claimed that the various steps taken by the town were irregular and insufficient to authorize the issuance of the bonds. Upon appeal from the judgment of the court below, awarding a writ of mandamus against the clerk commanding him to countersign the bonds, the Supreme Court said:

"The appellant being Town Clerk, the act of countersigning the bonds in question was a mere ministerial act. It was not the province of such clerk to determine whether the proper steps had been taken to authorize the issuance of the bonds. If valid reasons existed why they should not be issued, the law provides a mode in which that question could be properly determined. The People vs. Dean, 3 Wend., 438. The judgment of the court below must be affirmed."

The New York cases of the People ex rel. vs. Dean, thus approvingly cited by our own Supreme Court in support of the principle, was a particularly simple case. A person has been appointed a commissioner of deeds in the city of New York. Upon his appearing before the clerk of the proper court to take the required qualifying oath the clerk refused to administer it, on the ground that the appointee was under twenty-one years of age, and so incompetent to hold the office. On application for a writ of mandamus directing the clerk to administer the oath, the Supreme Court of New York said:

"A minor and an alien are incapable of holding a civil office within this state (1 Revised Statutes, 116, Section 1), but it is not the province of the officer to whom application is made to administer the oath of office to determine whether the person presenting himself is or is not capable of holding an office. It is the duty of such officer, on the production of the commission, to administer the oath. If an appointment has been improvidently, made, there is a legal mode in which it may be declared void. Let an alternative mandamus issue."

The rule is well stated in Section 523 of Mechem on Public Officers, as follows:

"It is not within the scope of the duties of a ministerial officer to pass upon the validity of laws, instructions or proceedings prima facie valid, and requiring his action. His only duty in such a case is obedience, * * * and he cannot excuse himself by undertaking to show the unconstitutionality or other invalidity of the law, or the irregularity of the proceedings."

The ordinance of February 25th, 1895, having been prima facie repealed by the repealing ordinance of April 10th, 1895, the latter ordinance should be taken by you as valid for the purposes of this application, and it necessarily follows that so far as you are concerned in this matter there is no ordinance under which the Ogden Gas Company is now authorized to lay its mains and pipes in the streets of this city. It is proper for me to add that what I have said above in discussing the rule under which you should act in such a case as this is not intended to imply that I consider the repealing ordinance invalid or ineffectual; indeed, my present impression is the contrary, although I have given the subject no special consideration.

I herewith return the papers.   Very respectfully yours,
WM. G. BEALE, Corporation Counsel.

March 23, 1896.
Hon. John O'Neill, Chairman of Special Committee.
Dear Sir—

In reply to your request for an opinion as to the extent of the powers that may be exercised by the special committee, appointed by resolution of the council March 16th, 1896, and especially in regard to the question as to whether or not said committee is invested with the power purported to be given to it by said resolution, of summoning witnesses, administering oaths and punishing for contempts, I desire to report that said matter has been carefully and fully considered in this office, and I am led to the conclusion that said committee cannot exercise the power of summoning witnesses, administering oaths and punishing for contempts, as specified in said resolution. The decisions of the higher courts bearing upon this subject, so far as the same relate to common councils of cities, are not at all numerous. One case, however, which affords much light on the subject, was decided some years ago by Hon. Horace Gray, then chief justice of the Supreme Court of Massachusetts and now one of the justices of the Supreme Court of the United States. His opinion in this case is found in Volume 120 of Massachusetts Reports, at page 118. In that case, one Whitcomb had been summoned to testify before a special committee of the common council of the city of Boston. This committee had been appointed with full powers to investigate charges against members in which it was alleged that certain members of the common council had received money or other valuable considerations to influence their action in relation to matters then pending before the council. And said committee, by order of the common council appointing it, had been given the power to administer oaths, call witnesses and punish for contempts, substantially the same as in the case of your committee. Whitcomb refused to answer the questions propounded. The common council thereupon passed an order committing him to the county jail for twelve days for contempt. He brought a habeas corpus proceeding to secure his release. This petition was decided in his favor, and he was ordered released by the court. In the course of this opinion the court, among other things, said:

"At the time of the adoption of the constitution of the commonwealth it was no part of the law of the land that municipal boards or officers should have power to commit or punish for contempt. . . . The city council is not a legislature. It has no power to make laws, but merely to pass ordinances upon such local matters as the legislature may commit to its charge, and subject to the paramount control of the legislature. Neither branch of the city council is a court or, in accurate use of language, vested with any judicial functions whatever. Nor are its members chosen with any view to their fitness for the exercise of such functions. To allow such a body to punish summarily by imprisonment the refusal to answer any inquiry which the whole body or one of its committees may choose to make would be a most dangerous invasion of the right and liberty of the citizen."

At the time this opinion was rendered there was in existence a general statute in the state of Massachusetts which professed to give authority to municipal councils to exercise the powers of administering oaths, punishing for contempts, etc., but the court held that this statute was inoperative and void as being in contravention of the constitution. In the state of Illinois there is no statute which professes to authorize any such action by the common council, and, therefore, the reason for holding that such authority does not exist is much **stronger** than it was in the case last referred to.

A standard law writer, considering this subject, says, "as to aldermanic boards, committees and other legislative bodies of cities," there is no authority to commit for contempt where a witness refuses to appear and testify. (Rapalja on Contempts.)

It was held by the Supreme Court of Connecticut (in the case of Noyes vs. Byxbee, 45 Conn., p. 385), that a statute which expressly authorized a certain commissioner to summon witnesses, compel their attendance and administer oaths, did not authorize a commitment for contempt for refusal to be sworn and answer questions.

It has been held that even the congress of the United States, the highest legislative body in the nation, has no authority to punish for contempts unless it be in relation to matters directly within the jurisdiction of congress. The constitution of the United States gives congress power to punish disorderly behavior of members or absence of members. In deciding contested election cases it may be it can punish witnesses. Also in impeachment cases. In one case involving these questions Justice Miller said:

"Whether the power of punishment in either house by fine or imprisonment goes beyond this or not, we are sure that no person can be punished for contumacy as a witness before either House unless his testimony is required in a matter into which that house has jurisdiction to inquire, and we feel equally sure that neither of these bodies possesses the general power of making inquiry into the private affairs of the citizen."

Kilbourn vs. Thompson, 103 U. S., 168 (1880).

This case was subsequently approved by Judge Field, of the United States Supreme Court, in an opinion in which occurs the following language:

"This (Kilbourn) case will stand for all time as a bulwark against the invasion of the right of the citizen to protection in his private affairs against the unlimited scrutiny of investgation by a Congressional Committee. The courts are open to the United States as they are to the private citizen, and both can there secure, by regular proceedings, ample protection of all rights and interests which are entitled to protection under a government of written laws and constitution."

Justice Sawyer in the same case used this language:

"A general, roving, offensive, inquisitorial, compulsory investigation conducted by a commission, without any allegation, upon no fixed principles and governed by no rules of law or of evidence, and no restrictions except its own will, or caprice is unknown to our constitution and laws; and such an inquisition would be destruction of the rights of the citizen, and an intolerable tyranny. Let the power once be established, and there is no knowing, where the practice under it would end."

This case decides that the congress of the United States cannot appoint a commission with power to punish contempts to investigate the affairs of the Central Pacific railway. In re Pacific Railway Company, 32 Fed. Rep., 241.

An eminent writer on legal subjects, in treating of the subject under consideration, uses the following language:

"No doubt sovereign legislatures, the houses of parliament, the houses of congress, and of our state legislatures, have the power to commit for contempts committed in their presence, or for disobedience to their orders, but not for contemptuous or libelous censures on their proceedings. But the power of committal for contempt under any circumstances does not belong to the inferior legislatures, such as town councils or town meetings. The remedy for disturbance in such case is binding over to keep the peace or indictment for disturbing a meeting."

Wharton's Criminal Law, 7th Ed., Vol. 3, Sec. 3445.

These expressions of the Judges in decided cases and of standard law writers treating on the subject all agree. I find no opinions contrary to the rules announced, and I consider that these expressions from judges and writers may be regarded as fully answering the points embraced in your inquiry. In my opinion, the committee, of which you are chairman, is not invested with nor possessed of the power and authority to compel the attendance of witnesses, to administer oaths or to punish witnesses for contempt in case of refusal to answer any questions that may be propounded.

And in case a witness should voluntarily appear and testify under oath, I doubt whether the administration of the oath would add any legal value to the proceeding or subject the witness to punishment for perjury in case he swore falsely. It will be understood, of course, that in this opinion I am endeavoring to confine myself entirely to the legal questions involved, and not to express any views respecting the policy or propriety of the investigation under consideration, which is something for the city council, and not for me, to determine. Of course it is always proper for the city council at any time to investigate the doings of city officers whenever in its judgment it thinks such investigation desirable. Respectfully submitted,

GEO. A. DUPUY, Asst. Corporation Counsel.

Approved:
WM. G. BEALE, Corporation Counsel.

March 24, 1896.

Philip Maas, Esq., City Collector.

Dear Sir—

In the matter of the transfer of the saloon license of A. Kenzle, of Brighton Park, referred to me, I am of opinion that under the saloon ordinance in force in the town of Cicero, in which Brighton Park was situated, at the time of annexation to the city, saloon licenses are transferable from one person to another, but not from one place to another, and I infer from the phraseology of the ordinance, which is not, however, explicit, that the transferee is not obliged to obtain new consents, but may take advantage of those obtained by his transfer. Very truly yours,

TIFFANY BLAKE, Asst. Corporation Counsel.

March 24, 1896.

P. O'Shea, Deputy Commissioner of Buildings.

Dear Sir—

The Corporation Counsel, Mr. Beale, has referred to me your letter requesting an opinion as to whether Section 65 of the Building Ordinance, passed March 13, 1893, confers right upon individuals to construct grand stands containing seats, etc., under the provision contained in said section providing for the construction of open shelter sheds not over twenty (20) feet high from the ground. The object of this section, it seems to me, is clear. It is to allow owners of large tracts of land to construct shelter sheds without sides or floors, having incombustible roofs, for the purpose of sheltering from the weather building material, lime, scrap iron, lumber, sewer pipes and hundreds of other things of like character. I do not think the language of the section can be tortured into giving individuals the right to erect such structures as you mention in your letter, viz.: a grand stand.

Very truly yours,

B. BOYDEN, Asst. Corporation Counsel.

March 25, 1895.

Hon. Adam Wolf, City Treasurer, City of Chicago.

Dear Sir—

I have given careful consideration to the subject matter of your letter of March 23rd.

The statutory provision requiring that a warrant shall show on its face the person to whom it is payable will, in my judgment, not be violated by the issuance of the proposed instruments, payable at specified banks, to persons named therein "or bearer," as, for example, "John Smith, or bearer." The addition of the words "or bearer" seems to involve no departure from the statutory requirement. Whether the words "or bearer" protect the original payee in case of loss of the warrant, as the words "or order" would do, does not concern the city. The question is as to the safety of the city and its financial officers. It may be that the proposed instruments are not "warrants" at all, but being payable at a bank, are to be regarded as city checks upon such banks. If this be so, the position of the city would perhaps be even stronger, because checks possess certain incidents to protect those who pay them in good faith not ordinarily attaching to municipal warrants. I see no reason to doubt that if such proposed instruments, called "warrants," are delivered to the proper payees respectively therein named, and are accepted by such payees, who receipt for their respective claims, the city and its financial officers will be protected, *except* in cases where payment is made, with knowledge or notice that the persons to whom payment is made have come into possession of warrants by means which would not entitle such persons, as against a former holder, to receive payment, such as by theft, by finding, etc. It is manifest that care should be taken to deliver these warrants in the first instance to the payees specifically named therein. Very respectfully yours,

WM. G. BEALE, Corporation Counsel.

March 27, 1896.

Hon. Joseph Downey, Commissioner of Buildings, City of Chicago.

Dear Sir—

Upon the question as to the control of the city of Chicago and its building department over the erection of structures in the various parks under park commissions existing independently of the city, I beg to say that the uniform ruling of this office has been that the city has no jurisdiction over such parks in respect to such structures. I concur in this view so far certainly as any ordinary cases are concerned. I can conceive it possible that cases might occur under which the courts would hold that the city had some jurisdiction in the premises, but such cases would be remote. In respect to the structure in process of erection in South Park, which has given rise to the present consideration of the matter, I think there is no doubt at all that the matter is under the exclusive control of the South Park commissioners, and that the city has no jurisdiction. In saying this I have in mind the provisions of the building ordinance which are probably to be construed as referring to parks under control of the city, such as the Lake Front Park, and if this is not so then these provisions are in excess of the city's powers. Very truly yours,

WM. G. BEALE, Corporation Counsel.

March 28, 1896.

John D. Murphy, Esq., Boiler Inspector, City of Chicago.

Dear Sir—

I have your letter of the 27th inst. with enclosures in the matter of inspecting boilers in Lincoln Park.

I have already had occasion to consider this general subject matter and have now given it further consideration, and I cannot feel any reasonable doubt that your department has no jurisdiction to inspect the boilers under the control of the Lincoln Park commissioners. So far as I can see, they have exclusive jurisdiction in the premises and cannot be compelled to pay the bill submitted in your letter, which I herewith return.

Mr. Dupuy some time ago, with my concurrence, advised you substantially to this effect, but perhaps less strongly, and we both agree in the conclusions of this letter. Very truly yours,

WM. G. BEALE, Corporation Counsel.

April 9, 1896.

James R. Mann, Esq., Chairman Judiciary Committee, Chicago.

Dear Sir—

Some days ago I transmitted to you the draft of an ordinance which I prepared as a substitute for an ordinance pending before the judiciary committee, authorizing the issuance of licenses or permits for the occupation of streets by movable booths, etc. In submitting the substitute to you I disregarded the question whether the granting of such street occupation permits would be within the powers of the city council, because I did not understand that any opinion upon that question was desired from me, but understood the desire of the committee to be merely that I should prepare an ordinance which would not be objectionable from a practical standpoint. Since sending the substitute to you the judiciary committee appears to have had a meeting, while you were away, at which it has considered the original ordinance and has requested my opinion as to the power of the city to lease portions of the public streets for private purposes. Although the request for an opinion is thus broadly expressed, I suppose and assume that it was intended to apply only to the scope of the proposed ordinance, and not to the broad general subject of the power of the city to lease any portions of the public streets under any circumstances. In responding to this request of the committee, therefore, I do not undertake to give an opinion upon this broad general question, but confine myself to the phase of its affecting the ordinance under consideration.

It is undoubtedly settled law, as applicable to this city, that the city having, subject to the paramount authority of the legislature, exclusive control over the public streets, may allow any use of them consistent with the public objects for which the streets are held; that the city cannot lawfully grant any permanent private use of the public streets which would be inconsistent or would interfere with the public use or enjoyment thereof; that it is the duty of the city to keep the public streets open, free and safe for public travel in all their parts; and that to permit a continuing and constant private use of any portion, however small, of a public street or sidewalk is legally beyond the city's power, though there be no actual inconvenience to the public.

Gregsten vs. Chicago, 145 Ill., 451.

Smith vs. McDowell, 148 Ill., 51.

Field vs. Barling, 149 Ill., 566.

A. M. Rothschild & Co. vs. City of Chicago, Circuit Court of Cook County, Horton, J., 28 Chicago Legal News, 216.

I understand that there are some practical considerations of public policy which favor the proposed ordinance, and that it is, therefore, not unlikely to be passed, on the theory that the commissioner of public works can exercise such discretion in granting permits as will tend to obviate all practical objection and leave only a technical legal objection in any case. Whether such an ordinance ought to be passed or not is not for me to determine, but it is obvious that such an ordinance, if passed, ought to be a guarded one. I have given further study to the substitute as prepared by me, and I think it should, if it is to be passed, have another section providing for a bond of indemnity to the city and reserving authority to the commissioner to cancel a permit whenever the public interests seem to require such action. I have, therefore, had the last page of the substitute re-written with such an added section and beg to enclose the new page to you to take the place of the last page of the substitute ordinance as heretofore sent you.

I return the papers received from the committee since its last meeting. Very respectfully yours,

WM. G. BEALE, Corporation Counsel.

April 10, 1896.

Charles W. Gindele, Esq., Secy. "Tax Commission," etc., Chicago.

Dear Sir—

You recently asked me on behalf of the commission the following questions:

1. Are safety deposit vaults considered part of the improvement on realty or do they come under personal property?

2. Are power plants installed on leased premises and for use of others than occupants of the building to be considered part of the improvements on realty or personal property?

3. Are expensive interior improvements and decorations on walls and ceilings of buildings, placed there by the lessee (exclusive of movable fixtures) part of the improvement on realty or personal property?

4. Are the land and office buildings of railroad corporations located outside of their right-of-way subject to taxation by the town assessors?

I think there can be no reasonable doubt that the subjects of your first three questions are to be regarded as parts of the respective real estate improvements with which they are connected. A power plant, installed for a brief period with a mutual understanding that it should be removed, would perhaps constitute an exception, but such an exception would doubtless be of rare occurrence.

The fourth question is equally free from reasonable doubt. Such land and office buildings are manifestly subject to assessment by local assessors. Very truly yours,

WM. G. BEALE, Corporation Counsel.

April 15, 1896.

C. H. Howell, Esq., Chairman Committee on Licenses.

Dear Sir—

Your committee requests an opinion from the Corporation Counsel on a proposed ordinance amending an existing ordinance concerning amusements. Mr. Beale has referred the matter to me for answer.

This ordinance seeks to change the existing fee required for a license to conduct theaters, etc., and in place of the sum now required for these privileges, viz.: $300 annually where the highest price of admission exceeds 50c and $200 annually where the highest price of admission does not exceed 50c to require the following amount: Ten per cent. and five per cent. of the gross receipts, respectively.

We presume your committee desires to know whether or not such an ordinance would be valid. The power conferred by the charter to license theatrical and other exhibitions, shows and amusements, authorizes the council to adopt any reasonable ordinance for that purpose, but the council cannot directly prohibit the business, nor can it adopt such unreasonable regulations as would tend to produce such a result, or be oppressive or injurious to the business.

Is this a reasonable ordinance is the first question to be answered. This is a practical question. Take for example the Chicago Opera House. The highest price of admission to that theater is, exclusive of box seats, 75c. This may well be considered an average price of all theaters in the city. I am informed that the gross receipts from a full house in this theater for an evening is something over $1,000. Ten per cent. of this amount is $100. Take two hundred days in the year as a fair average theater year, and the license fee of that theater, under the proposed ordinance, would be $20,000. The Appellate Court of this district in the case of Chicago vs. Ferris Wheel Company held that a license fee of $50 a day was prohibitory in its character, exorbitant and unreasonable.

The next question that arises is, is this ordinance in the nature of a tax on the business, or a public regulation?

It is clear that the power given to the council under Clause 41, Article V, of the act for the incorporation of cities and villages, is in the nature of a police regulation which finds its justification and limitations in the prevention of some threatened evil, and for the purpose of insuring proper police supervision whenever the character of the business is such that the absence of police supervision might occasion injury to the public. On these grounds it is competent for a municipality to require licenses and subjection to police supervision. In this connection Mr. Tiedeman in his work on Municipal Corporations, speaking of the various things that are necessary to be considered in fixing the amount of a license fee, says that the following items have been held to be proper to take into consideration:

First: The value of the labor and material in merely allowing and issuing a license.

Second: The value of the benefit of the license to the person obtaining the same.

Third: The value of the convenience and cost to the public in protecting such business.

Fourth: In some cases an additional amount may be imposed as a restraint upon a number of persons who might otherwise engage in the business.

If the above four items necessary to be considered in fixing the amount of the license fee, designated in the proposed ordinance, were taken into consideration at all it is apparent they were secondary considerations, and that the main object of the ordinance is for revenue. Our Supreme Court in the case of Chicago vs. Phoenix Insurance Company, 126 Ill., 276, uses the following language:

"The ordinance passed by the City of Chicago is one passed, as is apparent from its language, for the purpose of raising revenue—a subject foreign to the police power conferred on incorporated towns and cities by the statute."

If we are correct in our reading of the proposed amendments this fact would constitute a fatal objection to the ordinance as it stands.

Very truly yours,

B. BOYDEN, Asst. Corporation Counsel.

April 29, 1896.

Philip Maas, Esq., City Collector.

Dear Sir—

Your request for an opinion as to whether "dealers in railroad ties, telegraph poles, cedar posts, are to be classed under Sections 1808 and 1809, Municipal Code," has been referred to me.

This ordinance is plainly based on the 91st clause of Article V, of the cities and villages act, which gives the council power "to tax, license and regulate auctioneers, distillers, brewers, lumber yards, livery stables, public scales, money changers and brokers."

The ordinance itself provides: Section 1. "No person, firm or corporation shall keep or maintain, within the city of Chicago, any lumber yard, or other place where lumber is sold from the yard or place, without a license therefor." Section 2. "A license shall be granted to any person, firm or corporation to keep or maintain a lumber yard or place for the sale of lumber," etc.

Lumber is defined by the Century dictionary and by Webster as "timber sawed or split for use, as beams, joists, boards, planks, staves, hoops and the like." And a lumber yard is defined by the Century dictionary as "A yard or enclosure where wood and timber are stored for sale." It is true that technically and in the language of the trade, these definitions are too broad, the word lumber being technically restricted to material used for the construction of buildings. A consideration of the clause of the statute upon which this ordinance is based will throw light upon the scope of the term "lumber yard" as used in the statute and ordinance.

First, it is not to be presumed that the callings named in this 91st clause were arbitrarily grouped together, and indeed it is clear that each calling therein enumerated has a peculiar relation to the public at large, that all are quasi-public in their character. Thus auctioneers are, in a sense, public officers, and are therefore appropriately subject to "regulation," and brewers and distillers carry on a business peculiarly subject to police regulation. What then is the ground upon which lumber yards are included among these callings? Plainly because of the inflammability of the material which makes it a public menace in thickly settled communities. If this is the reason of their inclusion, clearly the broader definition of the word lumber yard as "a yard or enclosure where wood and timber are stored for sale" covers the legislative intent and gives the scope of this clause and the ordinance based upon it.

Following this line of reasoning I am of opinion that "dealers in railroad ties, telegraph poles, etc.," are within the spirit and intent of the ordinance and are, therefore, required to procure the license therein provided. Very truly yours,

TIFFANY BLAKE, Asst. Corporation Counsel.

May 4, 1896.

Noble B. Judah, Esq., Chairman Judiciary Committee, City.

Dear Sir—

The City Clerk has forwarded to me a proposed ordinance for a graduated license upon wagons and other wheel vehicles, requesting me to advise your committee whether, in my opinion, the ordinance would be valid if enacted, and also whether wagons now subject to license should not in any event be excluded from its operation.

An examination of the general city incorporation law and of the decisions of our Supreme Court, having more or less bearing thereon, seems to leave no room for doubt that the legislature has not invested cities incorporated under that law with the power to exact licenses in respect to vehicles used exclusively for the ordinary private business or pleasure of their owners. See particularly Farwell vs. City of Chicago, 71 Ill., 269; and Joyce vs. City of East St. Louis, 77 Ill. 156.

The proposed ordinance contemplates a license for all vehicles used for traffic, and it would, therefore, manifestly be invalid if passed as now drawn. Were its operation confined to vehicles subject to use by the public for hire I think the courts would uphold the principle of it. It is somewhat defectively drawn, as, for example, in requiring that the vehicles themselves shall pay the license specified rather than the persons who own or control the vehicles.

In a general way the second point on which the committee desired my opinion has been answered in the foregoing observations, but perhaps a more specific answer on that point will be better understood. So far as passenger traffic vehicles kept or used for hire are concerned, I am under the impression that all such are now reached or affected by existing provisions of licensing ordinances. These could not be properly excluded from an ordinance like the one under consideration. For in conformity with what I have already said, it will be noted that such vehicles are in fact the only passenger vehicles that can be legally included in and covered by such an ordinance. How far the existing license ordinances reach vehicles kept for transporting merchandise for hire I do not know, but probably all such wagons are reached by existing ordinances through the persons owning or controlling them about as fully as are public passenger vehicles. If this be so, then such merchandise wagons could not be excluded from an ordinance like the one proposed without leaving no merchandise wagons upon which such an ordinance could operate. The essence of this matter will be quickly perceived by referring to the Farwell case, in which the Supreme Court held that John V. Farwell & Co. could not be required to pay a license upon their wagons kept and used by them for the purpose of transporting goods between their store and depots and wharves for the sole benefit of themselves and their customers—such wagons not being open to the general public use, like public express wagons, cabs, etc.

The powers of the city in the premises are derived from clauses 42 and 91, in Section 1 of Article V of the general city incorporation law. The forty-second clause gives the city council power "to license, tax and regulate hackmen, draymen, omnibus drivers, carters, expressmen, porters, cabmen, and all others pursuing like occupations, and to prescribe their compensation."

The ninety-first clause gives the city council power, among other things, "to tax, license and regulate livery stables."

It was held by the Supreme Court in the case of Howland vs. City of Chicago, 108 Ill., 496, that a graduated license was proper and that the expression "livery stables" in the last clause mentioned meant livery stable keepers who kept vehicles for hire, and that the tax or license authorized by the clause, as well as by the forty-second clause, was an occupation tax or license. The plain import of this is that the power of the city in respect to licensing vehicles is confined to licensing certain occupations in connection with vehicles, that is, such public occupations as make the persons pursuing them common carriers, and that the city is without power to exact licenses from other persons directly or specifically on account of vehicles owned or kept by them. Of course, under other powers expressly contained in the general incorporation law, the city may and does exact licenses in connection with classes of business in which wagons are used, but the imposition of licenses in such cases is upon the business and is something quite different from a tax or license directly upon the vehicles or on account of the vehicles themselves. I herewith return the ordinance. Very respectfully yours,

WM. G. BEALE, Corporation Counsel.

May 6, 1896.

To the Honorable, the Judiciary Committee of the Common Council.
Gentlemen—

At the meeting of the council held May 4th, this department was requested to furnish an opinion to your committee, an order therefor having been passed as follows:

"*Ordered*, That the Corporation Counsel be and is hereby requested to furnish the judiciary committee an opinion as to whether or not the city council had authority to authorize the West Chicago Street Railway Company to lay its tracks on West Chicago Avenue across the boulevard, under the control of the West Park Commissioners."

The subject on which this opinion is requested has been carefully considered by the Corporation Counsel and myself, and he has requested me to furnish you our conclusions.

We are of the opinion that the jurisdiction of the city over the intersections of streets with boulevards is concurrent with the jurisdiction of the park commissioners. We are of the opinion that neither the city nor the park commissioners, without the consent and concurrence of the other, has the right to authorize the construction and operation of street railroads across these intersections. The question of the respective jurisdiction of the city and of the Park Board in a somewhat different case recently arose before Judge Tuley, and in his decision of the case he used this language:

"I am firm in the conclusion that the jurisdiction of the Park Commissioners and of the city over the street crossings of the boulevards must necessarily be concurrent. I think the Park Commissioners have no right to take the action they have taken without consultation with the city."

The action referred to in the decision of Judge Tuley as having been taken by the park commissioners was the building of a viaduct on the boulevard, which would have the effect of closing up one or more of the crossings. Very respectfully,

GEO. A. DUPUY, Asst. Corporation Counsel.

May 12, 1896.

Geo. A. Mugler, Esq., Chairman Committee on Elections, City of Chicago.

Dear Sir—

In answer to the inquiries made by you on behalf of your committee, respecting a re-districting of the city at the present time, I beg to say that, in my opinion, the city council may re-district the city whenever such action seems to it desirable, and that in doing so under existing conditions it must preserve the present number of wards. The matter seems free from any reasonable doubt.

Section 2 of Article III of the General City Incorporation Law, as amended in 1889, to prepare for the extended annexation of territory to the city in that year, provided in substantial effect that this city should have forty-eight aldermen and no more, unless an additonal number should be obtained through annexation in the manner prescribed in said section, and that there should be two additional aldermen for every annexed district of territory containing a specified number of inhabitants until the total number of aldermen should reach seventy, after which there should be a re-districting of the city

on a basis which would preserve the number of aldermen at seventy.
That number of aldermen has not yet been reached through annexation of territory, and, accordingly, I find that the number of aldermen in any re-districting must be limited by a provision of the action
of the section, which reads as follows:

"Whenever after such new territory shall have been annexed as
aforesaid said city shall be re-districted, the number of wards at the
time said city is re-districted shall be preserved."

Section 4 of Article LV of the same law provides as follows:

"The City Council of any city in this state * * * may from
time to time divide the city into one-half as many wards as the total
number of aldermen to which the City is entitled."

The foregoing appear to be the statutory provisions governing
the matter.   Respectfully yours,

WM. G. BEALE, Corporation Counsel.

May 12, 1896.
Joseph Downey, Esq., Commissioner of Buildings.
    Dear Sir—
    In response to your letter of inquiry of May 9th, in regard to
frame building erected on rear of 3240 State street, which letter is
accompanied by a petition of sundry property-owners, I beg to say, that
I have considered the matter, and that from these papers I understand
the fact to be that this is a wooden building constructed inside of
the fire limits, and that it is in direct violation of the building ordinances on that account.   If such be the fact, I think it is within your
power to summarily cause the removal and destruction of the building.   Section 11 of the building ordinance provides:

"The Commissioner of Buildings shall also have authority to direct the fire department after written notice has been served on the
owner, lessee, occupant or agent personally, to tear down any defective
or dangerous wall, or any building or any part thereof, which may be
constructed in violation of the terms of this ordinance," and Section
236 has substantially the same provision.

In the case of King vs. Davenport, 98 Ill., 314, the Supreme Court
considered carefully the powers conferred upon the authorities by an
ordinance which was substantially the same as the present ordinance
and which was passed by a city council having substantially the same
powers in relation to the matter as those of the city council of the
city of Chicago.

It was held that a building so erected in violation of the ordinance
could be torn down by the city marshal upon the order of the mayor
(as was provided in said ordinance) and that the owner had no cause
of complaint on account of damage done to her property.   In this case
she brought a suit and obtained a judgment against the city marshal
and the mayor for trespass, but the Supreme Court reversed the judg-

ment and held that she had no cause of action. In the course of the opinion, the court uses the following language:

"There can be no doubt, it seems to us, that the ordinance in question was a police regulation, proper, and made in good faith, 'for the purpose of guarding against the calamities of fire,' in a populous neighborhood; and we must regard it as an entirely reasonable regulation. There is no more frequent or admittedly proper exercise of the police power, than that of the prohibition of the erection of buildings of combustible materials in the populous part of a town, and the only means of making such prohibition effectual is by summary abatement. Every month's delay in the removal of the nuisance is constant exposure to danger. Before any judicial inquiry and hearing could be had in the matter, the whole evil sought to be guarded against might be produced."

In my opinion, this decision of the Supreme Court is decisive of your right, under this ordinance, to cause the removal and abatement of wooden buildings erected within the fire limits without any permit and directly in defiance of the provisions of the ordinance. I think this may be considered as a general rule having direct application to this and all other similar cases. Very respectfully,

GEO. A. DUPUY, Asst. Corporation Counsel.

June 3, 1896.

Philip Maas, Esq., City Collector, City of Chicago.

Dear Sir—

Some time ago there was referred to me from your office the question whether the street frontage of the South Parks should be taken into consideration in connection with petitions and remonstrances concerning saloons in Hyde Park local option territory. I have given this matter careful examination, and while the question may be open to some doubt, I am of the opinion that the law contemplates and requires that the park frontage should be considered.

In this connection I call to mind that the president of the South Park commissioners, as I am informed, recently submitted a protest against the place known as "Ye Tavern," on Fifty-first street. As I understand it, however, this communication represents simply the personal attitude of Mr. Ellsworth and is not to be regarded as the official action of the commissioners. Very truly yours,

WM. G. BEALE, Corporation Counsel.

June 4, 1896.

W. D. Kent, Esq., Commissioner of Public Works.

Dear Sir—

In reply to your oral request for an opinion as to whether the public have the right to make use of the docks along the margin of the Chicago river on either side thereof between Dearborn and State Streets, and as to whether or not the city has the right to construct

20

stairways from the bridges or approaches thereto at State Street and at Dearborn Street leading down to and connecting with such docks, I beg to say, that the matter has been duly considered by the Corporation Counsel and myself and we agree in the conclusions hereinafter set forth.

These docks on either side were formerly a part of what was known as the wharfing privileges or property of the city of Chicago. The deeds by which the real estate was conveyed to the present owners and their grantors contained a reservation in relation to a narrow strip abutting on the river (which strip was in some cases five feet and in some cases ten feet in width), substantially as follows: "Subject to the condition that five feet in width extending the whole length of the front of said premises of the river, shall forever remain an open wharf or dock, to be built and maintained in order and repair by said party of the second part, his heirs and assigns, for free passage of persons on foot, and that in no case, shall passengers by water be subject to any charges whatever for landing their ordinary traveling luggage and going over said wharf, and that the edge of said wharf shall be at all times perfectly and safely planked, or covered, so as to afford a secure passage for such passengers and luggage." We think this reservation clearly gives the public the right to pass over these docks in making landings for themselves with their ordinary luggage. This implies the right on the part of such persons to have safe and reasonable access to the intersecting streets. As the city has full authority and control over the grade of the streets, the right to elevate the surface thereof, to build bridges and viaducts, it would seem to clearly follow that incidental thereto it has the right to afford a safe and convenient passage way between the docks and the streets for the use of such persons as are entitled under this reservation to make use of the docks for the purpose of landing. We think, therefore, it is plain that the city may rightfully cause or permit the construction of a stairway or necessary passage way between the street and the surface of the docks. These stairways should be so constructed as not to substantially or unreasonably interfere with the use of the dock by the abutting property owner, who doubtless has the fee simple title to the docks. If these stairways can be built over the margin of the river without in any way interfering with the navigation, and in such way as to afford a connection with the dock, this would seem to be the better plan, because thereby the use of the entire dock by the abutting property owner will not be interfered with. If, however, this is impracticable, we think that a portion of the dock space might be reasonably claimed by the city for the purpose of affording a foundation for such stair or passage way.

We think it no objection to the construction of these stairways that the same be paid for by persons interested to have them built instead of being paid for by the city, if the work be done under the supervision of the city, and the stairways be for the free and common use of all persons who are entitled to make landings at the docks.

We desire to be understood as avoiding the expression of any opinion as to what are the rights of any vessel owner to make landings at these docks, either as against the abutting property owner or as against the other persons who are engaged in the navigation of the river. As to the former question the city is not interested, and as to the latter the harbor master will presumably protect the public interests. Very respectfully yours,

GEO. A. DUPUY, Asst. Corporation Counsel.

June 5, 1896.

H. J. Jones, Esq., Supt. Special Assessments.

Dear Sir—

Your letter of June 3d asking the opinion of this department as to the validity of stay orders of the council has been referred to me for an answer.

In my opinion, neither the council, nor any other authority of the city, has this power. Par. 165 of the charter of the city provides:

"All persons taking any contracts with the city or village, and who agree to be paid from special assessments, shall have no claim or lien upon the city or village in any event, except from the collections of the special assessments made for the work contracted for."

Now any contractor has a right to expect that the city will perform its duty and proceed to collect the special assessment. If the city were permitted to postpone the collection of the assessment, the one who is relying on the special assessment for the payment of his claim would be compelled to wait for his money indefinitely. The proper remedy in such case for the creditor to pursue would be by mandamus to compel the collection of the assessment. See *Dillon on Municipal Corporations, Section 614.*

In Higgins vs. Chicago, 18 Ill., 276, this seems to have been clearly decided.

In this case a person entitled to compensation for damages caused by the opening of a street asks for a mandamus to compel the collection and payment of a special assessment. The city made various objections to the assessment, among others that certain property was assessed too much and that the public square had been assessed. But the court held that after the confirmation by the court it was too late to raise objections and the only thing left was the collection of the assessment. They said:

"Where a street has been ordered to be opened or extended, commissioners for the assessment of damages have been appointed, and made and reported an assessment, which has been accepted and confirmed; a warrant issued for the collection of the amounts assessed for payment of such damages, and such street ordered to be opened; the parties entitled to such damages for property taken, etc., are entitled to have and collect such damages as of debt, and will be entitled to a mandamus to compel respondent to proceed to collect and pay over the same."

Since the creditors may compel this collection by mandamus, it seems clear that after confirmation of the special assessment the city authorities have no power to postpone it. Their only duty is to proceed to its collection.

Very truly yours,
E. B. BURLING, Asst. Corporation Counsel.
I concur in the above opinion.
WM. G. BEALE, Corporation Counsel.

June 8, 1896.

Hon. O. D. Wetherell, City Comptroller.

Dear Sir—

In reply to your request for an opinion as to the validity of the four per cent. gold bonds of the city of Chicago issued in place of and to retire prior issues of tunnel improvement bonds, I beg to say:

The city of Chicago is incorporated, and has been for twenty years last past exercising the functions of municipal government under an act entitled, "An Act to provide for the incorporation of cities and villages," which was in force July 1, 1872. By Article V of Section 1 of this charter it is provided that the city council shall have power:

"Sixth: To issue bonds in place of or to supply means to meet maturing bonds, or for the consolidation, or funding of the same."

Under the power thus conferred, the city council on April 2, 1896, passed an ordinance providing for the issuance of bonds for the purpose of providing means to pay the bonds issued July 1, 1866, known as Nos. 1 to 100 "P" inclusive. This ordinance was duly passed, published and approved by the mayor, and is the basis of the authority for the issuance of the bonds in relation to the validity of which you make inquiry. In my judgment no question whatever can properly be made that these bonds are legal and valid.

Respectfully submitted,
GEO. A. DUPUY, Asst. Corporation Counsel.

June 8, 1896.

Philip Maas, Esq., City Collector.

Dear Sir—

The other day when I was in your office talking with you and Mr. Schmit, you requested me to prepare an ordinance providing for the licensing of storage warehouses at an annual license fee of $200.00.

In my opinion, the city has no power to pass such an order as this. It is nowhere given specific authority to license storage warehouses, and it could only be justified as a police regulation, but the ordinance proposed would clearly not be of this sort; it would be of a revenue nature. It was held in the Phoenix Insurance Company vs.

The City of Chicago, 126 Ill., 276, that the city had no power under
this clause to raise a revenue from insurance companies. The same
reasoning would apply to the ordinance proposed.
Very truly yours,
EDWARD B. BURLING, Asst. Corporation Counsel.

June 10, 1896.
Hon. Geo. B. Swift, Mayor, etc.
Dear Sir—
In response to inquiries contained in letter of Wm. H. Wright
addressed to your honor and bearing date April 8, 1896, as to the
rights the public have to go through the turnstiles of the Illinois
Central Railroad Company for the purpose of reaching the lake
shore, which letter, together with the letter of Commissioner Kent of
date May 5th was sent by you to this office, I beg to reply:
That the public have the undoubted right to cross the tracks of the
Illinois Central Railroad for the purpose of reaching the lake shore
at points north of Park Row. The title to the lake and the ground
upon which the Illinois Central tracks are located north of Park Row
is in the city, and the Illinois Central has but a right of way over the
same. The public are, therefore, clearly entitled to the privilege of
crossing these tracks for the purpose of reaching the lake shore. This
was one of the points in controversy last summer in connection with
the Van Buren Street viaduct, and this position was asserted by the
city at that time and acquiesced in by the railroad company. In relation to the property south of Park Row, the situation is different. The
railroad company owns the fee simple title to the land upon which
its tracks are located. This carries with it in favor of the comapny
the right to the exclusive use of the property. In all cases wherever
a street has been opened up crossing the right of way of the railroad
company of Park Row, either by condemnation or otherwise, the
public are entitled to the privilege of crossing. This is, however,
true of but very few of the streets. Most of them end at the west line
of the right of way of the railroad company. Until such time as the
city council shall by condemnation extend these streets across the
tracks and right of way the public cannot claim the legal right to cross
the tracks in the line of such streets. It is undoubtedly a very great
hardship on the citizens living in this vicinity, as set forth in the letter
of Mr. Wright, to be deprived of the privilege of reaching the water's
edge, but this can only be obviated by some negotiation with the company whereby this right can be secured with the company's consent,
or by condemnation proceeding for the opening of streets whereby the
right can be secured without the company's consent.
Very respectfully,
GEO. A. DUPUY, Asst. Corporation Counsel.

June 27, 1896.

Hon. John M. Clark, Prest. Civil Service Commission, City of Chicago.

Dear Sir—

In response to the inquiries contained in your letter of the 15th inst., I beg to express my opinion as follows:

First: I do not see any legal impropriety in the adoption and use of an official seal by the commission, but I do not think there would be any legal import in its so doing. The law does not affirmatively authorize such a seal. In this sense, and only in this sense, it would be unauthorized. The commission not being a corporation and not being thus authorized to use a seal, there could be no legal advantage derived from one. It would be legally useless for any purpose. Having no legal effect it could hardly lend any official dignity or solemnity to any papers, and it might even have the contrary effect because of its lack of legal import. My own view is that it would be better for the commission not to adopt this useless form, but I do not know of any particular objection to it.

Second: I can find nothing in the law authorizing the commission to make a residence limitation applicable to city officers or employes after they have actually entered the service of the city, and I am clearly of the opinion that the commission is without such authority. Such a limitation imposed by the commission could be ignored by heads of departments and bureaus. Perhaps, however, the purpose which I assume the commission has in mind can be equally well accomplished by a rule providing that removal of residence from the city will be regarded by the commission as sufficient cause for discharge in all cases under the twelfth section of the Civil Service Law. I suggest this for your consideration.

Very respectfully yours,

WM. G. BEALE, Corporation Counsel.

July 14, 1896.

To the Honorable, the Committee on Judiciary.

Gentlemen— .

Your committee recently referred to this office the draft of a proposed ordinance in relation to the license and control of electrical contractors, etc., with a request that such draft be examined as to its form and validity and a report made thereon.

The matter having been referred to me, I beg to say, that I have carefully examined the ordinance and I believe it to be free from legal objection. I am of the opinion that it is within the power of the council to legislate upon the general subject matter of this ordinance. While the city charter does not contain any grant or power specifically covering the licensing and regulating of electrical engineers, contractors, etc., I think the proposed ordinance finds legal justification in certain provisions of the charter which seem to me to cover the subject in a general way. It is provided in the 63rd clause of the grant of powers to city councils that the city council shall have power:

"To prevent the dangerous construction and condition of chimneys * * boilers and apparatus used in and about any building or manufactory and to cause the same to be removed or placed in a safe condition when considered dangerous."

66. "To regulate the police of the city and pass and enforce all necessary police ordinances."

I assume that defective construction of electrical apparatus and appliances is dangerous; that it is very liable to lead to conflagration, and that skill and technical knowledge are required in order to do electrical work that will not be dangerous. If such assumptions are correct, it seems to me that electrical construction is a subject of police regulation, and that reasonable police ordinances fairly adapted to the avoidance of such hazard are necessary and proper police measures. I think substantially the same power exists to regulate electrical construction as to regulate plumbing, and it has not been doubted that the latter is a proper subject of police regulation.

It does not appear to be obligatory upon the board of civil service examiners to undertake the examination provided for in the ordinance. If, however, they are willing to undertake the examination, I consider that no reasonable objection can be made to the ordinance that it practically constitutes them a board of examiners. I therefore think that no reasonable objection can be made to the ordinance unless it be possibly to some of the minor details that can be readily remedied by amendment of the ordinance as occasion suggests or requires.

Respectfully submitted,

GEO: A. DUPUY, Asst. Corporation Counsel.

July 14, 1896.

Hon. Wm. D. Kent, Commissioner of Public Works.

Dear Sir—

I have to-day had a conference with Deputy Commissioner Moody, Mr. J. S. Cooper, street cleaning contractor for the Twenty-first and Twenty-fourth wards, and Judge Goodrich, Mr. Cooper's attorney, on certain questions submitted to me from your department concerning Mr. Cooper's contract, and I beg to advise you of my conclusions in respect thereto.

Upon the question whether the contractor is required to remove garbage, etc., from private premises in addition to streets and alleys, I think the fair interpretation of the contract is that it requires the contractor to make such removal from private premises (with the exception of certain specified hotels, boarding houses and restaurants); *Provided*, the boxes or other receptacles containing the garbage, etc., are put in places reasonably accessible to the contractor in private grounds and yards. The provisions of the contract and of the specifications forming a part of it are perhaps not entirely free from obscurity, but they seem to me fairly to impose the above requirement. On the other hand, it seems clear that the contractor is not required to enter buildings in the performance of his work. For the contractor to remove garbage from the interior of buildings might necessitate his going to the upper stories of high structures, such as apartment houses, and if this was contemplated there should have been something in the contract which would fairly show such intent. I do not find anything of the kind in the contract.

Respecting the right of the department to put additional men and teams upon the work at the expense of the contractor whenever the department deems necessary, I am of the opinion that the contractor is entitled, save perhaps in some extraordinary or exceptional instance constituting an emergency, to receive notice that the work is not being done to the satisfaction of the department and to have a reasonable opportunity to put on extra men and teams himself, or to otherwise satisfy the department, before the department exercises this right. It is not easy to lay down a general rule which should govern all cases under this particular subject, for each case must to a considerable extent be governed by its own circumstances and much must necessarily be left to the discretion of the officer charged with supervising the fulfillment of the contract. But it may be fairly said in a general way that whenever the department receives complaint or ascertains that the contractor's work is not being properly or adequately performed, it ought to notify the contractor and call upon him to remedy the condition found unsatisfactory under penalty of having more teams and men put on by the city at his expense. It would not be necessary to give the contractor a long notice for this purpose or even a formal notice. A telephone message would answer as well as any other notice, but where the city has the power so completely in its own hands it is manifest that there should be a high degree of fairness and reasonableness in exercising it. For the city to place extra men and teams upon the contract work without giving the contractor notice and an opportunity to take his own action would be quite likely to provoke an undesirable legal controversy over the question. Of course a disregard of the contract requirements might become so persistent or so flagrant that the department might be justified in acting without notice, but under ordinary circumstances the course I have indicated is the safe one to pursue.

Very truly yours,
WM. G. BEALE, Corporation Counsel.

August 15, 1896.
Mark Crawford, Esq., Superintendent of the Bridewell.
Dear Sir—

Some days ago you submitted to this department the question whether a police justice can impose costs upon a defendant when there is no judgment of fine or imprisonment rendered against him. In my opinion it is very clear that there is no such power. There is no incidental power in any court to impose costs of any sort upon either complainant or defendant. The power is entirely created by statute. A short answer to your question might be, therefore, that the statutes relating to costs do not give this power. It is the general policy of statutes allowing costs to allow them as an incident to the recovery of damages. It is considered only just that one who is entitled to recover should be indemnified for his expenses in establishing his rights. The city is in the attitude of a complainant seeking to recover a penalty for violation of an ordinance in an action of debt. If it does not recover any part of the debt it is surely unjust that a defendant, who is not liable in the action, should be compelled to pay the costs of a prosecution. I, therefore, answer your question in the negative.

Very truly yours,

EDWARD B. BURLING, Asst. Corporation Counsel.

August 17, 1896.

J. P. Barrett, Esq., Superintendent City Telegraph.

Dear Sir—

Your letter of August 13th, requesting the opinion of this office as to the right of the city to place underground conductors under the sidewalks has been referred to me.

In reply I would say that the city holds the streets in trust for public purposes and the stringing of electric wires above the ground or underneath the surface is undoubtedly one of these uses, and the city authorities have the power to select the portion of the street which shall be so used. The abutting owner cannot object to this use merely on account of his situation as abutting owner, but there are two things to be observed. The first is, that in putting in the wires care must be taken to do no damage to the abutting property. The second consideration is, that the city has in some instances granted to abutting property-owners, for a consideration, the privilege of using the space under the sidewalks for storage, but in my opinion even in such cases the city has a right to string its wires in this space, interfering as little as possible with the person using this space. The municipal authorities cannot grant away for a private purpose the exclusive use of this property, which is held by them in trust for public uses. Any private use must be enjoyed in subordination to the public interest. Very truly yours,

EDWARD B. BURLING, Asst. Corporation Counsel.

August 17, 1896.

Hon. J. J. Badenoch, General Superintendent of Police.

Dear Sir—

Some time ago there was submitted to this office an inquiry whether a justice of the peace sitting as a police magistrate could hold his court in some other town than the one for which he had been appointed. I have had the matter under examination, and have been constrained to take considerable time, because there was so little authority to be found upon the subject. There is no occasion for me to take any further time upon the question, for I am satisfied that it is somewhat unsettled, or at least that it cannot be regarded as decisively settled. The intimation, rather than the flat decisions of the courts, seems to be toward the view that a justice cannot sit lawfully in any other town than the one for which he is appointed. In this condition of things I am compelled to advise your department that it would not be safe, in my judgment, to have a police magistrate from another town sitting in any police courts.

Very truly yours,

WM. G. BEALE, Corporation Counsel.

September 2, 1896.

Hon. J. J. Badenoch, Chief of Police, Chicago.

Dear Sir—

Your letter of even date to the Corporation Counsel, in which you request an opinion as to whether you have "power to prevent bicyclists from using the tunnel" in La Salle Street in the manner complained of in Mr. Roach's letter, which is attached to your letter, has been referred to me.

The La Salle Street tunnel is a public highway, and the North Chicago Street Railway Company has no greater rights therein than such as are given it by the ordinance permitting it to lay its tracks and operate its cars therein.

It is true that as a consideration for the franchise the street car company has certain duties to perform, such as keeping the tunnel in a cleanly condition, in good repair, etc., but that does not give the company any more right to complain of bicyclists riding their machines through the tunnel than it would have to complain of their being run upon any other street upon which the street car company may have its tracks.

I can find nothing which would warrant you in prohibiting the use of the tunnel by bicyclists, and am, therefore, of the opinion that you cannot legally do so. Yours very truly,

WM. H. ARTHUR, Asst. Corporation Counsel.

September 3, 1896.

E. J. Phelps, Esq., Secy. Civil Service Commission.

Dear Sir—

I beg to acknowledge the receipt of your letter of the 2nd inst. (which, as you will note from your letter-press copy, was doubtless by inadvertence sent to a wrong address), asking my opinion upon the question whether the public vaccinators and medical inspectors referred to in your letter are to be regarded as in the classified service of the city, and stating that the suggestion has been made that they are not to be so regarded inasmuch as they are paid by a special appropriation made for the purpose.

In reply I beg to say that I do not think the method of payment, or of making appropriation therefor, is determinative of the question presented or really has any material bearing upon it. The substantial question is whether the persons mentioned are or are not employes of the city within the meaning of the civil service law. Your letter does not present the facts of the case sufficiently to enable me to pass definitely upon the question, but in a general way it will perhaps suffice for me to say, that if these vaccinators and inspectors are in the regular and exclusive employment of the city they come under the civil service law, while on the other hand if they are persons having independent vocations outside of their city employment and are merely performing special and transitory service to the city, as incidental to their regular work, they are in my judgment not to be regarded as under the civil service law. There is no difficulty about the rule to be applied. The difficulty is to apply it to any given case. A lawyer in the regular employ of the city with such employment constituting his main occupation, and his other and outside work being merely occasional and temporary, would be a city employe, but a lawyer in general practice engaged for a specific service for the city such as taking care of a certain litigation, precisely as he would take care of it for any other client, would not become, by virtue of such service to the city, a city employe as the term is used in the civil service law.

Very respectfully yours,
WM. G. BEALE, Corporation Counsel.

September 15, 1896.

L. B. Jackson, Esq., City Engineer.
Dear Sir—

In reply to your question as to whether or not the commissioner of public works has authority to make such changes as are in his opinion necessary for the public good in bridges and approaches thereto, notwithstanding such bridge or bridges may be crossed by the tracks of any street railroad company, which tracks will have to be altered on account of such change, I beg to say, that in my opinion such power exists in the commissioner of public works, and I advise you that he has full authority in the premises.

Very respectfully yours,
GEO. A. DUPUY, Asst. Corporation Counsel.

October 3, 1896.

Hon. John M. Clark, Prest. of Civil Service Commission, City of Chicago.
Dear Sir—

I beg to acknowledge receipt of your favor of September 22, requesting my opinion as to the meaning of the expression "heads of any principal department of the city" in Section 11 of the Civil Service Act. I understand that you desire to know what ought legally to be regarded as a "principal department" of the municipal government.'

In my opinion a principal department is one which, in the main, is subordinate only to the city council and to the mayor. Subordinate divisions of the municipal service, though they may be spoken of as departments, can hardly be regarded as principal departments within the meaning of the law. It would be more proper to call them "bureaus." For example, the city has two bureaus, commonly called the "Street Department" and the "Water Department." These are really subdivisions of the department of public works, and their heads are under the supervision and control of the commissioner of public works. The so-called street department and water department cannot be considered as principal departments under the civil service law. There are doubtless other cases of the same kind. The heads of these subordinate branches of the municipal service are not to be regarded as heads of principal departments and would not be exempt, as such, from classification in the classified civil service. There is some absence of uniformity in the method by which these bureau chiefs are appointed. Some of them are appointed by the mayor and confirmed by the council, in which case they would be exempt from classification in the classified service because all officers so appointed and confirmed are expressly exempted by the act. Other bureau chiefs are appointed by the heads of the departments of which they form a subdivision, and in such latter cases these chiefs would not be exempt from classification under the law no matter how important their bureaus.

Very respectfully yours,

WM. G. BEALE, Corporation Counsel.

October 3, 1896.

Hon. John M. Clark, President Civil Service Commissioner, City of Chicago.

Dear Sir—

In response to your letter of September 29th, and confirming what I have said verbally to the commission, I beg to advise you that in my opinion a fireman on the retired list is still to be legally regarded as a member of the fire department and subject to restoration to the place from which he was retired if upon examination it is disclosed that he is able to perform its duties. In other words, I think that such a retired fireman need not take the civil service examination required by an original applicant for a place in the fire department.

Very respectfully yours,

WM. G. BEALE, Corporation Counsel.

October 16, 1896.

Hon. Joseph Downey, Commissioner of Public Works, City of Chicago.

Dear Sir—

I have examined with care the question of the liability of the city for damages to property caused by blasting done by the contractors in the construction of the Northwest tunnel, and beg to give you my conclusions thereon substantially as I have heretofore expressed them verbally.

The question has a double aspect, namely: First, as to the primary liability of the city, and second, as to the ultimate liability of the contractors to indemnify or reimburse the city.

As this is a city work undertaken by the city and for its benefit, I have no doubt that any parties whose property is injured by it may recover their damages from the city, whether the contractors are also liable or not. It may be that such parties would also have a right to recover from the contractors as well as from the city, on the ground that both the city and the contractors are, legally speaking, joint wrongdoers so far as third parties are concerned. It seems to me clear that the city causing the damages cannot escape the liability and compel the injured parties to have recourse to the contractors who are performing the work. The ultimate responsibility of the contractors is primarily a matter between them and the city alone. Respecting the ultimate liability of the contractors to reimburse the city, the provisions of the contract, the specifications and the bond are, perhaps, not all that could be desired, but taken together I think they are reasonably clear, and that they make the contractors liable for all damages caused by the contractors.

The specifications contain the following paragraph:

"The contractor will be required to guard the public effectually from liability to accident during the whole progress of the work, both by night and by day, and will be held responsible for any damages the city may have to pay in consequence of neglect on the part of the contractor, or any of his agents, to protect the public against such accidents."

The contract contains a paragraph respecting damages growing out of the use of streets or public grounds in which it is provided, among other things, that the contractors "shall be liable for all damages * * * which may result from the carelessness of such contractor or contractors, his or their agents, employes or workmen."

One of the conditions of the bond is that the contractors "shall indemnify, keep and save harmless to the City of Chicago against all liabilities, judgments, costs, damages and expenses which may in any wise come against said city in consequence of the granting of such contract, or which may in any wise result from the carelessness or neglect" of the contractors or their employes.

Unless the city in some way waives the benefit of these foregoing provisions, or does some act equivalent to such waiver, I think the provisions are sufficient to fix upon the contractors ultimate liability for damages caused by them in the prosecution of their work. Whenever claims for damages are made against the city, the contractors should, of course, be notified of the claims and be given an opportunity to resist them, and no voluntary settlements of such claims can be made by the city in the absence of consent thereto on the part of the contractor without danger that the amount of such settlements cannot be established as valid claims against the contractors. I think also that care should be taken to warn the contractors about conforming to the requirements of their contracts, in order to avoid a possible contention on the part of the contractors that the city authorized or permitted the acts causing the damages in any case.

Very respectfully yours,

WM. G. BEALE, Corporation Counsel.

October 19, 1896.

Vere V. Hunt, Esq., Attorney, Department of Health, City of Chicago.

Dear Sir—

I have your letter of the 17th inst., and in reply beg to say, that, in my opinion, Section 16 of the milk ordinance, to which you call my attention, must be interpreted as requiring the milk dealer to take out only one license for his entire business—unless the ordinance elsewhere contains some other provisions than the one quoted in your letter, to which alone my attention is now directed. The requirement seems to be plainly that the fee is chargeable against the dealer for engaging in the business, and not against, nor in respect to, his different places of business, however many he may have.

Yours very truly,

WM. G. BEALE, Corporation Counsel.

October 30, 1896.

Hon. J. J. Badenoch, General Superintendent of Police.

Dear Sir—

Your request for an opinion from this office in relation to the powers and duties of deputy United States marshals, and of police officers, in relation to elections, has been referred to me, and in reply I beg to say:

1. All federal laws in relation to deputy United States marshals, their appointment, duties and compensation, were repealed by act of Congress of February 4, 1894. The several federal laws on this subject were repealed section by section. It was further provided in said act:

"Section 2. That all other statutes and parts of statutes relating in any manner to supervisors of election and special deputy marshals be and the same are hereby repealed."

There will therefore be no deputy United States marshals performing any duties at the approaching election.

2. In relation to the duties of police officers at elections, I had the honor to furnish to R. W. McClaughry, then superintendent of police, an opinion dated November 2, 1891, which is probably on file in your department, in which the duties of police officers are carefully considered. This opinion was substantially as follows:

"Referring to your communication of the 31st ult., inquiring as to what are the duties of the police in regard to enforcing certain provisions of the election law, I would say, that Section 28 of an act approved June 22, 1891, provides:

" 'Section 28. No person whatever shall do any electioneering or soliciting of votes on election day within any polling place or within one hundred (100) feet of any polling place. No person shall interrupt, hinder or oppose any voter while approaching the polling place for the purpose of voting. Whoever shall violate the provisions of this section shall be punished by a fine of not less than twenty-five dollars ($25.00) nor more than one hundred dollars ($100.00) for each and every offense; and it shall be the duty of the judges of election to enforce the provisions of this section.'

" 'Also that Section 9, of Article IV, of the Act approved June 29, 1885, provides as follows:

" 'Section 9. Said judges of election shall have authority to keep the peace and to cause any person to be arrested for any breach of the peace or for any breach of election laws or any interference with the progress of such election or of the canvass of the ballots; and it shall be the duty of all officers of the law present to obey the order of such judges of election; and an officer making an arrest by direction of any judge, shall be protected in making such arrest the same as if a warrant had been issued to him to make such an arrest.'

"I think the proper construction of these two sections would determine that the duty of enforcing the provisions of the election law rests primarily upon the judges of election. I think further that the po- and the votes are being counted. Police officers should be very careful not to in any way interfere with acts which they may suppose to be lice should be in strict subordination to the authority and order of such election judges during the time that the election is actually being held violation of the law, except upon the direction and under the supervision of the judges of election. The judges of election are strictly accountable to the Board of Election Commissioners for the enforcement of the law. The duty of enforcing the law rests upon the police, but only under the supervision and direction of the judges of election."

I think the conclusions then reached as set forth in that opinion were correct, and after careful consideration of the same, I am unable to add thereto anything of further importance.

Respectfully submitted,

GEO. A. DUPUY, Asst. Corporation Counsel.

November 5, 1896.

Hon. O. D. Wetherell, Comptroller, City of Chicago.

Dear Sir—

I beg to advise you of the conclusions to which I have come respecting the course best to be pursued in dealing with claims for special assessment rebates in cases where the specific rebates claimed have been previously paid out. I understand that the cases which are particularly troublesome are those where probably some one has wrongfully personated the rightful claimant and therefore drawn, upon proper papers, the money which should have been paid to the rightful claimant. The primary question is what you as city comptroller ought to do about paying the rightful claimant upon his appearing and convincing you to your satisfaction that the rebate has been improperly paid to some one else.

It seems to me that your proper course is to decline to take any action and to refer the claimant to the city council. These rebates are payable out of a special fund, each rebate being a proper proportion of the aggregate surplus in a particular special assessment proceeding. When the aggregate surplus has been properly apportioned to the property owners the surplus is exhausted, and I cannot see that you as city comptroller have any power to add to it out of any other funds. The cases present not so much a question of evidence respecting the rightfulness of the claimant's demand and the wrongful payment to some other party as they do a question of funds. If you assume a case where a property owner satisfies you beyond doubt that he is entitled to a certain rebate on an assessment paid by him; that the city has erroneously paid that rebate to some one else, and that the property owners should be paid the amount of the rebate by the city, the question nevertheless occurs, from what fund have you the right to take the money to pay the property owner. The rebate fund in that particular case is, strictly speaking, exhausted either by actual payment or by appropriation. I think a special appropriation would be required by the city council. There is further an element of policy involved in the fact that it may be necessary to charge up the amount of any erroneous payments heretofore made against some particular department or officer, and the city council will naturally have to settle such a matter in the end either directly or through its finance committee. It seems to me that it would be best to refer these claimants to the city council for relief. Very respectfully yours,

WM. G. BEALE, Corporation Counsel.

November 7, 1896.

Noble B. Judah, Esq., Chairman Committee on Judiciary, City Council.

Dear Sir—

There was recently submitted to this office a resolution pending before your committee under reference from the council, as follows:

"Whereas, it is charged that the Chicago Telephone Company

is putting in telephones in drug stores, hotels and other places in connection with slot machines, by which the use of said telephone is payable by the public inserting a certain amount in said slot machine contrary to the letter and spirit of the acts and ordinances of the City Council of Chicago granting the right to said Telephone Company to maintain a telephone service in the city of Chicago, therefore, be it

"Resolved by the Common Council of the City of Chicago that for the purpose of investigating the matter of the use of slot machines in connection with the telephone service of this city, and that said committee make proper report thereof to this Council."

In connection with this resolution this office is. formally asked "for an opinion (1) as to the rates which the Chicago Telephone Company has the right to charge, and (2) as to its power to place the slot machines in drug stores, hotels, etc., and (3) what power the City of Chicago has to regulate said Company's charges and rates." Informal inquiry is also made (4) as to the power of the city to impose a license in respect to telephones.

I am able to answer these inquiries without much difficulty or hesitation, particularly as the more important of them have heretofore been considered by this department.

(1) The ordinance passed January 4, 1889, under which the Chicago Telephone Company does business, provides in Section six (6) that the company during the life of the ordinance "shall not increase to its present or future subscriber the rates for telephone service now established," and that "there shall be filed by said company a schedule showing the rates charged by said company for telephone service at the date of the passage of this ordinance within the limits of the City of Chicago." This is the only provision of statute or ordinance known to me to be in force in this city bearing upon the subject. There is printed in Myers' Laws and Ordinances of 1890, Sections 4503 to 4515 inclusive, an ordinance passed October 15, 1888, in favor of the telephone company, prescribing different rates, but this ordinance of October 15, 1888, was never accepted' by the telephone company, and therefore by its own terms it never went into actual effect.

Pursuant to the ordinance of January 4, 1889, the telephone company filed its schedule of rates for telephone service established (see Council Proceedings of 1888 and 1889, page 846, February 11, 1889) and the rates therein mentioned I regard as its lawful maximum rates today to its subscribers for like service. In cases where by special arrangement the company installed the metallic return circuit and long distance instrument instead of the single wire and grounded circuit everywhere in use at the time the ordinance was passed, and still largely used, or installs its so-called "express service," or installs both of these improvements, it charges an extra price therefor, and I do not see why it may not rightfully do so. At least it can refuse to furnish the improved service at the prices for which it must furnish the ordinary service.

I assume that the committee does not desire me to set forth in detail the rates given in the schedules filed, as these schedules are equally accessible to the members of the committee, and that the foregoing general reference will be found sufficient.

(2) The "slot" machines, so-called, are merely telephones fitted with coin receiving and registering devices. The telephone company has the same power to install these combination instruments which it has to install any other form of telephone desired. It cannot force them upon anybody if they are not wanted. But I do not understand that these coin-collecting instruments are in fact furnished for private use at all. They are not rented to subscribers as ordinary telephones are rented, so as to become for the time being the telephones of the subscribers, but on the contrary the telephone company hires the room or the space in which to place them and installs them as its own telephones for public use. A person from whom space is thus rented apparently steps into the relation of agent of the telephone company to care for the instrument instead of having the partially independent control of it as an ordinary subscriber has of his telephone. The relation of the telephone company to these combination instruments so placed, appears to be legally the same as its relation to the instruments which it has in its own public exchanges. In one case it rents a little space in a store or office; in the other, it rents a room or several rooms, or perhaps a building. In both cases the telephone instruments stand on the same legal footing. There are apparently no "subscribers" in relation to them, and they do not appear to be affected by the above quoted ordinance provision.

(3) I think it is clear that the city of Chicago has no power to regulate telephone charges and rates. An extended opinion to this effect was given by Corporation Counsel Green in 1888, and is printed in the Council Proceedings of 1888 and 1889, beginning at page 677, under the date of December 21, 1888. His conclusions seem to be correct. I understand that a similar opinion was given by Corporation Counsel Winston, but it does not appear to have been printed.

The idea has been expressed that the above quoted language in the telephone ordinance gives the city the right to regulate the rates of the telephone company. This is plainly an erroneous view. In the first place, it is to be noticed that the phraseology of the ordinance provision is altogether insufficient for the purpose. It is a mere prohibition upon an increase of rates, which prohibition is valid only because accepted by the telephone company. Like any ordinary contract, if violated, relief must be had in the courts, for the city has not reserved in the ordinance any right of action in case of such violation In the second place, I think it may fairly be said that such a right or power as that of prescribing rates of compensation in any business cannot be effectually acquired by a city by virtue of its own ordinances. There must be charter or statutory authority underlying it. The City of St. Louis some years ago passed an ordinance in favor of a telephone company, in which it expressly reserved the right to fix the rates and charges for the use of telephones. Subsequently it passed an ordinance fixing telephone rates, but the Supreme Court of Missouri, in The City of St. Louis vs. Bell Telephone Company, 96 Mo., 623, held this regulating ordinance void on the ground that the city had no charter authority to regulate telephone rates.

The provision of the ordinance of January 4, 1889, prescribing the maximum telephone rates, constitutes a contract between the city and telephone company for the private benefit of telephone subscribers. If the city had power to enter into this contract provision, as I am inclined to think it had, the provision is valid and enforceable; otherwise it is not. Under a well-settled rule of law, any subscriber is entitled to substantially the same rights and remedies under this contract provision as if it had been made directly by such subscriber with the telephone company, unless such rights have been waived.

(4) The city of Chicago does not appear to possess any authority to impose a telephone license. This question also was carefully considered by Corporation Counsel Green on two different occasions, and you will find his opinions in the council proceedings for 1887 and 1888, on pages 151 and 535. I see no reason for changing the previous decision of this department on this question.

Very respectfully yours,
WM. G. BEALE, Corporation Counsel.

November 13, 1896.
A. S. Trude, Esq., 79 Clark St., Chicago.
Dear Sir—
I beg to acknowledge receipt of your letter of the 11th inst., relating to the proposed action of the Board of Education about placing its employes under the operation of the existing civil service law, and asking my opinion as to the legal propriety of such action, particularly in view of the provisions of the eighth section of the school pension law.

It has always seemed to me doubtful whether the civil service act could be legally applicable and compulsory in respect to employes of the Chicago Board of Education. In the Town of Lake annexation case of McGurn vs. Board of Education, 133 Ill., 134, Mr. Justice Bailey, speaking for the Supreme Court of the state, said that the Chicago Board of Education "in some points of view is to be regarded as a subordinate department of the city government, and in others as an independent municipal corporation." If the Board of Education thinks proper to waive the doubt and voluntarily place itself under the effect of the civil service law, I see no legal objection to its so doing. I believe further that such action would be wise and would be approved by the community. In this view I know that Mayor Swift concurs. It may be that some practical embarrassments in administration will result, but it is probable that these can be readily obviated by mutual forbearance and reasonableness on the part of the board and the civil service commission. There are always practical embarrassments in the administration of public affairs under any law.

There is a manifest repugnancy between Section 12 of the civil service law and Section 8 of the subsequently enacted school pension law, both relating to removals and discharges. The effect of this repugnancy seems to me clearly to be that the earlier civil service act must give way to the provisions of the school pension act in all cases where the latter is applicable. This view is in conformity with the well-settled rule of statutory interpretation. In respect, therefore, to school employes coming within the provisions of Section 8 of the school pension law, I think the judgment of the Board of Education would be final and conclusive, and not subject to the revision and approval of the Civil Service Commission. In practice it would probably be found that there is no real difficulty in applying the civil service law, as thus modified by this school pension law.

Very truly yours,

WM. G. BEALE, Corporation Counsel.

November 21, 1896.

Philip Maas, Esq., City Collector.

Dear Sir—

Your request for an opinion as to the power of the city to license wholesale malt liquor dealers in the prohibition districts of Lake View, Town of Lake and Hyde Park has been referred to me, and I have come to the following conclusions:

First. As to the Lake View or Ravenswood district the prohibition is absolute, the first section of an ordinance of the city of Lake View, passed June 27, 1889, containing the following: * * *. "No license shall at any time hereafter be granted to any person or persons to keep a saloon, dram shop or other place for the sale, exchange, giving away, or barter of any kind of alcoholic drinks."

Second. Section 22 of Chapter LVII of the Revised Ordinances of the Town of Lake (1887) provides that "No license shall be granted to any person to carry on the business of a wholesale liquor dealer within the districts where, by ordinance, saloons or dram shops are now or may be hereafter prohibited." Wholesale liquor dealer is defined by Section 19 of the same chapter as one who sells intoxicating liquor in quantities not less than one gallon at a time.

Third. The Hyde Park liquor ordinance, Chapter XV, Rev. Mun. Code, 1887, is not clear on the question of the sale of liquor by wholesale. It divides the traffic into two classes—dram shops or saloons (Sec. 2), and liquor or beer wagons (Sec. 4), defining the former as places where intoxicating liquors are sold in quantities less than one gallon at a time, and the latter as conveyances from which intoxicants are sold in quantities less than four gallons in one package. Section 6 provides that "The President and Board of Trustees, by resolution, may grant licenses to keep so many dram shops, saloons or *beer wagons* in the Village of Hyde Park, *outside of prohibited districts,* as they may think the public good requires, etc." Section 21 provides that "hereafter no license shall be issued to keep a *saloon or dram shop* within the territory described, etc."

The class created by our "malt liquor" ordinance is not coincident with either of the classes created by the Hyde Park ordinance, and you will notice that the latter does not require licenses for sales of four gallons or more. A license issued under our ordinance, however, would authorize sales in quantities of one gallon or more at a time. Furthermore, it is not clear that liquor or beer wagons must have been excluded from the prohibited districts. (Compare Sections 6 and 21 of the Hyde Park ordinance.)

The question, you will see, is not without difficulty, and in view of the disposition of this administration to protect effectually the residence districts of the city from the least invasion that might be hurtful, I should advise that you decline to issue licenses in the Hyde Park, as in the Lake View and Lake, prohibitory territories, and leave such applicants as desire to test the question to their remedy by mandamus. Very truly yours,

TIFFANY BLAKE, Asst. Corporation Counsel.

November 23, 1896.

Hon. Joseph Downey, Commissioner of Public Works, City of Chicago.

Dear Sir—

I have your request of this date for my opinion concerning certain points said to have arisen in connection with the application of the Chicago City Railway Company for a permit to change its motive power on Indiana avenue pursuant to the ordinance of July 16, 1894. I will take up these points in the order in which you mention them.

1 and 2. The ordinance authorizes a change of motive power to the overhead trolley system upon consent to such change of the property owners representing a majority of the frontage. It expressly provides that the mayor and commissioner of public works shall determine how the poles are to be placed. The consent of the property owners not being required by statute, but being merely a requirement imposed by the city, and the ordinance having reserved to the city authorities the question of deciding upon the location of the poles, I do not think the property owners have any control at all over this question. A condition placed in consents that there shall be side poles, or that there shall be center poles, as the case may be, seems to me wholly inoperative and ineffectual. The property owners must either consent or not consent, and any conditions which they seek to attach, attempting to limit the power of the city in the premises, are to be treated as surplusage. I believe this has heretofore been the uniform rule with respect to all such conditions, and it appears to me the only

practicable one. In my judgment these conditional consents should be counted and no attention should be paid to the conditions.

3. Revocations or copies thereof on file in the department received prior to the presentation of the consents, should, of course, be counted as cancelling all the corresponding consents appearing to have been given prior to such revocations. I confess to some hesitation respecting the proper course when the subsequently presented consents bear no date, but after careful consideration it is my opinion that the proper rule is to apply is to consider the consents as of the date when they were filed with the department. The question to be considered is what should be the proper rule for the department in all such cases, and not what the effect is going to be upon this particular railway company, or upon those who are opposing it. The verification of frontage consents is always a perplexing matter. Not long ago there came before me a case where one property owner had signed four different papers, two in favor of a thing, and two against it, and had signed both ways on the same day. Such consents are required in respect to saloons, in respect to livery stables, and in various other matters, and there must be some simple and practical rule for the city to work under. These consents are intended to be presented to the city authorities for their action, and it is only fair and reasonable that some degree of care should be required on the part of the people who give them, and that they should take the consequences of any want of due care on their part. I think the consents ought to speak as of the time when they are filed, except as against a revocation previously or concurrently filed with the department, and shown by proper dating to have been made after the consent was given. Any other rule will throw upon the department the burden of attempting to solve the Chinese puzzle of deciding disputed questions of date respecting such consents and revocations. Dating of papers is at best an unsatisfactory test as to the time when they were actually given in any case, because it is not unusual for papers to be dated back or dated ahead for special reasons, but where the papers show a specific date of consent, and a specific date of revocation, those dates probably ought to govern. The parties must then see that their dates are right. Where the consents are undated, therefore, I should treat them as having been made on the date when the papers are filed and as overcoming any previous revocation.

4. It has been the uniform ruling of this office, as I understand it, and I know it has been the uniform ruling since my incumbency of it, that revocations are not entitled to be considered if filed after the filing of the consents or petitions. There are excellent reasons for this. As already indicated, the papers are prepared to be presented to a public officer, and those who sign them know that they are intended as a basis for official action. If a man may sign a consent, say in July, upon which he knows that you may act at any time when it is presented to you, surely it is his business when he decides to revoke

that consent to notify you at once. After the consent has been filed with you I consider that his power to revoke it should be considered as gone, and if you accept revocations subsequently filed but asserted to have been previously made you are at once involved in the difficult task of deciding a controversy, which experience shows has frequently arisen, as to whether the revocation was actually made before the filing of the consents. The consents were filed in this case November 18th. It might be that some people could be induced to make and sign a revocation after that date and place upon it a date prior to the 18th, and seek to make use of such a revocation as having been made prior to the filing of the consents. Then would come affidavits and counter-affidavits, and a vast amount of difficulty for the department. Moreover, the door would be open for a lot of unfairness in the department in holding back a decision upon consents until revocations could be filed whose makers would assert that they were actually made prior to the filing of the consents, and interested people would be likely to charge such unfairness in many cases where none had occurred, thereby lessening public confidence in the department. Unfortunately all people are not honest, and the few dishonest ones are usually the cause of the most trouble. The opportunities for fraud should be minimized to the greatest possible extent, and a fixed rule should be adopted for this class of cases as far as practicable. It seems to me a reasonable and proper rule to require that revocations must be filed concurrently with or before the filing of the consents. If this rule is insisted upon in all cases the department will be free from the turmoil which usually ensues whenever a matter of frontage consents is under consideration, and in the end I believe the public welfare will be promoted.

5. Where an apparent signature to a consent is claimed to be a forgery or unauthorized, I do not see how you can avoid some investigation to determine the facts in each case. The courts have decided that an authority may fairly be presumed where a name appears to have been signed by another person, and I think this the only practical rule for the department to work under. I should therefore presume that signatures are authorized and genuine in the absence of claims to the contrary by the people whose names thus appear to have been signed. Where such claims are made I should hear both sides respecting the authority or the genuineness of the signature, taking care to confine the hearing to the exact question presented. The less you are compelled to go into investigations outside of the face of the papers the better it is in every case, and it would manifestly be improper to allow a property owner to go into proof as to whether he had changed his mind after he had in fact given his authority, and that authority had been acted upon. The sole question in such a case, for example, would be whether he had in fact given the authority.

6. Where revocations are on file in the department there is no difficulty in dealing with them under the rules above suggested, but I

can appreciate that great difficulty might arise over the loss of revocations in the department files. It is not to be expected that among the thousands of letters received by the department some loss will not occur, but for reasons already suggested to receive affidavits asserting that revocations have been filed where such revocations cannot be found, would open the door to a great deal of undesirable controversy and to fraud and to charges against the department. It would be well if 'the department could find it practicable to keep an index of such papers for its own protection, but I can see some embarrassment about this. The property owners can, however, easily protect themselves when they file revocations at any time in any such case by preserving a copy and having the department's receipt upon the copy of the originals as filed. The department will not then be compelled to rely upon the affidavits, but will have a paper shown by its own endorsed receipt to be a copy of the original, and showing that that original was filed in the department. This method of procedure is so plain and obvious that it ought to occur to any property owner filing a paper, and where papers cannot be found after careful and diligent search in the department, and there is nothing to show their filing, I think it is proper and reasonable to refuse to accept affidavits to their filing, and I would not accept such affidavits except in cases where their filing was admitted by the parties in the opposite interest.

7. In my judgment, for reasons already sufficiently indicated, such conditions as you mention under your seventh point should not be considered, but should be ignored and the consents counted.

8. I should not accept such affidavits as you mention under your eighth inquiry for reasons already suggested.

I answer your inquiries under some pressure, for, as you know, I am on the point of leaving the city to be gone for a short time, and I understand you desire my opinion before I go. If there are any portions of this letter not entirely clear to you I think Mr. Dupuy will be able to explain them, for he has expected that you would probably ask for an opinion in my absence, and he has therefore discussed these questions quite fully with me to ascertain my views. If there are any further points upon which you desire advice he will also give it to you promptly.   Very respectfully yours,

WM. G. BEALE, Corporation Counsel.

November 28, 1896.

To the Honorable, the City Council.

Gentlemen—

By an order of your honorable body, passed at your meeting held on the 23rd inst., this office was asked to furnish an opinion "as to the legality of an extended exclusion of traffic and ordinary public uses from streets within park districts, and as to whether or not any limit exists to the boulevarding of the public thoroughfares, highways and streets of this municipality, and the consequent deflection of our streets from their proper uses as channels of trade and highways of the people."

In reply I beg to say that the matter has been referred to me and that I think the act of the General Assembly in force July 1, 1895, which is referred to in the order asking for an opinion, answers these questions. This act provides "that every board of park commissioners or park authorities shall have power to connect any public park, boulevard or driveway under its control with any part of any incorporated city, town or village by selecting and taking any connecting street or streets, or parts thereof, leading to such park, boulevard or driveway * * * provided, that the consent of the corporate authorities having control of any such streets or streets so far as selected and taken, and also the consent in writing of the owners of a majority of the frontage of the lots and lands abutting on such streets, so far as taken, shall be first obtained." Under the language of this act any street or part of a street may be taken which connects any public park, boulevard or driveway with any part of any incorporated city, town or village. These words should doubtless be given effect according to their plain import. I think the passage of an act with these provisions is within the power of the legislature.

In regard to the question as to whether or not there are limitations upon the power of the park boards to select and take streets, I would say that the proviso in the act furnishes such limitations. It requires the consent of the municipal authorities and the consent, in writing, of the owners of a majority of the frontage of property abutting on such streets. These two limitations would seem to be ample to prevent the "deflection of streets from their proper uses as channels of trade and highways of the people." I know of no other limitations than these upon the power of the park boards in behalf. Respectfully submitted,

GEO. A. DUPUY, Asst. Corporation Counsel.

December 3, 1896.

John D. Murphy, Esq., City Boiler Inspector.

Dear Sir—

Yours of even date to the corporation counsel, in which you request an opinion as to your duty when you find a boiler in a dangerous condition, and after notifying the owner and user thereof of such fact he refuses to place same in a safe condition and continues to use it in disregard of your orders to the contrary, has been referred to me for the purpose of furnishing you the desired opinion.

In my opinion, the proper manner in which to deal with such a case is to refuse to allow the operation of the boiler while in an unsafe condition. Inform the owner and user of such boiler of your decision and of your intention to arrest and prosecute any person attempting to operate the boiler while in an unsafe condition. For that purpose I would have a police officer detailed to watch the boiler and carry out your orders.

By an ordinance passed July 9, 1890, amending Section 821 of the Municipal Code of 1881, it is made unlawful for any person to use a steam boiler or tank subject to steam pressure without a certificate from the boiler inspector that such boiler or tank may be safely used. In this case you have declared the boiler to be unsafe, and any person attempting to use it after such notice is engaged in an unlawful act, and is amenable to the law, and for the preservation of life and property I believe it is your duty to see that a boiler or steam tank in an unsafe condition be not used while in such condition.

Very truly yours,

W. H. ARTHUR, Asst. Corporation Counsel.

December 8, 1896.

Joseph Downey, Esq., Commissioner of Public Works.

Dear Sir—

In your letter of the 3rd inst. you ask for an opinion on the following question: Where the owner or persons in charge of vessels or boats tie or anchor them along the various docks in the Chicago river, has the city, or the department of public works, the power to compel their removal upon the complaint of the abutting property-owner?

The city of Chicago has as full power and authority over the Chicago river as it has over the streets and public grounds of the city. The river is a public and navigable highway, situated almost entirely within the limits of the city, and riparian owners have the same right to light, air and use of the dock along the river front as abutting property-owners have on the streets and highways of the city. There is no practical difference. One is a highway for pedestrians and vehicles, and the other is a water highway for vessels and other craft, and the privileges and rights of abutting property-owners in both cases must be determined by the same laws.

The act for the incorporation of cities and villages grants to the city council ample power over the Chicago river. Subdivisions 30 to 38 of Section 1, Article V, give the city council power "To deepen, widen, dock, cover, wall, alter or change the channel of river courses; to construct and keep in repair canals and slips for the accommodation of commerce; to erect and keep in repair public landing places, wharves, docks and levees; *to regulate and control the use of public and private landing places, wharves, docks and levees;* to control and regulate the anchorage, moorage and landing of all water craft and their cargoes within the jurisdiction of the corporation; to make regulations in regard to the use of harbors, towing of vessels, opening of bridges."

Under the powers thus granted the city council passed an ordinance, dated June 26, 1890, revising the harbor ordinances of the city, and this ordinance is now in full force and effect, and the powers therein conferred upon the harbor master may be legally exercised.

By the provisions of this ordinance the harbor master and his assistants are clothed with police powers for the purpose of effectually upholding the regulations of the city concerning the harbor, and for such purpose have all the power and authority of police officers (Section 1335). and are empowered to order the removal of all vessels and other craft necessary, even although the vessel ordered to be moved is tied up at the dock of a riparian owner and there discharging her cargo; but the harbor master's power in this latter extreme case can only be exercised where the removal is made necessary to facilitate the movements of other vessels or craft. (Sections 1324, 1337.)

It will not be claimed that Congress has assumed, under the power it is conceded to have to regulate commerce with foreign nations and among the several states, to enact any laws concerning the matters embraced in this ordinance. Ordinances and regulations concerning the use of the harbor pertain to local government with which it is hardly probable Congress will ever assume to interfere, and the Supreme Court of the United States has announced this doctrine in the case of Escanaba Company vs. Chicago, 107 U. S., 678, where the court uses the following language:

"But the states have full power to regulate within their limits matters of internal police, including in that general designation whatever will promote the peace, comfort, convenience and prosperity of their people. * * * The commercial power of Congress is exclusive of State authority only where the subjects upon which it is exercised are national in their character and admit and require uniformity of regulation affecting alike all the states. The regulations concerning local ports, nothwithstanding a general control over them for all commercial purposes is conceded to be in Congress, is wisely left with the state authorities within the limits of which such ports are situated. The non-action of Congress in such matters may be regarded as a declaration that the states or municipal authorities on which the duty may be devolved may be left free to make all needful regulations in respect to wharf boats, tug boats and other boats used within the harbors within their respective jurisdiction, and also regulations in respect to the use of such harbors in towing of vessels and the opening or passing of bridges, and with the exercise of such powers by the local municipal authorities Congress has not interfered where such regulations were thought to be necessary to the protection of property or the comfort and convenience of the people."

Very truly,

B. BOYDEN, Asst. Corporation Counsel.

I have examined the foregoing opinion by Mr. Boyden, and consider the same to be correct.

GEO. A. DUPUY, Asst. Corporation Counsel.

December 17, 1896.

P. O'Shea, Esq., Acting Building Commissioner.

Dear Sir—

In answer to your letter of inquiry I beg to say that a livery stable has been defined by the Supreme Court of one of our states to be, "a place where horses are groomed, fed and hired, and where vehicles are let" (Williams vs. Garinges, 30 La. Ann., pt. 2, 1094, 1095, cited in 13 Am. & Eng. Enc. Law, page 935.) I think this definition may be considered accurate. It would seem to follow that a stable cannot be classified as a livery stable where the horses therein kept are used only in the business of the person keeping the stable. I think it makes no difference that such business may consist in teaming, or hauling either passengers or freight, so long as the horses and vehicles kept in such stable are not let for hire. I do not think that the place can be classified as a livery stable. Very respectfully yours,

GEO. A. DUPUY, Asst. Corporation Counsel.

December 10, 1896.

John J. Badenoch, Esq., General Supt. of Police.

Dear Sir—

You ask me whether or not persons are guilty of violating the laws of the state, or the ordinances of the city, who are operating upon substantially the following plan:

A room or office is maintained ostensibly as a commission house where persons are permitted and invited to congregate, and where any one who chooses may deposit with the proprietor, or his agents, such money as he may choose, accompanied with an offer on his part to wager or bet the same on a horse race thereafter to take place in some other state. In such room are large cards on which are posted the names of different horses that are to participate in races on various race tracks and the odds against each horse, and on which blackboards are also posted, from time to time, the results of races after the same have been run. It appears from printed information conspicuously displayed on the walls that no bets or wagers are made in such room. Persons desiring to make wagers are informed that their wagers will be placed for them by the proprietor, or his agents, by telegraph, at points outside of the state of Illinois; that when such offer is made it is accordingly telegraphed to points outside of the state of Illinois, and if an acceptance of the bet is secured that the person who made the offer is notified; that his money is thereupon deposited with the proprietor before his offer is telegraphed, and the proprietor gives a printed slip or ticket, and the proprietor thereupon forwards the money to the point where the offer was accepted, charging and receiving therefor from the depositor a small sum for commission. After the event has occurred on which the wager was made, if the party who deposited the money was successful he presents his ticket and obtains the stake money, or obtains an order for it on the person with whom the bet was made. This I understand to be substantially the plan you outlined to me, though slight variations from it would not be important under the adjudicated cases.

I have no doubt that such acts on the part of the proprietor, or his agents, constitute a violation both of the Criminal Code of the state and of the ordinances of the city of Chicago. I am of the opinion that a place so kept is a gaming house, within the meaning of Section 127 of the Criminal Code, which prohibits keeping of gaming houses. Also, that such acts are a violation of Section 1 of an act passed in 1887, entitled "An act to prohibit book-making and pool selling," and further that such acts constitute a violation of an ordinance of the city entitled "An ordinance to abolish pool selling and pool rooms," passed September 16, 1889, and found as Section 2412 of the Laws and Ordinances of the city. This question is not new to the courts of this country. The Supreme Court of Tennessee, in the case of *Williams vs State*, found in 92 Tenn. Rep., at page 275, had occasion to consider a system of doing business in all respects substantially the same as the system adopted here, and it was held that the parties were properly convicted of gaming. In this case the court said:

"But under the facts as agreed on in this case, we are of opinion that the contract was not intended to be completed in Kentucky, and was not in fact consummated there, nor until the Kentucky parties had wired their willingness to accept the bet to the Nashville agents, and until they had communicated this fact to the Nashville customer. Until this is done, no money is paid by the customer, no ticket is issued to him; and until these things are done, it was not intended that the contract should be completed, and without these final transactions the bet would not have been effectuated or closed.

"The telegram from the Kentucky principals to the Nashville agents is nothing more than an authority to the latter to close the deal on the terms proposed; and this closing of the deal is done in Nashville by the Nashville agents, after receipt of such authority from their Kentucky principals. The money to make the bet is then paid in Nashville, the ticket evidencing the contract is then signed and delivered, and the deal is completed there.

"After the race is run, the winnings are paid in Tennessee, not in currency, it is true, but in a draft which the customer accepts as payment and treats as cash."

Substantially the same conclusion was reached in the case of *Ransome vs. State*, 91 Tenn., 716. A case strikingly similar to the matter now under consideration was decided by the Supreme Court of Michigan in 1892. See the case of *People vs. Weithoff*, *73 Mich. Rep., page 632*. In this case the court in its opinion said:

"The respondent was prosecuted under Section 2029 of Howell's Statutes, the information charging that the said respondent did, for hire, gain, and reward, keep and maintain a gaming room, contrary to provisions of said section. The section reads:

" 'Any person who shall, for hire, gain, or reward, keep or maintain a gaming room, or a gaming table, or any game of skill or chance, or partly of skill and partly of chance * * * shall be deemed guilty of a misdemeanor.'

"The evidence on the part of the prosecution showed that the respondent occupied and maintained a room, kept a telegraph operator therein, and, for a commission paid by any person, telegraphed to Guttenberg, N. J., the amount of money the person desired to bet, and the name of the horse chosen by him in the race at Guttenberg. The person desiring to have his money forwarded to Guttenberg first made out an order as follows:

" 'Please execute for me on the race track at the races to be held this day on the grounds of the.... .....in the county of.........., State of............, or at any other place or time, the sum of...... dollars, ...and do not, under any circumstances, accept odds on this race at the said track at a less price than........ I desire to be positively and distinctly understood, and for this reason only do place in your charge my money, for you to place my said money for me only on said horse above mentioned, and at no other place than on the grounds of said .... during the progress of the races this day; and for this purpose I make you my common carrier. For the expenses incurred by you in so placing my money—my special money —on the grounds of the said............I agree to pay you the sum of five cents.'

"A blackboard is kept in the room, upon which is recorded at brief intervals the position of the horses in the race. The man at the blackboard, who does the marking, is called the 'marker,' and the man at the ticket office is called the 'ticket agent.' There are also employed the telegraph operator and a 'helper.'

"The trial judge instructed the jury, basing his instructions upon the testimony given by one Crandall, as follows:

" 'If you believe beyond any reasonable doubt that on the 5th of January a horse race was about to take place at Guttenberg, N. J., and that at the room in question a person in the defendant's employ sold tickets for that purpose, sold to Crandall a ticket, for which $1.05 was paid, then and there gave Mr. Crandall the names of the horses that were to participate in the race then about to take place at Guttenberg, and he was about to place the money of Mr. Crandall ($1) on the horse named by Mr. Crandall, and Mr. Crandall then paid to the person so selling him a ticket in this room five cents commission, and the money was placed as agreed and the result of the race so announced as won by the horse on which Mr. Crandall placed his money, and you believe the money of Mr. Crandall was so placed as a stake or wager, then that room was a gaming room, and, if kept for that purpose, was evidently within the meaning of the statute.'

"The statute in question was exhaustively considered in People vs. Weithoff, 51 Mich.. 203. It was there held that betting on the result of a horse race is gaming; that a room used for the purpose of facilitating the betting on horse races is a gaming room, within the meaning of this statute; and that it is not essential to the offense either that those who bet or wager should be engaged in the game, or that the game upon which the bet is laid be conducted within the room.

"It is urged for the defense here that no actual betting occurred on the premises; that the defendant had no greater responsibility for the bets than the servant of a telegraph company, who sends dispatches directing that money be wagered; and that, as no bet or wager is actually made in the room, it is not a gaming room. We think this contention ignores the real substance of the transaction. The money is placed in the hands of the defendant by one party to the wager, and, if he wins, he receives the money won in this room; if he loses it, a knowledge of the loss is brought to him in this room. That it requires intervention of another agency does not relieve the respondent. *It would be a reproach to the law if it were possible that responsibility could be avoided by any such subterfuge and is apparent in the very scheme adopted by the respondent in the case.* That the purpose in fitting up this room was to furnish the information which enables persons to exercise their judgment in laying wagers; that money is paid into the hands of defendant irrevocably, to wager it; and that the gains of the wager are paid and the losses made known to those making bets within the room, are beyond question. We think this constitutes the room a gaming room, within the meaning of this statute."

The same conclusions substantially have been reached by Judge Cooley, an eminent judge of the Michigan Supreme Court, in the case of *People vs. Weithoff, 51 Mich. Rep., p. 203.* There are decisions in Missouri, and possibly in other states, which are to the like effect. A decision of the Supreme Court of Virginia has been called to my attention which announces the law to be substantially the contrary to that announced by the cases above cited. In this case it is held that an offer to bet on a horse race telegraphed from Virginia to New Jersey and accepted in New Jersey did not constitute an offense against the laws of Virginia. The court says:

"A bet is a wager between two or more persons. It involves a consideration of wills; that is, there must be an offer to bet made on one side and accepted on the other. When the offer is accepted, and not before, the betting becomes complete" (see Lascallet vs. Commonwealth, 17 South-Eastern Reporter, p. 546), and it is accordingly held that the offense, if any, was committed in New Jersey and not in Virginia. I consider this case to be clearly in conflict with the reasoning and the conclusions in the Michigan and Tennessee cases, as well as in the other authorities to which I refer, and I am clearly of the opinion that the Michigan and Tennessee cases are more in accordance with the views of our courts and that the same will be regarded as better authorities than the Virginia case, in so far as the Virginia case is in conflict with the other opinions.

The conclusions which I have here reached are supported by the decisions of our own local courts. In 1892 one Walter C. Lloyd, the secretary of the Mercantile Telegraph Company, was arrested on a charge of keeping a common gaming house in the city of Chicago. The business carried on by the company of which he was secretary and superintendent was not more clearly within the prohibitions of the criminal code than is the business to which I have above referred to; yet, his honor, Judge Adams, after a full and patient hearing of the matter, held that the business of the company was a violation of the criminal code, in a long opinion, a copy of which I herewith hand to you.

Respectfully submitted,

GEO. A. DUPUY, Asst. Corporation Counsel.

December 31, 1896.

Hon. Wm. R. Kerr, Commissioner of Health.

Dear Sir—

Your letter of December 22nd, requesting the draft of an order empowering you to recommend to the council certain improvements and also asking for an opinion as to the power of the council to provide summary means for the abatement of buildings dangerous to health, has been referred this day to me for an answer.

In response thereto I enclose the draft of the order requested. As to the second question, I beg to say that in my opinion there can be no doubt of the power of the council to provide by ordinance for the summary destruction of buildings dangerous to the public health. The charter of the city, paragraph 73, clause 75, gives the council power "to declare what shall be a nuisance and to abate the same; and to impose fines upon parties who may create, continue or suffer nuisance to exist." The 78th clause gives the council power "to do all acts and make all regulations which may be necessary or expedient for the promotion of health and the suppression of disease." The 84th clause gives the council power "to compel the owner of any grocery * * * or other unwholesome or nauseous house or place to cleanse, abate or remove the same." The power is thus plainly given to order the owners of such places as you mention to place the same in a good sanitary condition. Some means must be used to enforce the order. The council may of course impose a penalty by fine for failure to abate such a nuisance, but it also has unquestionably the power to provide for the summary destruction of such building in the manner that you suggest. This is quite like the power of the police to destroy buildings in the hope of arresting a conflagration. To arrest the progress of disease is of not less importance than to arrest the progress of fire. In King vs. Davenport, 98 Ill., p. 305, our Supreme Court upheld an ordinance giving the city marshal authority

to remove a wooden roof within the fire limits after failure to remove
the same upon notification. No doubt such ordinance should provide for reasonable notice to the owner of the building either to place
the same in a sanitary condition or to remove the same, but upon
failure to comply with such notice I am of the opinion that the council
can authorize you in the manner you suggest in your letter to proceed
to destroy the building.

Very truly yours,
EDWARD B. BURLING, Asst. Corporation Counsel.

December 31, 1896.

John J. Badenoch, Esq., General Superintendent of Police.

Dear Sir—

In relation to the right of the American Volunteers to hold public
meetings at the corner of Monroe and State streets, and to use drums
and other musical instruments at their meetings, through the noise of
which it is alleged that the occupants of the abutting premises are dis-
turbed—which matter you referred to me some time since—I beg to
say that I have carefully considered the same and report the following as my conclusions:

Section 65 of Article V of the general incorporation act of cities
and villages (Revised Statutes, Chapter XXIV), conferring powers
upon city councils, contain the following provisions:

"The City Council in cities * * * shall have the following
powers:

"9. To regulate the use of same (streets).

"10. To prevent and remove encroachments or obstructions
upon the same."

"72. To prevent and suppress * * * noises, disturbances
in any public or private place."

Under the foregoing powers the city council has passed an ordinance (Section 2177, Laws and Ordinances, 1890) as follows:

"No person shall engage in any game * * * or do anything
else in the streets * * * which shall collect any crowd of persons so as to interfere with the passage of teams or vehicles or persons passing along the streets and sidewalks."

The inquiry suggested by you resolves itself into two questions:
First, whether or not, despite these provisions of the statute and the
ordinances, the Volunteers have the legal right to assemble in the
streets if such assembling interferes with the passage of vehicles and
persons along the streets and sidewalks, respectively; second, whether
or not they have a legal right to make a noise such as is reasonably
calculated to seriously disturb the occupants of abutting premises. In
my opinion they cannot legally claim either of these rights. In the
two cases of the City of Chicago vs. Trotter, 136 Ill., Rep., p. 430, and
in Rich vs. City of Naperville, 42 App., 224, the courts considered
questions somewhat allied but in my opinion clearly distinguishable

from the questions now before us. It was held in these cases that ordinances which required parties desiring to parade to obtain a permit in one case from the chief of police and in the other case from the city council were unreasonable and void, because of their discriminating character. In each case it was said:

"This by-law is unreasonable, because it suppresses what is in general perfectly lawful, and because it leaves the power of permitting or restraining processions and their courses to an unregulated official discretion, when the whole matter, if regulated at all, must be by permanent. legal provisions, operating generally and impartially."

* * *

"The law abhors partiality and discrimination. All persons and all societies stand upon the same plane concerning their liberties, whether political, social or religious, and their full enjoyment is vouchsafed by our bill of rights."

And in one of these cases the court said:

"Ever since the landing of the Pilgrims from the Mayflower the right to assemble and worship according to the dictates of one's conscience, and the right to parade in a peaceable manner and for a lawful purpose, have been fostered and regarded as among the fundamental rights of a free people. The spirit of our free institutions allows great latitude in public parades and demonstrations, whether religious or political, and if they do not threaten the public peace, or substantially interfere with the rights of others, every measure repressing them, whether by legislative enactment, or municipal ordinance, is an encroachment upon fundamental and constitutional rights."

It will thus be seen that neither of these cases can be regarded as an authority on these questions, and the right to assemble in the street and hold public meetings therein which will interfere with traffic and the ordinary uses of the street is quite a different thing from the right to parade in the street, and the cases above quoted indicate that even that right may be regulated by a reasonable general ordinance and applying to all persons alike. The right to make loud noises such as materially interfere with the comfort and convenience of persons on the abutting property certainly does not exist, and especially where such noise is proposed to be made daily and at regular intervals through a long period of time. In other words, even if the right to carry musical instruments with a parade should be held to exist, it does not follow that such music may be made regularly upon public streets to the annoyance of others.

It is perhaps needless to say that the above conclusions apply not only to the particular case in question, but to any and every public meeting of any character proposed to be held upon the public streets. That the Volunteers are doing a praiseworthy and noble work, that they deserve to have and do have the sympathy of public officials in their work, that their work tends to lessen the prevalence of crime, and thereby to lighten the work of the police department, are things that cannot with propriety be considered in attempting to determine the purely legal phases of the question presented. I do not wish to be understood as suggesting that the police department should prohibit all such meetings or all meetings and gatherings on public streets. The question as to whether the police should under all circumstances prohibit such meetings, and the question as to whether the Volunteers have the legal right to hold such meetings are two quite different questions. My neighbor has no legal right habitually to walk across my premises, but it does not follow that I ought on that account prohibit his doing so under all circumstances. How far such meetings should be prohibited is purely a practical question for the superintendent of police in the exercise of a sound discretion to determine; but in my judgment the strict legal right on the part of persons so proposing to meet to hold such meetings in the public streets and to produce such noises as I have above referred to by means of music or otherwise, does not exist. Of course in the foregoing I speak only of meetings on the streets that "interfere with the passage of teams or vehicles or persons passing along the streets and sidewalks." Meetings that do not have this effect are not within the prohibitions of the ordinance. Whether meetings of this latter character are legal I have not considered, because I proceeded (perhaps wrongfully) on the assumption that any meeting at the place named, and at any hour of the day or evening, would necessarily interfere with passage and traffic.

Very truly yours,

GEO. A. DU PUY, Asst. Corporation Counsel.

December 31, 1896.

Hon. John M. Clark, Prest. Civil Service Commission, City of Chicago.

Dear Sir—

In accordance with your request I have had a careful examination made to ascertain what offices and places of employment under the municipal government of this city come within the exceptions of Section 11 of the Civil Service Law, and I believe that the list which I enclose covers all existing offices and places of employment which are excepted from the classified service *by virtue of said section.*

In this connection reference may properly be made to the places of employment under the commission. Section 11 is silent respecting them, but upon careful consideration of the purpose and scope of the law as a whole it is my opinion that the chief examiner and other examiners are not to be regarded as in the classified service of the city and as eligible for appointment only through competitive examination, but that the ordinary employes of the commission should be so regarded.

Very respectfully yours,

.WM. G. BEALE, Corporation Counsel.

LIST OF CITY OFFICERS OR EMPLOYES EXCEPTED FROM CLASSIFIED SERVICE UNDER SECTION XI OF THE CIVIL SERVICE ACT.

I.

OFFICERS ELECTED BY THE PEOPLE.

Mayor.
Members of the city council.
City Clerk.
City Attorney.
City Treasurer.

II.

ELECTED BY THE CITY COUNCIL.

Sergeant at Arms of the Council.

III.

APPOINTED BY THE MAYOR SUBJECT TO CONFIRMATION BY THE CITY COUNCIL.

Comptroller.
City Collector.
Corporation Counsel.
Prosecuting Attorney.
Commissioner of Public Works.
Deputy Commissioner of Public Works.
Inspector of Steam Boilers.
Inspector of Fish.
Inspector of Gas Meters.
Inspector of Oils.
Inspector of Weights and Measures.
Superintendent of Markets.
Superintendent of the Street and Alley Cleaning Bureau.
Harbor Master.
Assistant Harbor Master.
Vessel Dispatcher.
Assistant Vessel Dispatcher.
Bridge Tenders.
General Superintendent of Police.
Police Justices.
Police Court Clerks.

Police Court Bailiffs.
Pound-Keepers.
Commissioner of Health.
City Physician.
Commissioner of Buildings.
Fire Marshal.
Library Board.
Inspectors House of Correction.
Board of Examining Engineers.

IV.

OFFICERS SPECIFICALLY EXCEPTED UNDER SECTION XI OF ACT.

Members of Board of Education.
Judges and Clerks of Election.
Superintendent and Teachers of Schools.
One Private Secretary to Mayor.
Members of the Law Department.

January 5, 1897.

Philip Maas, Esq., City Collector.
Dear Sir—
Replying to your note of this date, making inquiry whether or not the city has authority to suppress a place of amusement which has not paid the license fee required of it, through the intervention of police officers, I beg to say that I have carefully examined what law I can find on the subject, and I have reached the conclusion that the city has not such right. In Beach on Public Corporations, Section 523, it is said: "If the manner of enforcing ordinances is prescribed by statute or charter, it is a cardinal rule that no other method can be resorted to." The method provided by our city charter for the enforcement of its ordinances is contained in these words: The city council shall have power "to pass all ordinances, rules, and make all regulations proper or necessary to carry into effect the powers granted to cities or villages, with such fines or penalties as the City Council or Board of Trustees shall deem proper." (Cl. 96, Sec. 1, Art. V, Chap. XXIV, Rev. St.) This implies that ordinances are to be enforced by means of fines and penalties rather than by direct act of the police department. The Supreme Court of this state (City of Pekin vs. Smelzel, 21 Ill., 468) had occasion to consider a question very similar to this, and in its opinion the court said: "This provision leaves it free from doubt that penalties by way of fine was the mode intended to compel an observance of ordinances restraining, prohibiting and regulating the sale of intoxicating liquors." I am therefore forced to the conclusion that the imposition of fines and penalties is the only proper method of compelling obedience to an ordinance in

such a case as the one about which you make inquiry.

I might add further that the city has no power to compel the payment of a license fee as such after the time has expired which the license would cover and for which the same should have been issued. The only remedy is to enforce the fine or penalty, and this remedy is not very effective after an unlicensed house or business has been permitted to run without license until the time has expired for which it should have obtained a license. Very respectfully,

GEO. A. DUPUY, Asst. Corporation Counsel.

January 8, 1897.

Hon. Joseph Downey, Commissioner of Public Works, City of Chicago.

Dear Sir—

Replying to your inquiry of the 7th inst., relating to certain street frontage petitions, I beg to say that in my opinion there is no difficulty where the petitions bear either a date of actual signing or a date of presentation to the council, which date of presentation may properly be regarded as the date of signing in the absence of some other stated or known date of signing. In all such cases the last expression counts, and if a property-owner in signing one petition has revoked his signature upon a previous one, the revocation should be recognized. For example, as I understand the matter, petitions have been presented at different council meetings, so that some petitions show a presentation on December 4th, and others on December 11th. A petition shown to have been presented December 11th in favor of one company, with a revocation of previous signatures in favor of another company, all signatures being undated, should be treated as revoking such duplicate signatures upon the earlier petitions in making your computations of frontage.

But in connection with this matter two points arise which are not free from difficulty, and which require separate consideration.

In the first place, you may happen to find undated petitions in behalf of two different companies, presented *on the same date*, containing the names of property-owners signing for the same property both petitions, and in each petition revoking their signatures to the other peition. In such cases there would in all probability be nothing before you to tell which signature was the later one. A property-owner having signed both on apparently the same day, and having on each of them revoked his signature on the other one, there would be no way in which you could determine whether to count both, or either or neither. In such a case I think you should not undertake to determine at all the question involved, but should report the exact facts to the council or the council committee for their determination. They will have their own opinion in any event and will not consider it obligatory to follow your determination, and the safe and prudent practice for the department in such matters as the one now before you is to report merely the facts and to avoid stating conclusions upon debatable points.

The other point is one which would have more importance for the council or council committee, but it is well enough for you to have it in mind. It has always been my view that where petitions are sought for different companies upon the same street and less than a majority of property is signed in favor of any one company, the city council probably has the lawful power to take the petitions as a whole, and to count the aggregate frontage as in favor of a street railway upon the street, and to confer the license upon whomsoever it will, without regard to the special beneficiary named in the petitions. I have always advised private clients in accordance with this view, as a matter of precaution in their interest. In this case, for instance, if thirty-three per cent. of the frontage on a certain street is in favor of one company and thirty-three per cent. is in favor of another company neither has a majority, but duplication of signatures aside) sixty-six per cent. of the frontage would be in favor of *a street railway upon the street*, and I am inclined to the opinion that a majority thus computed would comply with the statute and authorize action by the council. I should wish to examine this last question more fully before expressing a final opinion upon it but my present rule is as indicated. Respectfully yours,

WM. G. BEALE, Corporation Counsel.

Chicago, Jan. 27, 1897.
Isaac N. Powell, Esq., Chief Clerk Board of Election Commissioners.
Dear Sir—

In accordance with the request of Mr. Greeley in his letter of January 7, 1897, and following our conversation of this afternoon, I submit my conclusions as to the effect of the various annexations to the city upon the township relations of the territories annexed.

I may say generally that where annexation has been by act of legislature, and the act provides for the annexation of certain territory to the city, or that the city shall include certain territory, making no reference to the township, the township relations undoubtedly remain as before. (See City of East St. Louis vs. Rhein, 139 Ill., 116, and cases therein cited.) The township, particularly under our general township organization laws, past and present, is a civil division of the county, and exists as a municipal corporation, merely for the purpose of carrying on the state government. Its functions and those of a city or incorporated town or village are distinct. (See Greenwood vs. Town of La Salle, 137 Ill., 225; Village of Marseilles vs. Howland, 124 Ill., 547; People vs. Supervisors, etc., 111 Ill., 527; that Cook County is under township organization, see People vs. Brislin, 80 Ill., 423; C. & N. R. Co. vs. People, 83 Ill., 467.)

The first extension of the city was by act of legislature February 16, 1847. It did not affect the township. I do not find this act in the session laws of 1847,but its text appears in a municipal code of the city of 1856, page 524.

The second extension was by act of February 12, 1853, Laws of 1853, page 609. Town relations were undisturbed.

The third extension, by act of February 13, 1863, Laws of 1853, page 40, did not affect the township.

The fourth extension was by act of February 27, 1869, Laws of 1869, Vol. 3, page 342, which separated the part annexed from its original townships and added it to the town of West Chicago. The phraseology is as follows: (the territory annexed) "shall constitute part of the west division of said city and of the town of West Chicago; and said added or new territory shall cease to be a part of the several towns to which it now belongs or appertains."

As to the fifth and sixth extensions, I have met with difficulty. Although our Map Department maintains that they were made by acts of legislature, May 16, 1887, and April 29, 1889, respectively, I do not find such acts after the most careful search in the session laws of those years. It might be well to have a search made in the County Court for record of elections affecting these extensions.

All subsequent annexations were by election under the provisions of the general law, or by ordinance, and did not disturb existing township relations.

I believe the foregoing covers the points suggested in our conversation. If I can give any further assistance you may command me.

Very truly yours,
TIFFANY BLAKE, Asst. Corporation Counsel.

Chicago, February 4, 1897.
Honorable William R. Kerr, Commissioner of Health, City of Chicago.

Dear Sir—

I beg to acknowledge receipt of your letter of the 3rd inst., requesting advices from me about enforcing the ordinance of February 3, 1896, prohibiting traffic in horse flesh for human food.

In my opinion this ordinance is invalid and unenforceable, and the council committee, which originally had it, or one substantially like it under consideration, was advised by this office of its probable invalidity before it was passed. I do not think the city council has any more authority to prohibit the sale of horse flesh than it has to prohibit the sale of other meat. It may, however, regulate such sales.

October 7, 1895, an ordinance was introduced into the council to regulate the sale of horse meat and was referred to the Committee on Health and County Relations. (Council Proceedings 1895 and 1896, page 1022). Subsequently that committee requested this office to examine the ordinance, and also another ordinance prohibiting the sale of horse meat, which latter ordinance had been submitted to the committee, and I believe was in its substantial scope similar to the one ultimately passed and now under consideration. The ordinances were in

November, 1895, sent back to the committee with the opinion that the prohibitory. ordinance would not be valid if passed by the council, but that a proper regulating ordinance would be. It was further suggested to the committee that some modifications seemed desirable in the regulating ordinance submitted, and a substitute ordinance was prepared in this office with care and sent to the committee along with the two which had been received from it. On November 18, 1895, the committee reported the substituted ordinance to the council after having increased the license fee therein provided for and recommended that it be passed. (Council Proceedings 1895 and 1896, page 1311.) This report and substitute ordinance came under consideration of the council December 9, 1895, and again on January 6, 1896, on which latter date the ordinance failed to pass. (Council proceedings 1895 and 1896, pages 1471 and 1619.) January 9, 1896, the prohibitory ordinance was introduced into the council and was referred to the Committee on Judiciary. (Council proceedings 1895 and 1896, page 1641.) It was by that committee reported January 27, 1896, possibly with some changes, and with recommendation that it pass (Council Proceedings 1895 and 1896, page 1766), and on February 3, 1896, was passed unanimously. Council proceedings 1895 and 1896, page 1841.)

It would in my judgment be a waste of time, energy and money for your department to attempt the enforcement of this ordinance.

Very respectfully yours,
WM. G. BEALE, Corporation Counsel.

Chicago, February 4, 1897.
Hon. Joseph Downey, Commissioner of Public Works, City of Chicago.

Dear Sir—

Answering your inquiry of this date, I beg to say that I am not aware that the United States has any jurisdiction over the sidewalks surrounding the post-office block, and more than it has over the surrounding streets. This view is expressed on the assumption that the sidewalks are not laid on ground belonging to the United States, but are, like ordinary sidewalks, a part of the streets whose title is vested in the city. It may be that a portion of that sidewalk is in the street and a portion on land belonging to the United States, in which case there would be a divided jurisdiction, the United States controlling that portion of the sidewalk upon its own premises.

So far as I am aware, the city has the same jurisdiction over the streets and sidewalks and the space thereunder (not within the limits of the property owned by the United States) which it has over streets, sidewalks and space elsewhere—with this limitation, however, that the city cannot levy a special assessment against the United States for the care or improvement of abutting streets and sidewalks.

Very respectfully yours,
WM. G. BEALE, Corporation Counsel.

346

February 4, 1897.

Vere V. Hunt, Esq., Attorney Health Department.

Dear Sir—

Your letter of January 28th, relating to the fees of jurymen in justice courts, has been referred to me for answer.

In reply thereto, I beg to say, that there can be no doubt that the defendant must advance the fees if he wishes a jury. In Mc-Arthur vs. Artz, 129 Ill., 552, it was decided that since the statute on fees made it the duty of the county to pay the clerk's fees in cases of acquittal, the defendant could not be made to advance them, inasmuch as he could not recover them back as costs in case he were not convicted. This case was followed in Anderson vs. Shubert, 158, Ill., 75. Those cases turned entirely on the statute, the question being whether the clerk of the court should be paid his fees by the defendant in the case or by the county. It was held that he should look to the latter, since the statute says that in case of acquittal the fee should be paid by the county. Here the case is entirely different. There is no fund provided for the payment of jurymen. The statute says expressly that in every case where a jury may be called the defendant shall first pay their fees. By Chapter LXXIX, paragraph 48, it is provided that "In all cases either party may have the case tried by a jury if he shall so demand, and will first pay the fees of the jurors."

If the defendant does not pay the fee here no one will. In the other cases the county was ordered to pay the fees of the clerk. This is the difference between the two cases. The defendant need not have a jury unless he wishes. If he does he must pay the fees. A short answer to the controversy might be that it is the defendant's own business whether or not he shall advance the fees. If he can persuade six men to serve for nothing, he need advance no fees. The justice has no funds for this purpose. If he were to make payment out of his own pocket he could not reimburse himself. The statute says the defendant shall pay the jurors, and no provision being made for payment from any other source, he must do this if he wishes a jury.

Very truly yours,

EDWARD B. BURLING, Asst. Corporation Counsel.

Chicago, March 16, 1897.

Vere V. Hunt, Attorney Department of Health, City of Chicago.

Dear Sir—

Answering your inquiry of the 15th inst., as to whether it is unlawful under Section 8 of the recent cigarette ordinance, for a tobacco dealer to have cigarettes in sight in his place of business of he refuses to sell them, I beg to say, that in my judgment that section clearly does not prohibit such keeping and exposure of cigarettes. The section is directed against the having or keeping "for sale," or exposing "for sale," or offering "to sell," and your inquiry is based upon the assumption that in fact the dealer *does not sell.*

The evidentiary weight to be given to the possession and display of a quantity of cigarettes by a tobacco dealer is a question of considerable difficulty, and one respecting which it is not easy to lay down a general rule. Such possession and display would, of course, be suspicious, and I think might fairly be held to establish a presumption that the dealer had such cigarettes for sale. Very truly yours,

WM. G. BEALE, Corporation Counsel.

Chicago, March 16, 1897.

Honorable William R. Kerr, Commissioner of Health, City of Chicago.

Dear Sir—

In answer to your inquiry as to whether or not wholesale dealers in cigarettes who sell exclusively to the trade outside of the city of Chicago are required to have a license by the cigarette ordinance, I beg to say, that in my opinion such dealers do not come within the provisions of the ordinance, or if they do that the ordinance would be ineffective to prohibit such sales. There is no provision in the charter authorizing the city council to license dealers in cigarettes, and consequently the city council's authority in the premises must be referred to the grant of power to "make all regulations which may be necessary or expedient for "the promotion of health or the suppression of disease," or to the grant of power to "regulate the police of the city and pass and enforce all "necessary police ordinances."

I think the power of the council to pass an ordinance of this character as a sanitary or police regulation is unquestionable, but its operation as such police or sanitary measure must necessarily be confined to the city of Chicago. The sale of cigarettes by wholesale firms to the trade outside of Chicago where such cigarettes are not used or consumed within the city of Chicago cannot be fairly held to be an infringement upon any police regulation made for the benefit of this city. It therefore seems plain to me that sales of this character do not require a license, because not forbidden by the ordinance, or because, if forbidden by ordinance, the ordinance itself I think is ineffective to that extent, as being without the powers of the city council.

Very respectfully yours,

GEO. A. DUPUY, Asst. Corporation Counsel.

INDEX.

A

24

INDEX. 377

PAGE.